They Sought
a Country

MENNONITE
COLONIZATION
IN MEXICO

With an Appendix on Mennonite
Colonization in British Honduras

Harry Leonard Sawatzky

UNIVERSITY OF CALIFORNIA PRESS
Berkeley, Los Angeles, London 1971

University of California Press
      Berkeley and Los Angeles, California
University of California Press, Ltd.
      London, England
Copyright © 1971, by
      The Regents of the University of California

      ISBN: 0-520-01704-8

Library of Congress Catalog Card Number: 78-92673
      Printed in the United States of America

To Johann and Elizabeth Sawatzky

Foreword

The Mennonites, one of the oldest of the Protestant sects, originated in the Alps. They moved as colonists to the North German plain and to South Russia, arrived in Pennsylvania in 1700 and in the Canadian prairies about a hundred years ago, and settled in Mexico and Paraguay after the First World War. In their early years they suffered expulsion and occasional execution; later they migrated when restricted by governments in the exercise of their way of life.

Their creed, based on the authority of the scripture as interpreted by their own consensus, sets them apart from the dominant society. Their organization is congregational; the community determines its spiritual order and thereby also what is approved in material things and activity. Their separation from "the world" is declared by avoidance of ostentation, plain living, and plain dress. Congregational autonomy permits the revision of rules; and as a result numerous branches have been formed, including the communistic Hutterian Bretheren, who split off almost four hundred years ago.

Tolerance of apartness was found by becoming wholly rural communities *(Bauern)*. Mennonites colonized agricultural land and lived in villages, as they still do.

The quality of Mennonite society, its changes, dispersals, and removals to new and strange environments, form the first part of this book, which is set forth with great insight and knowledge.

Leonard Sawatzky grew up in Mennonite communities of Manitoba, founded by his people in the 1870s, immigrants of German speech from South Russia and pioneer wheat farmers in the Canadian prairies. He has been a qualified farmer in the tillage of different soils, the management of crops according to season and weather, and the economics of agriculture. Also he has the background of Mennonite ways, and is an acute observer and a field geographer who is concerned with man as an ecologic dominant and disturber.

In the First World War the Canadian Mennonites lost certain exemptions, in particular as to schools. The government of Mexico guaranteed the privileges desired, land thought suitable was available, and a large exodus from Canadian prairie to Mexican plateau got under way. The most conservative congregations moved en masse, reenforcing their apartness by going to a land of strange language and culture. Colonization was by villages such as they had built in Canada after the manner of their Russian settlements. Their keeping to accustomed ways brought them to the edge of disaster in Mexico because they continued to farm as they had in Canada; however, they did learn in time.

The main story deals with the exodus, the relocation in Mexico, the reluctant accommodation to a greatly different environment, what they learned and failed to learn, and the expansion to new colonies needed by their natural increase and economic changes. It is an intimately observant study, critical and understanding, a study of real people in situations construed according to their faith in the purpose of their being.

CARL SAUER

Acknowledgments

I wish to thank the Woodrow Wilson National Fellowship Foundation for its support of the extensive field research that was imperative to the treatment of the chosen topic.

Particular thanks are also due Mr. Walter Schmiedehaus of Cd. Cuauhtémoc, Chihuahua, who placed his entire archive of materials pertinent to the life of the Mennonite colonies in Mexico at my disposal, and who in conversation provided many insights and suggestions. Similarly, I owe a great deal to that genial patriarch and former Vorsteher of the Manitoba colony, Gerhard J. Rempel of Campo 22, Blumenort, for the exceedingly useful documents and correspondence he provided from his extensive personal files; and to the old schoolmaster, David Harder, of La Batea, Zacatecas, whose personal chronicle provided the time perspective on many important events in colony history. I am equally indebted to Elder Peter B. Loewen of the Kleine Gemeinde at Los Jagueyes, Chihuahua, for the materials he provided relative to his group. Others who particularly put themselves out to assist me were Secretary Menno Dueck of the Quellenkolonie at Los Jagueyes; Vorsteher Abram Peters of Ojo de la Yegua; Isaac I. Dyck, Campo 18, Manitoba colony; Peter G. Froese, Campo 112, Grossweide, Swift Current colony; surveyor Heinrich J. Martens, Campo 21, Neuenburg, Manitoba colony; Deacons Peter Harms, Jakob J. Peters, Diedrich Friesen, and Franz Guenther of the Manitoba, Swift Current, Ojo de la Yegua, and Hague colonies respectively; Heinrich Bergen, Jakob B. Wiebe, and Jakob Bartsch of the Hague colony; Johann Bartsch and Abram Rempel of Yermo; Peter S. Peters of Neuendorf, Manuél, Tamaulipas; teachers Daniel D. Peters and Helen Ens; nurse Katherine Fehr and agronomist Philip Dyck of the Comité Menonita de Servicios; Victor Mendoza of the horticultural division of the state Department of Agriculture, Chihuahua; Patricio Gonzales of the Alliance for Progress (Banco de México);

the management of the Celulosa de Chihuahua, Anáhuac, Chihuahua; John K. Reimer and Menno Loewen of Spanish Lookout, British Honduras; and Peter H. W. Wiebe of Blue Creek, British Honduras.

I was particularly appreciative of the warm-hearted gestures of the families of David B. Penner, Campo 2-B, Manitoba colony, and Jacob R. Loewen, Weidenfeld, Santa Clara colony, who invited me to make my headquarters with them when in their part of the country.

I wish also to thank all those friends whose interest in the project helped to sustain my efforts to its completion.

Finally, I wish to express my appreciation to Carl O. Sauer, James J. Parsons, and Harold J. Dyck of the University of California, Berkeley, for their sympathetic understanding of my purpose in attempting this study.

HARRY LEONARD SAWATZKY

Contents

Chapter I

Background of the Mennonites in Mexico

With few exceptions the Mennonites in Mexico are those who emigrated from Canada and their descendants. Others, numbering today perhaps less than a dozen families, came from Russia and the United States. Essentially all are the ideological descendants of the Anabaptist wing of the Protestant Reformation. More precisely, they have their ideological origins in that pacifist branch of the Anabaptist movement in the Low Countries which by the early 1540's had come under the leadership of Menno Simon, from whom the sect takes its name. Although in many respects they resembled other contemporaneously arising Protestant sects, the sum of the major facets of their ideological position—baptism only of adults upon confession of faith; insistence upon separation of church and state; refusal to bear arms; renunciation of participation in secular affairs of government; and refusal to take oath—sets them apart from the majority.

As a folk, the Mennonites came to be possessed of a strong agrarian tradition whose origins appear to lie in the earliest stirrings of the Anabaptist movement in the 1520's. Although in the Low Countries the Anabaptists emerged out of the textile towns of Flanders, their position there quickly became untenable because of the organized opposition of the Roman Catholic authorities. Because of close economic and political ties, Spain, as a bastion of orthodox Catholicism, exerted considerable influence in Flanders. The "heretics" therefore dispersed into the countryside, where they could more easily avoid detection and the attentions of the

Inquisition. Although they found new homelands in which they were officially tolerated, for over 200 years more the Mennonites were nevertheless to find it politic to continue to be *die Stillen im Lande*, the unobtrusive ones. This they have repeatedly found to be possible only from an agrarian base and rural habitat. The Mennonites now in Mexico—the descendants of conservative elements who were to migrate in turn to frontiers of settlement in Prussia, in South Russia, and in North America—early recognized that maintenance of the old order was dependent upon the staving off of cultural incursions from without. Mobility within the larger society leads to assimilation and the abrogation of the traditional way of life. It is only upon an unsophisticated agrarian base that the old ways can be at all maintained. To this end settlements in large, exclusive, self-regulating "colonies" within a relatively unsophisticated and linguistically, culturally, and ethnically different *Umwelt* have proven most capable of long-term survival. The maintenance of the "integrity" of such "cultural islands" rests upon strict conformity in secular and religious matters. In consequence, then, although in form the segregation of "church" and "state" is assiduously maintained, in effect each supports the other in exacting compliance with whatever norms of convention are seen as assuring continued survival of the traditional way of life. The avenues of permissible innovation are therefore narrowly circumscribed. Where divisions arising out of dissatisfaction with the existing ethic have gained momentum, the ultimate result has often been the withdrawal of the dissident faction, which then takes on an identity of its own. In consequence, there have emerged, over the generations, numerous "persuasions," encompassing a rather broad spectrum of attitudes, whose adherents—400,000 or more in Europe and the Americas—consider themselves Mennonite. Of these, the Mennonite colonists in Mexico today represent some of the most conservative factions.

The First Migration

Seeking economic opportunity and protection from religious persecution, groups of Mennonites, by the mid-sixteenth

century, had migrated from the Netherlands and established themselves in several colonies (*Dorfgemeinschaften*) in the region of the
delta and lower flood plains of the Vistula and Nogat rivers near
the Hanseatic Free City of Danzig, then under the Polish kings.
Small numbers of Mennonites continued to immigrate to the area
at least until 1565.[1] Although they were subjected to certain civil
disabilities and sporadic threats of expulsion, the Mennonite cause
always found champions among the noblemen whose lands bene-
fitted from their skills and industry. In consequence, "letters of
grace" (*Gnadenbriefe*) endorsed by the king and reaffirming their
rights to residence and the practice of their religion were repeatedly obtained for them.[2] It was under these conditions, over a period of 200 years and more, that the Mennonites established the
cultural solidarity and folk identity (*Gemeinschaftssinn*) which
have marked their group coherence ever since.

The Movement to Russia

With the advent of Prussian rule over most of the Danzig region after the first partition of Poland in 1772, the civil and
religious disabilities were somewhat modified by royal decree. The
established Lutheran Church, however, alarmed at a progressive
diminution of its tithe revenues owing to continuing Mennonite
acquisition of land, succeeded in the late 1780's in obtaining the
imposition of severe restrictions upon further Mennonite land

1. These marshy lowlands, lying from three to seven feet below sea level, had
been largely diked, drained, and occupied during the thirteenth, fourteenth, and
fifteenth centuries under the Teutonic Knights. During the 1520's and 1540's much
of this land was ruined and abandoned because of flooding. Thereupon Dutch
entrepreneurs offered to restore the lost lands. They brought in Mennonite settlers
to do the work of diking and draining, and then leased the land to them. Because
of their valuable contributions to the economy of the region, the Mennonites were
granted many liberties, including toleration of what was, at that time and in terms
of contemporary thinking, their heretical religion. The Mennonite settlements of
the Danzig–Vistula region persisted without interruption until the end of World
War II, when the territory became Polish and the former residents were expelled.
See *The Mennonite Encyclopedia* (Scottdale, Pennsylvania: Mennonite Publishing
House, 1955), III, 481–482, and Horst Penner, "The Anabaptists and Mennonites of
East Prussia," *Mennonite Quarterly Review*, XXII (1948), 212–225.

2. P. M. Friesen, *Alt-Evangelische Mennonitische Brüderschaft in Russland
(1789–1910)* (Halbstadt, Taurien: Verlagsgesellschaft "Raduga," 1911), I, 42.

purchases. This hindrance to their economic life and the threat to the future integrity of their social and spiritual organization provided motivation for the Mennonites' next migration, to South Russia.[3]

Their awareness of South Russia as a possible haven for settlement dated back at least to 1786, when the Russian government dispatched a colonization agent, Georg von Trappe, to the Danzig Mennonites with the special commission of persuading them to settle in South Russia. Von Trappe's efforts, aided by growing problems of landlessness and impoverishment among the Mennonites, resulted in the establishment, in 1789, of the first Mennonite colony in Russia, Chortitza, on a stream of that name, tributary to the Dnieper, near Alexandrovsk (now Zaporozhe). It was the first large-scale migration in Mennonite history. In 1804 another colony, Molotschna, was founded north of the Sea of Azov near Berdiansk. In all, some 1,150 families comprising about 6,000 persons were involved in the establishment of these colonies.[4]

As colonists, the Mennonites came under the provisions of the Russian Colonial Law of 1763, a statute calculated to serve as special inducement to immigration from the more advanced countries of Western Europe.[5] Apart from offering free land, the Colonial

3. "Frederick William II," *The Mennonite Encyclopedia*, II, 386. The disabilities to which the Mennonites in Prussia were subjected included, at various times, prohibitions on the purchase of additional land, proscription of the right to hold public assemblies (church services), and denial of the right of lay persons to hold services in places designated as hallowed by the Lutheran State Church. Under the rule of Frederick William II, land acquired by Mennonites from tithing persons continued to be subject to the tithe, although its purchase was no longer forbidden. Proscription of public assembly not only discouraged proselytizing by the Mennonites but also militated against the erection of large church buildings of their own. Prohibition of lay speakers on hallowed ground chiefly affected graveside burial services; in the event burial was in a public cemetery, an ordained Lutheran would have to attend since the Mennonites had only a lay ministry. (It appears likely that the occasional Mennonite practice of having a family burial plot in the foreyard of the farmstead may reflect a stratagem by which this regulation could be circumvented. Many of these plots occur in the older Mennonite settlements of Manitoba.) All of the foregoing may, in the light of the thinking of the times, be considered to have been, in fact, "intolerable" impositions.

4. P. M. Friesen, I, 74.

5. The Russian Colonial Law, a document of ten articles, offered:

    1. Freedom of religion and exemption from taking oath.

    2. A homestead of 65 *dessiatines* per family (a dessiatine = 2.7 acres).

Law provided for perpetual exemption from military and civil service, freedom of religion, the right to control their schools and churches, and the right (and obligation) of agricultural colonies to be locally autonomous. Such colonies answered directly to a special branch of the Department of the Interior.[6] These conditions, together with the proviso that colonists refrain from all proselytizing among the Orthodox Christian peoples of Russia, effected and perpetuated a high degree of linguistic and cultural separation between the closed colonies and the Russian host society. In consequence, a strong element of ethnic identification came to be added to the character of the Mennonites as a religious sect.

The situation created by the Colonial Law would appear to have been one made to order for the Mennonites. Under it they could pursue a life removed from "worldly" influences, yet they were accorded far-reaching opportunities for developing their economic and cultural life. However, it also meant that, in keeping with the concept of the separation of church and state, the simple institutions of village administration brought from Prussia were elaborated to administer the secular affairs of large colonies. Further, before a thriving agriculture could be brought into being in the subhumid steppe, the practices and techniques of farming brought from the polderlands of the Baltic coast had to be radically revised and altered. The administrative and agricultural techniques which were subsequently worked out in South Russia came

3. Freedom of enterprise.

4. Special rights to manufacture beer, vinegar, and brandy.

5. A monopoly of the retail trade in alcoholic beverages within the colonies.

6. Perpetual exemption from military and civil service.

7. Exemption from the extended quartering of soldiers and from the corvée; the duty to keep bridges and roads in repair

8. Full rights in property; right to implementation of own inheritance regulations and management of the estates of orphaned minors.

9. Ten to fifteen years free from taxes, after settlement.

10. Orders to all levels of government to respect and honor the above privileges.

Articles 1, 6, and 8 of the above have essentially been the basis of Mennonite requests to governments prior to emigrating to new lands from that time on. P. M. Friesen, I, 99.

6. The Fürsorge-Komitee (Guardians' Committee), headquartered in Odessa, and usually presided over by a German. C. Henry Smith, *The Story of the Mennonites* (Newton, Kansas: Mennonite Publication Office, 1957), p. 406. Later, supervision of the colonies passed to the Department of Crown Lands.

to be very much a part of the fabric of Mennonite institutions. Transplanted to America, these institutions have continued to this day, particularly among the more conservative of the Mennonite groups which are heir to the Russian experience, as the basis for the regulation of secular affairs wherever settlement has been made in closed colonies and as the prototype of their field husbandry.

Abrogation of the Colonial Law

The virtual autonomy of the Mennonite colonies in Russia was to be terminated by events which followed the liberation of the serfs in 1861. The rise of Pan-Slavism heralded the end of the era in which privileged colonies of foreigners could live aloof from involvement in the building of the Russian nation. The future status of the colonies was defined in 1870 through the issuance of an *ukas* by Tsar Alexander II. The separate administration of the foreign colonies under the Department of Crown Lands was to be abolished and the colonies incorporated into the prevailing Russian hierarchy of government.[7] This meant an end to their isolation and privileged status.[8] Most alarming to the Mennonites was the threatened extinction of their exemption from military service. Although the government intended to make provision for medical corps service by conscientious objectors, such duty was unacceptable to many Mennonites since it would still make them part of the military organization.[9] The question of emigration was broached. In 1873 a deputation was sent to the United States and Canada to investigate settlement possibilities there. The tsarist government, in a conciliatory gesture, responded by dispatching Adjutant-General von Todtleben, then Governor-General of all South Russia but acquainted with the Mennonites since the days of the Crimean

7. E. K. Francis, *In Search of Utopia* (Altona, Manitoba: D. W. Friesen and Sons, 1955), p. 32.

8. The immediate cause of the abrogation of the privileges of the foreign colonies in Russia, which included the Volga Germans and others, was related to affairs in Europe. Germany continued to have guardianship over the rights of German colonists in Russia, a fact abhorrent to the Pan-Slavists. In 1870 Bismarck made a deal with the Russian government whereby, in return for Russia refraining from involvement in the Franco-Prussian War, Germany relinquished its guardianship rights with respect to the German colonies in Russia.

9. P. M. Friesen, I, 493.

War, to seek a rapprochement and dissuade them from emigrating.[10]

In 1874 the military question was resolved in a manner acceptable to the majority of Mennonites once they came to grips with the idea that as citizens they must in the future render some form of service. Under the arrangement worked out, young Mennonite men might discharge their obligations by serving for three years in special cadres with the Forestry Department. Generally speaking, the more liberal-minded and propertied elements found it possible to reconcile themselves to the terms of the compromise. Many even welcomed the change of status from that of a tolerated sect to one of citizens with defined rights.[11] Many, however, found the compromise too much of an impingement upon the "perpetual" privileges promised their forefathers at the time of immigration, and determined to emigrate. Even so, a wait-and-see attitude might have prevailed had not the newly promulgated laws stipulated 1880 as the final year in which emigration visas would be issued. No doubt this proviso helped to force the issue.[12]

The matter of military service was, however, only one aspect of a wider spectrum of problems confronting the Mennonite colonies. Particularly severe were the problems of landlessness and inadequate alternative economic opportunity. Ideological dissension within the Mennonite brotherhood and a strong reticence to accept the implications of the equalization of their civil status with that of the rest of the tsar's subjects,[13] as heralded by the new laws, were further inducements to emigration.[14]

10. *Ibid.*, I, 497. Von Todtleben had been commander of the Russian forces in the campaign to relieve the beleaguered city of Sebastopol during the Crimean War (1854–1856). In that war many Mennonites from South Russia served as volunteers, hauling provisions overland to the besieged city and evacuating the wounded to South Russia. To commemorate these deeds the Russian authorities subsequently set up a memorial in the Molotschna colony.

11. Elder Jakob Wiebe of the Krimmer Mennonites at Karassan, Crimea, to Elder Johann Wiebe of the Alexandertal Mennonite Church, February 27, 1876. Quoted in P. M. Friesen, I, 512.

12. *Ibid.*, II, 53.

13. *Ibid.*, I, 511.

14. As early as 1872, a small unofficial party from the Molotschna colony visited the U.S. and Canada to assess these countries. The members of this party were later quite influential in causing the Mennonite migration to be directed toward North America.

As word of the imminent migration spread, outside influences quickly came to bear on the direction which the movement would take. Both the United States and Canada were at this time actively canvassing Europe for immigrants. In the United States, settlement was largely left to private initiative, although state governments did make some overtures. The government of the Dominion of Canada, however, having but recently assumed sovereignty over Rupertsland, gravely concerned over a determined U.S. expansionism aimed at the western territories, and desperate to expand the economic hinterland, was most eager to achieve effective occupation of the west. Accordingly it maintained emigration agents in various European centers. In 1872 the government, upon being apprised of the proposed Mennonite migration, dispatched such an agent, William Hespeler, then stationed in Strasbourg, to South Russia in the hope of diverting them to Canada.[15] At Berdiansk he arranged for a Mennonite delegation to visit Canada in 1873 at government expense.

In order to accommodate the Mennonites' preference for group settlement, the Canadian government in 1873 set aside eight townships twenty-odd miles southeast of Winnipeg for their exclusive use.[16] Once the delegates arrived in North America, however, railroad interests in the United States, over whose lines they had to travel in order to reach western Canada, and the governments of the states then on the frontier of settlement also began to court them, offering every possible inducement.[17] The result was that the

15. John Lowe, Secretary, Department of Agriculture, Ottawa, to William Hespeler, Special Emigration Agent, June 1, 1872, Public Archives of Canada, Department of Agriculture Papers, Letter Book Number 6, pp. 35–36; this communication is reproduced verbatim in Ernst Correll, "Mennonite Immigration into Manitoba," *Mennonite Quarterly Review*, XI: 3 (1937), 220.

16. Order-in-Council, March 3, 1873. Public Archives of Canada, Ottawa.

17. Kansas, Nebraska, and Minnesota passed laws exempting Mennonites from militia service. Both the Santa Fe and Northern Pacific railroads sent settler-recruiting agents to the Mennonite colonies in South Russia. The Northern Pacific Railroad also entered into a contract with the Mennonite delegates whereby lands it owned in Dakota Territory would be reserved from sale to others until July 1, 1878, in an effort to make it possible for the Mennonites to form a closed colony by acquiring the government-owned sections which alternated with the railroad grants. Appeals to Congress to reserve the alternate sections of public land were of no avail. See Georg Leibbrandt, "The Emigration of the German Mennonites from Russia to

delegates visited Manitoba last, after they had been exposed to the climatically and, consequently, economically more attractive conditions farther south. In the minds of some of the delegates these considerations seem to have modified, in some measure at least, the precise nature of the matters entrusted to them by their home communities, which had laid great stress upon a guarantee of military exemption and the right to form closed colonies.[18]

The Migration to Canada

The Canadian government, on the other hand, proffered in addition to reserved lands essentially those statutory provisions with respect to military service, language, and religion which the Mennonites had enjoyed under their royal privileges in Russia—the Privilegium—whose infraction was the ostensible prime mover in the migration.[19] With land reserved *en bloc*, village communities as well as the desired closed colonies could be established on the basis of homesteading alone, thereby greatly diminishing the need for capital.[20] It is not surprising, therefore, that those who elected to come to Manitoba were among the most conservative and economically least well-endowed of the migrants.[21] They represented four distinct subgroups of the Mennonite communities in South Russia—Bergthal, Chortitza, Fürstenland, and the Kleine Gemeinde (literally, little congregation).

---

the United States and Canada, 1873–1880," *Mennonite Quarterly Review,* VII: 1 (1933), 5–41.

18. Leonhard Sudermann, *Eine Deputationsreise von Russland nach Amerika* (Elkhart, Indiana: Mennonitische Verlagshandlung, 1897), p. 10.

19. The letter detailing the advantages and immunities which the government of Canada was willing to afford the Mennonites is contained in Department of Agriculture Letters Sent, VII (1873), 167–169, Public Archives of Canada, Ottawa.

20. Klaas Peters, *Die Bergthaler Mennoniten und deren Auswanderung aus Ruszland und Einwanderung in Manitoba* (Hillsboro, Kansas: Mennonite Brethren Publishing House, n.d.), p. 12.

21. It is also entirely probable that they were strongly influenced by one or the other of two Mennonites, Johann F. Funk of Elkhart, Indiana, and Jacob Y. Shantz of Berlin (Kitchener), Ontario, who accompanied them upon their land-seeking mission. Both of these men were involved with the Russian Mennonites throughout the rest of their lives.

Altogether the number of Mennonites who came to Manitoba between 1874 and 1880 was about 7,000.[22] The Bergthal and Kleine Gemeinde people occupied the original reserve (later known as the East Reserve), embracing the present boundaries of the municipality of Hanover (Township 7, Ranges 4, 5, and 6, Townships 5 and 6, Ranges 5 and 6, and Township 4, Range 6, east of the Principal Meridian [97° west longitude]). The Chortitza and Fürstenland people took up land west of the Red River of the North, where another block, the West Reserve comprising seventeen townships—Township 1, Ranges 1 East to 6 West, Township 2, Ranges 1 to 5 West, and Township 3, Ranges 1 to 5 West, sixty-odd miles south-southwest of Winnipeg—was set aside in 1876.[23] On this reserve they initially occupied, *en bloc*, the well-drained western portion. Of the Mennonites who came to Manitoba all but the Kleine Gemeinde had their origins in the old Chortitza colony, both Bergthal and Fürstenland [24] being daughter colonies. The Bergthal colony had led a separate existence since its founding in 1836. Fürstenland, while also independent of the mother colony, had been founded in 1864, just ten years prior to the migration. Its ties with the mother colony were therefore doubtlessly much stronger than those of the Bergthaler. Furthermore, whereas only a relatively small fraction of the Chortitza "old" colony emigrated, a majority of the Fürstenländer did so,[25] including their religious and civil leaders, who subsequently became Elder and Vorsteher,[26] respectively, of the combined group in Manitoba.[27] For the sake of

22. Their immigration, by years, was as follows: 1,532 in 1874; 3,258 in 1875; 1,356 in 1876; 183 in 1877; 323 in 1878; 208 in 1879; and 70 in 1880, for a total of 6,930. See Annual Reports of the Department of Agriculture, Canada, *Sessional Papers, 1875–1881*; these figures are reproduced in John H. Warkentin, "The Mennonite Settlements of Southern Manitoba," Ph.D. dissertation, University of Toronto, 1960. The groups were represented approximately thus: Bergthal—3,000; Chortitza—2,100; Fürstenland—1,100; and Kleine Gemeinde—800.

23. Order-in-Council, April 25, 1876. Public Archives of Canada, Ottawa.

24. So named because the land was rented from the heir apparent, the Grand Duke Michael Nikolaievitch.

25. The fact that the Fürstenländer were resident upon the land under a quitrent system rather than as outright owners probably served as a substantial stimulus to migration.

26. The office of Vorsteher or Oberschulze was roughly equivalent to that of reeve or executive administrator of a colony.

27. P. M. Friesen, I, 700.

brevity, the Chortitza and Fürstenland people will henceforward be referred to as Altkolonier, a name they later themselves adopted.

The Bergthal group, on the other hand, emigrated en masse, taking its civil and ecclesiastical establishments along. Furthermore, whereas the Bergthaler began the movement to Canada in 1874, the Altkolonier commenced to emigrate the following year, by which time it was evident that much of the land on the East Reserve was marginal in quality. They thereupon cast about for better land. The result was the creation of the West Reserve in 1876.[28] Geographical distance was thus added to the organizational separation of the Bergthal and Altkolonier groups.

The Kleine Gemeinde group came originally from the Molotschna colony, where it had its origins in 1812 as a fundamentalist reaction to a growing secularization within the existing Mennonite Church communities.[29] In 1865–1866, 120 families had founded a separate colony, Borsenko, near Nikopol. It broke up in the exodus to Canada. In Manitoba they settled in five villages of their own, three within the East Reserve and two outside of either reserve, west of the Red River.[30] Others, who had remained in the Molotschna colony, settled in the United States.

28. They actually began to occupy the area included in the West Reserve in 1875. The Altkolonier and Bergthal groups would have maintained separate existences in any event because of their doctrinal differences.

29. P. M. Friesen, I, 75.

30. The Mennonite village in Russia was a *Strassendorf,* or linear street village, surrounded by the village fields (*Flur*), laid out in the narrow strips of a *Streifenflur* (*Streifen*-strips), and a communal pasture. Under the colonial system in Russia, it had been relatively easy to maintain this occupancy pattern. The homesteading provisions under the Dominion Lands Act anticipated an individualistic form of ownership. Although the requirement that the homesteader reside upon his land was waived by the authorities in order to make it possible for the Mennonites to establish their traditional villages, it was nevertheless required that each homestead be entered in the name of an individual. The villages in Manitoba were therefore voluntary associations, without legal status, of owners who agreed to pool their land. Most of the Mennonites who came to Manitoba did initially enter into such arrangements. However, the attractions of an isolated compact farmstead captured the fancy of some right from the beginning. Moreover, anyone wishing to withdraw his land from the village "pool," for any reason and at any time, was entitled by law to do so. The Bergthaler never made much of an issue of the preference by some for the compact holding. The Altkolonier, however, invoked the ban, shunning, and excommunication against any member who "took his land out of the village" (literal translation from Plattdeutsch). (The same penalties were applied for infractions such as voting in municipal elections or other participation in "worldly" affairs.)

Each of these groups was noted for its ultra-conservatism and strictness, aimed at separation and isolation from "worldly" (that is, secular) influences, maintained by stern church discipline which encompassed authority over civic life and schools, building styles, household innovations, vehicles, clothing, and language.[31] All of them, as a result of schisms and in response to real or anticipated threats to the continued maintenance of their ideological group integrity, have participated in migration from Canada and in the establishment of the colonies in Mexico which are the objects of this study.

Intrustion of Provincial
Administrative Controls

For almost a decade the Mennonites in Manitoba came close to realizing the ambition of reestablishing their closed autonomous colonies on the Russian model. In 1880, however, the provincial legislature made provision for the inauguration of municipal government. Since this left local control in local hands, with higher echelons of government giving supervision only, this development need not have represented a serious infringement upon the status quo as far as the Mennonites were concerned. In the East Reserve, indeed, the transition appears to have been more or less painlessly made, since there were few requirements not already being fulfilled by the civic establishment brought from Russia. In the West Reserve, on the other hand, the Altkolonier, fearing interference from outside, objected to the new system. They refused to cooperate with the provincial authorities and generally ignored municipal matters.[32]

There also were important contemporaneous developments within the Manitoba Mennonite community. Owing to excessive summer rainfall and consequent flooding in 1876 and 1877, crops were lost on the East Reserve and many settlers began to cast about for a more favorable location.[33] Consequently they began, in 1878,

31. P. M. Friesen, II, 72.
32. This paragraph is based on John H. Warkentin, pp. 81–126 *passim*.
33. P. P. Epp, "Aus Meinen Erinnerungen," *Steinbach Post*, August 1, 1934.

to remove to the as-yet-unoccupied portions of the West Reserve.[34] Since these Bergthaler did not have the same aversion to participation in civic affairs as did the Altkolonier, they quickly came to occupy the available positions as municipal functionaries, realizing that the more efficiently they handled their own affairs the less formal intrusion into their communities there was likely to be. The Altkolonier, in contrast, appear to have regarded the government's action in establishing the municipalities as being little different from the incorporation of the Mennonite colonies into the *volost* system in Russia. A major cause of apprehension was the fact that, with the drawing of the municipal boundaries in 1883, English-speaking settlements were included with the Mennonites, ostensibly to assist with the work of organization, but quite probably also as an attempt to diminish the self-imposed isolation of the Mennonites.[35]

The Altkolonier, in order to present a unified front in opposition to these intrusions, used the disciplinary powers of the church to restrain dissident members. Although such measures were largely effective, it was not unusual for the Bergthaler to admit Altkolonier excommunicants to membership, thereby not only diminishing the effectiveness of Altkolonier church discipline but also deepening a growing rift between the two groups. Sanctions were invoked by the Altkolonier against the Bergthaler,[36] and the former, to reassert their integrity in membership and doctrine, assumed the new church name of *Reinländer Mennonites*.[37] A measure of the overall success of their resistance to change may be gauged from the fact that, until a majority of them left Canada in the 1920's, the Altkolonier tenaciously maintained an internal administration which was granted tacit recognition by municipal officers, who dealt with them through the Vorsteher.[38] What was to

34. Klaas Peters, p. 43.

35. John H. Warkentin, p. 85.

36. E. K. Francis, *In Search of Utopia*, p. 90. So acrimonious did relations between the two groups become that fraternization and intermarriage with Bergthaler were expressly forbidden by the Altkolonier church.

37. After the name of the village in which their Elder resided. In referring to them, however, the author will use the name Altkolonier throughout.

38. E. K. Francis, *In Search of Utopia*, p. 95.

be more important for the Altkolonier, however, was that the foregoing episode was only the first in a series of struggles with the Canadian authorities—struggles not so much *against* outside influences, really, as they were strivings *for* the maintenance of the status quo—which ultimately led to their emigration.

The Schools Question

The next major infringement upon the solidarity of the Mennonite community in Manitoba came through the medium of the schools. The document detailing the Mennonites' rights and privileges gave them assurance that they might educate their children "without any kind of molestation or restriction whatever." This was interpreted by the Mennonites to mean the right to complete autonomy in respect to schools, with instruction by their own teachers, exclusively in the German language and according to a curriculum of their own selection. For many years they remained free of government intervention. The pressure for change emanated this time from within a portion of the Mennonite community itself.[39]

In 1885, the Bergthaler in the West Reserve installed their own Elder, thereby becoming a separate, autonomous group. The action appears to have been taken merely out of recognition of the problems created by the distance separating them from the parent

39. Under the Manitoba School Act of 1871, a Board of Education was created, with Protestant and Catholic supervisory sections, under which local denominational schools could be established on local initiative and with local trustees. Such schools were subsidized by legislative grants through the agency of the board (see W. L. Morton, *Manitoba—A History* [Toronto: University of Toronto Press, 1957], p. 186). Essentially the act had been promulgated in recognition of the rights of the French Catholic minority in the province. The Mennonite parochial schools, however, by registering with the board, could receive the subsidies, although they then became part of the public school system. It appears that by 1878 this form of assistance had been accepted by a substantial number of Mennonite schools. The Altkolonier, however, kept severely aloof. Fear of possible hidden implications attendant upon acceptance of the school subsidies, together with a desire to maintain a united front among the noncollaborating districts, resulted in the early withdrawal of many of the Bergthaler and Kleine Gemeinde schools from the public school system, and by 1890 most of them had reverted to private status. See E. K. Francis, "The Manitoba School Problem," *Mennonite Quarterly Review*, XXVII: 3 (1953), 211–212.

body in the East Reserve. Shortly, however, a minority group of the West Reserve Bergthaler was to take action which led to serious inter- and intragroup conflict.

As the limited educational heritage of the Mennonites deteriorated owing to lack of cultural interchange, some of the more forward-looking of the Bergthaler—particularly businessmen in the emerging urban centers such as Gretna and Winkler on the West Reserve—began to agitate once more for the creation of public schools and for the teaching of English.[40] The provincial authorities actively encouraged these activities, pointing to the prevailing low educational standards among the Mennonites and emphasizing the assured need of English in the future.[41] In 1889 a group of West Reserve Bergthaler, including, significantly, their Elder and four ministers, opened a teacher-training school at Gretna—the present Mennonite Collegiate Institute. No doubt, in addition to the stated reasons, they were responding to the same motivation that prompted participation in municipal matters, namely that by looking after their own affairs to the satisfaction of the authorities they could forestall incursions from without.[42]

The Altkolonier and indeed the majority of the Bergthaler violently opposed the new school. To them, knowledge of the English language would give the young in particular access to the "world," while any diminution of the German being taught would seriously threaten the continued functioning of the church, based

40. There was, of course, the pecuniary advantage of government support for public schools, a not insignificant consideration, for the Mennonite settlements were still in the pioneering stage at the time. Also, in the homogeneously Mennonite communities there did not have to be any change in the curriculum or function of the school owing to a change in status from parochial to public.

41. E. K. Francis, *In Search of Utopia*, p. 167.

42. That they were correct in so doing was shown in 1890, when the Manitoba Public Schools Act was passed, requiring secular schools and English as the language of instruction. So vigorously did the French Catholic community oppose the act, however, that a compromise was ultimately worked out, providing for bilingual schools where ethnic minorities required them. One of the languages was required to be English—a stipulation which the Altkolonier refused to meet until after the migration from Canada. Since the act did not make school attendance compulsory, many Mennonite districts simply submitted to paying the school taxes while continuing to maintain their private schools.

as it was on the use of the German language.[43] Inter- and intra-group tensions during this period were intensified with the passage, in 1890, of the Manitoba Schools Act. The act provided that public schools would in the future be nonsectarian, with English as the language of instruction. It did not, however, stipulate compulsory attendance. The conservative Mennonites used this legal loophole and simply continued, or reverted to, the private school. In some mixed areas where progressives insisted on public schools, however, all ratepayers were taxed to support them, thereby imposing an added burden upon those who continued to support the private schools. In a few districts, under similar circumstances or because of jurisdictional disputes, no school at all was maintained. In 1890 the great majority of the West Reserve Bergthaler split away to form a new conservative church group, the Sommerfelder. The Bergthaler of the East Reserve,[44] to register their disapproval and sever connections with the renegade progressives, changed their name to Chortitzer.[45]

These issues and events, which threatened totally to disrupt the traditional Mennonite way of life, were next involved in a new development, the creation of daughter settlements away from the arena of conflict, in the Northwest Territories.[46] By 1890, good

43. The language of everyday communication among the Mennonites was Platt-deutsch, the dialect of the Danzig region. John Thiessen, *Studien zum Wortschatz der Kanadischen Mennoniten* (Marburg: N. G. Elwert Verlag, 1963), p. 26, describes it as "predominantly Lower Saxon, more accurately . . . Lower Prussian with a Netherlands heritage, including some Frisian elements, and with adoptions from Polish, Russian, particularly Ukrainian, Yiddish, Old Prussian, and lastly English." It is not a written language. The use of literary German was confined almost exclusively to the church. The continuation of the religious life of the community, in the eyes of the Mennonite church leaders, was therefore dependent upon the teaching of an adequate amount of German in school and hence the great emphasis on its exclusive use there. Actually, then, the introduction of English meant that the Mennonite child had to learn *two* foreign tongues in school. Furthermore, there were few Mennonites capable of teaching English, and non-Mennonite teachers were of course unthinkable.

44. The East Reserve church groups, the Bergthaler and Kleine Gemeinde, were about equally conservative, so that no serious intergroup clashes over the school issue developed there.

45. After the mother colony, Chortitza, in Russia.

46. In 1905 the provinces of Saskatchewan and Alberta were carved out of these territories.

land was becoming scarce and dear in the reserves. The portion occupied by the Altkolonier, roughly the western half of the West
Reserve, was becoming particularly overcrowded.[47] Nevertheless,
the desire to withdraw from the unsettled conditions in Manitoba
was a significant factor.

Beginning in 1890, Mennonites from Manitoba began to move
westward. Although reserves were not granted, it was later made
possible for them to take up contiguous mixed tracts of crown and
railroad land,[48] a concession particularly attractive to the Altkolonier. Sommerfelder, Chortitzer, and Altkolonier began settling
first in the Hague–Osler area north of Saskatoon, then Sommerfelder and Chortitzer in the vicinity of Herbert.[49] Another settlement, in the semiarid region south of Swift Current, was begun
by Altkolonier in 1900, on an "island" of relatively good land surrounded by broken range country, which afforded them a welcome
measure of isolation.[50] These settlements predominantly perpetuated the traditional form—agricultural villages and a local internal

47. There was still plenty of vacant land in Manitoba, but it was not available
in the contiguous blocks which the Altkolonier in particular held to be indispensable to their way of life. Because of the grouping of homesteads to form *Gewann*
(open-field) villages, there was from the first little vacant land in the Altkolonier
section of the West Reserve. Land fragmentation and migration were for them the
only available answers if their rural agrarian way of life was to be upheld. There
was one partly rough and wooded township in the extreme southwest of the West
Reserve, adjacent to the Altkolonier section but above the Manitoba Escarpment,
which the Mennonites avoided because it was believed to be unsuitable for the
growing of grain. However, in 1898 all remaining land on the West Reserve, including this township, was thrown open to general settlement by an Order-in-Council
(see John H. Warkentin, p. 200).

48. E. K. Francis, *In Search of Utopia*, p. 148.

49. In Saskatchewan the splinter groups of the Manitoba Bergthal church, the
Sommerfelder and Chortitzer, assumed the name Bergthaler once more. However, to
avoid confusion, the practice found in most writings about them will be followed;
that is, the name Sommerfelder will be used throughout to designate all conservative splinter groups derived from the Bergthaler.

50. After 1900 many Mennonites from Kansas, Oklahoma, Minnesota, Nebraska,
and the Dakotas came to western Canada to take up homesteads. There was also a
substantial trickle of immigration directly from Russia and Prussia. Considerable
numbers of these more liberal Mennonite elements settled in the vicinity of the
Altkolonier and Sommerfelder, particularly in the area north of Saskatoon. Their
compromises with the "world" displeased many of the conservatives and provided
motivation, if only in a minor way, for the later migration of the conservatives to
Latin America.

administration—to which these groups had adhered in Manitoba. The magnitude of the movement into the west is indicated by the census of Canada, which in 1911 reported 14,400 Mennonites in Saskatchewan, almost as many as the 15,600 in Manitoba.[51]

In Manitoba, during the 1890's and into the early years of the present century, significant educational progress was made among the Mennonites, and a substantial number of public schools teaching both English and German were once more created, even in some decidedly conservative communities.[52] There was, however, no participation from the Altkolonier, whose church leaders invoked excommunication and ostracism upon members who permitted their children to attend any but Altkolonier private schools. Nevertheless, a small trickle of Altkolonier and other conservatives was continually being won over to the "liberal" camp. This gradual process was, however, rudely interrupted through the precipitate action of the provincial government when, in 1907, it decreed that all public schools must henceforward fly the Union Jack.[53] The reaction among the Mennonites was predictable. Suspicious of the implied militarism of the flag-flying policy and fearful of its

51. The 1911 census lists another 1,524 Mennonites in Alberta, but since these were not involved in the migrations to Mexico, no further mention is made of them here. In Saskatchewan there was a combined total of thirty-two Altkolonier and Sommerfelder villages, seventeen in the Hague–Osler area and fifteen in the Swift Current area. A further indication of the magnitude of the movement of Mennonites into Saskatchewan may be gained from statistics on the numbers of Mennonites in Manitoba and Saskatchewan at the time of the censuses of 1901, 1911, and 1921:

	Manitoba	Saskatchewan
1901	15,246	3,751
1911	15,600	14,400
1921	21,295	20,544

It should be remembered that the above figures, particularly those from Saskatchewan, also include immigration from the United States and from Europe. However, the Russländer Mennonites who came to Canada after the Bolshevik Revolution did so after 1921.

52. This is shown by a list of German–English bilingual schools published in the *Manitoba Free Press* of November 26, 1910. It includes the names of several districts populated predominantly by conservative Sommerfelder. In addition, the Kleine Gemeinde and some Sommerfelder private schools were giving instruction in English as well as German. See A. Willows, "A History of the Mennonites," M.A. thesis, University of Manitoba, 1924, p. 68.

53. Hugh Ross, *Thirty-Five Years in the Limelight: Sir Rodmond P. Roblin and His Times* (Winnipeg: Farmer's Advocate of Winnipeg, 1936), p. 105.

implications for their military exemption in the future, they resisted.[54] One-quarter of the Mennonite public schools once more reverted to private status.[55]

Eventually the provincial government realized that the flag policy was not going to achieve its goals of instilling patriotism and a sense of the British tradition. In 1910 a German-speaking school inspector was engaged for the Mennonite reserves, to try and regain the ground lost over the flag issue. Indeed, so successful were the efforts of Inspector A. Willows [56] that between 1909 and 1916 the number of public school classrooms in the Mennonite districts rose from forty to eighty, the number of pupils in such schools more than doubled,[57] and the number of students in Grades 9 to 12 rose from two to sixty five.[58] From the twenty-odd Altkolonier districts there was, however, no cooperation.

It appears probable, however, that even the majority of the Altkolonier might have eventually been won over to acceptance of

54. I. I. Friesen, "The Mennonites of Western Canada, with Special Reference to Education", M.A. thesis, University of Saskatchewan, 1934, pp. 107–108.

55. In the absence of a law requiring students to attend public schools, school districts could, of course, forego the government grant and revert to private status, thereby escaping the flag-flying requirement. They did not, however, necessarily give up bilingual teaching. In the years 1907, 1908, and 1910 no new Mennonite public school districts were organized. This appears to have been owing at least in part to the incumbent school inspector and his relations with the Mennonite public, which may have reinforced the effects of the flag-flying policy of 1907. H. H. Ewert, Inspector of Schools from 1891 to 1903 and principal of the controversial teacher-training school, managed to establish forty-one Mennonite public schools during his tenure despite heavy opposition. From 1904 to 1910, only three Mennonite public school districts were created. See I. I. Friesen, pp. 106–107.

56. He had changed his name from Weidenhammer.

57. From 1,124 in 1909 to 2,593 in 1916.

58. A. Willows, p. 67. Progressive Mennonites hoped that these high-school students would become teachers and thus aid in building up an adequate teaching force for all Mennonite schools. Much of the credit for the increased public-school enrollment was owing, of course, to continuing efforts among the progressive Mennonites themselves. There was a total of some 100 schools in the Mennonite reserves in 1916; this statistic indicates that most of the Mennonite districts outside of the Altkolonier enclave in the West Reserve had been won over to the bilingual public school system by that time. Indeed, so good was the progress that in 1915 the bilingual Mennonite public schools rated considerable praise in educational reports, in contrast to schools in French, Polish, and Ruthenian districts. See C. B. Sissons, Bi-Lingual Schools in Canada (Toronto: J. M. Dent and Sons, 1917), p. 145.

the public schools and instruction in English as well as German [59] had not World War I intervened and precipitated events in a manner which resulted in Altkolonier emigration.

With the advent of the war and a rising (and assiduously nurtured) tide of nationalism, the Mennonites discovered themselves to be an alien minority group which, besides being conscientious objectors, was German in culture and language. In 1916 the wartime Manitoba government, taking advantage of nationalist feeling and support, moved to put an end to the bilingual public schools and to impose English as the sole language of instruction.[60]

To implement this policy, the provincial legislature in 1916 passed the School Attendance Act, making attendance in public schools mandatory for all children between the ages of seven and fourteen [61] unless they were receiving instruction privately at a standard satisfactory to the provincial authorities. Provision was

59. What the writer is postulating is that since there was some interest in improved education on the part of individual Altkolonier, the issue would have eventually come to a head in spite of reactionary official church policy. The ultraconservatives would ultimately have left the area, perhaps for other, more remote frontiers in Canada, leaving behind those more amenable to change. How such processes of change operate within Altkolonier society will be illustrated later on with reference to the Mennonite colonies in Mexico.

60. This is not to say that a change in school policy was neither necessary nor desirable. In many of the bilingual schools in Manitoba, English was being poorly taught. Furthermore, the law stated that if ten or more children of one nationality were attending school in one district, they were entitled to instruction in their mother tongue if they so desired. In ethnically homogeneous districts this was not a cause for dissension. There were, however, many mixed districts in the province, where two or more ethnic groups had the right to instruction in their own languages. The result was a great deal of dissension and infighting, stemming largely from a reactionary clergy who were not only unwilling to modify their ethnic consciousness, but fearful as well of losing, or having compromised, their positions of leadership.

61. C. B. Sissons, p. 151. The general desirability of enforcing compulsory attendance throughout the province is borne out by the fact that in 1915 absenteeism in German bilingual schools (mostly Mennonite but including a few Lutheran districts) was 36 percent. In Ruthenian–Polish districts it was 40 percent, and in French districts it was 53 percent (computed from statistics quoted by C. B. Sissons, p. 141). Although there are no statistics to substantiate this contention, the rate of school attendance in the Mennonite private schools cannot be said to have been higher than that in the public schools. Although attendance was ostensibly compulsory to age twelve, children of all ages were frequently kept out of school to help with farm work. The length of the school year in the various villages was not uniform, varying from a minimum of two months to a maximum of seven. (The foregoing is based on the personal recollections of the writer's parents.)

made to assist teachers in bringing their qualifications up to the prescribed standard.[62] Although the "bilingual" clause in the Public Schools Act, which had been responsible for much of the difficulty in which the provincial educational system found itself, was simply deleted, the way was left open for part-time instruction in other languages.[63]

The "progressive" Mennonite districts more or less readily complied with the new requirements. In more conservative areas the idea that the flag was purely a military emblem was gradually losing ground.[64] There were still many, however, who had as yet barely been persuaded of the desirability—or indeed, permissibility—of the forward-looking changes already in effect, among them the teaching of English. The subordination of German to English, together with the imposition of a curriculum which included such "worldly" subjects as history and geography, was perhaps too great a single step. The conservative clergy, for reasons previously cited, objected to these new and, to their minds, threatening innovations, which were furthermore regarded as being in direct contravention of the rights and privileges promised them in 1873. To their influence was ultimately added that of some teachers who, although the government expressed its willingness to help them raise their qualifications, eventually despaired of meeting the requirements and joined the reactionaries.[65] From the Altkolonier there was, predictably, no compliance whatever with the new law.

However, the reactionary Mennonite element was able to escape, for the moment at least, the requirements of the Attendance Act. On the advice of the incumbent member of the provincial legislature for Rhineland,[66] who at the time was also minister of agriculture, many Mennonite districts reverted once more to

62. C. B. Sissons, p. 153.

63. In the Mennonite public schools German-language instruction was subsequently given for one-half hour before and after regular classroom hours. In rural schools this was still, in the main, the case in 1965.

64. A. Willows, p. 74.

65. E. K. Francis, *In Search of Utopia*, p. 173. On the other hand, numerous more successful teachers became supporters of higher educational standards.

66. The Provincial Electoral Riding which included most of the Mennonite West Reserve.

21

private schools.[67] The advice was the more unfortunate in that, coming as it did from a senior member of the provincial cabinet, those who were guided by it were mistakenly led to believe that their position was unassailable by the school authorities.[68] Eventually the provincial administration, exasperated at seeing the purposes of its legislation thwarted, embarked on the course of action which ultimately precipitated the emigration of a large part of the Mennonite community. Under the provisions of the Public Schools Act, private schools were required to meet standards acceptable to the provincial authorities. In 1918 measures against the move toward private schools were instituted. Ratepayers in districts which were planning to revert to private status were warned against taking such action. If, however, they persisted, the district was placed under the control of an official trustee, and its school continued to operate as a public school. Next, the public schools which had earlier reverted to private status were revived by the same expedient. Finally, in the areas where no public schools had theretofore existed, the private schools were condemned as inadequate and public schools created.[69]

In Saskatchewan the ultimate course of events was much the same as that in Manitoba. When the school legislation was framed at the founding of the province in 1905, the unfortunate aspects of the Manitoba education laws were already manifestly apparent. In consequence, uniform standards for all Saskatchewan schools, public and sectarian, were written into the law from the beginning.[70]

67. A. Willows, p. 75. This was the second major instance of political "advice" with respect to the Mennonite school question. In 1903 Inspector H. H. Ewert was dismissed as a result of political maneuvering aimed at winning the Altkolonier and Sommerfelder vote.

68. *Ibid.*, p. 75. This episide reflects the autocratic thinking the Mennonites brought from Russia, where the hierarchy of authority culminated in the person of the tsar. The idea that various levels of government could have absolute jurisdiction in any matter was strange to them.

69. I. I. Friesen, pp. 116–117. These measures evoked a period of obstructionism, particularly on the part of the Altkolonier. Local lumber merchants, under threat of boycott, dared not supply materials for school construction. Workmen and supplies were brought from Winnipeg. Land for building sites was refused and had to be expropriated.

70. C. B. Sissons, pp. 158–159.

Since the new province was for some years to come still in a pioneering state, the government chose not to impose uniform English-language schools at once.[71]

The situation in Mennonite communities in Saskatchewan was in some ways comparable to that in Manitoba, with "progressives" and "conservatives," both church-group oriented, taking opposing positions. The majority of Saskatchewan Mennonites never offered resistance to public schools.[72] The Altkolonier and Sommerfelder, however, who had settled in the province when the entire region was still under federal jurisdiction as the Northwest Territories, had established their customary private schools. When the government of Manitoba imposed compulsory attendance, Saskatchewan followed suit. The premier of Saskatchewan, after personally satisfying himself as to the standard of education offered in Mennonite rural private schools, informed the Altkolonier Elder in the Hague–Osler district of his unfavorable impressions. If the Mennonites wished to retain their private schools, they must conform to Department of Education standards.[73] At Swift Current, the inspector of schools reminded the Mennonites that the School Attendance Act was binding upon them in Saskatchewan as in Manitoba.[74]

The response of the Altkolonier and of some of the other conservatives was to simply ignore the public schools. In the fall of 1918 the Manitoba authorities abandoned attempts at persuasion and resorted to the courts. Parents who failed to show valid cause why their children were not attending a recognized school were fined and, when that failed to achieve the desired compliance, imprisoned. The same course of action was taken in Saskatchewan, where the measures resorted to were, if anything, harsher and more peremptory. Most of the other conservatives quickly capitulated. The Altkolonier, however, were in a real dilemma. Undoubtedly many would have chosen to obey the law rather than suffer in-

71. *Ibid.,* p. 164.
72. I. I. Friesen, p. 136. Those who did not resist would include the Mennonites who had immigrated directly from the United States, Prussia, and Russia.
73. *Ibid.,* p. 139.
74. *Ibid.,* p. 136.

carceration or be gradually impoverished by fines [75] had such compliance not meant excommunication and ostracism. Some attempted to evade the issue by moving into as-yet-unorganized districts. Needless to say, great unrest prevailed among the Altkolonier in both provinces. Few of them ever understood fully the implications of the education laws. To their leaders it was a test of the faithful by which unity and like-mindedness could once more be established. There was talk of emigration.

World War I and the Conscription Question

The education laws were, however, only one test of the Mennonites' traditional concepts during this time. Late in 1916, the Dominion government let it be known that, in order to determine the manpower situation in the country, all males between the ages of sixteen and sixty-five must register with the authorities. Although there was no mention of a draft, this announcement caused consternation among the Mennonites. Many feared registration was preliminary to a military call-up. A combined delegation of five men from Saskatchewan and Manitoba was immediately dispatched to Ottawa to remind the government of its promise never to require military service from the Mennonites. They were given assurances that the government would honor its commitment. It is believed that most of the Mennonites ultimately registered. The Altkolonier of Manitoba and Saskatchewan called a joint conference (*Bruderschaft*) which sat in the village of Reinland in the West Reserve. Some of the leaders were persuaded that the registration was not unlike a census and could therefore be complied with. Others were convinced of its militaristic intent and suggested emigration in preference to compliance.[76] This occasion marks the beginning of the sentiment for migration.

75. Some men regularly paid the fines for as long as four years and finally submitted to the regulations only because of insolvency.

76. Gerhard Rempel, Campo 22, Colonia Manitoba, Chihuahua, Mexico. Rempel's father was a delegate to the meeting from the Swift Current district of Saskatchewan. United States land agents played upon the Mennonites' fear of a military draft in

The suspicions regarding the intent of the national service registration were to some extent justified. In 1917 military conscription was imposed in Canada. Young Mennonite men were called up like any others. When they proclaimed themselves conscientious objectors, they were hauled into court. Their trial may be considered to have been a test case, for the crown scrupulously adhered to its commitment guaranteeing them exemption from military service. The trial, at which the defendants acquitted themselves rather inadequately when questioned closely as to the basis of their scruples with respect to military service, was well publicized,[77] however, and served to intensify public resentment against the privileged status of the Mennonites.[78]

Resort to the Courts on the School Issue

Meanwhile, during 1917, 1918, and 1919, the pressure for acceptance of the public schools continued to mount. In Manitoba

---

the hope of selling them land in the U.S., which was not yet in the war. The new 640-acre homestead provision in the U.S. also evoked considerable interest in Mennonite circles, but fear of U.S. entry into the war kept the Mennonites in Canada from taking advantage of it. The *Steinbach Post* of 1917 carried a great many advertisements offering land in the U.S.

77. The *Winnipeg Tribune* of January 4, 1918, gives an account of the proceedings.

78. The fact that their ethnic and linguistic character was that of the enemy was played up by numerous "patriotic" pressure groups. Although the efforts of such groups to have the Mennonite draft exemption abrogated were unsuccessful, it is nevertheless likely that they had some influence on government attitude. The *Winnipeg Free Press* has extensive files on this type of agitation. In 1916 persons of German origin and conscientious objectors were deprived of the franchise. This move was of little consequence to the Mennonites because their conscientious-objector status had not yet been tested in the courts (they were simply exempt on the basis of the Order-in-Council of August 13, 1873, which detailed the privileges the Mennonites were to be guaranteed). Furthermore, they had traditionally considered themselves as being of Dutch, not German, origin and had registered as such. In 1917, however, Mennonites, Doukhobors, and Hutterites were specifically deprived of the vote. As a punitive measure it must have failed, because the conservatives who had most aggravated the authorities did not exercise their franchise anyway. In 1919 the Canadian immigration laws were amended to bar the entry of persons belonging to any of the above-named sects. Again the Mennonites in Canada were not directly affected, but these measures did cause alarm and unrest. However, for the Mennonites in Manitoba and Saskatchewan, the school question was by that time the main issue.

all remaining rural Mennonite private schools were condemned in the fall of 1918.[79] When the provincial authorities brought a test case before the Manitoba Court of Appeals in August of 1919, it was ruled that, notwithstanding promises made to the Mennonites by the federal government in 1873, the province of Manitoba had the right to enact and enforce the education laws.[80] The ruling generated considerable feeling among the Mennonites that the Dominion government had cynically deluded them in order to persuade them to settle in Canada at a time when immigrants were desperately needed to secure effective occupation of the west and broaden the economic base of the country. The judgement of the Manitoba Court of Appeals was protested, ultimately to the Privy Council in London, but to no avail.[81]

The Sommerfelder, who had never taken as adamant a stand against the school legislation as had the Altkolonier, appear to have accepted the decision of the Manitoba court as final. They appealed once more to the provincial government, expressing their willingness to cooperate wholeheartedly in "placing [their] schools above just criticism." [82] "As a matter of conscience, [however,] your Petitioners cannot delegate to others the all important responsibility of educating their children, convinced as they are, that instruction in other than religious schools would result in the weakening and even loss of faith, and would be generally detrimental to the moral and spiritual welfare of the children." [83] Even a relatively uncharitable interpretation of the Schools Act should have conceded them the right to retain their private schools as long as these met the standards required by the Department

79. E. K. Francis, *In Search of Utopia*, p. 185.

80. W. J. Tremeear, ed., *Canadian Criminal Cases*, XXXI (Toronto: Canada Law Book Company, 1920), 419–425 (*Rex* v. *Hildebrand*). The Dominion government, it was ruled, having delegated authority over education to the province by the Manitoba Act of 1870, was legally incompetent in such matters when the guarantees to the Mennonites were given in 1873.

81. E. K. Francis, *In Search of Utopia*, and "The Mennonite School Problem," *Mennonite Quarterly Review*, XXVII: 3 (1953), 232; *Winnipeg Evening Tribune*, July 30, 1920.

82. Petition of the members of the East Reserve Sommerfeld church, Chortitzer, to the government of Manitoba, January 13, 1920.

83. *Ibid.* This statement was repeated in a joint petition of the Sommerfelder of both reserves on October 14, 1921.

of Education.[84] The government of Manitoba, however, chose not to allow the petition, "For, it was no more a question of educational standards which prompted the authorities to destroy [the private schools] once and for all, and to replace them by English public schools. It was part of a consistent national policy aimed at the assimilation of ethnics to safeguard national unity and cultural uniformity." [85]

Apparently if, as had been established, the provincial government had sole jurisdiction over educational matters, then it could frame regulations aimed at particular minority groups. Furthermore, the government recognized no difference between the several Mennonite groups involved in the school dispute. Indeed it appears likely that the uncomprising stand of the Altkolonier prompted the denial of the privilege of maintaining private schools of proper standards,[86] as the Sommerfelder had expressed a willingness to do.

Decision to Emigrate

The Altkolonier, recognizing that the introduction of English and a more secular curriculum were hardly to be avoided, had already determined, at conferences held in both Manitoba and Saskatchewan during July 1919, that emigration was the only way out. It was decided to dispatch delegates to Argentina—possibly because it was known that there were substantial numbers of Germans there—to ascertain whether a Privilegium might be forthcoming from that country's government.[87]

The Sommerfelder reached the decision to emigrate only after

84. This privilege has actually always been conceded by the government to religious groups. Even the liberal Bergthal Mennonites on the West Reserve were operating two private schools at the time, and these were never threatened with dissolution.

85. E. K. Francis, "The Mennonite School Problem," *Mennonite Quarterly Review*, XXVII: 3 (1953), 233.

86. The Altkolonier never indicated a willingness to teach English or to introduce into their schools the curriculum demanded by the government.

87. David Harder, "Chronik," a hand-written manuscript detailing significant events in Altkolonier history from just prior to World War I to the present. The manuscript is in the possession of its author, David Harder, Blumenhof, Campo 2, La Batea, Zacatecas, Mexico.

it became evident that not the least conciliatory gesture from the government would be forthcoming. They too, therefore, "with a heavy heart" felt "compelled to seek another home." [88] For both groups there followed then the agonized search for new lands, which in the course of the 1920's was to see the Altkolonier take themselves off to new frontiers in Mexico, the Sommerfelder to Mexico and Paraguay.

The Kleine Gemeinde [89] were also greatly disturbed by the innovations in education during these times, and by the possible implications of the wartime regulations for their future military status. Of the conservative Mennonite groups, they had offered the least resistance to the public schools. Indeed, by 1903 six of the seven predominantly Kleine Gemeinde villages had been organized into public school districts.[90] With the proclamation of the flag-flying requirement in 1907, all of them adopted the legal strategem of reverting to private schools,[91] but eventually returned to the public school system of their own accord. World War II, however, was to revive their unrest and result in a body of conservatives among them establishing a colony in Mexico in the late 1940's.

Certain it is that had not the pressures of World War I complicated matters, more patience and good will might have been brought to bear on the problem of getting the conservative Mennonites to generally accept the new educational requirements. Most of those who eventually emigrated never really understood the true nature of the series of events which finally led to the decision to leave Canada.

88. Petition of the combined Sommerfelder congregations of Manitoba to the provincial government, October 14, 1921.

89. The Kleine Gemeinde in Manitoba had undergone a split about 1882, when about half the group went over to the Church of God in Christ (Mennonite), an evangelical church organized in Ohio in 1859 by John Holdemann. In Manitoba they are generally referred to by other Mennonites as Holdemänner.

90. This statement is based upon district names mentioned in the *Manitoba Free Press* of November 26, 1910. They are Rosenhof and Rosenort in the rural municipality of Morris, and Steinbach, Blumenort, Blumenhof, and Grünfeld in the East Reserve.

91. I. I. Friesen, p. 111. They did not, however, cease to teach English.

Other Mennonite Immigrants in Mexico

The few Mennonites in Mexico who do not derive from the settlements in Canada represent three small groups which came to Mexico in the 1920's, two from the United States and one from Russia. In 1924 three Kleine Gemeinde families from Meade, Kansas, purchased land in Chihuahua. In 1927 a Holdemann (Church of God in Christ) Mennonite group from Isabella, Oklahoma, composed of four brothers and their families, also went to Chihuahua. The motivation behind both of these small groups was escape from what they felt were excessive secular influences, particularly upon the rising generation. The small Russian Mennonite group consisted of refugees from the Bolshevik Revolution; in most cases they had family members who, for reasons of health, could not meet the requirements of U.S. and Canadian immigration laws. During 1924 and 1925 attempts were made by the Mennonite Board of Colonization to establish these people in a number of locations in the states of Guanajuato, Durango, and Chihuahua.

Conclusion

The causes of the Mennonite migrations to Mexico thus were several. One was the simple and inescapable fact of scarcity of land in existing Mennonite communities, which had resulted in their diffusion over the western provinces of Canada. That it influenced the thinking in relation to emigration is a fact not to be denied. The more apparent reasons for migration were the disturbing influences upon the traditional Mennonite way of life by the Canadian host society, with the threat these implied to the authority of the leaders and the cohesiveness of the community. More particularly there were the threats posed to the conservative elements by the existence, within the Mennonite community, of a substantial body of liberals who, for several reasons, preferred to collaborate with the world at large. These issues were sharpened by direct governmental intervention in Mennonite community affairs in the sensitive areas relating to local administration and exemption from military service. The "liberals" adjusted to prevailing conditions. The response of the "conservatives," as had been the case in Prussia and Russia before, was to seek escape from unwelcome impositions and impingements through the traditional device of emigration to new frontiers where the old order might once more be recreated. These frontiers were to be, this time, in the wastes of highland Mexico.

Chapter 2

Preparations for
Auswanderung

When the Altkolonier arrived at the decision to emigrate, in July of 1919, steps were at once taken to seek a suitable tract of land in a country which would undertake to guarantee them the concessions they sought with respect to language, religion, and schools. Word of the impending migration was of course carried in the press, and the Altkolonier were shortly besieged by offers of land from railroad companies, land dealers, and speculators in such widely separated places as the southern United States (Mississippi, Florida, Alabama) and Brazil. It was agreed among the three Altkolonier settlements that if at all possible a single tract large enough to accommodate them all should be purchased. Accordingly, a delegation of six men was dispatched to South America in early August of the same year.[1] The delegates proceeded first to Ottawa, the national capital, where were joined by their legal advisor. Ostensibly the stop in Ottawa was for purposes of ascertaining that their citizenship papers were in order,[2] and of establishing contact with the Argentine Consulate.[3] While in Ottawa, however, they visited various

1. The delegates were: Klaas Heide and Cornelius Rempel from Manitoba; David Rempel and Rev. Julius Wiebe from Swift Current; and Johann Wall and Rev. Johann P. Wall of the Hague–Osler district.

2. In getting their papers in order, the Altkolonier delegates experienced difficulties which in all fairness can be attributed only to obstructionism on the part of the immigration authorities. For those of the delegates who had been born in Russia, it was extremely important to have all papers in order so as to assure their readmission into Canada.

3. The Argentine Consulate took special pains to determine if the Russian-born delegates were, perhaps, Bolsheviks. Argentina was known to have a substantial

departments of the federal government in the company of their lawyer, in what appears to have been yet another attempt to win from the federal authorities the concessions which, if granted, would keep them in Canada.[4] Although they received admissions from a few of the officials with whom they gained audience that their cause had a certain merit in view of the legalistic approach taken toward the school question by the authorities, nothing could, of course, be done. The delegates therefore, with some trepidation, proceeded upon their journey to South America.

The delegation arrived in Sao Paulo in September 1919. After an audience with government officials, they traveled inland to Curitiba in the state of Paraná, where the Brazil Railroad Company wished them to inspect some land. They arrived in Buenos Aires on October 6.[5] The Argentine government, although at the time actively encouraging immigration, appears to have responded to their visit and request for a Privilegium with something less than enthusiasm. European emigrants, victims of World War I, asking no special rights or privileges, were streaming into South America. Under such circumstances the preconditions set by the Altkolonier enjoyed little likelihood of being met.[6] Nor, to all appearances, were they given any encouragement.

German population, and it is this fact which appears to have directed Altkolonier attention there, since there were no overtures from that country. An agent of the Brazil Railroad Company had visited Swift Current, and had generated interest in his country.

4. David Rempel, "Personal Diary," *passim*. Their lawyer, in addressing several members of Parliament and senators, presented the Altkolonier thus: "These are delegates, they wish to go to Argentina and we are driving them out." It is rather evident that this technique was calculated to disconcert the government and possibly at the last minute to gain the Altkolonier their objective.

5. This itinerary is recounted here to establish the lack of likelihood that the Altkolonier delegates conferred with Uruguayan officials, as some students have postulated. They left Curitiba for Montevideo late on Wednesday, September 30, and departed from Montevideo for Buenos Aires on Monday, October 5. Since travel time between Curitiba and Montivideo would have taken a minimum of two days, this leaves little time during which Uruguayan officials could have responded to the Mennonites' petition; everywhere else in Latin America, such responses from officials usually took several weeks. Moreover, October 4 was a Sunday, and the Altkolonier would have undertaken no labor on that day.

6. In his diary David Rempel related that he and the others in the party visited the harbor area, where thousands of immigrants from Germany and Austria were disembarking.

Offers of Land in the U.S.A.

Even before the delegates departed for South America, the Altkolonier had been offered at least one block of land in Alabama. Indeed it appears that a few families went there.[7] Then, early in 1920, a land agent from Mississippi offered them 200,000 acres in that state, extending, at the same time, prospects of obtaining for the Altkolonier the privileges which were an imperative precondition for any purchase. Delegates from Manitoba and Saskatchewan were at once dispatched to investigate the offer. They returned with word that the necessary concessions had been promised by the state government, although no document to that effect was as yet available.

In April of 1920 another delegation went to Mississippi to pursue the prospects of establishing a settlement. On April 29, Rev. Johann P. Wall of the Hague–Osler settlement stated, in an interview carried in the *Winnipeg Evening Tribune,* that Governor Russell of Mississippi had pledged the desired privileges in writing, and that U.S. Attorney-General A. Mitchell Palmer had promised immunity from military service. Furthermore, he said, the Altkolonier were awaiting a formal document from the U.S. government covenanting it to respect the Mennonites' privileges in perpetuity.[8] At the time of the interview, Rev. Wall was waiting upon officials of the Saskatchewan government to inform them that unless the Mennonites' military and school privileges were continued, 8,000 of his people would leave Canada.

7. David Rempel, "Personal Diary." In a letter to his family, dated Curitiba, Brazil, September 25, 1919, he states that the plantation crops he saw near Sao Paulo reminded him of "die Auswanderer nach Alabama" (the emigrants to Alabama).

8. *Winnipeg Evening Tribune,* April 30, 1920. The Mennonites *did* receive a letter stating that they would enjoy the rights of conscientious objectors. Religious freedom was of course guaranteed by the Constitution. Such promises were repeatedly made to the Mennonites during their search for land. It appears certain that the Altkolonier delegates, under pressure not only from the provincial governments because of the school laws but from their own people as well, chose to see these promises in the best possible light. On the other hand, it is highly unlikely that eager land agents or states desirous of settling wastelands with pioneers of proven ability took the trouble to discover precisely what cultural peculiarities, beyond the most apparent ones, lay behind the Altkolonier migration movement. The *Tribune* erroneously identified Rev. Johann P. Wall of Hague as Elder Wall of Swift Current.

His purpose in seeking audience with them, he said, was to discover what the government's reaction to such an exodus might be. He was assured there would be no official hindrance.[9] A few days later Governor Russell denied having made promises such as the Altkolonier claimed, which would contravene either federal or state laws.[10] Nevertheless on May 4, at a conference held in Reinland, Manitoba, it was determined to go ahead with plans to purchase land, and ten days later yet another group went to Mississippi for this purpose. On the strength of the progress reported upon their return, the Altkolonier communities were canvassed to determine the acreage each individual wished to reserve. A deposit of $2 per acre was collected, and early in June a delegation of four was dispatched with these monies to make the down payment. When they got to the U.S. border, however, they were turned back.[11]

Although the Altkolonier were loath to give up the idea of migrating to Mississippi, the realities of the situation now precluded such a move. The project could not be so quickly abandoned, however, because certain commitments had been entered into by the delegates with respect to the contemplated land purchase.[12] Litigation was narrowly avoided.

9. It is transparently evident that Rev. Wall's statements to the government were meant to drive home the magnitude of the potential economic loss to the province if the Mennonites left, and thereby perhaps to gain some concessions. This technique is strongly reminiscent of the techniques repeatedly employed against the tsarist government in the early 1870's, which at that time resulted in concessions that were satisfactory to the majority of the Mennonites in Russia.

10. *Winnipeg Evening Tribune,* May 7, 1920.

11. David Harder, "Chronik," *passim,* and *Steinbach Post,* December 22, 1920. The precise reason why they were refused entry has never been publicized. It is known that the American Legion had made representations to the government against the proposed Mennonite immigration into Mississippi. However, the immediate reason may have simply been that the four delegates did not have their papers in order. The agent of the land company which was hoping to negotiate a deal with the Mennonites asked the U.S. immigration office in Winnipeg about the admissibility of the Mennonites. He was informed that no special status would be granted them.

12. In June of 1921, H. A. Emerson, representing the Aberdeen Land and Chattel Company of Yellow Pine, Alabama, stated in Winnipeg that the Mennonites had contracted for the purchase of 100,000 acres in Wayne County, Mississippi. He pronounced himself ready to sue if an out-of-court settlement for damages could not be reached. *Winnipeg Evening Tribune,* June 25, 1921.

Faced with this setback to their plans, the Altkolonier leaders directed yet another plea to the Manitoba government: "Is there any place in Manitoba, where none other can live, in which we could found a colony, apart from the world, where we could bring up our children, unhindered by common laws, in the true faith of our forefathers?" They were told that the law applied everywhere, that a country within a country was impossible to contemplate in Canada. The Altkolonier thereupon determined to reopen negotiations with Brazil.[13] Greater urgency was imposed upon the migration movement by the refusal, in July of 1920, of the Mennonite appeal to the Privy Council[14] concerning the imposition of the school laws.

To Quebec?

By August of 1920 it was evident that no Privilegium would be forthcoming from Brazil.[15] However, sometime during the summer of that year the Altkolonier became aware of the fact that the government of the province of Quebec was actively assisting settlement in the Abitibi region of the Great Clay Belt. Now a concerted drive was mounted to win the desired concessions in Quebec–exemption from military service, with full religious and educational freedom, including the right to the exclusive use of German. On August 13, 1920, the first of a series of delegations left for Quebec in an effort to obtain the desired guarantees. The course of events was reminiscent of the Mississippi deal. The first delegations returned with high expectations for the full realization of the Altkolonier's hopes. There followed then the gradual attrition of these hopes as it became apparent that Quebec was not really interested in encouraging the settlement of others than French-Canadians, while the federal government would no more guarantee them privileges in Quebec than anywhere in Canada.[16]

13. *Manitoba Free Press*, May 18, 1920.

14. *Winnipeg Evening Tribune*, July 30, 1920.

15. Delegates went to New York in the summer of 1920 to consult with Brazilian officials there. When the Privilegium proved unattainable, the Altkolonier abandoned the idea of migrating to that country.

16. David Harder, "Chronik," *passim.*

The Strain Begins to Tell

It was about this time that the unity of the three Altko-lonier groups began to break down. First, the continuing investigations of land in the U.S. and Canada encouraged numerous private individuals to join the delegated groups on these relatively short journeys. These persons returned with their own evaluation of the lands they had seen and inevitably broadcast their prejudices at home, with decidedly divisive effects. Second, the repeated failures to find a suitable place to which to migrate were cause for grave concern to the Altkolonier leaders, who feared a total accommodation to the education laws by their younger people if an emigration could not be realized soon.

The Quebec venture was undertaken without the support of the Hague–Osler group in Saskatchewan. Independently of the others, it sent a delegation to Mexico in September of 1920.[17] The real instigator of this venture was one John F. D. Wiebe, a member of the Krimmer Mennonite Brethren who had immigrated from Kansas,[18] owner of a real estate and insurance business in Herbert, Saskatchewan. Wiebe, aware of the extensive land reforms to be undertaken in postrevolutionary Mexico, and anticipating the entrepreneurial possibilities inherent in a massive land deal such as the anticipated Altkolonier migration would entail, went to Mexico City and established contact with Arturo J. Braniff, brother-in-law of Alvaro Obregón, the incumbent President. Wiebe returned to Canada and informed the Altkolonier of his findings,[19] as a result of which the Hague–Osler delegation was dispatched to Mexico.

While the Manitoba and Swift Current groups were still actively pursuing the diminishing prospects of moving to Que-

17. *Ibid.*
18. See above, Chapter I, note 50.
19. Jacob A. Wiebe, Cd. Cuauhtémoc, Chihuahua, Mexico, personal communication. Wiebe is the son of John F. D. Wiebe and the grandson of the founder of the Karassan Krimmer Mennonites, Jakob Wiebe. The Altkolonier did not retain John F. D. Wiebe as their agent. Wiebe, however, had a commission arrangement with the Braniff interests.

bec,[20] the Hague–Osler delegates returned from Mexico with high hopes that a Privilegium would be forthcoming from that country's government. In the meantime, in September of 1920, the Altkolonier of Manitoba directed yet another plea to the provincial government. This time it was a request for a moratorium on the enforcement of the school attendance laws for two years, to give them time to wind up their affairs and leave the country.[21] When word of the Hague–Osler group's relative success got abroad, the other two settlements dropped the unpromising Quebec venture and turned their attentions to Mexico. At a conference held in Reinland, Manitoba, it was agreed to send a joint delegation from all three settlements to Mexico. Because the passports of the Manitoba delegates were not in order, only the representatives from Swift Current and Hague–Osler were able to go. When they returned to report continuing bright prospects of obtaining a Privilegium yet another delegation, this time representing all three groups, was dispatched to Mexico in January of 1921.[22] They were accompanied by John F. D. Wiebe, the man who had directed the Altkolonier's interest upon this venture.[23]

They arrived in El Paso on January 28, 1921.[24] Wiebe had been actively making contacts with various persons and agencies desirous of disposing of lands in Mexico. In El Paso the delegates received a letter of welcome from the Mexican president and the minister of agriculture, and were joined by an interpreter.[25] The

20. The Altkolonier Elders Johann Friesen of Manitoba and Abram Wiebe of Swift Current went to Ottawa to seek guarantees from the federal government that it would uphold any promises made by the Quebec provincial authorities. Quebec did not at that time have a compulsory school attendance law.

21. *Winnipeg Evening Tribune,* September 20, 1920. The *Tribune* reported that the Altkolonier leaders were experiencing an alarming incidence of compliance with the education laws, particularly among the younger people, who furthermore did not have any wish to emigrate.

22. David Harder, "Chronik," *passim.*

23. David Rempel, "Personal Diary," January 21, 1921.

24. This delegation consisted of Klaas Heide, Cornelius Rempel, and Rev. Julius Loewen of Manitoba; Benjamin Goertzen and Rev. Johann Loeppky of the Hague–Osler district; and David Rempel from the Swift Current settlement.

25. The interpreter, Daniel Salas López, subsequently served the Mennonites for many years as their contact man with the government in Mexico City. His role is difficult to define, but he appears to have had influential friends in the government.

group crossed the border at Nogales, Arizona, on February 3, in the company of one Enlow, a land agent from Los Angeles who had met them in Tucson. Enlow had numerous parcels of land, both irrigated and unirrigated, to offer the Mennonites, from Hermosillo southward through the states of Sonora, Sinaloa, Nayarit, and Jalisco. None of these properties, however, appealed to the Altkolonier as being suitable for the establishment of a Mennonite colony. At Hermosillo, Sonora, they were offered 120,000 acres of desert land at $.60 to $.75 (U.S.) per acre. Although the Altkolonier were appreciative of the fertility of the land when placed under irrigation—"in spite of the dryness the land appears to be good; where irrigated, we saw several orange orchards laden with fruit"—it did not appeal to them. Again in the vicinity of Culiacán, Sinaloa, they were impressed with the cactus and thorn scrub-covered landscape, "so thickly overgrown, that cattle are visible for no more than fifty yards. . . . the ground is hard and dry, and it does not appear that planting could be successful here . . . [but] where watered, it grows magnificently, sugarcane and bananas . . . [At Ciudad Ruiz, Sinaloa] when one digs a hole in the earth, it steams. The water from wells is warm . . . the climate is said to be very unhealthy." It is evident from David Rempel's description that they had serious reservations about the possibilities of life in the tropics. Furthermore, they were unwilling to consider irrigation farming,[26] while dry farming on the cactus and thorn scrub-covered range lands appeared to them to offer little hope for the establishment of a successful agriculture. What they were really looking for was a land complex which offered prospects of being amenable to the pursuit of the same agricultural practices the Mennonites had been accustomed to in Russia and Canada.

26. The reluctance to undertake the purchase of irrigated land was partly owing to its high price and to the Mennonites' lack of experience in irrigation farming. However, a further consideration by the Altkolonier was the fact that the territory surrounding such lands would inevitably be settled by Mexicans. The Altkolonier wanted more isolation. Their itinerary took them from Hermosillo to Mexico City via Guaymas, Culiacán, Mazatlán, Cd. Ruiz, Tuxpan, Santiago, Tepic, Ixtlán, San Marcos, and Guadalajara.

The delegates proceeded via Guadalajara to Mexico City, where, on February 17, they were joined by A. I. Villareal, the Minister of Agriculture, and Arturo J. Braniff, who accompanied them to the presidential palace for an audience with Alvaro Obregón. They presented their request for a Privilegium to the president, who expressed enthusiasm at the prospect of acquiring for Mexico so large a group of enterprising farmers. There followed then a period of nine days during which the particulars of the Privilegium were worked out. President Obregón was at first reticent to endorse the clause referring to sectarian schools and the exclusive use of German. However, when it became apparent that without this guarantee there was no prospect of the Mennonites settling in Mexico, he finally let it stand as the Altkolonier wished.

The delegates were hopeful of taking the completed and endorsed Privilegium with them. They were also anxious, however, now that this major hurdle had been cleared, to get on with the search for suitable land. Accordingly, they left Mexico City on February 27 for Durango, in the company of Braniff, having been assured that the Privilegium would be sent to them as soon as completed in proper official form. Braniff arranged for them to view numerous properties which he had on hand for liquidation, including part of the Valle de Guatimapé in which the Hague–Osler group ultimately settled several years later. In Durango, Braniff introduced them to the governor, who promised to honor the Privilegium endorsed by the president, and to aid the Mennonite immigration in every way possible.[27] The Privilegium, signed by President Alvaro Obregón and Minister of Agriculture A. I. Villareal, was received by the delegates while still in Durango:

To the representatives of the Old Colony Reinland Mennonite Church, Rev. Julius Loewen, Johann Loeppky, Chairman Benjamin Goertzen, and members Cornelius Rempel, Klaas Heide, and David Rempel.

In answer to your appeal of 29 January of this year, in which

27. The preceding two paragraphs are based upon the diary of David Rempel, February 16 to March 5, 1921.

you express the desire to establish yourselves as agricultural settlers in our country, I have the honor to inform you of the
following, in answer to the concrete questions which your aforementioned appeal contains.

1. You are not obligated to military service.
2. In no case are you required to make oath.
3. You have the most far-reaching right to exercise your religious
   principles and the rules of your church, without being in any
   manner molested or restricted.
4. You are entirely authorized to found your own schools, with
   your own teachers, without the government in any manner
   obstructing you.
5. Concerning this point, our laws are most liberal. You may
   administer your properties in any way or manner you think
   just, and this government will raise no objection if the members
   of your sect establish among themselves economic regulations
   which they adopt of their own free will.

It is the particular wish of this government to favor colonization by elements of order, morality, and toil, such as the
Mennonites, and it will be pleased if the foregoing answers are
satisfactory to you, in view of the fact that the aforementioned
franchises [privileges] are guaranteed by our laws and that you
enjoy them positively and permanently.

> *Sufragio efectivo, no reelección.*
> *México, a 25 de febrero de 1921*
> *El Presidente Constitucional de los*
> *Estados Unidos Mexicanos*
> *Signed: A. Obregón*

El Secretario de
Agricultura y Fomento
Signed: A. I. Villareal

Increasing Urgency

As the legal pressure with respect to the enforcement
of the Canadian school attendance laws mounted, and with it
the urgency of those who desired to emigrate on this account,
a kind of minor panic reigned in the Altkolonier settlements.
Although no suitable land had yet been found elsewhere, there
were those who, on the strength of the promising prospects

reported from Mexico by the first Hague–Osler delegation, urged the sale of property in Canada so that there might be no further impediment to the migration once a satisfactory destination was discovered. The Hague–Osler group put up its land for sale early in 1921 and quickly found a buyer, at $40 per acre, who, however, failed to meet his obligations. The deal fell through, and the Mennonites repossessed their land. The Swift Current group also offered its land for sale about this time, through a legal firm in Swift Current, agreeing to pay a commission of $4 per acre for the finding of a bona fide buyer. Against the advice of Elder Jakob Wiens of Hague and of one of their own ministers, Rev. Julius Wiebe, the Swift Current Altkolonier accepted as agent for their land the same man who had handled the abortive purchase of the Hague–Osler land.[28] While the combined delegation from all three Altkolonier settlements was still in Mexico in the spring of 1921, the Swift Current people received, through this agent, an offer of land in the U.S. A certain James J. Logan and one James P. Taylor proposed to sell them a large tract of land in Florida, taking in exchange 107,000 acres in the Swift Current district at an average valuation of $45 per acre, upon which they intended to settle farmers from the United States.[29] The deal must have generated considerable interest in Florida, for shortly thereafter the secretary of agriculture from that state visited the Swift Current area. He informed the Mennonites that while school attendance was compulsory, there was no specification as to the *kind* of school, whether public or private. On the question of military service, he assured them that this was connected with the religious freedom guaranteed by U.S. law, and that they need not fear conscription.[30] At least a few Altkolonier families appear to have responded to these blandishments. By June of 1922 at least one family, formerly from Saskatchewan, was appealing to the Canadian Department of Immigration and Colonization for aid to return to Canada.[31]

28. David Harder, La Batea, Zacatecas, Mexico, personal communication.
29. *Winnipeg Evening Tribune,* June 7, 1921.
30. *Ibid.,* July 12, 1921.
31. *Ibid.,* June 14, 1922. In his letter the regretful emigrant stated that his "intentions were never to leave Canada, but I was talked up to do so, and [I am] very sorry that [I] did."

The law firm acting for the Mennonites demanded of them a guarantee of its commission, should they produce a buyer. To satisfy this demand the owners of a total of 10,200 acres in the Swift Current settlement were persuaded by their leaders to sign releases of their property. When the Florida deal also fell through, for lack of performance on the part of the American promoters, the law firm nevertheless demanded its commission for performing its legal obligations in locating a bona fide buyer. Court action resulted. The law firm was given judgment and took possession of the land given by the Mennonites as surety.[32] The questionable legality of the confiscation proceedings is indicated by the haste with which the entire property was immediately mortgaged to the hilt, then sacrificed to the loan company by default of payment. The loan company then proceeded to rent the land back to the dispossessed former owners.[33] The authorities of the Swift Current settlement attempted to make good a part of the loss of those who were dispossessed, through a levy of $2 per acre on the remaining land. Willingness to participate in this plan manifested itself so poorly that the issue was dropped and the losers were abandoned to their misfortune.[34]

32. The Altkolonier were given judgment by the Judicial Court of Saskatchewan, the Saskatchewan Court of Appeal, and the Supreme Court of Canada. The plaintiffs thereupon carried the case to the Privy Council in London, which reversed the earlier decisions. No further appeal was possible, and the Altkolonier forfeited 10,200 acres of land in lieu of the judgment of $221,000 and costs. *Steinbach Post,* December 10, 1924. The fact that British financial interests were involved makes the Privy Council's reversal of the Canadian Supreme Court's ruling appear all the more as a "managed" miscarriage of justice.

33. David Harder, La Batea, Zacatecas, Mexico, personal communication. The particulars are vouched for by Johann Martens, Campo 8, Nuevo Ideal, Durango, Mexico, who is one of those who lost their land through this action.

34. One can only guess at the motives of the leaders in so quickly abandoning this eminently just, if unpopular, enterprise. It appears not unlikely that it was done to avoid increasing the factionalism which was making the whole emigration movement ever more difficult to handle. It is known that those who were dispossessed of their land were subsequently told by their leaders that their misfortune was a design of the government to get them to leave Canada (Johann Martens, Campo 8, Nuevo Ideal, Durango, Mexico, personal communication). In view of the lack of comprehension that characterized most Mennonite contacts with government authorities, it appears likely that the leaders of the Swift Current settlement were themselves convinced that such was the case.

While the various dealings for the acquisition of suitable land were dragging on and the several colonies were making independent attempts to liquidate their properties in Canada, it had become progressively more difficult to maintain any semblance of the unity of purpose and action which had characterized the emigration movement at the beginning. However, when the delegates to Mexico returned in March of 1921, sufficient unity was once more forged to warrant a survey to establish the acreage each aspiring emigrant wished to reserve. On the strength of this, another delegation was dispatched in April to complete final arrangements for a land purchase. There was interest in locating in the Valle de Guatimapé, in the Municipio of Canatlán, about eighty miles northwest of the city of Durango. An agreement with Braniff was reached and a contract made for the purchase of the Guatimapé lands.[35]

A Growing Rift

During the extended dealings, it had, however, become apparent to the representatives from Manitoba and Swift Current that the Hague–Osler brethren were generally less well-endowed financially than the others. Fears were therefore aroused that if a joint land purchase of sufficient size to accommodate all three groups were transacted, the Hague–Osler group might prove unable to meet its financial obligations. In that event the others would have to make good or run the risk of having the entire colony foreclosed. When the leading delegate from the Hague–Osler settlement, the forceful Rev. Johann P. Wall, discovered the existence of this sentiment on the part of the others, he challenged them on it. The result was a complete rupture of the plans for a unified purchase.[36] The Hague–Osler group thereupon tem-

35. David Harder, La Batea, Zacatecas, Mexico, personal communication.
36. The episode referred to occurred in the Hotel Posada Durán in Durango. Details were supplied by David Harder, La Batea, Zacatecas, Mexico, and were vouched for by David B. Penner, Campo 2-B, Cd. Cuauhtémoc, Chihuahua, Mexico. Penner's father was present on the occasion referred to. The rupture of relations appears to have been mainly attributable to a personality clash between Klaas Heide of Manitoba and Rev. Johann P. Wall, both of whom were reputed to have been very forceful characters.

43

porarily abandoned the idea of moving to Mexico and picked up the threads of an ephemeral connection with Paraguay.[37] A delegation which went to that country returned disenchanted with the prospects of settling there. In the meantime the postwar economic boom had run its course, property sales were difficult to make, and the Hague–Osler group was forced to shelve its emigration plans for several years. The Guatimapé deal, of course, disintegrated.

The Land Is Found

While the ill-fated deal with Braniff was still pending, John F. D. Wiebe had established an office in El Paso, from where he hoped to be instrumental in directing the movement of the Mennonites once the projected migration began. In El Paso he established contact with the Newman Investment Company, which, like Braniff, had on hand numerous Mexican properties for liquidation, from owners who feared confiscation of their lands once the agrarian reforms were brought into effect. A property which held particular promise of meeting the Mennonites' requirements was the Hacienda Bustillos, part of the estate of Carlos Zuloaga,[38] some sixty miles west of the city of Chihuahua. To this

37. It appears that the Altkolonier delegates had, on a previous journey to New York (possibly when negotiations with Brazil were resumed following the breakdown of the plans to remove to Quebec), come into contact with Colonel Samuel McRoberts, who directed their attention to Paraguay. McRoberts later played a major role in a Sommerfelder migration to Paraguay in 1926 and 1927.

38. The Hacienda Bustillos was part of the Zuloago *latifundio* (group of landed estates) of several million acres. Prior to 1725 western Chihuahua was an important mining and ranching region, with numerous mining towns, presidios, haciendas, and missions. There ensued then over a century of "Apache troubles," with Apache tribes plundering and destroying most of the settlements. During the eighteenth and early nineteenth centuries western Chihuahua was gradually pacified through the creation of numerous military settlements. In 1832, however, the Apaches resumed their relentless guerrilla war. Ranching, agriculture, and mining came almost to a standstill. In such circumstances land was cheap, and a few men, envisioning the end of the Apache threat through concerted military action, began to acquire vast holdings. Among them were General—later Governor—Luis Terrazas, who ultimately owned nearly one-half of Chihuahua, and General Félix Zuloaga, founder of the latifundio Zuloaga. (Félix Zuloaga was proclaimed Vice-President of Mexico in 1857 under President Comonfort.) The Bustillos property belonged first to Luis Terrazas, from whom it was acquired by the Zuloagas through a third party. Details of this devel-

Wiebe directed the attention of the Swift Current and Manitoba groups. The Northwestern Railway of Mexico, which was interested in the future traffic that an agricultural colony within its territory would generate, made Wiebe its agricultural agent for purposes of expediting the anticipated migration. This enabled him to obtain free transportation for himself and the Mennonite delegates over U.S. and Mexican railroads.[39]

The Altkolonier delegates were enthusiastic about the agricultural prospects in Chihuahua. At Bustillos, corn, oats, barley, and potatoes were being grown without irrigation.[40] On September 6, 1921, the Manitoba Altkolonier purchased 150,000 acres from the Zuloaga estate.[41] About the same time the Swift Current delegates contracted for the purchase of an adjacent 75,000 acres. The price was $8.25 in U.S. gold per acre, the land to be selected by the Mennonites. The purchase previously arranged with Braniff, for the Llanos de Guatimapé, was unilaterally abrogated, much to Braniff's dissatisfaction, although he retained the money already paid. Later Wiebe took him in as an associate on the Bustillos transaction, and Braniff thereupon dropped all further claims against the Altkolonier.[42]

The purchase agreement between the Manitoba Altkolonier and the Zuloaga interests stipulated a down payment of $2 in gold

---

opment are not clear. The Zuloaga family was connected by marriage to that of Francisco I. Madero, leader of the revolution of 1910 and President of Mexico until his assassination in 1913. Doña Luz Zuloaga, daughter of Carlos Zuloaga, was the wife of Alberto Madero, a relative of Francisco I. Madero. The name Madero, however, occurs *twice* in the contract of the sale between the Zuloagas and the Mennonites, suggesting that there may have been a further connection. (The above information is derived from Donald D. Brand, "Northwestern Chihuahua," Ph.D. dissertation, University of California, Berkeley, 1933, *passim*, from Benjamin Keen, ed., *Readings in Latin American Civilization* [Boston: Houghton-Mifflin, 1955], pp. 274–275, and from a personal communication from Señora Julietta M. de Coughanoar of Cd. Chihuahua.)

39. The Northwestern Railway of Mexico placed a private car at the disposal of Wiebe and the delegates.

40. Klaas Heide, Gretna, Manitoba, to Arturo J. Braniff, September 15, 1921.

41. Gerhard J. Rempel, Campo 22, Cd. Cuauhtémoc, Chihuahua, personal files. Rempel was for many years Vorsteher of the Manitoba colony.

42. Arturo J. Braniff to David Rempel and Rev. Julius Wiebe, Wymark, Saskatchewan, October 19, 1921.

per acre, with the balance to be spread over eight years at 6 percent interest. The vendors agreed to insure that all squatters would vacate the property, and to use their good offices in obtaining confirmation of the presidential Privilegium from the state authorities also. When the Altkolonier accordingly addressed themselves to the governor of Chihuahua on the latter issue, endorsement was quickly forthcoming.

Before the purchase of the Zuloaga lands could be considered entirely completed, the Mennonites, as foreigners seeking to acquire property in Mexico, had to obtain formal permission from the federal government. Indications are that Arturo J. Braniff took care of this matter himself, for the necessary certificate was quickly forthcoming.

Liquidation of Canadian Holdings

Although the destination of the migration was now determined, there remained the problem of liquidating their Canadian assets—a problem which was to strain to the limit the coherence of the Altkolonier community. At a conference held in Reinland, Manitoba, in May of 1921, to hear the reports of the latest delegations to Mexico, the consensus of opinion was that the migration would, this time, materialize. It was therefore determined, at the suggestion of their leaders, to pool all fixed property—land and buildings—and to endeavor to sell the entire parcel in one transaction. A uniform price per acre was to be asked, regardless of the condition or quality of the land. Buildings were to be included with the land; however, in the case of those who owned no land, a valuation was to be allowed for buildings.[43] Although there was objection from those who considered their farms to be in a better state of improvement than the average, and from the landed who could not well accept the stipulation that they receive nothing for their buildings while the landless should, never-

43. Under the Mennonite *Gewanndorf* (open-field village) system, every landless person resident in the village had a right to a plot in the village communal pasture, where he could erect his own buildings. These were his property, but he acquired no proprietary interest in the land he occupied.

theless it was possible to obtain sufficient agreement to put all the land up for sale in one block. Initially this agreement was set to terminate on August 21, 1921, after which date each person was to have the right to sell independently. When, however, no sale had been accomplished by the deadline, extensions were made, over the strong objections of a growing number of individuals who saw in continued fruitless attempts to sell *en bloc* only a delay in achieving the desired goal of emigration.[44]

Indeed, a buyer did materialize, in the person of the same man who had previously operated in the abortive Hague–Osler and Swift Current deals. After repeated postponements and renegotiations of the proposed sale, this entire venture also collapsed. Canada was entering its first post-World War I economic slump. Land prices were falling precipitously, keeping pace with and even anticipating the drop in prices for agricultural products. In the spring of 1921 prospects for realizing an average price of $75 per acre had appeared good. As prices fell, some, desiring to emigrate but determined to get as good a price as possible for their property, simply broke their promise and sold privately. These were taken to task for their action and required to clear themselves with the congregation. If they refused, their leaders denied them the special immigration papers which the Mexican government had provided to facilitate the migration. Others, viewing with dismay the steadily diminishing value of their property, determined not to emigrate at all. Stern disciplinary measures were invoked, including excommunication and ostracism.

The Altkolonier leaders had reason to desire a large-scale sale of the property. First, it was needed in order to realize the monies necessary to make the stipulated payments on the land purchased in Mexico. Second, such a sale would free a large number of people to emigrate in a body and set up the new settlements. Third, the sale *en bloc* was designed to foster the purchase of the Altkolonier properties by a large outside corporation. Not only would this effectively block opportunistic "back-sliders" from increasing their holdings at bargain prices, but it would almost certainly guarantee

44. David Harder, "Chronik," *passim.*

that a substantial number of people of various ethnic backgrounds would enter the district. Such an eventuality, the Altkolonier leaders reasoned, would so thoroughly upset the accustomed way of life of those who remained behind that they would soon be prompted to follow to Mexico and, promising obedience in the future, seek reinstatement in the church.

These were especially trying days for the Altkolonier leaders in Manitoba. As efforts to sell out failed repeatedly, it became ever more difficult to maintain order and unity in the community. More and more lost interest in the cause of emigration and began to obey the education laws. Finally, in January and February of 1922, the Elder and ministers of the Altkolonier church in Manitoba canvassed the community to discover who would undertake to stay with the congregation and obediently and dutifully emigrate with it.[45] The rest were eventually excommunicated.[46]

At the time of the land purchase in Chihuahua, the Altkolonier leaders were still involved in fruitless attempts to sell the Canadian property *en bloc*. When word of the purchase reached Canada, many would-be emigrants began to sell off their chattels (which were not included in the agreement for a common sale of land and buildings) by public auction. All through the autumn of 1921 and the spring of 1922 the sales continued. Prices realized were very low, in part because of deteriorating economic conditions generally, in part simply because sellers outnumbered buyers.

Although the Altkolonier authorities never officially abandoned the plans for a communal liquidation of property, by early 1922, in view of the obligations contracted in Mexico and of the diminishing enthusiasm of many, land sales were permitted to pass more and more to private initiative. By February of 1922 a substantial group had indicated its readiness for immediate departure. The Altkolonier leadership also directed strong efforts to the promotion of an early removal. By late February enough would-be emigrants

45. *Ibid., passim.*
46. Some of those who remained behind eventually joined other Mennonite churches. Others never joined any church again. Still others founded a new and somewhat more liberal Altkolonier church, which, however, was never recognized by the parent body in Mexico.

were organized to warrant the chartering of four trains to carry them and their chattels to Mexico. Meanwhile, two trainloads were also organized in the Swift Current settlement. Between March 1 and March 11, 1922, all six of these trains left for Mexico, arriving after some eight days at the tiny cattle-loading station of San Antonio de los Arenales (now Cd. Cuauhtémoc) on the edge of the valley which was to be the Altkolonier's new home.

The haste with which these earliest emigrant trains were assembled gave many little opportunity to sell their land. For those who had already disposed of their animals and equipment, there was little point in remaining in Canada, whereas if they left for Mexico early enough they might yet be able to put in some crops there.

Thus, many of those who were among the first to emigrate did so without having sold their property in Canada. Such persons often gave their land over to a friend or relative who was not yet leaving to sell as opportunity might dictate. When such people in turn prepared to leave, they exhibited a strong tendency to accept whatever was offered for the property entrusted to them.[47] In consequence, land prices in the Altkolonier area of the West Reserve dropped to as low as $12.50 per acre, buildings included. In the Swift Current settlement land prices went as low as $5 per acre.[48] Later, in 1923, 1924, and 1925, many Altkolonier were able to sell at somewhat better prices to newly arrived Russländer Mennonites, refugees from the Bolshevik Revolution, thousands of whom were assisted in their emigration by the Canadian Mennonite Board of Colonization.

The Altkolonier migration continued sporadically through 1922, 1923, 1924, and 1925, and scattered families continued to come to Mexico for a decade thereafter. In 1924 a small part of the Hague–Osler group purchased 3,000 acres in the Valle de Guatimapé of Durango, where the earlier abortive transaction with Braniff had been negotiated. Later, as colonists—eventually, over

47. This and the foregoing two paragraphs are based upon David Harder, "Chronik", *passim*.
48. David Harder, La Batea, Zacatecas, Mexico, personal communication.

the years, some 950 Mennonite émigrés entered the Valle de Guatimapé—continued to arrive, more land was acquired, usually through rental-purchase agreements.[49] Unlike the Swift Current and Manitoba groups, the majority of the Altkolonier in the Hague–Osler area remained in Canada. By the time they were able to sell their land at a price which would give them enough capital to make a new beginning in Mexico, unfavorable reports of the hardships of pioneering there were already current in Canada. Many had simply accepted the school system and no longer wished to emigrate. Others were simply too poor to go, while the church coffers, from which financial aid might otherwise have come, were in no position to provide it.

The Sommerfelder Emigration

Meanwhile, the Sommerfelder, after the final appeal for retention of their private schools was denied by the government of Manitoba in October of 1921, also began in earnest to plan a departure from Canada. They were aware of the Altkolonier attempts at obtaining a Privilegium in South America and early turned their attention there.[50] Later that year they sent a fact-finding delegation to Paraguay, where the government accorded them the desired Privilegium in all particulars.

Sometime during the early winter of 1921–1922 a Chihuahua banker became aware, through the Altkolonier, of the impending Sommerfelder migration. He was David S. Russek, member of a banking family of Chihuahua and one of the heirs to the Hacienda Santa Clara—one of 17 haciendas comprising the vast Terrazas *latifundio* (it covered almost one-half of the state of Chihuahua)—which bordered the Zuloaga estate on the north. The heirs, fear-

49. Jakob Bartsch, Campo 9, Grünthal, Nuevo Ideal, Durango, Mexico, personal communication and local church records.

50. The Altkolonier, however, did not provide them with details of their experiences in South America. Eventually, in 1926 and 1927, the bulk of the emigrating Sommerfelder established Menno colony in the Paraguayan Chaco.

ing, as had the Zuloagas, the possible confiscation of their property when and if the agrarian reforms promised by the revolutionary leaders were imposed, were eager to sell. Russek therefore came to Canada early in 1922 for the purpose of offering Santa Clara to the Sommerfelder. Delegates were invited to come and inspect the land. Prior to Russek's visit, Sommerfelder emigration sentiment had been rather uniformly directed towards South America. Now the Elder on the West Reserve in Manitoba changed his mind and became a booster for migration to Mexico. There were substantial attractions to such a move. First, if they settled on Santa Clara, they would be relatively close to the existing Mennonite colonies founded by the Altkolonier. Second, emigration to Mexico entailed a relatively short journey overland, which would consume a much smaller portion of available capital than would the lengthy journey to South America. Furthermore—and it is not to be denied that this thought was entertained by many—it was a step much less irrevocable than migration to South America.

The Sommerfelder church leaders of the East Reserve refused to participate in the Mexican venture. The appearance of Russek therefore resulted in a division of purpose within the Sommerfelder ranks, similar to that which the various offers of land and privileges had caused among the Altkolonier. On the West Reserve there was substantial interest in the idea of removing to Mexico. In the early summer of 1922, Julius Harder, Franz Voth, and Derk Doerksen went to inspect the Russek land offer at first hand. Russek expected the entire Sommerfelder congregation to move to Santa Clara and promised to build a railroad to their colony. The Sommerfelder delegates were not that optimistic. They contracted for the purchase of 12,000 acres at $12 (U.S.) per acre. However, anticipating that many would-be migrants to Paraguay might decide to come to Mexico after all now that concrete steps to establish a Sommerfelder colony in Chihuahua had been taken, they took an option on an additional 50,000 acres. The Mexican government complied with their request and extended to them a Privilegium based on the one offered in 1921 by the government of Paraguay.

This Privilegium, although in all other particulars the same as that granted the Altkolonier, contains two additional clauses derived from that proffered by Paraguay: "There is imparted to you for all time for your lives and properties, the protection of the law. There is tendered to you complete liberty to leave this Republic when it is deemed convenient." The final clause confers these same privileges, under the same terms, upon their descendants as well.

Russek made two trips to Manitoba to promote the land deal. He also sent a representative, one John MacDougall, a U.S. citizen, to Manitoba and Saskatchewan to promote his proposition among the Sommerfelder.

In determining whether or not he would emigrate, the individual Sommerfelder was a much freer agent than his Altkolonier counterpart. The Sommerfelder community was much less tightly organized than those of the Altkolonier. The latter had an ecclesiastical and a secular organization which, though separate, would support each other in exacting compliance from the individual. With regard to secular affairs, the Sommerfelder community, on the other hand, simply participated in the normal functions of municipal government. From the time the controversial education question was broached, it had been generally left to the individual's conscience whether or not he would accept the provisions of the Schools Act. Many Sommerfelder lived on isolated farmsteads. All in all, they may be considered to have been much more individualistic and less group-oriented than the Altkolonier.

This individualism manifested itself as soon as as the first forerunners of the Sommerfelder reached Mexico to inspect the Russek land. When Russek showed them a smaller tract (part of the Zuloaga estate which he had on hand to sell) less than half as far from San Antonio de los Arenales as Santa Clara (thirty miles, as against seventy-five), two men, Jacob Sawatzky and John Fehr, purchased 3,125 acres there. Yet another group found a location to its liking near Cusihuiriachic, some fifteen miles south of San Antonio.[51]

51. The information pertaining to Santa Clara was provided by Peter P. Penner and Jacob R. Loewen, both of that colony.

Conclusion

In view of the reluctance of other Latin American nations to grant the Mennonites a Privilegium, it is rather surprising that these concessions were so easily gained in Mexico. Mexico had just emerged from a protracted revolution. That a large body of foreigners as culturally and linguistically strange as the Mennonites should be encouraged to immigrate into the country under guarantees of special rights and privileges seems unusual to say the least. Mexico was, however, just beginning its reconstruction from the chaos of revolution—a reconstruction which the Mennonites might materially aid. Moreover, President Alvaro Obregón, in his election manifesto of 1920, had committed himself to invite persons of capital and enterprise, nationals and foreigners equally, to participate in the development of Mexico's riches.[52]

52. "For the development of the natural riches of my country, I propose to extend an invitation to all men of capital and enterprise, nationals and foreigners, who are disposed to invest their capital in the development of the said riches, based on a spirit of equity, with the result that there will be obtained for our national treasury and for the workers who cooperate with the said capital, participation in the benefits which logically must accrue to each". (From the election manifesto of Alvaro Obregón, Piedras Negras, Coahuila, March 10, 1920, in the Silvestre Terrazas Collection, Bancroft Library, University of California, Berkeley. Translation by the author.)

The idea of encouraging and even sponsoring immigration was not a new one. During his thirty-year term of office (1880–1910), President Porfirio Díaz actively encouraged the founding of colonies of foreigners and repatriated Mexicans. As a result some sixty colonies were created, thirty-seven of them being of foreign stock. Of the latter, five were sponsored by the Mexican government, and thirty-two were privately financed. They included French, Belgian, Spanish, Boer, Japanese, Russian, Puerto Rican, and American elements. These colonies appear to have enjoyed varying degrees of success, ranging from total failure to relative prosperity. Their combined population appears never to have exceeded 4,000 during the Díaz era. *La Colonización en México* (Mexico City: Talleres de Impresión de Estampillas y Valores, 1960), *passim*. Most conspicuous of the colonies founded during those years are the still-surviving Mormon settlments in northwestern Chihuahua, in the region of Nuevo Casas Grandes. The Mormons, too, received a Privilegium; in their case it was the guarantee, from the Díaz government, of the right to continue the practice of polygamy. Owing to harassment during the anarchical period of the revolution of 1910–1920, it appears that all the Mormons left Mexico, their position having become particularly untenable after the withdrawal of General Pershing's expeditionary force, which effected a military occupation of much of Chihuahua from March 1916 to February 1917. After the revolution many of them returned once more to Mexico.

Nevertheless, it would be of interest to know what effect the anticipated large sales of land to the Mennonites by a close relative of the president had upon the ease with which the Privilegium was gained.

That the majority of the Mennonite emigrants to Mexico had no clear notion of the country to which they were going, or of the physical and climatic conditions which prevailed there, is certain.

It is also evident, from the frequent appeals to various levels of government, that the Altkolonier hoped somehow to avoid leaving Canada. Difficult to understand is the fact that in these appeals and in their endeavors to find a suitable place either in Canada or the United States, the Altkolonier repeatedly asked for guarantees from provincial and state governments which did not have the authority to grant such guarantees. Exemption from military service is a case in point. Similarly, they sought assurances from the federal governments of both Canada and the U.S. relating to matters such as education, which were entirely under provincial or state jurisdiction. Even considering that there was a problem in communication because few of the Mennonite leaders and delegates possessed an adequate command of English, there nevertheless appears room for doubt as to the quality of the efforts put forth by their own legal advisors and by government officials to bring them to a clear understanding of the issues involved. On the provincial level at least, the authorities were glad to have the matter resolve itself through a general departure of the recalcitrants.

The Altkolonier attempts to win concessions by reminding the authorities of the economic losses which would ensue upon their departure were patently an error in judgment. After having repeatedly stated that they would take their people out of Canada unless their terms were met, the Altkolonier leaders were constrained to make earnest of their intentions once they had explored all avenues and exhausted all stratagems. The truth of this allegation is admitted by many senior members of the Altkolonier community in Mexico today.

Internal dissensions disrupted the original plans for settling all the Altkolonier migrants upon a single land complex. It is perhaps not too strong a statement to say that the petty power structures extant within each of the groups precluded the mounting of a unified colonization effort. Ultimately, although other factors which influenced personal decisions were involved, it was one's sense of obedience to his own church and secular authorities which governed individual participation in the migration.

Chapter 3

The Colonies in Mexico

With the desired Privilegia satisfactorily in hand and the real estate transactions completed, the Altkolonier and Sommerfelder Mennonites from Manitoba and Saskatchewan could move to take possession of their newly acquired lands in Chihuahua.

The several groups differed in the manner in which they took possession and assumed responsibility for the retirement of the indebtedness against the land. Among the Altkolonier of Manitoba it was agreed to take a single deed for the entire 150,000-odd acres. The land was then to be sold to individuals at the acquisition price of $8.25 (U.S.) plus a surcharge to cover costs incurred in the protracted travelings and dealings which finally led to the purchase. This brought the price to $9 per acre.[1]

The Swift Current Altkolonier group adopted a somewhat different approach. They divided the block acquired for their colony into plots, each of which was large enough to accommodate a single village with arable and pasture lands—usually a block four kilometers square, containing about 4,000 acres. Deeds were drawn separately for each village. The land was then sold to individual settlers in the same manner as that of the Manitoba Altkolonier—at $8.25 (U.S.) per acre plus a $.75 surcharge.

1. The $.75 surcharge per acre was necessary principally in order to liquidate the loss of $50,000 incurred through the abrogation of the contract with Braniff when relations among the delegates collapsed. The Manitoba and Swift Current groups were assessed $30,000 of the loss and the Hague–Osler group $20,000. The entire amount was levied against the land purchases in Mexico. The amount per acre was relatively small for the other two, but the Hague–Osler group, which initially bought only 3,000 acres in Durango, was forced to surcharge its purchase by nearly $7.00 per acre over and above the purchase price of $4.00! (Information relating to the Hague–Osler group was supplied by Jakob Bartsch, Campo 9, Grünthal, Nuevo Ideal, Durango, Mexico, personal communication.)

Both methods greatly reduced the amount and expense of the legal services required to effect transfer of title from the Mexican owners to the Mennonites, as compared to what these would have been had each settler individually obtained title. Furthermore, large acreages which were not at once taken up were covered by the general or group titles.

The Manitoba Altkolonier proceeded to found two holding companies, each in the names of two prominent members of their community—Klaas Heide and Peter Neufeld, and Johann W. Rempel and Cornelius Wall—and a trust organization known as the Waisenamt to take titles to the property acquired by them. These companies, duly registered under Mexican law, in which the entire Manitoba Altkolonier emigrant community was included as "unnamed members," committed themselves to the administration of these lands, the collection and payment of taxes, the retirement of the residual debt, and such other affairs as might from time to time require regulation. In short, they were to represent the secular arm of colony administration.

The Santa Clara Purchase

The method of conveying title to the lands reserved for the Sommerfelder by their delegates raised a serious crisis in that group even before its departure for Mexico. The church leaders, supported by others, wanted a common deed similar to the one taken by the Altkolonier, with the individual to hold his land only in right of a document issued by the colony authorities. Some six persons, recognizing how such a device could compromise individual initiative, balked and insisted on separate deeds. Those who supported the idea of a communal title insisted that separate deeds were impossible. Russek, who was in Canada at the time to expedite the land deal with the Sommerfelder, became aware of the controversy, although he was not conversant with the basic issues. He suggested clearing up the impasse by issuing separate titles. The faction supporting a communal deed was thereupon accused by the other would-be emigrants of deliberate misrepresentation in order to arrogate power and influence to itself. Eventually the issue was glossed over by the issuing of a communal deed in the name of Harder, Voth, and Doerksen for the group desiring it, and separate titles for the others.[2]

The Sommerfelder Migration

So much delay was occasioned before the matter of the mode of acquisition of the land in Mexico was settled that the first Sommerfelder did not emigrate until November of 1922. They too experienced the difficulties in resolving their affairs in Canada that had beset the Altkolonier emigration effort. Like the Altkolonier, they chartered trains to transport themselves and their effects to Mexico. Three trains left southern Manitoba between October 16 and November 11 of 1922.[3] Their rail destination was Agua Nueva, about 100 kilometers north of the city of Chihuahua on the Mexican National Railroad.[4] From there a wagon road led some forty miles up a canyon penetrating the Sierra del Nido, a range of the Sierra Madre Occidental, to their lands on Santa Clara. The group which chose to settle with Jacob Sawatzky and John Fehr on the 3,125 acres which those two had bought, nearer San Antonio de los Arenales, chartered a separate train which carried them to San Antonio. The few participating families of Sommerfelder from Saskatchewan[5] chartered individual railroad cars which were then coupled onto Altkolonier trains. Single families and small groups

2. During 1944 and 1945, after the death of one of the original holders of the communal deed, that land too was individually deeded to its respective owners. (One of the original three delegates and deed holders, Julius Harder, was living in 1965 in the small, predominantly Sommerfelder Mennonite colony in the state of Tamaulipas).

3. Two of these trains left Altona, Manitoba, on October 16 and November 11, 1922, arriving at Agua Nueva on October 22 and November 18, respectively. The train carrying the group which settled on the 3,125 acres bought by Sawatzky and Fehr nearer San Antonio de los Arenales left during this time also, from Rosenfeld, Manitoba. Information supplied by Peter Penner, Santa Clara, personal communication.

4. Agua Nueva has since been renamed Parrita.

5. The Saskatchewan Sommerfelder who joined this migration appear to have all come from the Herbert area, west of Regina,

of Manitoba Sommerfelder who followed later also attached their cars to Altkolonier trains.

Taking Possession

Before the Mennonites could take actual possession of their lands, it was necessary, of course, to run detailed surveys. The Valle de Bustillos had been granted by the Spanish authorities as a hacienda in 1745. It was bounded, as was the custom in making such grants, by the crests separating the Bustillos *bolsón*, some thirty-five miles long and fifteen wide, from other drainage basins. Initially, the Altkolonier representatives had been offered the entire Bustillos hacienda. The Altkolonier, however, were interested only in the portions which, to their eyes, were "useful"—that is, which showed promise of being amenable to Mennonite agricultural practices. The surveys were run during the autumn of 1921 by two Mexican engineers.[6] They were accompanied at every stage by Klaas Heide, who went ahead of the party, scanning the land, determining where the boundary should run. When the traverse was closed, Heide had the land measured into blocks two kilometers square. The resulting plan was taken to Canada and the future villages were blocked out before the migration began. This was possible because persons intending to participate in the migration were required to reserve in advance the amount of land they wished to take up in the new colonies. It shortly became evident that considerably less than the 225,000 acres purchased would be initially taken up. Much of the land indeed remained unoccupied and unused for many years.

The original Zuloaga offer, as has been stated, was of the entire latifundio, which included all the lands of the Bustillos drainage basin, some 3,000 square kilometers.[7] The price asked for the entire property—some 750,000 acres—was a lump sum equal to the amount later paid for the 225,000 acres (at $8.25 per acre) pur-

6. They were Carlos Haerter and Victor Muñoz. Haerter spoke German.

7. The actual area of the drainage of the Bolsón de Bustillos is 3,083 square kilometers, as determined by planimeter.

chased by the Altkolonier for the establishment of the Swift Current and Manitoba colonies. The Altkolonier thus rejected over two-thirds of the proffered domain. The rejected portions included forests of oak and ponderosa pine, many thousands of acres of range land, and the sheltered reentrant valleys along the mountain fronts, which contained much timber and potentially arable land.

The reasons for this seeming lack of foresight in failing to acquire the bordering uplands were several. It was considered by some, particularly church leaders, that overt preparation for anticipated future need was an act of little faith which put the bounty of God into question and might, indeed, invite His retribution. Moreover, owing to the difficulties experienced in liquidating Canadian assets, land reservations were lagging, and it was becoming evident that there would be a substantial surplus even among the 225,000 total acres whose purchase was contracted. Again, because of the difficulties in selling their properties in Canada and the generally low prices realized, there was a shortage of money among the Altkolonier, and they were unwilling to pay taxes upon surplus land for which they had no immediate use.[8] In any event, they appear to have had little or no knowledge of the potential value of the lands they rejected out of the Zuloaga estate. Furthermore, there is the persistent tradition among the Altkolonier that it is the Mennonites' calling (*Berufung*) to be tillers of the soil.[9] Although this does not entirely preclude other lines of economic endeavor, the effect is to discourage activity that is not directly contributory to the farming base. Finally, the Mennonites had, and continue to this day to have, a typical flat-landers' fear of the forest

8. The Altkolonier also had rather fixed ideas about what size a family farm should be. Very few initially purchased more than 200 acres. Therefore, if the total purchase price were spread over an ever greater acreage, as would have been the case had they taken the entire Zuloaga estate, the total revenue which could be immediately realized from land sales to meet commitments to the Zuloaga heirs, already embarrassingly small, would have been smaller still. Most of the rest of the Bustillos land, by one means or another, came under new ownership during the decade following the revolution.

9. Justification for this position can be found in I Corinthians 7:20, "Let every man abide in the same calling wherein he was called."

and the mountain, which was sharpened in Chihuahua by apprehension at being isolated among a Spanish-speaking Catholic population.

The arrival of the Mennonites in the Valle de Bustillos heralded a tremendous economic upsurge for this region, ravaged as it had been by a decade of revolution. Overnight, as it were, the valley was to be densely populated, with villages rising upon its floor, with the cattle population restored, and with all the appurtenances of mechanized farming being applied to land which had hitherto supported an economy based on grazing and subsistence agriculture. Walter Schmiedehaus, a German-born businessman of San Antonio de los Arenales (now Cd. Cuauhtémoc), witnessed the arrival of the Altkolonier trains:

When we think of migration, there comes to mind that dramatic picture we might time and again have witnessed in the great harbor cities of Europe . . . : pale, poverty-marked and fear-filled people amid the bundles of their pitiful possessions. . . . Privation-worn women upon whose faces the tears of farewell from the homeland were not yet dry . . . The flight for *Lebensraum*, from poverty or persecution, the stride into the unknown, into adventure, the great gamble of the homeless, the homeseeker . . . the *Auswanderung* of the Mennonites from Canada to Mexico is altogether different. A closed colony of several thousands undertakes a journey . . . through half a continent. They are . . . well-to-do, self-assured farmers, come as a solidaristic group with documented privileges, to take possession of . . . [their] lands. . . . Was this the goal? Was that boundless highland, that appeared so inexpressably wild and worlds away in the pale shimer of moonlight, the new *Heimat* one had exchanged for the familiar things of Canada? . . . And then they were standing about in groups, speaking amongst themselves as at home, by the hundreds, out there in the wild prairie under a lowering Mexican moon—Plattdeutsch! With first light began the unloading. Holstein cows and great Belgian horses, chickens and geese, grain tanks and bundle wagons, farm implements and great heaving tractors, coils of barbed wire, roofing and corrugated iron, furniture, bedding . . . By noon all was ready, and the long caravan of horse- and tractor-drawn wagons snaked down the hill of San

61

Antonio, out on the valley floor, where the new villages were to rise.[10]

Eventually, a total of some thirty-six chartered trains carried the emigrants to Mexico. The emigrating Mennonite knew where he was going. His land was surveyed, awaiting his arrival. He did not embark upon the journey alone, but in the company of a train load of his friends and neighbors,[11] who carried with them, as did he, all the chattels desired, occasionally several boxcar loads per family. He did not need to master a strange language, nor wrestle with strange customs in a foreign land—the entire familiar framework of language and institutions emigrated with him and continued to function uninterrupted. He could depend upon his neighbors, and they upon him, to assist in the erection of the first shelters. There were manifest weaknesses in the emigration—in the lack of knowledge relating to soils and climate and to suitable crops and tillage practices—but these were offset to a substantial degree by the Mennonites' tradition of mutual assistance.

Land hunger has played a part in every Mennonite migration of consequence throughout their history.[12] Usually it has had an important, even dominant role. While it certainly provided motivation for some in this migration, statistics, which are sketchy, suggest that the urge to expand was one of the lesser factors operating in the Altkolonier move to Mexico.[13] For example, statistics from

10. Walter Schmiedehaus, *Ein Feste Burg ist Unser Gott* (Cd. Cuahtémoc, Chihuahua, Mexico: G. J. Rempel, 1948), pp. 113–119 *passim*. Translation by the writer.

11. Several Altkolonier villages in Manitoba ceased to exist as a result of the emigration. Among them are Kronsthal, which was completely depopulated, and Blumengart, which was purchased by Hutterites from South Dakota and converted into a *Haufendorf* (an irregular, sub-circular village). Other villages—Reinland, Blumenort, Rosenort, and Gnadenthal, to name but a few—continued to exist as Strassendörfer because of sales to other Mennonites, principally Russländer but including other Canadian Mennonites and a few Mennonite families from the U.S.A. All of the Manitoba villages, however, abandoned the *Gewannflur* (open-field system) with the Altkolonier exodus.

12. The migration of the Russländer Mennonites in the 1920's after the Bolshevik Revolution might be regarded as an exception. Nevertheless it was the prospect of once more owning land which helped to prompt many, even if only in a marginal way, to emigrate to North America.

13. There are a number of related factors which perhaps provide as much motivation to migrate as does land hunger per se. One is the possibility of getting out

two Manitoba Altkolonier villages, showing as of March 1921 the amounts of land to be sold in the West Reserve and the amounts reserved by the same villages in Mexico, indicate an increase in total acreage of only 12 percent.

Most of the Altkolonier seem not to have been ambitious to greatly increase their holdings through the move to Mexico. Indeed, it appears that a substantial number of the larger farmers elected to reserve smaller acreages in Mexico than they had owned in Manitoba. On the other hand, many of the smaller farmers chose to modestly increase their acreage. The landless Altkolonier from Manitoba also appear to have been modest in their aspirations, most being satisfied with eighty acres or less. In the Swift Current colony the average individual holding appears to have been initially somewhat larger than the average individual holding in the Manitoba colony. However, the Swift Current Altkolonier also rather closely followed a trend to acquire farms of roughly the same size as those they had left in Canada.[14]

It is at once evident that in framing the articles of incorporation of the holding companies, the Altkolonier authorities sought

of debt by selling the existing holdings at a price which exceeds the cost of acquisition in the new colony. Another is the chance (where there is not significant debt) of obtaining a holding of the desired size in the new colony at a low cost, and then using the money left from the liquidation of assets in the old colony to acquire more machinery, implements, and so forth. An important aspect of the sale of higher-priced properties in the old colony is the opportunity it often affords farmers of using the capital to provide farms for their children, which they might not otherwise be able to do. Once a new colony is decided upon and land for it is found, a speculative factor may also become involved, with persons acquiring land at the low initial price and selling it later at a profit. One other factor which has a bearing upon individual decision-making is the reluctance to break up the family. Young people in particular, married and unmarried, frequently migrate with their elders simply because of filial loyalty. On the other hand, those who would otherwise refuse to accompany the migration can often be swayed to do so by parental threats to withhold economic assistance or, on occasion, to disown them. The writer personally knows of several instances relating to the Altkolonier migration of the 1920's in which fathers refused to sell the family land to sons desirous of remaining in Canada. He is also familiar with cases where sons who initially refused to go to Mexico were later persuaded to do so because, lacking aid in obtaining a start on their own in Canada, they were able to acquire land only by obeying their elders' wishes.

14. Farms in the Swift Current Altkolonier settlement of Saskatchewan, being in the semiarid belt, were generally substantially larger than those in the Manitoba settlement.

to obviate the fundamental weaknesses which had threatened the cohesiveness of their communities in Canada since the time of their founding. As the sole legal owners of the colony land, in effect representing the combined civil and ecclesiastical organizations, these Altkolonier companies assumed complete control. The individual was effectively insulated from contact with the Mexican governmental machinery, all taxes and other imposts being collected and paid through the *Vorstand*,[15] the elected civil authorities of the colonies. In assuming legal ownership, these holding companies were able to exercise absolute control over the sale and resale of land, thus guaranteeing against the incursion of "alien" elements into the community. In Manitoba particularly, many of the Mennonite villages had been broken up through the withdrawal of individual homesteads from the land pool necessary to maintain the existence of the traditional villages. Others had been disbanded owing to foreclosure of mortgaged homesteads. Under the conditions of ownership by which the individual was to hold his land in the Altkolonier colonies in Mexico, it would be almost impossible to mortgage real property to outside lenders, and certainly foreclosure was impossible as long as the colony authorities chose not to permit it. The actual and implied control over individual initiative that this condition fostered has been and continues to be an extremely important factor in Altkolonier life, in ways which will be treated more fully in a subsequent chapter.

The Consequences of Exodus Are Felt in Canada

The Altkolonier exodus, once begun, proceeded with considerable dispatch. By the end of 1922 the Manitoba colony in Mexico had a population of over 2,000,[16] of a total of approxi-

15. The Vorstand was represented in the individual villages by the Schulzen (mayors), who in turn answered to the Oberschulze or Vorsteher, whose office is that of general superintendent of colony affairs.

16. Elder Isaak M. Dyck, Manitoba colony, personal communication. The Swift Current colony numbered 1,258 in 1926, the first year for which the records are available (Jacob J. Peters, Swift Current colony, Campo 114A, Hoffnungsthal).

mately 6,000 who would locate there by 1926. Indeed, the economic losses which the Altkolonier leaders had implied would result from their emigration, but which had left provincial authorities unimpressed, seem to have been sufficient to evoke concern on the part of the Canadian Pacific Railway and influential Winnipeg business interests. As the trek to Mexico continued, it began to appear that, in view of the slow sales of Altkolonier land,[17] a substantial portion of the rich Mennonite West Reserve might, in fact, become largely destitute of population. In January of 1923 a group of prominent Winnipeg businessmen formed an ad hoc organization which was to attempt to halt the further exodus of the Mennonites.[18] Recognizing that relations between the Altkolonier and the provincial authorities had deteriorated to the point where direct negotiation was no longer a realistic possibility, they offered to act as mediators. It was their hope that some minor concessions on the education question might possibly be obtained from the government. In view of repeated reports of lack of enthusiasm for the migration on the part of the younger Altkolonier particularly, even limited concessions, it was believed, might tip the balance in favor of remaining in Canada.[19] No such concessions were, however, forthcoming.

17. It was not until later in 1923, and in subsequent years, that the rapid influx of Russländer and others radically altered these prospects.

18. *Winnipeg Evening Tribune,* January 16, 1923. Taking the initiative were D. K. Elliot of the R. J. Whitla Company, J. H. Ashdown of the J. H. Ashdown Hardware Company, and E. J. Hutchings of the Great West Saddlery. *The Steinbach Post* of June 13, 1923, reported that T. O. F. Herzer of the Canadian Pacific Railway, which served both reserves in Manitoba and the Swift Current area, visited Mennonite settlements in Manitoba and Saskatchewan during May of 1923. He promised to work toward a settlement of differences between them and the authorities. He consulted with the premiers of Manitoba, Saskatchewan, and Alberta, and tried to persuade the Mennonites not to leave before the results of his efforts were known. His efforts appear to have had little or no effect.

19. Any concessions which fell short of meeting all of the Altkolonier's demands would have had little effect. It is doubtful if these businessmen had much, if any, understanding of the social controls inherent in Altkolonier society, which took most of the element of personal initiative out of any decision to emigrate. Had their activities been directed toward gaining concessions for the Sommerfelder, who had already expressed a willingness to meet the educational requirements of the province if permitted to keep their private schools, the response might indeed have been a positive one.

The Migration Continues

By the end of 1923, despite the delays in disposing of their Canadian properties, the Altkolonier had founded forty-seven of the sixty-seven villages in existence today in the Manitoba and Swift Current colonies in the state of Chihuahua.[20] They were concentrated in a solid block of land in the eastern two-thirds of the Manitoba colony and in the southern, eastern, and central portions of the Swift Current colony. Two important considerations were involved in the establishment of this settlement pattern. First, all the villages were located either on low ground where shallow wells could successfully be dug or near one of the spring-fed streams—the arroyos known as Casa Colorada, Napavechic, and Sauces—where water could always be obtained. Second, in view of the large initial surplus of land, the settlers reasoned that if things went badly, unoccupied portions of the colonies might ultimately have to be relinquished. In that event, unless the Altkolonier settled *en bloc*, there existed a possibility that Mexican settlements might come into being among their villages. This was a possibility which they wished in all events to forestall.

Indeed, the Swift Current colony very shortly was forced to face up to just such a situation. Lacking both the numerical and economic strength of the Manitoba colony, the Swift Current settlers soon realized that effective occupation of the entire block intended for them was impossible. In consequence the northern portion, extending toward El Porvenir, which had been platted for Campos 108 and 116, was returned to the former owners and never settled by the Mennonites.[21]

20. One of these forty-seven villages, Friedensruh, established in 1922 about one and one-half kilometers north of the present site of Silberfeld, Campo 26, Manitoba colony, was dissolved in 1925–26. The reasons will be discussed later.

21. The land thus relinquished was subsequently incorporated into the Mexican *ejidos* (agricultural communes) of La Quemada and El Porvenir. The present Campos 108 and 116 date from 1945 and 1956 respectively; they were founded as the result of purchases of separate blocks of land from Mexican owners who feared expropriation in the face of *agrarista* importunings.

The Agrarista Question Broached

Although the occupation of the Valle de Bustillos by the Mennonites was peacefully achieved, it was not uneventful. During the revolutionary period, the cattle empire of the Zuloagas had fallen victim to various raiders and poachers. The *hacienda* headquarters at Bustillos had been abandoned, and gradually the more favored locations, principally on stream sites on the margins of the valley where the soils were lighter and more easily tilled than those on the valley floor, were occupied by squatters who settled in the clustered ranchos characteristic of the Mexican rural scene. In keeping with the slogan of the revolutionary general Emiliano Zapata, "The land belongs to him who tills it!" these agraristas insisted they had a right to it.

Whereas only one such agrarista settlement, Ojo Caliente, was actually located on Mennonite colony land, the rest were all near its margins and extended their land use onto the colony. At first the Altkolonier, whose contract with the Zuloagas expressly made it the latter's responsibilty to remove any resident Mexicans from the land, contented themselves with making representations to the former owners. When it became apparent that the agraristas would not leave, even in response to promises of land elsewhere, concern mounted.

The Shadow of the Revolution

To add to these troubles, the Mennonites' livestock and other wealth proved a tremendous attraction to the revolutionary raiders still active in the Sierra Madre.[22] While no large-scale raids

22. Pancho Villa was still operating in the Mennonite area at the time. On at least one occasion he and his band purchased provisions in the Mennonite villages. This action by Villa is in stark contrast to his usual dealings with foreigners. From 1914 to 1920, during which time he was in control of much of Chihuahua, he deliberately attempted to embarrass the federal government by harassing all foreigners, even to the extent of systematically hunting them down and killing them. In 1920, however, he made an agreement with President de la Huerta to desist from such activity. Donald D. Brand, p. 143.

on the colonies were carried out, thefts and highway robberies were frequent. The Mexican government, concerned about its image abroad in the event the defenseless Mennonites were attacked, publicly guaranteed them protection and stationed troops in the colonies.[23] Some of the more faint-hearted of the Altkolonier began to agitate for a return to Canada. They were told by their church leaders to remain in Mexico or face excommunication. Nevertheless, later that year the Altkolonier leaders saw fit to ask the Mexican government for official documented assurances of protection and of liberty to leave Mexico at any time they chose.[24]

The Agrarista Problem Intensifies

The continued influx of Altkolonier during 1923 and 1924 steadily pushed back the limits of the land occupied by the Mennonites. This led to angry confrontations between them and the agraristas, with the latter disputing the Mennonites' right to displace them.[25] Free-ranging Mexican cattle repeatedly destroyed Mennonite crops. When the Altkolonier built a stout fence along the western boundary of the colony to keep these animals out, it was cut time and again.

The actions of the Mexican country people must be regarded as stemming from dislike not so much of the Mennonites per se as of foreigners generally. They had been peons under the Spanish *hacendados* (hacienda owners) and, more recently, the *mineros* in the foreign-owned mines such as that at Cusihuiriachic near the southern limit of the Mennonite colonies. The revolutionary leaders had promised them land, and they were convinced that occupa-

23. *Winnipeg Evening Tribune*, April 25, 1922.

24. The full text of the reply to the Altkolonier request is reproduced in H. L. Sawatzky, "Mennonite Colonization in Mexico: A Study in the Survival of a Traditionalist Society", Ph.D. dissertation, University of California, Berkeley, 1967.

25. This episode is reminiscent of a similar occurrence during the occupation of the Mennonite West Reserve in Manitoba. Anglo-Saxon squatters had settled on the timbered western margin of the reserve. Although the Mennonites did not wish to live there, they needed the timber. When they moved to dispossess the squatters, the latter attacked and drove them off. Eventually a compromise was negotiated through the intercession of government officials. *Manitoba Daily Free Press*, June 14, 1881.

tion and use would guarantee them title to it once the legal machinery caught up with the details of the promised massive post-revolutionary land reforms.

The Altkolonier directed repeated petitions to state and federal authorities, asking that their rights to the land be secured and the agraristas removed. In the autumn of 1923 a commission did indeed arrive in the Mennonite colonies to regulate the issue. However, it soon became apparent that its real interest lay much more in solving the conflict between the agraristas and the Zuloagas than in assisting the Mennonites to gain full possession of their land. Nevertheless, since the entire land deal continued to be dependent upon the Altkolonier receiving full and undisputed possession, the former owners were eager to have the matter solved to their satisfaction. It was not until early in 1925, however, following intercession by the state governor and a direct appeal to the president, that this was accomplished.[26]

Several thousand hectares in the immediate vicinity of San Antonio de los Arenales were expropriated for the accommodation of the displaced agraristas.[27] This is the origin of the Colonias Santa María, Ejidal, Delicias, and San Antonio and the Ejido Cuauhtémoc,[28] in the immediate environs of Ciudad Cuauhtémoc.[29] The

26. Mexican business interests in San Antonio de los Arenales influenced the Governor of the state of Chihuahua, Jesús Antonio Almeida, to defend the Mennonites against some of the grosser injustices—among them exploitation by minor officials—being perpetrated against them. In so doing he was influenced by the Mennonites' threat that they would in the future refuse to pay taxes upon colony land which was in fact in agrarista hands. As a conciliatory gesture the governor rescinded the taxes on such land until the Mennonites obtained full possession. To a substantial degree the delay in settling the land question was owing to the change of government in 1924, when Alvaro Obregón was replaced in the presidential office by Plutarco Elias Calles. The change necessitated an almost complete re-presentation of the problem to the new hierarchy of government officials.

27. Several thousand acres of the expropriated land belonged to the Manitoba colony; the rest belonged to the Zuloagas. Although the Mennonites had to relinquish the land, the Zuloagas absorbed the loss by subtracting its value from the amount still owed them.

28. There is a difference between a *colono* and an *ejidatario* in that the former possesses his land in fee simple, while the latter enjoys only the equivalent of freehold tenure.

29. The name of San Antonio de los Arenales was changed to Cd. Cuauhtémoc about 1928. In the anticlerical postrevolutionary period, most place names of a

Zuloagas were required to pay each agrarista family 200 pesos (U.S. $100) to cover the costs of removal and to provide wood enough to complete a dwelling and a yard fence.[30] In addition, the former owners had to construct a dam and reservoir on the Arroyo de la Casa Colorada below the hill of San Antonio, to furnish water to the new Mexican settlements.[31] By mid-1925 the last of the agraristas had left the Mennonite colonies. To forestall any return the Altkolonier dynamited the remaining buildings. The fact that the agraristas finally vacated the colony land without any apparent residue of bitterness toward either the Mennonites or the Zuloagas is a tribute to the unparsimonious way in which the latter met the terms of the settlement.[32] It appears reasonably certain from the single-minded tenacity with which the Altkolonier pursued their objective of securing removal of the agraristas from colony land that they never gained an insight into the issue from the agrarista point of view. Their thinly veiled implications that the economic upsurge which their substantial importations of capital had brought to the region might be terminated by their withdrawal had the desired effect. The governmental hierarchy of Mexico, with supreme power vested in the president, bore a much greater similarity to their own autocratic society and to the still-remembered tsarist administrations than had the democratic regime of

religious character were changed to secular names that were often reminiscent of figures of local or national historical significance. Cuauhtémoc was the name of the nephew of Moctezuma, King of the Aztecs at the time of contact with the Spaniards under Hernán Cortez. Cuauhtémoc himself fought valiantly against the conquistadors.

30. The amount of wood needed would be limited to roof timbers and fence posts—not a great amount.

31. Rainy-season freshets shortly filled the reservoir with debris. Cd. Cuauhtémoc thereupon turned to the drilling of wells—a much more sanitary source—to supply its water needs.

32. The writer is indebted to Mr. Walter Schmiedehaus, businessman of Cd. Cuauhtémoc and Chihuahua, and German Consul for the state of Chihuahua, for the information relating to the removal of the agraristas. Mr. Schmiedehaus was given power of attorney by the Altkolonier to present their case before President Calles. The writer knows of no other case in which the Altkolonier have delegated such power to someone not a member of their group. Mr. Schmiedehaus was at that time an employee of the banking firm of Baltazar Meléndez in San Antonio de los Arenales.

Canada. This, and the fact that only under autocratic rule can there be minorities with Privilegia, they appear to have understood. Since that time, the Altkolonier have consistently addressed themselves to the person of the president in seeking their ends.

The Sommerfelder Settle Their Lands

In taking possession of their land, the Sommerfelder experienced none of the difficulties with Mexican squatters that beset the Altkolonier. However, they had their own very substantial problems, the most immediate of which was that of obtaining a reliable supply of water.[33] When their delegates inspected the land with Russek in 1922, they had been shown a number of dug wells (*norias*), with water at eight to ten feet below the surface, upon which were focused numerous wagon tracks. It has proven impossible to establish precisely what land the delegates were shown, but on the strength of the favorable impression gained during the inspection trips, contract was made for the purchase, at $12 (U.S.) per acre, of the 12,000 acres (4,800 hectares) upon which the villages of Silberfeld, Neuanlage, and Sommerfeld are centered.

When the first Sommerfelder trains arrived at Agua Nueva (Parrita), the colonists proceeded at once via the canyon road westward to Santa Clara. When they arrived upon their land, they found the "wells" to be dry. The conclusion reached was that the delegates had been duped, that the "wells" were pits to which water had been hauled. Furthermore, while the delegates had reported the soil to be good, much of it was in fact extremely stony.[34]

The immediate consequence of the shortage of water was that only one village, Neuanlage, where a spring and stream-front location beckoned, was founded in 1922. The rest of the arriving

33. The fact that there were no Mexican squatters on the land was probably an indication of the dearth of water.

34. Local legend has it that the delegates were supplied with free spirits and cigars throughout the land-inspection trip. This appears to offer a plausible explanation of some of the more baffling aspects of the land deal, for some of the Sommerfelder had a reputation for hard drinking in Manitoba. If the foregoing is true, then it may be that they were duped and that the land actually purchased was, at least in part, different from that which the delegates had inspected.

colonists were forced to remain at Ojos Azules, some six kilometers east of the present site of Weidenfeld, and at other Mexican ranchos. One result of these initial disillusionments was a further impairment of intragroup confidence and cooperation. As the lack of water backed up the incoming colonists as far as the debarkation point of Parrita, pressure mounted for a move onto their land. Those already located, however, recognizing that available water could never sustain such numbers, exerted counterpressures to discourage them. The impasse thus generated stimulated the immediate return of some of the less determined emigrants to Canada, where the word of their disillusionment quickly made the rounds. The result was an abrupt cessation of the movement of the Sommerfelder to Mexico.

The Russek interests, meanwhile, in anticipation of a wholesale migration of Somerfelder to Santa Clara, had begun the construction of the promised railroad from Parrita. Indeed, by the time conditions with regard to the water supply on Santa Clara deteriorated to such a degree as to halt the migration, the roadbed had already been laid from Parrita well into the mouth of the canyon through which rail access to Santa Clara was possible. Recognizing that this entire effort was futile if the Sommerfelder immigration ceased at this point, Russek took steps to revive it. He purchased a drilling machine and had three deep wells drilled, locating them roughly in the center of each of the 4,000-acre blocks upon which the villages of Sommerfeld, Neuanlage, and Silberfeld are located.[35] The Sommerfelder, however, failed to respond as expected, and the migration ended.

35. Because these wells were from 500 to 700 feet deep, wind motors were inadequate to drive the pumps. It was therefore necessary to install internal-combustion engines for this purpose. Intragroup dissensions, however, resulted in failure to maintain the wells and machinery in proper order, and the wells were abandoned. Indeed some of them eventually became partially or completely, by accident or design, filled with debris. During the hard years of the 1930's, the machinery disappeared; it was sold for salvage, it is said, by persons whose resources were exhausted, in order to purchase provisions. In 1952, after four years of unbroken drouth, water on Santa Clara became so scarce that many had to haul it from the Santa Clara River, fifteen kilometers distant. This crisis generated sufficient unity to cause the abandoned wells to be cleaned out and placed back in production. In 1965 the cost of water was 70 centavos (5.6¢ U.S.) per 200 liters (54 gallons).

Much of the Santa Clara land had been resold to individual Sommerfelder, without prior inspection by the new owners, before they left Canada. In addition to the disillusioned returnees, many still in Canada and now dissuaded from going to Mexico had also bought land on Santa Clara. The result was that a good deal of property already purchased and paid for was abandoned by its owners. Furthermore, since the disillusioned returnees had the effect of discouraging further Sommerfelder migration to Mexico, the attention of those still intent on leaving Canada was diverted to Paraguay, their ultimate destination. Others decided not to emigrate at all.

The Sommerfelder who chose to settle on the Sawatzky–Fehr block of 3,000-odd acres and those who went to Cusihuiriachic appear not to have experienced the various peculiar difficulties which from the first beset the Altkolonier and Santa Clara Sommerfelder. The village of Halbstadt, Campo 55, was established on the Sawatzky–Fehr block. Two villages—Eichenfeld and Sommerfeld—were founded near Cusihuiriachic by eighteen of the twenty-seven Sommerfelder families from the Herbert area of Saskatchewan.[36]

The First Assessment of the New Land

There is much evidence of inexperience and naiveté on the part of both Altkolonier and Sommerfelder in acquiring the land for their new colonies. Proud of their tradition of having possessed the most fertile lands in the polders of Prussia, the South Russian steppe, and the prairies of Manitoba, they are not known to have sought advice from informed sources as to the potential of the region and the lands selected. They relied mainly upon their own observations, taking heed of the fact that certain familiar types of crops would grow, and of the fortuitous advice to seek lands where forested slopes round about gave evidence of a certain reliability of rainfall. That the lands of the Valle de Bustillos would

36. Jacob Loewen, Campo 76, Santa Clara, personal communication. Eight of the Saskatchewan Sommerfelder families settled at Santa Clara, and one family located at Halbstadt, Campo 55.

not be as productive as the farms they left in Canada, the delegates at least appear to have recognized. However, there is reason to believe, on the basis of informed opinion on the part of the Altkolonier pioneers, that their leaders saw the recognized shortcomings of the environment as a factor in favor of the maintenance of the precepts of their conservative society. The rich soils of the Agassiz Lake Basin of Manitoba had, perhaps, too amply rewarded the farmer. With the means to such ends available to the individual, it had proven impossible for the Altkolonier leadership to hold the line against innovation and luxuries. The Valle de Bustillos was by nature much less generously endowed. This factor, it is said, suggested itself as a positive one. If but a modest livelihood could be coaxed from the soils of Bustillos, this fact of itself would guarantee against preoccupation with innovation and radical ideas. In the light of this reasoning, the encircling mountains too were a positive factor, for they would preclude the development of a neighboring group of progressives such as that which had breached Altkolonier insularity in Canada.

The prices paid by the Mennonites for the land upon which they established their colonies show a complete lack of familiarity with conditions existing in the Mexican land market at the time. It is evident that the criteria applied to price were those of Canada. By prevailing standards of post-World-War-I land values in Mennonite settlements in Manitoba and Saskatchewan, the price of the Zuloaga and Russek lands—$8.25 to $12 (U.S.) per acre, in gold— was reasonable (although later, as the Canadian market slumped, it came to approach, and even exceed, the price eventually realized by many an Altkolonier and Sommerfelder emigrant for his Canadian holdings). Although the capabilities of land in the Canadian settlements varied, little of it was poor in terms of Mennonite standards. "Land is land" had come to be the sentiment of many, and this helps to explain the extensive sales of land sight unseen to persons desirous of emigrating. That the Altkolonier and Sommerfelder grossly overpaid for their initial acquisitions in Mexico is borne out by the fact that, in spite of improved political stability, prices of land adjacent to theirs were on the order of 3 pesos ($1.50 U.S.) per acre a few years after the founding of the colonies.[37] Only in very recent times have prices of new acquisitions by the Mennonites in the vicinity of their colonies ever exceeded those originally paid in 1921–1922, and that perhaps largely because Mennonite land hunger has driven prices back up to that level.

The "Kansans"

Notwithstanding the colonists' early difficulties and disillusionment, other smaller groups of Mennonites shortly entered the Bustillos region. The first of these, in 1924, were the "Kansans." Three family groups of Kleine Gemeinde Mennonites from Meade in southwestern Kansas purchased 2,000, 2,000, and 1,000 acres respectively in a contiguous block just north and east of the Manitoba colony—the present locations of Heuboden, Campo 30, and Hoffnungsau, Campos 31 and 32.[38] Campo 31 was settled first, the families clustering together for safety in view of the likelihood, real or imagined, of attack by nocturnal marauders. The following year, however, three families, finding Campo 31 "too crowded"— they had been accustomed to isolated farmsteads—moved to Campo 30, Heuboden. The Kansans have not maintained a separate identity. One family group returned to Kansas in 1926. The other two intermarried with the Altkolonier. Altkolonier purchased parcels of the "Kansan" land, and today little remains of the original Kansas stock in Campos 30, 31, and 32. Administratively, they have been absorbed by the Ojo de la Yegua colony.[39]

37. Information on land prices was obtained from Jacob R. Loewen, Weidenfeld, Campo 51, Santa Clara, and from Heinrich Martens, Neuenburg, Campo 21, Manitoba colony. The Mexican currency then had a value of 2.15 pesos to the U.S. dollar.

38. One of the patriarchs of the group, Jacob Reimer, was a great-grandson of Klaas Reimer, founder of the Kleine Gemeinde in South Russia in the early nineteenth century (*Familienregister der Nachkommen von Klaas und Helena Reimer* [Winnipeg: Regehr Printing, 1958]). The Kleine Gemeinde Mennonites in the Meade area had come from Jansen, Nebraska, in the early years of this century.

39. Gerhard Enns, Heuboden, Campo 30, personal communication. Until the founding of the Ojo de la Yegua colony, the "Kansan" area was administratively a part of the Manitoba colony.

The Russländer

The Russian Revolution and its aftermath, which pre-cipitated the emigration of thousands of Russländer Mennonites to Canada, also led in 1924 to the establishment of several small Russländer groups in Mexico. The fact that they came to Mexico was owing more to circumstance than choice.

In Canada, in 1922, a Mennonite Board of Colonization was created to assist Mennonite refugees from Soviet Russia to remove to Canada. The efforts of this board were complicated by the fact that the Mennonites were one of the sects which, as pacifists, were, by the 1919 amendment to the Immigration Act, expressly barred from entering the country. However, a direct appeal to the prime minister succeeded in getting this discriminatory legislation res-cinded in June of 1923.[40] During the following decade some 23,000 Russländer came to Canada.

The Canadian Mennonite Board of Colonization approached the Mennonite Church communities of Kansas—most of which were of the same stock as those in western Canada, having also come from South Russia in the 1870's—in an effort to enlist their support in assisting the Russländer emigration to Canada. The Kansas group, however, decided to form a separate Board of Colonization, which subsequently strongly advocated the settle-ment of the Russländer in Mexico. There is reason to suppose that it would have preferred to assist the Russländer in emigrating to the United States. However, under the Johnson Act of 1921, immigration to the U.S. was based on a quota system related to the ethnic structure of the foreign-born population according to the census of 1910. This provision had the effect of making the East European and Asiatic quotas very low. The Russländer

40. That the way was opened for Russländer Mennonite entry into Canada may be ascribed in part to the lack of success of various post-World War I settlement schemes, both government- and railway-sponsored, in western Canada. In part it was also owing to the personal intervention of Prime Minister William Lyon Mac-kenzie King, who had lived among the Mennonites in Ontario, had sat as M.P. for the strongly Mennonite district of Waterloo North, and was sympathetic to their cause (E. K. Francis, *In Search of Utopia*, pp. 202, 203.)

Mennonites were classed as Russians, and consequently had little hope of entering the U.S. in large numbers. Very few were able to enter the U.S. directly.

The Kansas-based Mennonite Board of Colonization placed itself in communication with the Mexican government and with the Mennonites in Russia who were hopeful of emigrating. Meetings were held in Newton, Kansas, on March 3-5, 1924, at which Mexican officials, among them J. B. Rowland, land and industrial commissioner for the Mexican National Railways, were present.[41] Rowland undertook to provide free transportation for the Russländer Mennonites from port of entry to their destination in Mexico. Also in attendance was Mr. Göldner, German Consul for the state of Chihuahua, who promised to assist the board in obtaining a loan to cover the costs of resettling the Russländer in Mexico.[42] By April of 1924, the Board of Colonization had a list of 1,001 persons who were ready to leave Russia for Mexico.[43] Efforts were made to prepare for their arrival, but there appear to have been delays in acting upon these preparations. As a result, the first Russländer groups, fearful of remaining longer in Russia, embarked for Mexico without Board of Colonization sponsorship.[44]

41. The Mexican representatives were Senator Rafaél V. Balderrama; Carlos M. Peralto; B. Coutú, Consul of the Federal Republic of Mexico in Kansas City; B. T. Abot of the Mexican Department of Agriculture; and J. B. Rowland, land and industrial commissioner for the Mexican National Railways, also acting in behalf of the Department of Finance. "Mennoniten-Wanderung," *Steinbach Post*, August 6, 1924.

42. "Zur Mennonitischen Einwanderung in Mexico," *Steinbach Post*, August 27, 1924. Sureties posted by individuals and groups in the United States were to guarantee the loan. The Board of Colonization also contacted steamship lines and obtained promises of reduced rates for the Russländer emigrants.

43. "Mennoniten-Wanderung," *Steinbach Post*, May 14, 1924.

44. The reasons for the delay in achieving positive action to assist the refugee Russländer appear to hinge on the fact that the Board of Colonization was under the sponsorship of six groups—the Mennonite Church, the Evangelical Mennonite Church, the Holdemann, the Mennonite Brethren, the General Conference Mennonites, and the Krimmer Mennonite Brethren—and it took some time to obtain agreement among them as to the course of action to be taken. The first group of Russländer to arrive at Vera Cruz had hoped to go to Canada, but could not apparently, in their estimation, safely remain in Russia until clearance to enter Canada was obtained.

When the board was advised of the imminent arrival at Vera Cruz of the first Russländer group, a delegate was hastily dispatched to meet them.[45] No suitable land on which the Russländer might settle had yet been found. Rowland and the German Consul, Göldner, acting as agents for the owner of a 14,000-acre property, Barajas, near Pénjamo in the state of Guanajuato, offered it as a suitable place. The Board of Colonization delegate, however, after inspecting the land, decided it was unsuitable and dispatched a cablegram to that effect to the Mennonites in Russia.[46] Both Rowland's offer of free transportation within Mexico and Göldner's offer of aid in obtaining financing for the resettlement venture were thereupon withdrawn.[47]

The delegate from the Board of Colonization proceeded to Vera Cruz to meet the arriving Russländer—six families, a total of thirty-six persons. On the advice of this delegate, the group accepted an offer, by a land agent who had property to sell there, of free transportation to Musquiz, Coahuila.[48] Musquiz, however, is a semidesert area, and the Russländer's situation there quickly became untenable. John F. D. Wiebe, the land agent who had

45. He was J. W. Wiens of Kansas. In Mexico City, Wiens got in touch with Daniel Salas López—the man who accompanied the first Altkolonier land-seeking mission to Mexico—and with Rowland. See above, Chapter II, note 25, for the role of Daniel Salas López in Mennonite affairs in Mexico.

46. Apparently one purpose of the cablegram was to stall the movement of Russländer to Mexico until provision for their settlement could be made. The Board of Colonization, however, was still performing in an indecisive manner. The delegate in question had been to Mexico before in regard to the colonization of the Russländer. During this previous encounter, both Rowland and Göldner had taken a dislike to him and had asked the board not to send him on the same business again. Much of their later truculence may be ascribed to their displeasure with the Board of Colonization for nevertheless sending him to Mexico once more, against their advice.

47. Rowland's explanation for his failure to honor the offer of free transportation was that travel warrants were available to immigrants only upon application by landowners engaged in bona fide colonization projects. Since the incoming Russländer had no firm final destination, they were not entitled to the travel warrants.

48. Musquiz is some 100 miles south of Eagle Pass, Texas. Although it has not been possible to substantiate this, it appears certain, because of the early involvement with this Russländer group of John F. D. Wiebe, the man who initiated Mennonite colonization interest in Mexico, that the agent was Daniel Salas López, with whom the Mennonites in Chihuahua had had several dealings.

directed Altkolonier interest to Mexico, by this time was involved with them and decided to assist them in removing to Chihuahua, to the vicinity of the Mennonite colonies there.[49] Wiebe applied to Rowland for travel warrants for the group. However, relations in that quarter were such by this time that these were refused. The Russländer thereupon removed to Chihuahua at their own expense, with some private assistance from Wiebe and one of the Colonization Board delegates. They ultimately located at Rosario, near La Junta, some thirty miles to the west of the Altkolonier colonies in the Valle de Bustillos.

In July of 1924 two more groups of Russländer, of two and four families, arrived at Vera Cruz. The two-family group proceeded to Baja California. They had relatives in California, through whose direct intercession with the immigration authorities they hoped to obtain admittance to the United States. The other four families went to the state of Durango.[50]

On August 14, 1924, nine more families landed at Vera Cruz. The Board of Colonization sent three delegates from Kansas to meet them.[51] On their way to Vera Cruz, the delegates stopped in Mexico City to request travel warrants for the new arrivals. Rowland was agitated over the cablegram sent to Russia by their

49. Businessman Walter Schmiedehaus of San Antonio de los Arenales (Cd. Cuauhtémoc) directed a plea to the Board of Colonization that the Russländer be settled in the proximity of the existing Mennonite colonies in Chihuahua. He drew attention to the difficulties certain to beset small groups settling by themselves in remote parts of the Republic and pointed out the existence of the market center of San Antonio, whose growth was almost entirely attributable to the Mennonite colonies. San Antonio could serve the Russländer as well, while their settlement in the immediate region would make them part of a larger community of people of similar ethnic, linguistic, and cultural background. Walter Schmiedehaus, "Zur Kolonisations- und Landfrage," *Steinbach Post*, December 31, 1924. The letter was originally written to *Der Herold*, a Mennonite newspaper in Newton, Kansas, a short time after Schmiedehaus' return from Mexico City, where he had successfully represented the Altkolonier in the agrarista question.

50. "Mennoniten-Wanderung," *Steinbach Post*, September 24, 1924. It appears probable that they founded the ill-fated colony at El Trébol, which will be referred to again later in the text.

51. They were D. E. Harder, J. M. Suderman, and P. H. Unruh. Unruh, however, was not able to leave Kansas immediately and was not present therefore at the arrival of the Russländer and did not accompany them on their first land-seeking mission. "Mennoniten-Wanderung," *Steinbach Post*, October 1, 1924.

predecessor and demanded its negation. The delegates refused to recall the cable, but did agree to inspect the Barajas property in the company of Rowland, the newly arrived Russländer, and the owner, one Enrique de Lascurain. On the basis of this agreement, Rowland issued travel warrants to Vera Cruz for the delegates and return tickets from there to Barajas for the entire group.

Both the delegates and the Russländer subsequently spoke favorably of the Barajas property. Of the 16,000 acres, 14,000 were cropland, 10,000 of which were irrigable. However, most of the land was very heavy clay and would require a great deal of power to work it effectively. Furthermore, they considered the price of $100 (U.S.) per hectare (over $40 per acre) too high, particularly since the irrigation works were in poor repair. Moreover, there were numerous squatters, who might be difficult to persuade to move, already upon the land. In view of all these considerations, the Russländer decided they wished to look elsewhere, to compare situations and prices, before committing themselves. They returned to Vera Cruz, whence they too proceeded to Chihuahua at their own expense.[52]

Rowland declared to the delegates that unless the damaging cablegram sent to Russia by their predecessor was recalled, further arrangements for Russländer immigration into Mexico would be impossible. Against their better judgement, but in order that negotiations for further immigration might once more be opened, the delegates agreed to dispatch a cable dictated by Rowland to the Mennonites in Russia: "Göldner [is] authorized Government and Railroad Representative. Has suitable lands for colonization."[53]

Four or five more families of Russländer arrived—at Tampico —during the late summer of 1924. They too came at their own

52. The delegates from Kansas meanwhile were taken by Rowland to inspect some other lands, also irrigated, in the vicinity of Irapuato, in the state of Guanajuato. It appears likely that this was the land on which the short-lived San Juan colony was founded (see below in the main body of the text).

53. "Mennoniten-Wanderung," *Steinbach Post,* October 15, 1924.

expense. Because matters for their reception and resettlement continued to be poorly regulated, little practical aid was extended to them. In any event, the cablegram sent to Russia at Rowland's behest appears to have had no effect in persuading the Mennonites there to redirect their emigration efforts towards Mexico. By this time the movement of the Russländer to Canada, a much-preferred destination, was proceeding rapidly, redirecting much of the motivation for a move to Mexico which might otherwise have existed.

According to J. M. Suderman, one of the delegates dispatched from Kansas to assist the arriving Russländer, a total of 124 families ultimately came to Mexico.[54] However, a majority of these must be regarded as having merely used Mexico as a corridor to their real destinations in the United States and Canada. The number who seriously attempted to locate in Mexico appears not to have exceeded 60 families, and might have been even smaller had it not been for a "hard core" who, because of health and quarantine regulations, were inadmissible to Canada or who had family members who were thus barred.[55] Mexico enforced few regulations of a like nature and therefore beckoned as an alternative to the breaking up of family units.[56]

The first groups of Russländer who settled at Rosario comprised eleven Mennonite Brethren families. They were joined somewhat later by a small group of General Conference Men-

54. J. M. Suderman, "Mennonite Colonization Board," *The Mennonite Encyclopedia*, III, 617.

55. The reasons for the choice of Mexico as the destination to which the Kansas-based Mennonite Board of Colonization would assist the Russländer appear to have rested solely on impressions gained by an influential Mennonite, P. H. Unruh, on a trip to Mexico. He had been impressed by the climate and fruitfulness of the country. His subsequent strong advocacy of Mexico would therefore seem to be the major source of motivation behind the choice of that country as the one to which the Russländer were to be assisted. (Rev. John H. Enns, Winnipeg. Rev. Enns was in Russia at the time and kept in close touch with emigration developments.)

56. The main health problem of the Russländer was a relatively high incidence of trachoma, a serious disease of the eyes. Most of the Russländer afflicted by this or other diseases remained under quarantine in Germany until cured and then came to Canada to rejoin their families.

nonites.[57] Doctrinal and attitudinal differences made unity of purpose and action difficult if not impossible, and the infant colony shortly disbanded.[58] It appears that the majority of those of the Mennonite Brethren affiliation ultimately went to the United States. Most of the General Conference people eventually emigrated to Canada.

In 1925 a group of thirty or thirty-two Russländer families took up small acreages of irrigated land at San Juan in the state of Guanajuato, near the city of Irapuato. Small-scale farming operations were begun, raising corn, beans, and melons, with about fifteen acres per family. This settlement also failed. The settlers lacked capital. Moreover, insecurity owing to the unsettled state of civil order and heightened by a sense of isolation within a strange society and culture prompted the families to leave one by one for Canada as this became possible. Such capital as had been invested in the colony was simply abandoned.

In 1925 also, a family group—a widower together with four of his children and their families—settled at Las Animas in the state of Guanajuato. They too shortly abandoned the project and are presumed to have gone to the United States. The patriarch of this group, one Abram Rempel, had already lived for a short time in the U.S. It appears likely that he went to Mexico to join his children as they arrived from Russia.

Not all of these colonists proceeded directly to Canada or the United States. In about 1926, some families from the disbanded colony at San Juan, Guanajuato, moved to El Trébol, Durango, in the Valle de Guatimapé and only a few miles to the southeast of the already existing Altkolonier colony at Nuevo Ideal. There

57. The distinctions between the Mennonite Brethren and the General Conference Mennonites hinge on doctrinal differences concerning the form of baptism, the attitude toward proselytizing, the proscription of stimulants and amusements, and so forth. In general, the General Conference Mennonites take a more permissive stand.

58. There are some of the General Conference group who blame the influence of U.S. Mennonite Brethren organizations for the failure of the colony at Rosario. Economic aid from these U.S. sources is said to have been reserved for members of the Mennonite Brethen group, a situation which created internal disruption and hastened dissolution of the colony.

they rented land from the same hacendado from whom the Hague–Osler Altkolonier made their first purchases. At its greatest strength the group numbered twenty-one families, some of whom, in contrast to those from San Juan, had come directly from Russia. However, once more lack of capital and the effects of a continuing numerical attrition owing to opportunities for one family or another to go to the United States or Canada doomed the tiny colony to failure. In a short time but three families remained, and they ultimately removed to Chihuahua.

In addition to the causes cited, a major factor in the failure of the Russländer colonization attempts was the fact that the Russländer groups were generally composed of persons who were more or less strangers to each other. There was, therefore, little or none of the commitment to neighbors, friends, and relatives which had characterized the transplantation of entire communities, such as the Altkolonier. A few Russländer families have, however, remained in Mexico. All have gravitated toward the Mennonite colonies in Chihuahua, where they have become active in the business life of Cd. Cuauhtémoc, the main Mennonite market center. As far as we know, only one of these families took up farming, and it has since removed to Canada.[59] Today only three small family groups of the Russländer—themselves much decimated by emigration to the United States and Canada and continuing to undergo numerical attrition in this way—are left in Mexico.

The "Oklahomans"

In 1927 a group of Holdemann Mennonites (Church of God in Christ) from Isabella, Oklahoma, purchased 1,100 acres at Cordovana, Campo 45.[60] Their reasons for leaving the United States appear to have centered on the increasing educattional exposure of their children to ideas and concepts which were

59. The family in question established itself at Weidenfeld on the Sommerfelder Santa Clara colony. There they built the first cheese factory to be established among the Sommerfelder colonists.

60. They were the brothers Ben, Henry, Ed, and Cornelius Koehn, with their families.

at variance with the fundamentalist precepts of the Holdemann persuasion. That they chose to settle at Cordovana may be in part explained by the existence nearby of the Sommerfelder village of Halbstadt. In 1945 the group from Oklahoma moved to irrigated land near Saltillo, Coahuila, and the Holdemann church purchased the entire Cordovana property from them. Since then it has been operated as a clinic and mission station,[61] with Mexican converts farming most of the land.

War Ends the Migrations

More stringent application of border-crossing regulations by Mexican authorities and the depression of the 1930's gradually phased out Mennonite travelings between Canada and Mexico. World War II put a complete stop to them. When efforts at colonization were once more mounted, the motivation behind them was directly related to events of World War II and the years immediately following.

The Amish and Old Order Migrants

In 1943 a group of six families—four of them Old Order Mennonite and the others Old Order Amish, totaling thirty-six persons—from Pennsylvania, Indiana, and Ohio moved to Mexico with the intention of setting up a colony there.[62] Their stated reasons for leaving the United States centered on withdrawal from the conscription laws and rigid educational requirements

61. Information on Campo 45 was provided by Leola Willard. Cordovana today has a medical clinic and a school staffed by personnel from Canada and the United States. The Holdemann group is the only one which has sought contact with the Mexican population. A number of Mexican converts, each farming about twenty hectares, also live on Cordovana or on one of the nearby Mexican settlements such as Colonia Ortiz, which is a short distance to the north.

62. J. Winfield Fretz, Waterloo, Ontario, personal communication. The Old Order Mennonites and Old Order Amish are the most conservative of the Mennonites of the eastern United States. In their attitude toward technological change, they take a stand very similar to that of the Altkolonier. The Old Order Mennonite families here referred to were those of Aaron Martin, David Newswanger, Daniel Martin, and John Martin, all from the Lancaster area of Pennsylvania. The Old Order Amish were Phineas Borntrager and Rudy Troyer and their families. Borntrager was from Indiana, Troyer from Ohio. Aaron Martin was the acknowledged leader of the group.

prevailing there, and the increasing hazards and inconvenience experienced with their horse-drawn vehicles on roads becoming progressively more crowded with motor traffic.

Initially upon coming to Mexico, they spent a season with the Altkolonier in Chihuahua. However, the dry farming in that semiarid region did not appeal to them, nor did they have much in common with their Altkolonier neighbors.[63] They therefore cast about for a more suitable location. Their search carried them into eastern San Luis Potosí, where they were attracted by the higher rainfall and the anticipated greater productivity of the land. Apparently quite by accident they met a Texan, Sid Taylor, who invited them up to his ranch at Rascón, offering them the opportunity of living there rent-free for a year, during which time they could decide whether or not they would buy. The Mennonites accepted the offer and returned to Chihuahua to fetch their families. The first of them settled at Rascón in January of 1944. Their colonization attempt was short-lived; they remained at Rascón for only one year. During the rainy season they were plagued by insects and malaria. Unable to cope, they chose to remove to Rayón, in the semidesert of central San Luis Potosí. There they remained for nine months more. However, the region was too dry for agriculture, and in 1946, following the death of their leader, the effort dissolved in a general return to the United States.[64] Ignorance of suitable agricultural practices, lack of capital,

63. The Old Order Mennonites and Old Order Amish are of Swiss–German origin. Their forebears emigrated to America during Colonial times. Culturally they differ considerably from the Altkolonier. Linguistically, too, there is little similarity between the dialect of the Old Order Mennonites and Amish and the Plattdeutsch of the Altkolonier, although by now the former groups have almost entirely adopted the English language. Moreover, having come from the moist regions of the eastern United States, they found the raising of crops in Chihuahua a disheartening experience.

64. Taylor interceded with the governor of the state of San Luis Potosí to permit the Mennonites to acquire land there. It was Taylor's hope, and eventually the governor's, that many more Mennonites might thus be encouraged to come and would develop the area agriculturally. Rascón is some 130 miles west of the gulf coast city of Tampico. Information obtained from Dr. J. Winfield Fretz, Conrad Grebel College, Waterloo, Ontario, personal correspondence (Dr. Fretz visited the Mennonites in San Luis Potosí during June of 1944), and from a report by John and Fannie Martin, then living at Hohenwald, Tennessee, carried in the *Steinbach Post* of June 25, 1947.

isolation within linguistically and culturally strange surroundings, and, finally, loss of their leader would appear to have been the causes. Some, however, not content to pick up the threads of their lives in their old home communities, sought the isolation they thought necessary to their chosen way of life by removing to remote parts of Tennessee and Alabama. A small group under the leadership of David Newswanger subsequently emigrated to Costa Rica.

Post-World War II Migration from Canada

During World War I the Canadian government had honored its original commitment not to require military service from the Mennonites. In 1940 a national manpower registration was once more carried out. Those men of draft age who proclaimed themselves conscientious objectors and could acquit themselves for their stand before a selective service board were given the opportunity to perform alternative service. Such men were placed where needed in agriculture, forestry, mining, or other industry essential to the war effort, or in hospitals. A majority of the Canadian Mennonites who were eligible under the draft regulations were ultimately placed in these classes of service.[65] Most Mennonites recognized the realities of the wartime situation and realized that they must render some form of service.[66] Nevertheless, real concern was caused to many who feared that in any future conflict no buffer between themselves and direct involvement in military action might be provided. From about 1941 on, there came to be a growing sentiment, which by the end of

65. During the early part of the war the attitude of the Canadian authorities was such that alternative service draftees were usually placed at a considerable distance from their homes so that in this respect they would not appear to be receiving better treatment than men in the armed services. Later, it was not uncommon for young Mennonite men under the alternative service provisions to be placed with their fathers, if labor requirements were such that they were eligible to have a man placed with them.

66. Mennonite church authorities cooperated with the government in carrying out the alternative service program. Generally speaking, through this service they avoided the accusations which had been leveled against them during World War I, i.e., that they remained at home and prospered from the wartime boom.

the war had reached substantial proportions among several Canadian Mennonite groups, to emigrate to some place where such involvement would not be likely soon to overtake them.[67] In consequence, when with the end of the war international travel once more became possible, the quest for such a country was actively taken up. Involved were elements of the Sommerfelder, Altkolonier, and Kleine Gemeinde. Ultimately each of them participated in migration to Latin America, the Sommerfelder to Paraguay and the others to Mexico.

The Sommerfelder took the initiative first. Since there already was a Sommerfelder colony in Paraguay,[68] attention was turned there, and it is not known that they considered any other destination. In 1948 some 1,600 Sommerfelder left Canada to found Bergthal colony in eastern Paraguay.

The Kleine Gemeinde began casting about for settlement opportunities under guarantees of freedom of conscience[69] very shortly after the cessation of World War II. Initially they turned for suggestions and advice to the Mennonite Central Committee (M.C.C.), which at that time was embarking upon a massive resettlement program to the New World of European Mennonite displaced persons and refugees. The M.C.C. sent inquiries requesting information regarding immigration and the possibility of obtaining Privilegia to all Latin American countries. Kleine Gemeinde attention was particularly directed to Mexico, South America, and Alaska.[70] Investigations into all of these areas were carried out simultaneously. The executive secretary of the Mennonite General Conference Board of Mutual Aid strongly

67. There was concern as well with regard to the actual maintenance of their pacifist principles. During World War II a substantial number of Mennonites joined the armed forces as volunteers.

68. Menno colony in the Gran Chaco, founded in 1926–1927 by Sommerfelder Mennonites from Canada.

69. The term "freedom of conscience" may be interpreted invariably as referring to exemption from military service and the right to maintain separate educational facilities, thus insuring that the exposure of the Mennonite children to ideas which might be considered to be at variance with religious doctrine may be circumvented.

70. Kleine Gemeinde Elder David P. Reimer, Giroux, Manitoba, to J. Winfield Fretz, Executive Secretary of the Mennonite General Conference Board of Mutual Aid, August 14, 1945.

recommended Alaska as offering opportunities superior to those of Latin America in terms of climate, agricultural possibilities, and relations with neighboring people. In consequence the Kenai Peninsula and the Tanana and Matanuska valleys were for some time considered for possible settlement. However, since the United States, in terms of law and attitude, was less favorably inclined toward conscientious objectors and the granting of special terms to minority groups than was Canada, the idea of removing to Alaska was dropped.

While these first tentative steps were being taken by the Kleine Gemeinde, the Elder of the Altkolonier group in the Hague–Osler district of Saskatchewan was attempting to interest his flock in migrating to Mexico to rejoin the main body of Altkolonier.[71] The participation of the Altkolonier in Manitoba was also invited. Before the end of 1945 a delegation of nine, representing the Saskatchewan and Manitoba groups, went to Mexico; they traveled first to Chihuahua[72] and thence to Mexico City to seek the desired Privilegium.

The visit of the Canadian Altkolonier delegation came to the attention of Isaak J. Reimer, originally from the Manitoba colony, who had for some time been in the employ of Mexican hacendados, in positions of trust, and knew a good deal about the possibilities of obtaining a tract of land suitable for the establishment of the envisaged new Altkolonier colony.[73] At the time, the owners of the Hacienda Los Jagueyes, some twenty kilometers west of the

71. He was Elder Johann M. Loeppky, a delegate on numerous Altkolonier missions prior to the migration of the 1920's and the "Johan Loeppky" named in the preamble to the Privilegium. His half-brother was Isaac M. Dyck, Elder of the Manitoba colony. Rev. Loeppky's congregation was the largest group of Altkolonier remaining in Canada. Owing to the severing of relations between its delegate and the other Altkolonier while on the search for land in Durango, and because of economic difficulties and a general diminution of interest in the migration, over two-thirds of the Hague–Osler group failed to emigrate in the 1920's.

72. One of the purposes of the visit to the Chihuahua colonies was to negotiate the status of the Altkolonier from Canada should the migration materialize. As has been previously stated, those who remained behind in Canada in the 1920's were no longer considered by the Altkolonier leaders in Mexico to be of "their people."

73. He had worked for the Almeida family (Don Jesús Antonio Almeida was the Governor of the state of Chihuahua who interceded on behalf of the Mennonites in the agrarista question), owners of the Hacienda Tepejuanes, which occupied the region between the Altkolonier colonies and Santa Clara.

Sommerfelder's Santa Clara colony, A. E. Estrada and his partner, one Luna,[74] fearing expropriation in the face of agrarista demands for land in that area, were eager to sell off their property. When Reimer apprised them of the potential immigration, Estrada and Luna sent him as their agent to Canada to offer the Altkolonier the Los Jagueyes ranch.

Meanwhile, independently of the Altkolonier groups, the Kleine Gemeinde had also been investigating prospects of moving to Mexico. By letter they approached Rev. Johann P. Wall[75] of the Hague colony in Durango with a view to enlisting his advice and aid in petitioning the Mexican government for a Privilegium. The year 1946, however, was a presidential election year in Mexico, and action upon the Kleine Gemeinde petition was delayed pending the establishment of the new government. While the Kleine Gemeinde were waiting for a reply, the Sommerfelder delegates from Canada who had been dispatched to Paraguay returned with reports of good prospects of founding a new colony in that country. The attention of the Kleine Gemeinde was therefore diverted for some time from Mexico to Paraguay, and plans were made to send a delegation with the Sommerfelder emigrant ship when that migration, which appeared imminent, was undertaken.[76]

Reimer had transmitted the Estrada–Luna offer to the Altkolonier in Manitoba. They in turn informed their brethren in Saskatchewan. On the basis of the interest shown and the indications of potential participation, it quickly became apparent that the Altkolonier had no hope of being able to purchase Los Jagueyes—52,700 acres—alone.[77] Elder Johann M. Loeppky, who

74. Both Estrada and Luna were Spaniards. The fact that they were not native Mexicans, it is believed, weakened their positions in the face of agrarista agitation for expropriation.

75. He is the same man who played a major role in the migration of the 1920's. Rev. Wall was born in the Fürstenland colony in South Russia in 1875. He came with his parents to the West Reserve in Manitoba in 1892, moving to the Hague area in 1899. He spoke Russian and German, learned English in Canada, and later acquired a good working knowledge of Spanish in Mexico.

76. David P. Reimer–Johann P. Wall correspondence, 1945–1947, *passim*.

77. Estrada and Luna were unwilling to sell only a part of their property. Under Mexican law, subdivisions of this nature weaken the owner's position against expropriation in favor of the agraristas.

was aware of the Kleine Gemeinde plans to emigrate, thereupon established contact with Elder David P. Reimer and suggested the possibility of a joint purchase of the entire tract. This had the effect of directing Kleine Gemeinde attention once more to Mexico, and the planned investigations in Paraguay were not carried out.

The Kleine Gemeinde enlisted the help of the Vorsteher of the Manitoba colony, Gerhard J. Rempel, to determine the attitude of the government of the state of Chihuahua toward further Mennonite immigration.[78] Rempel, after a personal interview with the former governor, reported considerable enthusiasm from that quarter.[79] The Kleine Gemeinde, however, were still loath to enter into any land dealings in Mexico without having made the prior acquaintance of the vendors. A delegation met with Estrada in Canada in September of 1947. Agreement in principle on the projected purchase was reached, pending the raising of the necessary funds for the down payment. The price was $7 (U.S.) per acre. Fund-raising was actively pursued throughout the autumn of 1947. By early January of 1948, the Kleine Gemeinde had $48,244 Canadian on deposit toward the purchase. The Altkolonier groups, particularly that from Saskatchewan, were lagging badly. A further complication was created by the fact that Canada was at the time experiencing a foreign exchange crisis, and the conversion of Canadian currency into U.S. funds was severely curtailed. The impasse was finally resolved when the sellers agreed to accept the equivalent of the agreed price in Canadian funds.[80] Then a new difficulty arose. Luna had been in Mexico City and had arranged immigration permits for the would-be emigrants. When the Altkolonier proved unable to raise sufficient funds to make good on their end of the deal, extensions had to be arranged for the permits, and these were difficult to obtain.[81]

78. David P. Reimer to Gerhard J. Rempel, September 16, 1946.

79. Gerhard J. Rempel to David P. Reimer, September 28, 1946.

80. A. E. Estrada to David P. Reimer, January 10, 1948.

81. Oscar Soto (lawyer for the Kleine Gemeinde) to David P. Reimer, January 23, 1948. The immigration permits, covering 150 families, were issued on November 21, 1947.

Furthermore, the permits had been issued subject to an obligation on the part of the Mennonites to make an investment of 1,250,000 pesos exclusively in agricultural development on Los Jagueyes, and on the assumption that 150 families would immigrate.[82] Failure to obtain the participation of the anticipated 150 families seriously threatened the ability of those who did emigrate to invest the amount promised.[83]

The Privilegium, too, had proved inordinately difficult to obtain. Eventually, the federal government agreed not to issue a separate Privilegium, but to provide for the inclusion of these later Mennonite immigrants under that issued in 1921.[84] On February 2, 1948, the land deal with Estrada and Luna was finalized, and on February 13 the Kleine Gemeinde deposited $20,000 (U.S.) in a Chihuahua bank as earnest money and part payment, pending the immigration of the first families from Canada.[85]

Up to this point, the entire purchase had been viewed as a joint venture by the Kleine Gemeinde and the Altkolonier. The Saskatchewan Altkolonier, however, had experienced four successive crop failures in the years immediately preceding, they were having great difficulty selling their land, and thus they consistently failed to meet their part of the bargain. The Kleine Gemeinde, therefore, before further payments were made, insisted on a separate deed for their portion of the purchase, to avoid being caught up in the anticipated failure of the Saskatchewan group.[86]

82. Licenciado Ernesto P. Uruchurtu, Under-Secretary of State, to Oscar Soto, lawyer for the Mennonites, November 22, 1947. A guaranty bond in the amount of 200,000 pesos was required to be deposited with the Banco de México, of which half was to be refunded when proof of the specified investment was provided, with the balance to be left as a guarantee that the Mennonites would not take their capital out of Mexico.

83. The exchange rate at the time was 4.85 pesos to the U.S. dollar.

84. Jacob M. Wiebe, formerly of Osler, Saskatchewan, and now of Hochstadt, Campo 8, Nuevo Ideal, Durango, is generally credited with obtaining inclusion in the Privilegium.

85. Personal files, Peter B. Loewen, Elder, Kleine Gemeinde, Los Jagueyes.

86. David P. Reimer to A. E. Estrada, July 30, 1948. During the years since the initial migration of the Altkolonier to Mexico, the Hague–Osler group in Canada had split into two camps, liberal and conservative. This fact furnished some motivation for emigration to the conservatives, but the prime mover was the determined ambition of Elder Loeppky to lead his people to Mexico to rejoin the parent body

An agreement was reached whereby the Kleine Gemeinde assumed responsibility for 35,133.33 acres, at a total value of $245,933.34 (U.S.) [87] It had always been assumed that the Kleine Gemeinde and Altkolonier groups would settle separately, and the boundary between their respective blocks had already been decided. Later the Manitoba Altkolonier group, alarmed at the continuing failure of the Saskatchewan group to pay, also asked for a separate deed, offering to pay all cash for 3,850 acres plus the attached mountain land,[88] leaving the Saskatchewan group to work out its problem alone. The similarity between this episode and that which led to the disruption of plans to purchase lands from the Braniff interests in Durango, in 1921, is obvious.

Despite these numerous difficulties and delays, by late March of 1948 some Kleine Gemeinde people had already disposed of their possessions in Canada and were ready to move. The original immigration permits had expired, however, and new ones, in spite of the efforts of Estrada and Luna to expedite matters, were not yet available.[89] To the would-be emigrants this was a very serious matter, for, having sold their farms in Manitoba, they would have to live off their capital until they harvested a first crop in Mexico. Unless the immigration permits were shortly forthcoming, it would not be possible to plant a crop in 1948. Others, equally interested in emigrating, refused to sell their land until they had assurance of being admitted to Mexico. As matters dragged on, they planted their crops in Canada, thereby precluding a move until after the harvest of 1948. The funds which should have

---

of Altkolonier. These factors must, however, be considered in the light of the fact that there was a very real overriding concern for the future military status of the Mennonites.

87. By the end of June 1949, $206,875 of this amount had been paid.

88. The land was divided so that 70 percent of each block was arable and pasture land, and 30 percent was mountain land.

89. David P. Reimer to A. E. Estrada, March 25, 1948. Estrada's and Luna's exertions are attributable to their interest in seeing the land deal go to a satisfactory conclusion, in view of their fears of expropriation. They are believed to have spent very substantial sums in smoothing the way for the issuance of the immigration permits.

become available for the land deal in Mexico, from sales of property in Canada, were therefore lacking. The entire effort was threatened with collapse. Then, early in the spring of 1948, Mexico instituted a head tax of 500 pesos ($72.78 U.S.) to be levied on all immigrants over the age of fifteen.[90] Besides representing a very substantial burden, the tax was regarded by the Kleine Gemeinde as an indication that the Mexican authorities now disapproved of their admission after all and meant to discourage them. Estrada did his best to reassure them to the contrary and promised to get them a government subsidy equal to the head tax.[91] In order that there might be no impediment to the migration once the permits became available, he suggested that Canadian properties be liquidated at once. When the permits still failed to arrive, Estrada advised them to enter Mexico on tourist permits pending the completion of proper immigration procedure. Some people took his advice, and by the end of May the first arrivals were plowing on Los Jagueyes.[92] When the immigration permits still did not materialize, great anxiety resulted. First, there was the fear of losing the immigrant-duty exemption on their belongings. Second, and this was much more serious, the activity on Los Jagueyes began to attract the attention of the local Mexican population. When Los Jagueyes had been uncultivated range land, it had been possible for the owners to stave off agrarista importunings by insisting that the land was good only for grazing. Now that it was being cultivated, and inasmuch as the title had not yet been transferred to the Mennonite purchasers, it was exceedingly vulnerable should the agraristas institute proceedings.[93]

90. A. E. Estrada to David P. Reimer, April 8, 1948.

91. A. E. Estrada to David P. Reimer, May 31, 1948. The vendors eventually agreed to absorb one-half of the head tax and one-half of the exchange on the Canadian dollar. No subsidy with respect to the head tax was ever granted by the Mexican authorities.

92. A. E. Estrada to David P. Reimer, May 31, 1948.

93. A. E. Estrada to David P. Reimer, November 23, 1948. The agraristas later did take action, unilaterally, to get possession of Los Jagueyes, but without success. The matter will be discussed further in the text.

Finally, on July 21, 1948, permits for the immigration of sixty-seven families were granted by the Ministry of the Interior.[94] It was not until December of the following year that the last of the Kleine Gemeinde group obtained the permits which allowed their legal immigration into Mexico. Individual families continued to come until 1952. Altogether the Kleine Gemeinde migration involved some 595 persons;[95] it was a movement that continued to be plagued by obstacles. Although household effects, livestock, machinery, and provisions could be exported from Canada without restriction, Foreign Exchange Control Board regulations strictly limited the amount of liquid capital that could be taken. A few families were able to take advantage of the fact that, with the Canadian border once more open, small numbers of Altkolonier and Sommerfelder were returning to Canada. Arrangements could be made with such persons for an exchange of bank deposits, thus circumventing the exchange controls.[96] Another hardship was imposed by the Mexican authorities when they rescinded the promise to permit all chattels to enter Mexico free of duty.[97]

The Altkolonier from Manitoba—116 persons in 20 families—began arriving at Los Jagueyes in the summer of 1948, but it was too late to put in a crop. The Saskatchewan group—18 families totaling 130 persons—did not come until December of that year. Financially, the Manitoba contingent was much better off. Having had a series of good crops, they had some cash reserves. Further-

94. The delay had been occasioned mainly by a "palace revolution" in the Ministry of the Interior, in which the minister was deposed. Luna therefore had to present the entire matter again, to the new officials. Further difficulty was then caused by the fact that five families which had been on the list of the sixty-seven who obtained permits were now not included. (David P. Reimer to the Mexican Ministry of the Interior, October 5, 1948.)

95. This number included approximately 218 adults and 377 dependent children. Elder Peter B. Loewen, Los Jagueyes, personal communication.

96. This capital was vitally needed in Mexico if the 1.25 million peso investment specified as a condition of immigration was to be made.

97. Particularly heavy imposts were levied against motor vehicles. Some could not pay them. Having been exported from Canada, however, the vehicles were not readmissable under existing regulations, nor could they be sold in the United States. As a result, some vehicles were simply abandoned in El Paso.

more, they had been able to sell their land in the West Reserve of Manitoba at good prices. Those from Saskatchewan, having experienced four successive crop failures, had little or no reserves, and in many cases had been unable to sell their land. Much of their motivation had been furnished by Elder Loeppky's determination. When the Manitoba group insisted on a separate deed to a specified portion of the Los Jagueyes property, the situation of the Saskatchewan group became hopeless. A number returned to Canada without even unpacking. Elder Loeppky, discouraged, also went home, leaving one minister with the group in Mexico. When he in turn found himself unable to resolve the dilemma, he also returned.[98] Legal procedures to deed the land according to Mexican law had, however, gone almost to completion. Many of the persons named in the deeds were no longer in Mexico and, never having been legal residents, were not entitled to have property registered in their names in any event. Not only could those who remained in Mexico not obtain title unless the persons named released the property, but the entire legal proceedings had to be gone through again, at great expense.[99] Furthermore, there was considerable agrarista agitation against the purchase of the land by these foreigners, which jeopardized the entire colonization effort. Indeed, in 1947 agraristas in the area had hired a surveyor to measure out lands on Los Jagueyes for themselves. When the Kleine Gemeinde established residence and proceeded to survey the land, the agraristas kidnapped two men and, although they were not harmed and Mennonite ownership

98. Rev. David Wall later returned to Mexico and remained for a while to serve the remaining Altkolonier on Los Jagueyes. However, only three of the Saskatchewan families stayed there, and he returned once more to Canada. Ten families of the Saskatchewan group went back to Canada, whereas eight remained in Mexico. Of the Manitoba group, four families remained in Mexico and fourteen returned to Canada. Those who remained were living in 1965 in various Mennonite colonies in the states of Chihuahua, Durango, and Zacatecas. Two families, one each from Manitoba and Saskatchewan, have migrated to British Honduras. The Altkolonier remaining on Los Jagueyes have joined the Santa Clara Sommerfelder church. (Jacob B. Wiebe, Campo 8, Hochstadt, Nuevo Ideal, Durango, and Jacob P. Neufeld, Kleindorf, Campo 252, Los Jagueyes, personal communication.)

99. Jacob P. Neufeld, Kleindorf, Campo 252, Los Jagueyes, personal communication.

was not contested further, the agraristas held the men for a ransom equal to the amount they had expended on the survey.

In settling their portion of Los Jagueyes, the Altkolonier first occupied the southern portion now containing Campos 252, 253, and 254. This was done so that if they were unable to meet their obligations it would be easier for the Kleine Gemeinde group to acquire the still-vacant land, which would thus be adjacent to theirs. Indeed, it very soon became necessary to take advantage of this provision, for, with the withdrawal of the majority of the Saskatchewan Altkolonier, it was impossible for the few remaining to even consider trying to retain full possession.

The survey of Los Jagueyes—the property was renamed Quellenkolonie (Spring Colony) owing to a number of springs found in the area—was conducted along lines of square kilometers, with concrete markers placed one kilometer apart. Upon this system were imposed several innovations relating to the system of land surveys in Canada. The meridian and range—but not the township—were implemented, with the principal meridian running through the approximate middle of the colony. On cultivated lands the acre was established, on the basis of 4,000 square meters to the acre, 250 acres to the square kilometer. The mountainous western portion of the original colony did not have this system imposed on it, and the metric system prevailed.

The entire colony was divided into blocks which met the existing Mexican laws with respect to proprietorship in land, which here permit an individual to own not more than 40 hectares irrigated, 200 hectares *temporal* (unirrigated arable), or 800 hectares of grazing land. The colony, however, maintains complete authority over the land, in a manner not dissimilar to the "holding-company" system of the Manitoba colony. Individuals, even though certain lands may be deeded in their names, hold real property only in right of a title issued by the colony. The colony reserved a strip five meters in width running the length of the western and southern sides of each square kilometer, and retained expropriation rights to land—at the prevailing price for land in general—intended for public use. All transfers of ownership were subject to approval by the colony authorities, and persons not resident on the colony were excluded from owning land there.[100]

Conclusion

The number of Mennonite immigrants to Mexico prior to World War II was about 7,000, grouped in four main colonies. Of these all but a few hundred came from Canada, the rest from the United States and Russia. In the post-World War II era, another 800 or so arrived, chiefly from Canada. In all, of the approximately 7,800 who came to Mexico, perhaps 20 percent were ultimately to return to their country of origin. Those who remained were to increase and spawn other colonization efforts in response, mainly, to shortages of land. Not all have been successful. All of them will be treated in a subsequent chapter.

100. This was a device aimed at retaining colony lands for the benefit of colony residents and at reserving available land for the rising generation. Failing implementation of such rules it was feared that land-hungry Altkolonier and Sommerfelder from neighboring colonies would drive land prices up and would also introduce the disruptive phenomena associated with splinter groups. (The colonies hold only surface rights to their land, inasmuch as all subsurface rights in Mexico are vested in the federal government.)

Chapter 4

The Physical Environment

Of the Mennonite colonists in Mexico thus far discussed, only those who came directly from Canada were to be successful to the degree that they have achieved "permanence." The colonies that these "successful" groups originally founded are: the Altkolonier Manitoba and Swift Current colonies and the small original outlier of the Santa Clara Sommerfelder colony, Halbstadt, Campo 55, in the Bustillos basin in Chihuahua; the Santa Clara Valley colonies of the Sommerfelder and Kleine Gemeinde in Chihuahua; and the Altkolonier Hague colony in Durango.

In terms of physical environment and climate, these colonies are all very similarly situated, at elevations of between 6,500 and 7,500 feet, in the upland and basin country which characterizes the eastern flank of the Sierra Madre Occidental. This is a region of northwest-southeast-trending mountain ranges and intermontane plains. The plains or basins between the ranges are practically continuous, normally merging along scarcely perceptible water divides which separate the region into a number of bolsones, or basins of enclosed drainage. These bolsones characteristically are structural depressions composed of pediment slopes and sedimentary bottoms floored with water- and wind-borne materials. Through erosion the pediments have advanced mountainward, leaving outlier hills along the ranges—*inselbergs* ("island" hills). Expansion and junction of pediments along water divides have led to the formation of pediment passes or saddles leading from valley to valley. The great mass of the mountains is composed of rhyolites, andesites, flat-bedded volcanic tuffs, porphyry, diorites, and basalt, from which the alluvial valley fill and, ultimately, the soils are derived.

Both the Guatimapé and Bustillos valleys are basins of enclosed drainage. Characteristically for such basins, their lowest portions are occupied by saline lakes, the *lagunas* Santiaguillo and Bustillos. The Santa Clara Valley, which is separated from the Bustillos basin by a low saddle, is drained by the Río Santa Clara and its tributaries into the Río Carmen, which empties into the Laguna de los Patos, a few miles northeast of Villa Ahumada. The valley floors consist of series of coalescing fans built by streams which, emptying onto the pediment slopes, have spread materials radially outward from the reentrant mountain valleys, laying an alluvial apron of varying texture over the pediment slopes and valley floors. Although shallow over the upper portions of the pediment slopes, in the central portions of the valleys the alluvium reaches a depth of several hundred feet. At present the mountain streams characteristically feed into the valleys along fanhead trenches incised considerably below the level of the apices of the fans. Along their lower courses they exhibit a marked tendency to follow the lines of coalescence of the fans.

Climatically this region, in which the earliest of the Mennonite colonies in Mexico were founded, is somewhat continental, shut off as it is from the Pacific Ocean, less than 200 miles away, by the backbone of the Sierra Madre. It may be defined, under the Köppen system of climatic classification, as BSkw, indicating semiarid temperate steppe conditions with a pronounced summer precipitation maximum, subject to a generally low level of humidity, intense sun, a high potential evaporation level, and large seasonal and daily temperature variations. In view of the low latitude— 29°N to 30°N in the Chihuahua colonies and 25°N in Durango— and of the desert conditions which prevail below about 4,000 feet to eastward, elevation must be regarded as being the prime factor in establishing this climatic province; it thrusts these areas more into the precipitation zone and, by reducing overall temperatures, thereby increases moisture effectiveness. The season of maximum precipitation, characteristically for regions in these latitudes situated to eastward of continental divides, comes during high summer, from late June or July to September or early October, when strong heating of the continental land mass results in reduced atmospheric pressures and, through the overcoming of the dominant westerly wind movement, in the consequent drawing in of moisture-bearing air from the Gulf of Mexico, some 500 miles to the east. Rarely is the rainy season of more than three months' duration. Since the region lies well southward of the main cyclonic storm tracks, it is only sporadically, and principally in winter, that cyclonic systems wander into the area and occasionally result in widespread precipitation. When they do, they appear to be associated with massive cyclonic storm systems centered over the lower Mississippi Valley and eastern Texas. Under their influence, in winter, snow may for a short time—a few days at most—fall on the valley floors and for longer periods accumulate on the surrounding hills.

Nevertheless, much the greater part of annual moisture receipts arrives in the form of localized, often very patchy, convectional showers of erratic distribution whose occurrence is concentrated in the months of high summer. Associated with them are extreme levels of electrical phenomena and a high frequency of hail. Characteristically for regions of marginal moisture adequacy, the annual areal and time distribution of precipitation is highly unpredictable. Averages obtained at a single station therefore have little general validity, even in the localized areas of the colonies, except insofar as seasonal and cyclical trends toward greater or lesser moisture abundance are concerned. Year-to-year precipitation amounts also are highly variable, and may readily fluctuate by as much as 50 percent above or below the mean.

In the colonies some precipitation may be expected on approximately seventy days per year, heavily concentrated in the rainy season of high summer.[1] This precipitation regime is characterized by a maximum at the onset of the rainy season (usually, July), followed by somewhat of a lull (August), and succeeded by a lesser

1. *Boletín Meteorológico*, No. 6, Estado de Chihuahua (August 1963), p. 84, based on the average of five years of record, 1958–1962, for Cd. Cuauhtémoc, Chihuahua. Rainfall records obtained from private sources in the Hague colony in Durango indicate that the situation there is very comparable. During drouth years, however, the number of days with rainfall may fall below fifty.

maximum toward the end (September, occasionally extending into October), as illustrated by the following record for Cd. Cuauhtémoc:

	June	July	August	September	October [2]
Rainfall (inches)	0.6	5.0	3.3	4.2	2.0

Not infrequently a single heavy rain of short duration heralds the end of the rainy season. To all appearances this phenomenon is triggered by a massive westerly flow which underruns warm air of high humidity (possibly conditionally unstable and of gulf origin), reestablishing the west winds which dominate the dry season but yielding one last rain. Limited records from the Mennonite colonies in Chihuahua and Durango suggest that the latter has, on the average, a slightly heavier annual rainfall—sixteen inches as against thirteen.[3] A partial explanation of this fact may lie in the nature of the terrain. Not only is the Guatimapé Valley much narrower than those of Bustillos and Santa Clara—ten to fifteen miles as against twenty to thirty—but the flanking hills are considerably steeper, thus enhancing the chances that orographically induced precipitation might extend out over the valley floor. Furthermore, the Guatimapé Valley is open to the southeast, the direction of rain-bearing winds from the Gulf of Mexico, whereas the mountains flanking the valleys of Bustillos and Santa Clara have a north-south orientation and lie athwart the direction of these winds. A strong limiting factor on the precipitation potential of gulf air reaching the Guatimapé Valley, however, lies in the necessity for it to first cross the Meseta Central, the highland of Zacatecas, which strips it of much of its moisture. Furthermore, the Hague colony lies some 4° to 5° equatorward and 500 feet below the elevation of

2. *Boletín Meteorológico,* p. 51.

3. Based on records, 1953–1964, privately kept at Gruenfeld, Hague colony, Durango, and by Peter G. Froese, Campo 112, Grossweide, Swift Current colony, Chihuahua. The reason for using these sources is that they represent values actually recorded on the colonies. There is no official meteorological station maintained within the Mennonite colonies, and the state of Durango publishes no meteorological data, according to Professor Jorge Acosta of the Instituto Tecnológico de Durango.

the Bustillos and Santa Clara valleys. Expectable temperatures in the Durango location therefore tend to be slightly higher, with a corresponding diminution of moisture effectiveness. Water deficiency in both the Chihuahua and Durango colonies is severe, potential annual evapo-transpiration values being five to six times the average precipitation.[4] In sum, then, the potential moisture situations in both regions are very comparable and verge on the arid.

A similar comparability in the physical environment of these colonies exists in the daily and annual temperature regimes, which substantially reflect the environmental factors heretofore discussed. Owing to elevation, overall temperatures are low for the latitude. In the colonies near Cd. Cuauhtémoc in Chihuahua, only three months of the year—June, July, and August—have mean temperatures in excess of 70°F (see Table 1).[5] At the Hague colony in Durango, where temperatures are generally a few degrees higher, May and September may also have means above 70°F.[6]

The annual temperature range at Ciudad Cuauhtémoc—27.5°F—is somewhat lower than the daily range, which varies from 33°F in January, the coldest month, to 36°F in June, the warmest. This relationship is expectable. Cloudiness in winter is rare, thus more nearly permitting maximum sunshine than is the case in summer. This condition, together with the relatively low latitude, tends to inhibit the annual temperature range. Because of the prevailing low humidity levels, however, the air near the ground constitutes a heat sink of low capacity. Under clear skies the heat accumulated during the day in the surface layer of the ground and in the lower atmosphere is quickly dissipated by reradiation during the hours of darkness. The result is pronounced nighttime cooling. This condition applies to a substantial degree during the rainy

4. *Boletín Meteorológico*, pp. 48, 71. Whereas average precipitation values range from 350–400 millimeters per annum, potential evapo-transpiration values are on the order of 2,000–2,500 millimeters.

5. *Ibid*, p. 15.

6. No detailed records are available for the Hague colony, but casual observations by older Mennonite farmers there, in particular as to frost and other temperature factors related to crop production, lead to this conclusion.

Table 1
ANNUAL MAXIMUM, MINIMUM, AND MEAN TEMPERATURES
AT CD. CUAUHTEMOC, CHIHUAHUA
(degrees in Fahrenheit)

Month	Average Maximum	Average Minimum	Mean
January	62	29	45.5
February	72	33	52.5
March	72.5	34.5	53.5
April	81	44	62.5
May	88	49	68.5
June	91	55	73
July	83	57	70
August	88	56	72
September	81	54	67.5
October	78	48	63
November	73	35	54
December	61	33	47
Annual Averages	77	44	60.5

season also, for the cloud cover associated with convectional thunderstorm activity normally dissipates by nightfall. However, July, the wettest month, has the smallest daily range—26°F—a reflection both of the greater heat capacity of the soil and the air at that season and of an appreciable level of cloud cover. That the annual march of temperature peaks in June instead of, as one might expect, somewhat later in the year, is owing to the fact that, whereas solar heating potential at that time is at a maximum, it is still before the rainy season, and skies are predominantly clear. The rate of heat build-up in the soil is therefore at a maximum. Absolute and relative humidity levels, owing to the approach of the rains, are already high. The heat capacity of the air is therefore enhanced, thus aiding its retention and accumulation. With atmospheric moisture content high, occasional muggy days, with high actual and perceptible temperatures, may occur.

In winter, occasional temperatures as low as 10°F in the Chihuahua colonies and 15°F in Durango may be expected in any year. Absolute minimums experienced in the colonies in Chihuahua have been on the order of 5° to 8° below zero, Fahrenheit.[7] Although days on which temperatures do not rise above freezing are rare, the high reradiation levels which prevail throughout the year occasion the occurrence of frequent night frosts during the period from October to May. Associated with them is cold-air drainage down the valley slopes, into the bottom lands. Frost hazard on the valley floors is therefore very closely related to factors of local relief. Since, under dry-land practices, agricultural land use is closely linked to the rainy season, which normally does not commence until July, the reliable "usable" frost-free period is little more than 100 days in the Chihuahua colonies, though somewhat longer in Durango.

The soils, too, of the valleys of Bustillos, Santa Clara, and Guatimapé reflect similarities in the physical environment. Predominantly they are the water-borne, water-worked, and water-laid erosion products of the country rock, mainly calcium carbonate- and gypsum-bearing andesites and tuffs, of the adjacent mountains. In the alluvial fans they are extremely variable, although generally they are coarse-textured adobes and sandy loams containing 60 percent or less of clay liberally admixed with coarser material of sand- to cobble-size, not infrequently underlain by stratified, poorly cemented gravels and cobbles. They are low in humus content. Most of the soils of the Manitoba, Swift Current, and Hague colonies and, except for narrow bands along the lower reaches of stream courses where finer-textured soils of higher humus content may occur, all those of the Santa Clara Valley are of this type.

On the floors of the valleys of Bustillos and Guatimapé, extending outward from the present western and northwestern limits of the lagunas, there are extensive areas of uniform-textured, dark, somewhat pebbly, gypsiferous—and, where ground water is high, saline—clay soils. Where well drained, they exhibit a columnar

7. Peter G. Froese, Grossweide, Campo 112, Swift Current colony, Chihuahua, recorded a sunrise temperature of −18° Réaumur (−8.5° F) on February 14, 1965. This he claimed to be the lowest temperature observed at that location since he began keeping casual records in 1927.

structure and, at depths of two to four feet, a horizon of calcium accumulation. They are high in humus and, where well drained, closely resemble chernozems. Examination of the terrain has led to the conclusion that the lagunas were of substantially greater extent at some time in the past, possibly during a pluvial period in the Pleistocene era, and that these clays are lacustrine deposits.[8]

The supposition with respect to an amplified condition of the lagunas, to help explain the nature of the present-day soils in the Guatimapé and Bustillos basins, is further based on the existence of a continuous broad band of very sandy soils extending in a northwesterly direction from the northeastern shoreline of the Laguna Bustillos (which has a very substantial beach development), to the northern limits of the Swift Current colony, in the vicinity of Campo 107, Burwalde, and beyond. This band of soils is marked by several well-defined beach ridges.[9] That no similar band of beach deposits exists along the southwestern and western margin of the (presumed) lake clays can be satisfactorily explained by the fact that, for most of the year, the wind blows consistently, often at high velocity, from a direction shifting between southwest and northwest. Wave action is therefore almost entirely restricted to the eastern and northeastern shore. It is to this sector that the beach deposits are confined. There are granodiorites in the headwaters of the Arroyo de los Sauces, which may be the source of some of the Bustillos beach sands. To the south and southwest the clays merge with the adobe soils of the fan deposits.[10]

8. R. H. Burrows, "The Geology of Northern Mexico," in the *Boletín de la Sociedad Geológica Mexicana*, VII, 88–89, believes, in fact, that some of the basins of this region which do not now have lagunas did have them during the moister era of the last glacial epoch.

9. Dr. John E. Kesseli, Professor of Geography at the University of California, Berkeley, 1931–1962, was in the field with the writer at the time the possible origin of these sandy soils was being studied. A further study of three small lagunas, all less than a mile in extent—one beyond the boundary of the Swift Current colony, west of Schoenberg, Campo 113; one in the vicinity of Edenthal, Campo 108; and the third southwest of Weidenfeld, Campo 28—revealed the same shoreline and bottom characteristics as the Laguna Bustillos. All had pebbly clay bottoms, shorelines of the same material on the west and southwest, and sandy beaches along their eastern and northeastern shores.

10. A similar history of soil development appears to have prevailed with respect to the Laguna Santiaguillo. However, since the beach deposits do not continue into

One other soil type which appears worthy of mention is found only on very small areas within the colonies. It is a red to chocolate-brown, gypsiferous clayey loam which occurs on the upper slopes of the pediments, adjacent to the mountain wall, and only between the stream channels. As far as can be determined, this soil derives directly as a weathering and erosion end-product of the tuff and andesite country rock. On the Manitoba colony it occurs only in the extreme northeast, in the vicinity of Hochstaedt, Campo 14B. On the Swift Current colony it is confined to small areas in the extreme west.

In their virgin state, these were predominantly grasslands, treed along watercourses and with some open forest. Principal grasses of this region are gramas (*Bouteloua*), curly mesquite (*Hilaria belangeri*), bunch grasses (*Sporobulus*), needle grasses (*Aristida*), false buffalo grass (*Munroa squarrosa*), tobosa grass (*Hilaria mutica*), and Mexican love grass (*Eragrostis mexicana*) in well-drained locations, sometimes associated with *Opuntia* (cacti). Poorly drained, saline soils support salt grasses, among them *Distichlis spicata* and *Eragrostis obtusiflora*.[11] Stream galleries often contain poplars (*Populus wislizeni*), willows, and walnuts (*Juglans rupestres* and *Juglans major*), among others. Yew-leaf willow (*Salix taxifolia*) is well distributed away from watercourses also, in the dark-soil zones where ground water is fairly near the surface.

In wooded areas, the Mexican live oak (*Quercus mexicanus*) is dominant to about 7,000 feet, intermingled with juniper and cedar and, in Durango, *huisache* (an acacia) and agaves. Above 7,000 feet there is a transition to pine (*Pinus ponderosa* [western yellow pine] and *Pinus arizonica* [Arizona pine]), associated with Mexican live oak and Douglas fir (*Pseudotsuga mucronata*).

From the foregoing brief description, it is evident, notwithstanding the Mennonites' own, largely subjective evaluation of its

lands of the Hague colony, no further investigation was made. Further weight is lent to the pluvial theory by the fact that inselbergs such as the Tortugas, within the Bustillos clay-soil belt just west of Waldheim, Campo 23, Manitoba colony, have substantial sand deposits on their southwestern flanks.

11. The writer is indebted to the Department of Botany, University of California, Berkeley, for some of the plant identifications.

potential amenability to the imposition of their accustomed land-use practices, that the basin and upland country of Chihuahua and Durango, although in some ways comparable to former homelands, presented environmental conditions very different indeed from those of prairie and steppe on which their agricultural practices and techniques were evolved.

Chapter 5

Accommodation to the
Mexican Homeland

Inasmuch as the survey of the acquired lands and the platting of the future location of the villages were largely carried out prior to the Mennonites' arrival in Mexico, only relatively minor logistical adaptations had to be made in this regard once they arrived upon the scene. Other problems were to prove more difficult of resolution. Some, such as the securing of building materials and reliable and adequate supplies of water, were immediate and urgent. Others, such as tillage practices, the selection of suitable crop varieties, and the proper season for planting, were largely worked out over the first few years. But the Mexican business community was not at first geared to the supplying of their particular needs and wants; neither was it equipped to absorb the surpluses of the Mennonites' commercially oriented agriculture. To economic difficulty were to be added the hardship of epidemic disease and the insecurity implicit in the restlessness and sporadic lawlessness of a revolution-conditioned host society. The initial fifteen years in particular—and especially in Chihuahua—were to try the resolve of even the most steadfast among the colonists.

The Early Period (1922–1926)

When the survey of the colony lands, under the direction of the various delegates, was completed, the plans were taken to Canada and the future villages platted. Since substantially less than the total acreage in the Manitoba colony of the Altkolonier in Chihuahua was immediately reserved (107,307 acres out of 150,000), only three villages were originally platted on that portion south of the right-of-way of the Mexican Northwestern Railway. The rest of the southern portion, together with considerable land along the western margin of the colony, was not subdivided and, for the time being, was left as unoccupied "farmland" or *Gemeindeland* (that is, land not allocated to particular villages).[1] The Swift Current group, unable to assume all of its contracted obligations, rationalized its economic position and geographic solidarity by relinquishing the area originally intended for Campos 108 and 116. Each person reserving land in Mexico was entitled to select the village in which he planned to reside. The location of his *Hauskoerl*[2] and other fields, or *Koerls*,[3] which altogether made up the total acreage he had reserved, was decided by lot. Usually, of course, people chose to emigrate with their neighbors to a village in the new homeland which bore the same name as the one left behind in Canada.

The most immediate tasks confronting the first arrivals in Mexico, the construction of dwellings and the breaking of land for the planting of crops, had to be tackled simultaneously. Many lived in tents while the first permanent shelters were being constructed; others lived in structures already existing on the land.

---

1. "Farmland" and *"Gemeindeland"* are the terms applied by the Altkolonier to land not included in a village field plan or *Flur*. "Farmland" usually is represented by relatively small areas left open between village Fluren. "Gemeindeland" normally consists of substantial blocks of vacant land. Such land may be sold to qualified persons in smaller parcels, or it may be laid out for new villages and systematically occupied as more land is needed to accommodate an expanding population. The equivalent of the term in English would be "community land," meaning essentially a reserve pool of land.

2. *"Hauskoerl"* is the term applied to the individual fields of the Streifenflur (strip-field plan) which front on the village street; on the forward portion of such fields the farmers build their houses and establish their farmyards.

3. This term is of ancient Germanic origin and refers to the individual narrow fields of the Streifenflur. Transliteration from Mennonite Plattdeutsch usage has led to another spelling, *kagel*. Tacitus, in his writings on the Germanen, spoke of their fields as *coerls*. The present spelling is adopted for the sake of phonetic clarity and will be used throughout. Denman W. Ross, *The Early History of Landholding among the Germans* (Boston: Soule and Bugbee, 1883), describes the coerl as being one *Tagwerk*, or a day's work, in areal extent.

The Mennonites had brought substantial amounts of building materials with them from Canada. Further supplies of lumber were obtained from sawmills already located in the mountains near the colonies or set up there by the colonists themselves, and from lumbering centers along the Mexican Northwestern Railway at Madera, Pearson, and elsewhere. It was not until several years after the Mennonites' arrival in Mexico that adobe brick gained general acceptance among them as a construction material.

The delays in getting the migration underway generated considerable concern among the Altkolonier leadership. Once the movement began, some four years elapsed before it had more or less run its course. Yet had the pace of the migration been even somewhat more methodical, it could possibly have been to the Mennonites' advantage. The first several train loads arrived in March of 1922, some months before the rainy season and the prospect of fresh fodder for the hundreds of cattle and horses they had brought with them. The entire Bustillos Valley had been burnt over by prairie fires, so that there was not even dry grazing available for the animals. When the feed reserves brought from Canada were exhausted, the situation was at once critical. Very quickly the Altkolonier were reduced to seeking feed supplies from the few large Mexican ranching operations still functioning in the region. These, however, were predicated upon free-ranging cattle and were not in the habit of putting up feed. The best available—though hard to obtain—was corn straw. The Canadian cattle and heavy draft horses, unaccustomed to poor and inadequate fodder, fared badly. Indeed, for the next several years what buoyancy can be imputed to the agricultural economy the Mennonites were imposing upon the Sierra Madre landscape can be largely ascribed to the supplying of grain and fodder to the newcomers as they arrived. For purposes of the migration as a whole, it was fundamentally necessary, even though not so planned by the Mennonite leadership, for a relatively small group to go in and raise crops which could help sustain the new arrivals as they came.

The most immediate concern, once the problem of complete

and effective occupation of the land— to forestall indigenous "infiltration"—was met, was that of obtaining adequate supplies of water. In the clay belt which extends in a broad band to either side of the Arroyo de los Sauces and flanks the southwest shore of the Laguna Bustillos, surface wells, fifteen to thirty feet in depth, yielded limited but dependable supplies and could be constructed at relatively low cost. In Durango, too, on the Hague colony, potable water could be obtained from dug wells. Stream density over much of the Manitoba and Swift Current colonies is such that most of the villages not able to obtain water from shallow wells had fairly easy access to this alternative source. No locational changes in villages were made out of considerations of water supply. The streams are spring-fed and normally carry a reliable if limited flow throughout the year. As the migration ran its course the villages assumed more or less their present occupancy pattern, expansion of human and animal populations necessitated the digging of wells adjacent to or in the arroyo bottoms, thereby tapping subsurface flow in addition to surface yield. Water haulage from stream sources, however, diverted considerable manpower from other tasks. One village, Gnadenfeld, Campo 2-B, eventually laid a pipeline from the village to the Arroyo Napavechic, a distance of some three-quarters of a mile. Springs provided a further limited supply. A number of them occur at no great distance from the lower limits of the fans, where they merge with the clays.[4] However, deep wells ultimately provided the answer to water supply for most of the colonies. The Manitoba Altkolonier had not been accustomed to deep, drilled wells in Canada. Those from Saskatchewan, however, were. Although during the initial settlement period drilling machinery was not at once available, drilled wells were soon attempted in some of the locations with less favorable surface water supplies. However, the problem of water supply for

4. The possibility exists that, since the presumed retreat of the Laguna Bustillos from much of the valley floor, the alluvial fans have to some degree extended themselves outward over the lacustrine clays. The latter therefore possibly form a stratum of low permeability underlying the outer tongues of the fans, with the result that soil water moving downslope emerges in springs where the fan deposits thin out.

domestic and farmyard use, away from the zone in which shallow wells are possible, was one which made major claims on manpower and capital for many years.[5]

The Occupancy Pattern

In Canada, the Altkolonier had practised a landholding system which adapted the *Strassendorf* and *Gewannflur*—a linear one-street village with its surrounding fields and pasture—to the sectional survey and the requirements of the Dominion Lands Act. These occupancy features were transplanted to Mexico and imposed upon the metric survey of that country. The 160-acre homestead, known as a *Wirtschaft*, consisting of a *Hauskoerl*, several other *Koerls* (strip fields) in various parts of the village "plan" (*Streifenflur*), and a fixed acreage in the communal pasture,[6] was made the basis of landholding. Normally a village was laid out in from eighteen to twenty-four full homesteads (*Wirtschaften*), although fractional homesteads were also permitted. Once the village land was fully taken up or occupied, persons residing in the village but desirous of further acquisitions could take up unoccupied "farmland."

Initial Adjustments

One aspect of the future occupancy pattern, the orientation of the villages and their arable lands, laid out in the strip fields (Koerls) characteristic of Streifenfluren, was left to be determined in Mexico. According to custom, the Koerls were laid out on the basis of a calculated attempt to equalize as nearly as possible the soil quality of all homesteads in the village. The orientation of

5. In the Sommerfelder village of Halbstadt, Campo 55, which was founded in 1922 on land purchased by Sawatzky and Fehr through the Russek interests, the water-supply problem was not solved until 1963, when a battery of wells was drilled about one kilometer north of the village, at the site of some springs from which, up to that time, all water had to be hauled.

6. This *Weiderecht*, or pasture right, is an integral part of the *Wirtschaft;* a colonist may not sell this right or withdraw his pasture land from the communal pasture.

the Hauskoerls determined that of the village. Thus, the different parts of the Streifenfluren were laid out in relation to their merits as assessed by the colonists.

In practice, the size of whole homesteads varies between 160 and 200 acres, normally containing at least two Koerls in addition to the Hauskoerl, and from thirty to forty acres in the pasture. In the case of two villages, however, this did not apply. The people who settled Hoffnungsfeld, Campo 12-B, generally considered themselves incapable, for material reasons, of assuming standard-sized farm units. Homesteads of eighty acres, consisting of a Hauskoerl, one Koerl, and eighteen acres in pasture, were therefore decided upon.

Blumenfeld, Campo 16, is the only village whose position was changed from that on the original plan out of consideration of terrain. On the original colony plan, the intention was to locate it approximately one mile north of its present position. However, the land there proved to be low-lying and subject to flooding from the Arroyo de los Sauces. Furthermore, the water table is very high, and the soils are saline and unsuited to tillage. Blumenfeld was therefore sandwiched between Osterwick, Campo 18, and Friedensruh, Campo 17. Because of the limited amount of potentially arable land on the Blumenfeld plan, these neighboring villages were persuaded to relinquish some of their acreage to it. Blumenfeld was then able to establish Wirtschaften of 110 acres. This was a compromise solution. Since commitments were made in Canada, prior to the migration, it was not possible for either individuals or the entire village to simply locate elsewhere. The only area to which Blumenfeld might have been relocated was the as-yet-unsubdivided land south of the Northwestern Railway right-of-way. However, this would have placed the village at the extreme limits of the Manitoba colony, in an area devoid of a readily accessible water supply. Furthermore, since Blumenfeld was the seat of the Elder of the Manitoba colony, a central location was desirable. The expedients described were therefore resorted to. It is not known that other alternatives were considered.

One further innovation upon the plans drawn up in Canada

was subsequently made in Mexico. Some of the Altkolonier villages in Manitoba had for some time been experiencing severe land shortages. This had been the primary cause of the founding of the daughter settlements in Saskatchewan. However, at the time of the migration there were numerous landless families—*Anwohner*—in the Manitoba settlement. Most of the Anwohner who took part in the migration reserved some land in Mexico, according to their real or anticipated ability to pay. The colonies therefore accommodated these persons by permitting fractional farm units.[7] Since the entire (or nearly entire) population of some of the Manitoba villages participated in the migration, the result was that many a projected village in Mexico was to have a substantially larger number of landholders than was the case in the parent village in Canada. This required the provision of additional Hauskoerls fronting the village street. By itself, this would have resulted in a doubling of the length of some villages. Moreover, there was a general desire among the migrants to establish a larger Hauskoerl than had been the custom in Canada, where it had customarily incorporated about sixteen acres.[8] Since the rear portion of this Koerl was most conveniently located to the farmyard, it was much used for the growing of fodder. Many had found the sixteen-acre site, which left only some ten acres of arable land outside of the farmyard, too small for this purpose. The new size agreed upon varied from village to village, but the Hauskoerl was generally increased to have a frontage of 300 to 400 feet. The maximum depth was two kilometers. The range of sizes therefore was from about twenty-five to approximately fifty acres. This caused a further substantial distension of the dimensions of the villages, to the extent that certain functional relationships of the Strassendorf threatened to become unworkable. School children would have excessive dis-

7. For example, twenty-one persons from the Manitoba Altkolonier villages of Blumenfeld and Neuhorst, who reserved land in Mexico, appear to have been *Anwohner,* as they listed no land for disposal in Canada. Of these, two reserved 160 acres; three, 100; nine, 80; three, 50; three, 40; and one, 5 acres.

8. Often the Hauskoerl in the Manitoba Altkolonier villages was sixteen rods (264 feet) wide by one-half mile in depth. This permitted the establishment of twenty Wirtschaften on two facing quarter-sections, ten to either side of the village street. Other dimensions, varying slightly from the above, were possible.

tances to walk, cattle would have too far to go to pasture, and outer fields would be inconveniently far away. Out of these considerations, then, it was decided to divide some of the more unwieldy villages. The result was the establishment of seven sets of "twin" villages, with each village a separate entity.[9]

Early Agricultural Progress

Despite the substantial mechanical sophistication of the Mennonites' implements, the records available do not show that they achieved a great rate of progress in subjugating the grasslands of their Sierra Madre valleys to agricultural use. During almost all but the few months of the rainy season, the clay and adobe soils were inordinately stubborn, impenetrable to the moldboard plows that had been brought from Canada. When wet, the soils stuck to the plowshare and failed to scour, while their frequently high content of rocks and gravels proved exceedingly wearing on machinery. Ground broken during the summer, after the first rains, dried brick-hard and could seldom be sown the same year. Winter precipitation was unusually copious during the first few years, yet the Mennonites were unwilling to plow at that time, fearing that the land would then be poor.[10] Statistics from the Manitoba colony in 1924, set forth in Table 2, give some idea of the progress of cultivation. Colony records further reveal that in Au-

9. They are Blumenort and Blumenthal, Campos 22 and 25; Gnadenthal and Gnadenfeld, Campos 2-A and 2-B; Hamburg and Steinbach, Campos 3-A and 3-B; Rosenthal and Rosenort, Campos 6-A and 6-B; Rosenfeld and Rosengart, Campos 7-A and 7-B; Schoenthal and Hoffnungsfeld, Campos 12-A and 12-B; and Kleefeld and Neuendorf, Campos 1-A and 1-B.

All the Mennonite villages in the colonies in Chihuahua and Durango were required to be given a numerical designation, since the traditional German names were confusing to the Mexican government and postal authorities. Suffixes, either alphabetical or numerical, applied to villages other than those listed above, have resulted from the subsequent establishment of villages on originally unoccupied Gemeindeland, i.e., Campos 14-B, 14-C, 1-C, 4½, 9½, and so on. (Gerhard J. Rempel, Blumenort, Campo 22, Manitoba colony, personal communication.)

10. The belief that ground, either sod or cropland, which was plowed "on the frost" would yield poorly and be very weedy the following year was held in Manitoba but may go back to Russia. As far as can be determined, there is no sound basis for the belief.

Table 2

EXTENT OF CULTIVATED LAND IN MANITOBA COLONY

IN *1924*

Village	Campo Number	Population	Cultivated Acreage
Schanzenfeld	19	101	632
Eichenfeld	14-A	131	532
Kronsthal	9	136	647
Einlage	11	67	410
Reinfeld	8	49	324
Blumenfeld	16	61	236
Hoffnungsthal	12-B	60	222
Hochfeld	10	10	36
Gnadenfeld	2-B	64	500
Gnadenthal	2-A	100	700
Blumenort	22	166	1,050
Friedensruh	17	42	130
Schoenwiese	20	75	442
Hamburg	3-A	131	823
Rosengart	7-B	112	980
Blumengart	15	135	700
Rosenthal	6-A	97	525
?	?	14	90
Waldheim	23	93	844
Reinland	4	68	478
?	?	138	654
?	?	97	560
Totals		1,947	11,515

SOURCE: The records of the Manitoba colony, compiled in mid-August 1924. The list is incomplete.

gust of 1924, 175 farmers in 10 of the oldest villages had a total of 6,129 acres under cultivation, for an average of 35 acres per farm. There were still few tractors. Horses, owing to shortages of good feed, were often in poor shape and unable to perform as much work as might otherwise have been expected of them.

The results of the Mennonites' first cropping attempts were not encouraging. A series of reports during 1923 from Milpillas, near Cusihuiriachic, a little south of the Manitoba colony, where eighteen Sommerfelder families from Saskatchewan had founded the villages of Eichenfeld and Sommerfeld late in 1922, gives a good indication of their problems. In April, when they observed the agraristas planting corn, the Mennonites also went out to plant —corn and potatoes. The seed either failed to germinate at all, or, if it did, the plants died long before the summer rains. They laid it to the fact that their new breaking was cloddy and had not held the moisture from the past winter's few rains. This, however, appears to have been only a partial explanation. The Mennonites had mechanical planters which placed the seed at only a few inches' depth. They failed to recognize that the agraristas used an iron-tipped planting stick to place the seed into the subsoil moisture at a depth of six to eight inches. By the time the summer rains began in July, the agraristas' corn was three to four feet high, while that of the Mennonites was faring badly or had, indeed, expired.[11]

Although the vast majority of the Mennonites, Altkolonier and Sommerfelder alike, simply attempted to pursue the same type of farming to which they had been accustomed in Canada, there was nevertheless a significant amount of experimentation undertaken by a few individuals during the first few years. Unfortunately for the morale of the colonists, most of the results were negative. The necessity of waiting for the rainy season was impressed upon them when they sowed after a few light rains in April or May. The seed might germinate, but plants died back for lack of moisture long before the rains properly set in in July. However, the need to postpone seeding until that time meant that crops had to grow and mature during the diminishing days of late summer, when the hazards of early fall frosts assume imposing proportions. Flax, barley, corn, oats, and spring wheat—all familiar from Canada—received the most attention, but spring rye, winter wheat, and winter rye were tried as well,[12] as was grain sorghum. The winter

11. The Altkolonier and Sommerfelder from Manitoba, particularly, were familiar with corn, but mainly as a fodder crop.

12. 1923, 1924, and 1925 had inordinately wet winters, which prompted the attempts with winter grains. Following limited initial successes with them, the colonists quickly abandoned them when more normal winter precipitation regimes reasserted themselves.

grains, wheat and rye, did not usually survive through the dry spring. Spring wheat (Marquis) succumbed to rust. Flax and corn, although susceptible to frost, showed promise. Sorghum, although about as successful as corn, yielded no more fodder than corn and did not produce a marketable grain crop if spared from frost. Much the same held true for barley and summer rye, since the Mennonites did not use them as bread grain. Oats appeared to show the most initial promise. Its moisture requirements were, if anything, less than those of corn, and it was less susceptible to frost. During the initial years of settlement there was, moreover, a good internal market in the colonies for locally grown oats; this crop supplied the needs of newcomers until they too, hopefully, became self-sufficient.[13] It was particularly vital as feed for the heavy draft horses brought from Canada. This internal market rendered oats largely immune to the vagaries of a shaky—and often ephemeral—Mexican market, although its production and sale under these circumstances represented not an influx of new wealth to the colonies but merely a redistribution of capital brought from Canada.

The Cropping Pattern Becomes Established

Beans, being unfamiliar to the Mennonites as a field crop, did not at once find a vogue. However, since beans and corn were the only field crops for which there was any active demand on the Mexican market, these, along with oats, were, by 1926, dominating the cropping practices of the more forward-looking of the Mennonite farmers. Flax, although it showed promise as a first crop on new breaking, dropped out of the cropping picture after a number of years. If damaged by frost, a real danger in every year, it was a total loss, whereas under similar circumstances the other crops would at least yield fodder. Furthermore, there was little market for it, and its price, in relation to other crops, was dis-

13. The Santa Clara Sommerfelder and those at Halbstadt, Campo 55, thus enjoyed a good market for oats for several years. They teamed it south to the Altkolonier colonies, where it fetched 1.00 to 1.10 pesos per bushel (at an exchange rate of 2.15 pesos to the U.S. dollar).

advantageous.[14] Nor were the soils well suited for it. Once their initial meager endowment of humus from the thin sod was gone, they puddled and caked readily at the surface, entrapping the seedlings and preventing their emergence. Attempts to raise wheat persisted considerably longer, partly because of a determination by some to continue Canadian farming practices, partly because of a desire to make the colonies self-sufficient in bread grain. Eventually the attempts at wheat-growing, too, died out.[15]

The years during which the principal migration took place—1922 to 1926—appear to have been the peak of a wet cycle. Once the march of the seasons was understood and the necessary adaptations in planting made, some very fine yields—to offset the numerous failures and disappointments—were realized from the virgin soils. In 1925 corn yields ran as high as forty to forty-five bushels per acre (one-and-a-half wagonloads of ears), flax yields ran five to fifteen bushels, winter wheat yields ran six to twenty bushels, and oats yields were as high as thirty and more bushels per acre. The highest—and by now legendary—yield ever realized was seventy-one bushels per acre of Canadian "Golden" oats on the Santa Clara colony in 1925. Such yields, although far from general, persuaded many who, in view of the unsettled civil state of the country and other problems, were approaching pioneering in Mexico with some trepidation, to see things through, at least for a while longer. The promising results of the 1925 harvest, together with the Mennonites' general appreciation of the milder winters, were strongly instrumental in convincing many that success could yet be wrung from this colonization venture.

Important to the agricultural evolution of the colonies was the gradual abandonment of Canadian crop varieties and the adoption of climatically better-adapted ones in their place. A development of

14. In July of 1927, the first date for which records are available, corn was 68 pesos per metric ton (2,200 pounds), flax was 100 pesos, and oats was 85 pesos. Since both oats and corn normally far outyielded flax, at such prices the latter was at a decided market disadvantage.

15. In recent years wheat-growing, employing climatically better-adapted varieties, has once more been undertaken. The implications of this trend will be discussed later.

particular significance was the adoption of "Texas" varieties of oats, which were better adapted than the Canadian varieties to the latitude and prevailing moisture conditions. These appear to have been first brought in by the "Kansans" who settled Campos 30 and 31. By the late 1930's they had completely replaced Canadian varieties.

Epidemic!

The same wet summers which, through 1925, held out promise for the agricultural future of the colonies also brought with them manifestations which harbored a very real threat to their continued existence. Each year, with the onset of the summer rains, malaria, in epidemic proportions, ravaged the region. The Mennonites, coming as they did from a country where it was not known, had no resistance to it. In 1925 alone, some 130 deaths were attributed to it.[16] There were no public health facilities, but in that year a Mexican doctor moved to San Antonio de los Arenales. Before, the only doctor within reach was at the mining town of Cusihuiriachic,[17] more than fifty miles from the more distant Altkolonier villages and nearly a hundred from Santa Clara.

The wet summers brought with them high ground water and, in the low-lying areas adjacent to the Arroyo de los Sauces, substantial flooding. Since practically all water was taken from shallow wells and surface sources (streams and springs), a general contamination of water supplies must have occurred,[18] for the malaria epi-

16. Contained in a report written in January 1926 by Johann W. Wiebe of the Manitoba colony and carried in the *Steinbach Post* of February 3, 1926.

17. Cusihuiriachic was owned by the Cusihuiriachic Mexico Mining Company. Its mines produced chiefly silver, with some zinc, small amounts of lead, and minute quantities of gold and copper. The company's head offices were in Duluth, Minnesota, and there were branches in El Paso and Chihuahua. The chaos of the revolutionary period, during which all but a handful of Americans fled the state of Chihuahua, together with low ore prices, punitive taxation of foreign-owned property, and labor-union agitation during the postrevolutionary period, finally forced closure of the mines in the 1930's. The town today, although inhabited, is in ruins. (Ignacio and Gilberto Delgado, Cd. Cuauhtémoc, Chihuahua, personal communication, together with the writer's observations.)

18. Although spring water might not have been contaminated at the time of fetching, it was customarily kept in barrels of doubtful hygienic condition; as a result, it might have been no safer than that from streams or shallow wells.

demics were complicated by the spread of typhoid. Then, in the spring of 1926, there followed an outbreak of smallpox. Since the Mennonites had little knowledge or appreciation of—nor, for that matter, faith in—immunization, these diseases simply ran their course. The center of contamination, from which these epidemics radiated outward, appears to have been Eichenfeld, Campo 14-A, which is on low ground, had shallow wells, and was several times flooded. Largely out of ignorance of the nature of communicability of these diseases, no quarantine was attempted in an effort to isolate the afflicted. Indeed, sick persons from severely ravaged villages were often transported to hitherto unaffected parts of the colonies for care, thereby intensifying the epidemics' sweep. At least one village, Friedensruh, established in 1922 about one mile north of the present site of Silberfeld, Campo 26, ceased to exist as a result of these epidemics. In 1925 it was so badly decimated that the few remaining families relocated elsewhere and the site was abandoned. The name was transferred to the village presently answering to it, Campo 17 in the east-central part of the Manitoba colony.

The Waverers Return to Canada

Despite the prospects that the problems of wresting a livelihood from the highland valleys on the flank of the Sierra Madre could yet be solved, many were disheartened by initial reverses and, despairing of exhausting their capital in fruitless attempts at discovering viable techniques of cropping and land use, abandoned the colonization effort to seek their fortunes once more in Canada. Among the Sommerfelder, numbers had, of course, turned back at once or very shortly after arrival in 1922. Among the Altkolonier, whose social controls were stronger, the first dissidents did not return to Canada until 1923, after making at least a token attempt at establishing themselves in Mexico. Many had been half-hearted participants in the migration and had gone only under a certain amount of ecclesiastical, community, and family duress. Others had had exaggerated notions of the climatic and other benefits of life in the subtropics and were quickly disillusioned by the stark realities of pioneering in so difficult a region.

Some—the poor—of the Swift Current and Manitoba Altkolonier Gemeinden [19] had come partly or entirely at community expense, and had little personal economic stake in the success of the colonization venture. Such persons were often easily diverted from any resolve they might have had with respect to emigration, and the reasons for it, from Canada. Returning oftentimes to their old communities, they spread descriptions, frequently exaggerated, of Mexico which led many a would-be emigrant to doubt the wisdom of such a move. The Mennonite authorities in Mexico were put to great pains to discredit and dispel these stories and keep the migration moving. To a pronounced degree they were successful. First, the return to Canada did not assume major proportions before the main migration was essentially concluded in 1926; and second, for those still in Canada who wavered in their determination to emigrate there was still the adamant position of the school authorities to take into account. All in all, the numerical attrition experienced in the first few years was not sufficient to greatly impair the colonization effort.

The Hague Colony

The Hague colony in Durango, although small to begin with, suffered very little attrition through a return to Canada. The migration of this group did not begin until 1924, by which time opposition to the compulsory education requirements had substantially diminished. Only the most sincere opponents of the education laws therefore emigrated. Furthermore, the Hague Gemeinde (church community) was too poor to assist its indigent members on the migration. Everyone, of however meager a capital endowment, came at his own expense and on the basis of his own decision. The average determination of this group to prevail in Mexico was therefore likely stronger than that of their Swift Current and Manitoba brethren, while its financial capacity to give up and return to Canada was considerably less. Taking stock of their limited capacity for

19. The term *Gemeinde* denotes the church community, which in the case of the Altkolonier is identical to the secular community.

absorbing economic reverses, and under the able urging of Elder Jakob Wiens, the Hague colonists made little attempt to farm on the basis of traditional crops and concepts of agriculture, but adopted the indigenous Mexican beans and corn at once. They were thus spared many of the disheartening reverses which punctuated the early years in Chihuahua.

The Majority Continue the Struggle

Even for those who gave no serious thought to giving up the attempt in Mexico, the initial failures to raise crops which would carry them through forced many to seek ways of arresting the attrition of their often meager capital. Those who had machinery enjoyed some success in hiring out their services to Mexican ranchers, breaking land or threshing. Many returned to Canada for the busy summer season to earn enough money to carry on.

Very real difficulties confronted the Mennonites in obtaining the necessary supplies and services indispensable to their substantially mechanized agriculture and the maintaining, more or less, of their accustomed way of life. The raison d'être of San Antonio de los Arenales prior to the arrival of the colonists—except for some months in 1916 when it was the headquarters of the Pershing punitive expedition against Pancho Villa [20]—had been to serve as railway cattle *embarcadero* and cavalry outpost. As such, it boasted little more than a huge adobe-walled corral, the cavalry post, a restaurant, *cantina,* and a few small retail establishments.[21] Such items as hardware, machine parts, harnesses, tractor fuel, and the indispensable wheat flour were difficult and at times impossible to obtain. The Mexican business community (if such it may indeed

20. The United States Cavalry, under General John J. Pershing, mounted a punitive expedition into Mexico in 1916 against the revolutionary General Pancho Villa, following the latter's attack on the border town of Columbus, New Mexico. Later, the expeditionary force was shifted to the vicinity of Hidalgo del Parral, in the extreme southwest of the state of Chihuahua.

21. Eyewitness account, Walter Schmiedehaus, Cd. Cuauhtémoc, Chihuahua, personal communication.

be called) of the local region was simply not geared to the supply of what were, to the Mennonites, fundamental necessities. Flour was particularly critical. Eventually the Mexican government came to the Mennonites' assistance by providing free railroad passes to delegates sent to seek supplies of flour and wheat. Some flour was brought in from the south (Aguascalientes and Gómez Palacio), but when it was learned that wheat was available at Madera, 188 kilometers "up the line" of the Northwestern Railway, future supplies were procured from there and ground into coarse flour in the colonies. The government paid the freight.

New Problems

To a degree, the problems of supply were initially solved by colonists going to El Paso in advance of the arrival of emigrant trains from Canada; there they would purchase flour, replacement parts, and other necessities. These were then added to the freight complement of the arriving trains and brought into Mexico as settlers' effects, thus escaping duties and import bans. Newcomers were also afforded the benefit of their forerunners' experience in terms of advice as to what they should buy for their own future needs prior to crossing the border. It was legal for arriving immigrants to make these purchases in the United States, and these were allowed entry into Mexico in the same way as the chattels brought from Canada. There was thus nothing to prevent them from doing someone a favor by bringing in extra items. At first the Mexican authorities either were not aware of this practice or else turned a blind eye to it. The colonists, for their part, regarded it as a justifiable tactic, for they had had no good prior advice as to how best to prepare for their material needs in the new homeland. Then, in 1925, without prior announcement, customs duties were levied on all goods carried by the immigrating Mennonites, whether bona fide settlers' effects or not. Whether there was a causal relationship between the earlier Mennonite strategem and the imposition of the duties cannot be established. Following a direct appeal to President

Plutarco Calles in November of 1925, the duties were rescinded, but not retroactively.

The Awakening Response of the Mexican Market

As the first years of the colonization effort wore on, the Mexican market made a strong response to Mennonite demand, a demand stimulated by their substantial importation of capital—estimated at four million dollars [22]—much of which was to be spent in transforming the countryside into an agricultural landscape. Indeed, the Mexican market proved much more capable of developing lines of supply catering to Mennonite demand than it was of creating the machinery for absorbing their impending agricultural surpluses. The Mennonite colonists, for their part, had brought with them the appurtenances of, and a dedication to, mechanized agriculture predicated on the production of surpluses for outside markets. Their institutional framework, however, was not geared to encourage—or, for that matter, accommodate—either private or group initiative in aggressively pursuing and developing market opportunities.[23] Of their own accord, Mexican markets were slow to respond and develop.

The large and continuing Mennonite importations of capital from Canada soon attracted a number of enterprises to San Antonio de los Arenales. Among the first to respond were the Russek interests, which established a branch bank there before the end of

22. Based on estimates by Jacob A. Wiebe and Walter Schmiedehaus, both of whom were engaged in the earliest banking operations in San Antonio de los Arenales, following the arrival of the Mennonite colonists.

23. The reasons for this are several. First, marketing activity was regarded as being speculative and, by implication, of questionable honesty. Second, it meant direct and continued contact with the outside world, which was not permitted the Altkolonier, although the Sommerfelder took a less adamant stand on this issue. Third, the request for the Privilegium explicitly stated that the Mennonites wished to settle in Mexico as agricultural colonists. There was some fear, therefore, that engagement in commercial activity could be regarded by the Mexican government as a breach of faith which might invite an attack upon the Privilegium. A few Sommerfelder, however, immigrated as *comerciantes*, not as *agricultores*.

1922. Another firm, that of Baltazar Meléndez, which originally functioned only as an exchange to convert the Mennonites' dollars to pesos, soon broadened into banking operations as well. Before the end of 1923, the brothers Cardón, Mormons from Colonia Dublán near Nuevo Casas Grandes, had opened an agency for gasoline and machinery. A large hardware company based in Chihuahua and El Paso opened a branch, and a lumber company established a large sales yard in response to the unusual demand for lumber created by the Mennonites' initial insistence on building with wood. Over the next few years many more businesses were established at San Antonio, and by 1925 there was a resident doctor in town. At Estación Patos (now Nuevo Ideal), Durango, the rail point nearest the Hague colony, events assumed much the same pattern, although they moved more slowly and were smaller in magnitude, as the opportunities inherent in doing business with the Mennonite colonists manifested themselves. Eventually, both San Antonio de los Arenales (later Ciudad Cuahtémoc) and Nuevo Ideal were to become regional market centers owing to their proximity to the Mennonite colonies, and were to far outgrow older, established towns.

Largely because of the linguistic barrier between the Mennonites and the Mexican businessmen eager for their trade, the growth of San Antonio and Nuevo Ideal—but particularly San Antonio—attracted and provided opportunities for a substantial number of German nationals, adventurers and opportunity-seekers, in Mexico at the time.[24] Later their numbers were swelled by a small number of Russländer Mennonites who also entered the business community. Since they spoke German, they not only could readily communicate with the Mennonites but also quickly gained their confidence. In 1924 Walter Schmiedehaus, a former army officer, represented them in the agrarista question. Very soon they assumed most of the positions of trust in the banks and other business establishments, or went into business for themselves, catering mainly to the Mennonite market. Not a few started out as pedlars, hawking

24. Some had been officers in the Mexican Federal Army, others were bona fide colonists seeking to escape the economic chaos of post-World War I Germany.

their wares from village to village in the colonies,[25] then later set up businesses in Cd. Cuauhtémoc which by local standards became flourishing enterprises and continue to this day. One such individual has left an enduring mark on the colonies. Among other lines, he had an agency for fruit trees—apples, peaches, apricots, and plums—from an American firm. These he sold from door to door in the colonies and was thus instrumental in the establishment of many of the numerous front-yard orchards still to be seen in the Manitoba and Swift Current colonies.

Conclusion

By the end of 1925, in spite of disappointments, epidemics and numerical attrition through return to Canada, it was evident that the Mennonites' numerical and economic strength was great enough to absorb these reversals. It was also evident that their commitment to the colonization attempt and their accommodation to the new homeland—and of Mexico to them—were sufficient, barring calamity, to promise their survival.

25. In Canada the Mennonites were very familiar with this type of retailing. There, the pedlars were mainly German-speaking Jews.

Chapter 6

Economic Evolution, the Privilegium, and the Attainment of Permanence

Because of the postrevolutionary unrest still prevalent in the country, the Mexican government went to considerable lengths to protect the Mennonite colonies. This was particularly so in Chihuahua, which for almost a decade after the end of the revolution in 1920 was plagued with armed insurrections by political malcontents. Although there were no direct incursions upon the colonies, the unstable civil state of the country hindered their progress in establishing the conditions under which a livelihood might be wrested from their valleys on the flanks of the Sierra Madre.

The First of the Bank Failures

The first of a succession of direct and indirect economic blows to the colonists, resulting from the unstable state of the country, was the failure in late 1923 of the firm of David S. Russek and Company, reputedly the largest banking organization in the state of Chihuahua. Divested of its liquid capital during the abortive uprising of former Provisional President Adolfo de la Huerta against the regime of Alvaro Obregón, the Russek organization sank into insolvency, with a loss to Mennonite depositors in the San Antonio branch of several hundred thousand pesos.[1] In the

1. Walter Schmiedehaus, Cd. Cuauhtémoc, personal communication. Schmiedehaus was an employee of the San Antonio branch of the Russek bank at the time of its failure. Partial restitution was made by the Russek organization in that it made over a block of land four kilometers square to its Altkolonier creditors.

same year a local rebellion against the state government of Chihuahua, led by Dolores Miramontes—"Don Lolo"—resulted in direct raids on the cash resources of business establishments and banks in San Antonio de los Arenales.

The Government Evaluates the Colonies

Such misfortunes only added to the very real hardships with which the colonists had to contend. Nevertheless, significant progress continued to be made. This was recognized in a glowing tribute by a Mexican government commission sent on a tour of inspection to the Altkolonier colonies in Chihuahua late in 1924 or early in 1925; the purpose of the commission was to determine the desirability of having additional colonies of Mennonites established in the Republic.[2] The commission concluded:

Perhaps it will be possble to settle Mennonite colonies throughout the Republic; that would surely be the practical way to spread the use of modern farm machinery and also to get the heavy breeds of horses established in the country. A similar result might be obtained with cattle, poultry and swine, for all these animals, brought with them by the colonists, are of the best quality.

Only one criticism can be raised against the colonists, that they assimilate so little in the country. For they have maintained their German speech although they left Germany 140 years ago . . . This criticism would be justified if one did not consider that a large number of the settlers will leave the colony to engage in other businesses . . . among the people of the country.[3]

Such observations, although highly laudatory of the Altkolonier's methods, institutions, and accomplishments, showed a considerable lack of realistic understanding of the suitability to

2. The real reason for the commission's trip to the Altkolonier colonies lay in the unsatisfactory relationship that existed between the Mennonite Board of Colonization, which was attempting to assist Russländer Mennonites in emigrating to Mexico, and the Mexican government. The findings of the commission were to aid the government in arriving at a policy decision regarding further Mennonite immigration.

3. *Steinbach Post*, May 27, 1925, quoting the magazine *Der Deutsche Kolonist*. Translation by the author.

the environment of some of their introductions, and of the desirability of implanting them among the Mexican rural population. The Mennonites' wooden houses cost a great deal more than those built of adobe brick. Furthermore, unless well insulated, they offered considerably less in terms of comfort, their interior temperatures fluctuating much more directly with those outside. They were therefore colder in winter and hotter in summer than comparable adobe sturctures. Although the commission members were impressed by the heavy horses brought from Canada, their use was in fact to be discontinued by the Mennonites themselves before many years had elapsed. Such horses could work well only on superior feed and did not have the wiry strength and survivability of the Mexican horse of recent feral ancestry. The Mennonites' cattle, too, although well able to stand comparison with their Mexican counterparts, were generally of nondescript breeding, a partial legacy of the communal pasture. Similarly their poultry and swine were inconspicuous for quality by North American standards.

Perhaps the most significant misinterpretation of the Mennonite colonies and their inhabitants lay in the confidence expressed that they soon would mingle freely in the host society and, in practical fact, merge with it. Mexican authorities appear not to have realized at all that it was precisely a determination to avoid such a rapprochement with the world at large which prompted the Mennonite migration in the first place.

However the commission interpreted its findings, its report appears to have spawned considerable interest. On November 17, 1925, the President of the Republic, General Plutarco Elías Calles, arrived in San Antonio de los Arenales to inspect the Mennonite colonies in person. With him were the minister of agriculture and the governor of the state of Chihuahua.

Harvesting was at full tempo in the colonies. The summer had been one of ample rainfall and crops generally were good (in fact the best, in per-acre yields, that have been achieved throughout the colonies' history). The villages nearest San Antonio were already well built up. President Calles pronounced himself greatly impressed with the colonists' high level of activity and the ample evidence of their enterprise. At the end of his visit he was presented with a memorial scroll which the Altkolonier had had prepared in Spanish and German. After pointing out their accomplishments despite the hardships encountered in Mexico, and the economic benefits they had brought to the region, it followed the custom with respect to such occasions—as, indeed, had also been the custom in tsarist Russia—and asked a boon of the president. It was a request that customs duties on the chattels and provisions of those yet to come be rescinded, and that those recent arrivals who had been forced to pay them be given a refund. The tenor of the document was one of high optimism. It represented the Mennonites' hope that by holding forth on the benefits their colonization had already brought to the region as well as the favorable economic implications for the future, present concessions might be won.

The Milpillas and Ensenillas Failures

That all was not going as well in the colonization effort as the memorial scroll suggested is indicated by the dissolution of the nearby Sommerfelder colony at Milpillas in the same year. Disappointing results from the colonists' first planting in 1923 prompted some members—as was also the case in the other colonies—to return at once to Canada. Malaria, too, and other diseases took their toll. Those with little capital were quickly reduced to seeking expedients whereby they might carry on. Not infrequently families were left in Mexico while their menfolk went to Canada to earn money working in the harvest. Water was in chronically short supply, and apparently the capital for drilling deep wells was lacking. Conditions were ameliorated somewhat in 1924, when there was a wet summer and the water situation improved greatly. Furthermore, a satisfactory crop of oats, corn, and barley was harvested that year, although wheat was destroyed by rust. The colonists found an attractive if limited market for produce in the nearby mining town of Cusihuiriachic, as did some members of the Manitoba colony.[4] Nevertheless, by late 1924 four more families were preparing to leave for Canada, and another was moving to Halbstadt, Campo 55. Fifteen families remained at Milpillas,[5] none of them committed to staying.[6] As in the Russländer colonization attempts, there were internal dissensions which impaired the prospects for survival.

Early in 1925 a group of three men from Milpillas went to look for land elsewhere. Eventually, together with a small group from Santa Clara, they settled upon the purchase of 1,000 acres—to be surveyed into 100-acre lots—some three miles north of Ensenillas, at no great distance from the point where the canyon road from Santa Clara emerges from the Sierra del Nido. The price was $4 per acre, which included two wells to be constructed at government expense.

During the summer and fall of 1925, the year of the worst malaria and typhoid epidemics ever to strike the colonies, people kept leaving Milpillas, either to join their Sommerfelder brethren at Santa Clara or to return to Canada. By December of that year only five families remained. They had a fairly good crop in 1925, partly from their own planting and partly from the abandoned fields of their erstwhile neighbors. Within the next year or so, however, the colony dissolved. The colony at Ensenillas fared no better and also shortly disbanded. The Milpillas episode must be regarded, like the Russländer attempts in the same years, as a case of a colonization attempt by too small a number, of too high a degree of individuality, who acted independently with little regard for the repercussions of their actions upon the rest of the community, to which they appear to have felt but a limited commitment. Whenever numerical attrition following on colonization attempts

4. Butter fetched a peso ($.46 U.S.) per pound, lard $.26 per pound, and eggs $.40 per dozen, all prices that were considerably higher than those for the same products in the Prairie Provinces of Canada at the time.

5. The apparent disparity in the number of families remaining, when compared with the original eighteen, is owing to the fact that several new family units had been created in the interim.

6. Report by Peter Schulz, Cusihuiriachic, December 18, 1924, carried in the *Steinbach Post* of January 7, 1925.

by the Mennonites in Mexico has reached a certain point, it has invariably been succeeded by a kind of panic at the prospect of being isolated among the native population, and the entire colony breaks up.

Growing Disquietude

For the other, larger, surviving colonies there continued to be some realistic cause for optimism through 1926. However, the wet cycle which had characterized the years since 1922 had apparently spent itself, and more normal conditions prevailed. There was drouth in 1926, but soil moisture reserves were good, and there was a middling crop. Further significant adjustments in land use and agricultural techniques were being made. Beans, corn, and oats had come to dominate the cropping picture. The Mexican method of maximizing yields of feed and fodder from corn— the practice of "coppicing"—was finding favor.[7] The disk plow, which is much better suited to the turning of the difficult soils of the region than is the moldboard plow, was also coming into use. Finally, the virtues of the smaller, tougher Mexican horses were coming to be appreciated, and they were beginning to replace those brought from Canada.

Offsetting these positive trends was the cessation of the influx of Canadian capital when the migration ended in 1926. In the colonies there was a vital dependence upon this capital. Although

7. The word "coppicing" is introduced by the author to describe a particular practice, or set of practices, related to maximizing the combined grain and fodder yield from corn (maize). Specifically the term refers to the harvesting of wood from live trees, whereby branches are systematically cut back without destroying the tree; the wood so obtained is usually used as fuel. In the "coppicing" of corn, the green parts of the plant are harvested by hand, with the aid of the sickle, after the ears are set. All portions of the plant above the maturing ears are removed. This phase of the harvesting procedure takes place in September. Then, in late October or November, when the ears are ripe, they are snapped, again by hand. Then the mature stalk is cut to the stubble with the sickle. The "coppicing" procedure yields a grade of fodder—*forraje verde*—that is superior in quality to the dry stalks— *rastrojo de maíz*—obtained at the final cutting. If the "coppicing" operation were not resorted to, all the fodder yield would be of the lower quality of the final cutting.

there was some revenue accruing out of agriculture, this was still far from adequate for sustaining current expenditures and further development. The internal economy of the colonies, too, was substantially predicated upon these funds, for the dominant avenues of economic opportunity lay in the provision of services—building, land-breaking, and so forth—and sales of feed and fodder to the newcomers. The annual payments on the Bustillos lands, since new wealth was not yet being created at an adequate rate, could be made only on the basis of a heavy dependence on an influx of immigrant capital. In addition, the local banks—San Antonio once more had two, that of the Meléndez organization and another founded by Jacob A. Wiebe, son of John F. D. Wiebe—depended heavily for their operations on the new deposits made with the arrival of each immigrant train. They did some business with the colonists, but their main avenues of lending were in mining and ranching. Although these were probably, in the main, sound risks, they represented substantial long-term commitments. As long as money continued to come from Canada, the banks could maintain their liquidity on the strength of new deposits. When these suddenly ceased to accrue in the by now expected fashion, the banks were faced with a difficult transition period, until their extended-term loans came in.

The Privilegium Is Attacked

There is little doubt that the banks could have weathered the transition had it not been for factors beyond their control —political unrest and the first direct incursions upon the Mennonite Privilegium.

In 1927 Don Jesús Antonio Almeida, Governor of the state of Chihuahua, who three years earlier had interceded on behalf of the Mennonites in the agrarista question, was deposed in a coup d'état. His successor, Don Fernando Orozco, a man of evidently greater revolutionary zeal, set about enforcing the revised Constitution as adopted by the government of President Calles. Singled out for particular attention were two articles of the Constitution:

Article 3, which required the establishment of socialist curricula in schools, "without religious influence, fanaticism, or prejudice"; and Article 27, which provided for severe curtailment of religious activity and for the closing and confiscation of churches.[8] At first the Mennonites were unaffected, but then, as churches were closed and the offices of the Roman Catholic Church were denied the populace, resentment against the apparent immunity of the "aliens" led to denunciations of their privileges. The *presidente* of San Antonio de los Arenales set about enforcing Articles 3 and 27 in the Mennonite colonies, apparently on instructions received from higher authorities.

The threatened termination of the Mennonite colonies' privileged status appears to have served as the signal for local bureaucrats and political activists to reap what material or political advantage they could out of the situation. Complaints were entered against the Mennonite schools, which gave religious instruction. The practice of each village having its own place of burial was denounced, and only one cemetery was to be permitted each colony. The Waisenamt, which holds in trust the estates of widows and orphans, was attacked as an illicit banking organization and threatened with heavy penalties. Obscure regulations were recalled, and all vehicles, of whatever description, were required to be licensed, retroactively to the date of immigration. The Mennonites regarded these developments as deliberate harassment. The Vorsteher arranged an audience with Governor Orozco and obtained the withdrawal of all those charges which directly impinged upon the terms of the Privilegium. Then the taxation and license matters were dealt with, and an agreement was reached whereby the colonies received remission of the retroactive demands and reductions on the current levies.[9]

8. The model for the purge emanated from the state of Tabasco on the south coast of the Gulf of Mexico. Its Governor, Tomás Garrido Canabal, was dedicated to stamping out religious influence in Mexico. Graham Greene, *The Power and the Glory* (Don Mills, Ontario: Bellhaven House, 1965), tells a graphic story of the antireligious measures taken in Tabasco by the Canabal regime.

9. The license fees on vehicles were ostensibly to pay for government expenditures on roads, drains, and bridges in the colonies. This, however, was a fabrication, since the colonies performed all such work themselves, out of their own levies.

As time wore on, the actions against the Mennonites diminished. The colonies' status, and that of the Privilegium, remained unchanged. Nevertheless, the events described had created serious unrest among the colonists. By May of 1927 two sizeable groups from Chihuahua had left for Canada and another was preparing to leave in June.[10] The withdrawal of their reserve capital put serious strains on the local banks. That year, also, there was serious drouth. Many colonists had a poor crop and were forced to draw on their capital, thus further straining the banks' resources. Since the flow of money from Canada was essentially at an end, the bulk of the annual land payments to the Zuloagas also had to be made from funds on deposit in the San Antonio banks.

More Bank Failures and Continuing Attrition

Then, in June, the Bustillos cavalry commandant staged a revolt designed to restore the recently deposed Don Jesús Antonio Almeida to the governorship. The revolt failed, but some important people in San Antonio were suspected of involvement and subsequently arrested. To forestall a run on the banks by the alarmed Mennonites, it was decided to temporarily close them. Although the crisis passed, confidence had been seriously impaired. Further losses such as those experienced with the closing of the Russek bank in 1923 were feared. Gradually the Mennonites withdrew their capital. Meanwhile deposits were few and small, and early in 1928 the Meléndez bank closed, freezing some one million pesos of Mennonite deposits. However, a plan was proposed whereby, under supervision of the National Bank Commission, the bank would be kept in operation and the Mennonites' money would be returned as outstanding loans matured and came in. At a meet-

10. *Steinbach Post,* June 1 and 15, 1927. There was considerable interest in the Peace River area of Alberta. Numerous Altkolonier, particularly from Saskatchewan, had already settled there. One of the attractions of the region for the Altkolonier was the fact that it was still in a pioneering stage of development. It was therefore relatively easy to settle more than three miles—the limit for compulsory attendance—from a public school in an organized district.

ing held in Hochfeld, Campo 10, the colonists unanimously committed themselves to refrain from demanding payment of their deposits until the bank could resolve its difficulties. Some of the colonists, however, did not hold to the agreement made by their Vorsteher and representatives of the Waisenamt, and began to withdraw their deposits. This set off a run on the Meléndez bank, and it was shortly forced into bankruptcy, with a net loss to the Mennonites of some one-million pesos ($230,000 U.S.). Then, in 1929, General Gonzalo Escobar launched his revolutionary movement, the Renovadora, thus bringing further unrest to the country and consternation to the business community. The Wiebe bank, already under severe pressure, had difficulty collecting its outstanding loans and could not withstand the run by its depositors. It, too, went into bankruptcy.

Both the Meléndez and Wiebe organizations made substantial efforts at restitution. The Wiebe bank ultimately met all but approximately 100,000 pesos of its debt to depositors. The Meléndez organization, which had numerous other business interests in Cd. Cuauhtémoc, as San Antonio began to be called in 1928, took to holding auctions of goods and cattle, at which depositors could bid against the still outstanding balances of their accounts.[11]

The Mennonites' losses from the several bank failures totaled on the order of three-quarters of a million pesos. Considering their total importations of capital, estimated at four million dollars in cash and half that amount again in chattels, these losses should not have been crippling. However, most of them were incurred at a time when the bulk of the Mennonites' capital had already been committed to sustaining and developing the colonies. The losses therefore represented a large percentage of their still liquid assets. A number of business failures in Cd. Cuauhtémoc followed shortly after, reflecting the curtailed purchasing power of the colonists, who, in the years following, were also to experience progressively

11. The result of this tactic was, of course, a terrific inflation of prices, inasmuch as persons bid as much as three and more times the actual value of articles in an effort to salvage something of their lost capital. Information about the bank failures was obtained from Walter Schmiedehaus and Jacob A. Wiebe, both of whom were personally involved.

greater difficulty in meeting the contracted payments to the Zuloagas, until finally the balance had to be renegotiated and new repayment terms set.

Despite the bank failures and resulting hardships, there continued to be progress on some fronts. Gradually, grain buyers established themselves at Cd. Cuauhtémoc. A large grain storehouse (*bodega*) was built in 1928. The market, however, remained unpredictable and was easily flooded. Moreover, Cd. Cuauhtémoc buyers paid approximately a third less than prevailing Chihuahua prices.[12] Furthermore, 1928 and 1929 were drouth years with much hail and, although a few fortunate persons could claim that they were making some economic headway—owing to price rises provoked by shortages—many others began to experience real hardship and privation. Over much of the colonies, farmers, particularly those with small acreages, could not even harvest enough feed for their horses. Then, when the time came to plant, their animals either had had to be sold or were too weak to work. Seed, too, was scarce and dear. For either or both of these reasons some people were unable to put in a crop in 1929. Such persons were reduced at once to seeking day labor, which paid little and was not often available.[13] Some, their resources exhausted, found work in the Morman colonies in northwestern Chihuahua.

12. Santa Clara farmers were able to team grain to a market in Chihuahua via the canyon road, a seven-day round trip. Teaming to Cd. Cuauhtémoc took five days. Besides the added two days, however, hauling to Chihuahua required the carrying of more feed, which substantially reduced the payload. At first oxen were used for some hauling, as they could forage better than horses. In 1928 two Santa Clara farmers bought trucks. These could haul substantially larger loads than wagon teams which, depending on the distance and the condition of the trail, could carry a payload of from 800 to 1,300 kilograms (1,760 to 2,860 pounds). Teaming and trucking charges from Santa Clara to Cd. Cuauhtémoc were 15 pesos per metric ton; to Chihuahua, they were 20 pesos.

13. Wages for day labor averaged from 50 centavos to a peso (23¢ to 46¢ U.S.) per day. By the month, the rate of pay was from 4 to 6 pesos, board added. Mennonites were usually paid slightly more for the same type of labor than were Mexicans. Mennonite employers have consistently shown a preference for the hiring of Mexicans, partly because the employer-employee relationship is more impersonal. Employment opportunities for Mennonites in the colonies have therefore been limited, particularly in agricultural labor. In more recent times, in the several small industries which have become established in the colonies, the preference has, on the other hand, been overwhelmingly for the hiring of Mennonites.

The Situation in Durango

The Hague colony in Durango, although it, too, experienced difficulties during its early years, was spared much of the economic dislocation that beset the colonies in Chihuahua. Because of its original small beginnings and the fact that the colonists had little capital in excess of immediate needs, no banking or large business establishments were created in response to an effective or anticipated demand for these services. There were therefore no bank or business failures related to political unrest, as was the case in Chihuahua. Moreover, the Mennonites in Durango had no initial problems with agrarista squatters. They also escaped particular attention during the antireligious campaign which embroiled the Chihuahua colonies in numerous difficulties in 1927. Their adjustment to the indigenous crops had been accomplished very early. Although there was economic hardship, it did not contrast so starkly with the conditions which the Hague colonists had known in Canada.[14] For all these reasons, then, there was less unrest in the colony and less pressure for a return to Canada. Indeed, so different were prevailing attitudes of the Hague colonists as compared to those of many in Chihuahua that their brethren in Canada, far from being deterred by reports from Mexico, continued to arrive well into the 1930's, during a period when numbers of people annually left the Chihuahua colonies to return to Canada.

The Lowest Ebb and a Gradual Upturn

The few hopeful indications of a possible reversal of the economic attrition which characterized the years to 1929, particularly in the Chihuahua colonies, were quickly dashed by the onset of the depression of the 1930's. Although it appears doubtful, in view of the realities of drouth and other natural hazards, that significant capital accumulation could ever have been achieved out of the Mennonites' agricultural economy, the depression effec-

14. As has been previously stated, the Hague–Osler Altkolonier were much less well materially endowed in Canada than their Swift Current and Manitoba brethren.

tively erased any such possibility. In 1931 the price of corn dropped to 12 pesos per metric ton ($4.20 U.S.),[15] and even at those prices there was little demand. Produce prices, however, in relation to commodity prices, remained relatively high. The colonists reacted with a gradual swing to the production of dairy, meat, and poultry products in conjunction with the accepted field-crop commodities.

Under normal conditions of vegetation growth, it was only through utilization of crop residues that the livestock sector of the Mennonites' agricultural economy could be at all maintained. The growing relative importance of animal products therefore had a pronounced effect in terminating fruitless attempts at the growing of unsuited crops and in crystallizing land use around a field-crop spectrum incorporating corn, oats, and beans. In the event of a crop failure, except if destroyed by hail, these nevertheless produced fodder. If the crop matured successfully, the residues still made valuable feed, a consideration which did not, for instance, apply to wheat or flax.

Since the successful raising of poultry and hogs requires substantial quantities of grain, the raising of cattle, which does not require grain and which allows for both meat and dairy production, offered the best prospects within this adjustment to land use and market opportunities. The outgrowth of this accomodation to existing conditions was the development of the Mennonite cheese industry. For many years now cheese has been one of the colonies' major sources of income, second only to the combined production of field-crop commodities.

The Cheese Industry

The cheese industry of the Mennonites in Mexico appears to have had its beginnings in the village of Rosengart, Campo 7-B, Manitoba colony, in 1931.[16]

15. Other commodity prices that year were: beans, 60 pesos per ton; eggs, 5 centavos each (23¢ U.S. per dozen); butter, 1.10 pesos per kilogram (19¢ U.S. per pound); lard, 75 centavos per kilogram (13¢ U.S. per pound). The rate of exchange in 1931 was 2.85 pesos to the U.S. dollar. Prices obtained from an observer's report, written November 26, 1931, published in the Steinbach Post of December 17, 1931.

16. Actually, the first attempt at commercial cheese manufacture in the Mennonite colonies was made in 1930, when a German national tried to set up a factory

In 1929 Peter G. Friesen left the Manitoba colony and found work as the manager of a small irrigated farm owned by a German pharmacist in the Mormon settlement near Nuevo Casas Grandes. A cheese factory owner whom he got to know offered to teach him the art of cheese-making. In 1931 Friesen returned to the Manitoba colony and began making cheese in Rosengart. Lacking financing, he interested two farmers, Peter Blatz and Abram P. Martens of Rosenthal, Campo 6-A, in his venture. They in turn persuaded a Mormon cheese-maker to come to the Manitoba colony as a technical advisor and aid them in establishing the industry among the Mennonites.[17]

Cheese is a highly regarded, even a prestige item of the diet in highland Mexico. Once it came to be produced in the colonies, the market developed with little promotional exertion by the Mennonites. However, they sold their cheese at first through a Chihuahua wholesale firm. Following the establishment of the connection with the Mormons, it was also marketed through a cheese factory owner from Nuevo Casas Grandes. By 1936 the demand was such that the Mennonite-owned cheese factories severed connections with these middlemen and marketed their product directly.

There was at first some reticence by the Altkolonier farmers to conform to the requirements of cheese factories in terms of promptness of delivery and regularity of supply. The economic advantages to the farmer inherent in regular deliveries, however, soon established the necessary level of conformity to the factories' requirements. The supplying of milk to cheese factories was to become, and in general continues to be, the most reliable single producer of revenue to the vast majority of the Mennonite farmers in Mexico. It frequently becomes the sole avenue of earning when field crops fail.

---

in Reinland, Campo 4, Manitoba colony. However, it came to nothing, apparently because of a lack of capital and difficulties in obtaining milk supplies. The actual development of the cheese industry in the Mennonite colonies is not related to this event.

17. Information obtained from Peter G. Friesen (the person mentioned in the text), Nuevo Ideal, Durango, and Abram Blatz, son of one of the co-founders of the cheese industry in the Manitoba colony.

In 1935 Chihuahua Mennonites introduced the cheese industry into the Hague colony in Durango. The reaction to this development was, if anything, more positive than in Chihuahua.[18] Most significant, perhaps, was the gradual change in cattle breeds set in train there by the cheese industry. Previously, dairying had been predicated upon the production of cream and butter. With the advent of the cheese industry, emphasis turned to milk. Interest came to center on breeds noted for high milk production rather than for high butterfat content. Cows dominantly of Holstein-Frisian ancestry were gradually to replace other breeds.[19]

The Santa Clara Sommerfelder did not respond as readily to the prospects inherent in the market for cheese. The first cheese factory there was not built until 1942. Then it was a Russländer Mennonite, who had acquired a farm at Weidenfeld, who built and operated it.[20]

Had the dairying and cheese-producing sector of the colony economies gained momentum a few years earlier, the Mennonites might have been spared a good deal of economic hardship. The Altkolonier of Chihuahua in particular might have been able to avoid a major threat to their progress and, for that matter, their continued existence.

The Land Debt

The poor crops and falling prices of the late 1920's and early 1930's made it impossible for the Altkolonier of the Manitoba

18. Jakob Wiens, the Altkolonier Elder in Durango until his death in April 1932 and himself an able and dedicated farmer, was a strong proponent of advancement in agriculture. In Chihuahua the influence of the Altkolonier Elders has been generally in the opposite direction.

19. It was formerly believed that breeds such as Shorthorn, whose milk has a higher butterfat content than that of Holstein-Frisian cows, would yield more cream. It was subsequently found that the Holstein-Frisian breed also showed a net advantage in cream production, a fact which helped to stimulate the change in breeds.

20. When the owner died shortly after the factory at Weidenfeld, Santa Clara, was built, management passed to an Altkolonier. Although some of the smaller farmers derive a large part of their income from milk deliveries to that cheese factory, in general the commitment to dairying is substantially smaller among the Sommerfelder than among the Altkolonier.

and Swift Current colonies to meet their commitments to the Zuloagas. The Swift Current colony had relinquished a substantial portion of its initial acreage soon after the founding of the colony. This had been the more readily possible because deeds to the colony lands were based on individual villages. The return of the land to the Zuloagas had therefore not entailed a renegotiation of the entire purchase. Possession of the Manitoba colony, on the other hand, was registered in the names of the two "holding companies," Heide, Neufeld and Reinländer Waisenamt, and Rempel, Wall and Reinländer Waisenamt. The relinquishing of any portion of these blocks of land, had it been attempted, would therefore have required the issuance of new deeds. Such an attempt might well have laid the entire colony once more open to agrarista attack.

In order to meet the obligations to the Zuloagas, it became necessary for the Gemeinde [21] leaders of the Manitoba colony to apply considerable moral suasion to those members who still possessed substantial amounts of liquid capital; [22] these members were asked to lend it to the colony for application to the outstanding debt. As time wore on and the economic situation worsened, it became ever more difficult to extract from unwilling lenders the funds necessary—and then only at high interest rates—to continue the payments and keep the colony from collapse.[23] Eventually, the balance—930,920.52 pesos—had to be renegotiated.[24] Before this was accomplished, however, a great part of the funds held in trust by the Waisenamt, representing the estates of widows and minor heirs, had been diverted to the repayment of the land debt.

The Swift Current colony experienced difficulties very similar to those of the Manitoba colony in meeting its commitments to the Zuloagas. There was, however, a difference in that no blanket deed

21. The term Gemeinde, as it applies to the Altkolonier, encompasses both the religious and the secular community.

22. In most cases such capital was on deposit in Canadian banks, these having been quite rightly regarded as being more secure than their Mexican counterparts.

23. David Harder, "Chronik," *passim.*

24. The last of this debt was finally discharged in 1948. (David Harder, La Batea, Zacatecas, personal communication.)

covered the entire colony. The colony authorities did not elect to make the retirement of the combined debt of the several villages a united colony responsibility, as was the case in the Manitoba colony. Each village was therefore left to solve its own problems of survival. Consequently, between 1932 and 1936, six villages—Rosenhof, Campo 104; Neuanlage, Campo 105; Shoenfeld, Campo 106; Gruenfeld, Campo 109; Neurecht, Campo 111; and Hoffnungstal, Campo 114A—were forced into bankruptcy. Grossweide, Campo 112, arrived at an agreement with the Zuloagas whereby one-half of its land was relinquished to the former owners and any payments already made on that portion were credited to the remaining half.[25]

The effect of these bankruptcies was to raise at once the fear than Mexicans would now buy into the colony and disrupt the structure of the Altkolonier settlement pattern. Once again considerable suasion was brought to bear on persons known to possess substantial liquid capital in order to buy back the forfeited lands. For their part, the Zuloagas, fearing renewed agrarista agitation over the repossessed lands, were eager to sell it again to the Mennonites, and, indeed, at greatly reduced prices.

Because the Swift Current colony deeds covered entire villages, when a village underwent foreclosure all of its residents shared the same fate. Those who had their farms entirely paid for were dispossessed along with others who were still heavily mortgaged. Situations arose where persons who in fact had had their farms completely paid for were offered the "opportunity" of purchasing them once more from the Mennonite investors who had bought the foreclosed villages from the Zuloagas. A few, not content to accept the situation, instituted proceedings. After protracted litigation, however, they were found to have no supportable claim in law. Incensed at this injustice, many who were in the position of having had their land largely or entirely paid for left the Swift Current colony. Some who were able returned to Canada. Others moved some miles north to Saucito (now Altenau, Campo 35) or

25. The land thus given up was subsequently incorporated in the ejido of Rancho San Ignacio.

took up land in the still-vacant portions of the Manitoba colony. A few joined the Hague colony in Durango.[26] A small number of destitute families squatted for some years on vacant land south of Rancho Tepehuanes, in the vicinity of the present site of Campo 71, Neuschoenwiese.

The repurchase of the foreclosed lands on the Swift Current colony resulted in significant changes in the structure of the villages affected. In every case the field patterns were broken up or strongly modified. All the communal pastures were dissolved. Koerls were enlarged, or they were altogether dispensed with and compact farms were established. Although very few isolated farmsteads came into being, the villages evolved into much more dispersed linear settlements than those which retained the Streifenflur with its numerous narrow Koerls.

Institutional Breakdown under Stress

Owing to the attrition of their resources, the years of the late 1920's and early 1930's are generally regarded as having been the most difficult ever experienced by the Mennonite colonies in Mexico. Under the stress of their economic and other difficulties, serious inadequacies in the institutional structure of Altkolonier society began to manifest themselves. For example, those who lost their land owing to the foreclosures in the Swift Current colony were left to their misfortune, and the Manitoba colony, although its landholding was so structured that there was a colony-wide commitment to the retirement of the mortgage debt, was also unable to prevent injustices. The Waisenamt as custodian of substantial sums in the form of the estates of widows and orphans held in trust, had either borrowed these funds to meet the mortgage payments to the Zuloagas, had lost them in the bank failures, or had lent them to borrowers who, because of the depressed economic conditions, were unable to meet their obligations. As the financial circumstances of the holders of Waisenamt notes deteriorated, their desperation to salvage something of their capital led to massive

26. David Harder, La Batea, Zacatecas, personal communication.

note devaluations, to one-third and less of the face value. There was some effort to stabilize the situation; devaluations of Waisenamt notes were forbidden. Nonetheless, they were resorted to anyway, particularly by persons attempting to raise money for a return to Canada. In transactions involving Waisenamt notes, however, a cash levy of 5 percent of the amount involved in the transaction was made in order to establish a fund to aid the destitute.

Some who did not panic were able to turn the Waisenamt's difficulties to their own advantage. The still-vacant land of the Manitoba colony was thrown open to purchase against Waisenamt notes. This measure was of some advantage to those who legitimately held the notes. However, it also offered speculative opportunities to those who could purchase the notes for cash, at a small fraction of their value, and then use them to make land purchases from the colony at 100 percent of their face value. Similarly, persons who were in debt to the Waisenamt could purchase the notes cheaply, then use them as currency, instead of cash, to extinguish their obligations, thus preventing the Waisenamt from obtaining the funds it needed to meet its obligations to the legitimate holders of its outstanding paper.[27] All in all, very substantial transfers of wealth occurred as a result of the Waisenamt's difficulties, with the advantage, generally speaking, accruing to those who had managed to remain solvent.

A New Dilemma

If those years of the late 1920's and early 1930's were ones of difficulty and unrest in the Mennonite colonies owing to economic uncertainty and hardship, the situation was by no means alleviated by the state of civil order in the country. The poor crops of 1927 and the years following, together with a diminution in job opportunities in the Mennonite villages, rendered the rural Mexican population in the settlements around the colonies destitute.

27. Gerhard J. Rempel, Blumenort, Campo 22, and Heinrich J. Martens, Neuenburg, Campo 21, Manitoba colony, personal communication. Eventually, in 1939, it was ruled that in the future no more than one-half of amounts owing to the Waisenamt could be discharged with Waisenamt notes.

The colonies, hard put to answer their own most immediate needs, experienced a great increase in the numbers of beggars roving the countryside. Thefts and armed robberies once more became frequent.

Because of the generally poor crops, commodity prices remained high in relation to purchasing power through 1930,[28] and it may be said with considerable justification that the Mennonites' Mexican neighbors were driven to stealing from them. Although the Mennonites were in difficulties, they were in any event generally better off than the Mexican peasantry.

During the early years of colonization, losses to thievery had been significant enough. Indeed, in 1922 the Mexican government had found it expedient to station federal troops in the Altkolonier colonies in Chihuahua for the protection of the settlers. In those days, however, thefts centered on provisions and cash. Now a disconcerting element had entered into the thefts and robberies, reflecting, no doubt, the rising involvement in agriculture of the *ejidatarios* and *colonos* (Mexican peasants): harnesses, implements, and workhorses, as well as seed stocks, became prime objects of theft. By late 1929 the situation had become so serious that the colonies once more felt themselves forced to ask for federal protection. By the end of that year soldiers were stationed in the Altkolonier villages, and later a headquarters was built for them by the colonists in Steinbach, Campo 3-B.

The presence of the troops resulted in an overall abatement of petty crime. However, driven perhaps by desperation, some formed armed gangs to counter the troops and nocturnal and even daylight robberies increased. The Mennonites were in a real dilemma. Armed protection appeared a mandatory prerequisite for even a minimum level of security. However, if their pacifist principles forbade resort to violence, was it proper, or even permissible, for them to appeal for military protection and have the soldiers, so to speak, commit acts of violence in their behalf? Recurrent shoot-

28. Prices for beans and corn, the commodities most important to the Mexicans, varied between 1928 and 1930 from 6 to 10 centavos per kilogram for corn and from 15 to 25 centavos per kilogram for beans. For the relation between these prices and customary wages, see note 13, above. There was, moreover, little work available.

ings, involving several killings during robbery attempts and including the apparently senseless murder of an entire Mennonite family on an isolated farmstead near Cd. Cuauhtémoc,[29] could not be met by a stance of defenselessness. Some Mennonites began to arm themselves and, under provocation, to shoot back. At night it was common for groups of several families to cluster together for safety.

In Durango the situation did not deteriorate to the point where an appeal for military protection was made until 1933. Soldiers, as many as four to a village, were set on patrol, to good effect. So effective, indeed, did the military patrols in the colonies in Durango and Chihuahua prove, that the Mennonites soon discovered themselves on the horns of another moral dilemma. The officers had judicial authority and rights of summary trial and sentence. Summary executions were carried out in both the Swift Current and Hague colonies. This was more than the Mennonites had bargained for. Knowing the likely consequences to the accused, they hesitated to give information even against malefactors whom they could positively identify.[30] Nevertheless, the executions appear to have had a very substantial salutary effect, for afterwards there was a very marked reduction in the incidence of thefts and robberies.

Growing Sentiment to Depart Mexico

The more or less lawless conditions prevailed until the mid-1930's, with troops continuing to be stationed in the colonies. Although there is some reason to suppose that the harassment of the colonies was partly inspired by radical political sentiment against the alien Mennonites, this cannot be firmly established.[31]

29. The family of one Peter Schellenberg was brutally murdered in the autumn of 1933, apparently by a robber.

30. These facts were taken from a variety of observers' reports appearing in the *Steinbach Post* during the years in question and were verified by Jakob Bartsch, Campo 9, Grünthal, Hague colony, Gerhard J. Rempel, Blumenort, Campo 22, Manitoba colony, and other witnesses to the events related.

31. There are some in a position to hazard an educated guess who believe that crimes against the Mennonites and their property, particularly in 1933 and 1934, when there were numerous threats and acts of violence against them, were related to the resentments generated by the systematic deportation of Mexican nationals from the United States during the depression years.

In any event, the fears and uncertainties generated by the unsettled civil state of the country, coupled with the economic hardships of the times, served as a powerful stimulus to many to seek their fortune elsewhere.

Early during the period of unrest in Chihuahua, quite a few people left the colonies there to join the Hague colony in Durango, where conditions were still more stable.[32] Most of those wishing to leave, however, desired to return to Canada, but money was scarce, and the obtaining of sufficient cash for the journey not infrequently necessitated the sacrifice of practically all of a family's possessions. Indeed, some were reduced to peddling their household furnishings to Mexican villages, for whatever they could fetch, in the attempt to raise sufficient money for the trip. Others appealed to relatives in Canada for assistance, but the depression reigned there too, and it was not always possible for those in Canada to lend aid, even when they wished to do so.[33]

There were, moreover, by this time, new problems which frequently caused delays and embarrassment in the passage between Mexico and Canada. In 1931, because of the depression, Canada altered the interpretation of its immigration laws. As a result, immigration was drastically curtailed. This became a serious impediment to many Mennonites attempting to return. Because of the special papers provided by the Mexican government to facilitate the migration, it had not been necessary for the Mennonites to have passports. Many of the returnees, therefore, although born in Canada and otherwise entitled to return, could present no satisfactory proof of their citizenship. Failing regularization of the matter, they were refused entry and had to return to Mexico. In 1931, however, Mexico also established restrictive practices with respect to

32. Some of the removals from Chihuahua to the Hague colony were, of course, as has been previously mentioned, related to the foreclosures in the Swift Current colony in 1932 and later.

33. Such appeals were often met with little sympathy from relatives in Canada. Having been excommunicated for their refusal to migrate to Mexico and having, furthermore, on occasion been denounced for it by the very persons now seeking their aid, such relatives often had little or no motivation to respond to appeals for help.

immigration, and there were new and unanticipated difficulties in crossing the boundaries of that country as well.[34]

The establishment of a satisfactory state of civil order would probably have resulted in an early phasing-out of the return movement to Canada. Life in Canada, during the depression, was difficult too, and it was very hard to make a new beginning there. However, events, whose implications were seldom fully understood by the colonists, seemed to recur at critical times and kept alive the desire to leave Mexico. In 1932 the Mexican government carried out a registration of all aliens, in the course of which the head of each alien household was assessed 10 pesos ($3.12 U.S.).[35] The money thus raised was intended for use in assisting destitute nationals being repatriated to Mexico from the United States. The Mennonites, however, interpreted it as a national manpower registration not unlike that carried out in Canada in 1918, to which they had given only the most grudging compliance. Such suspicions of the government's intentions with respect to them, in spite of its record of having honored the Privilegium during the antireligious campaign of 1927, and in spite of the fact that the government had gone to considerable lengths to ensure the security of the colonists' lives and property, created once again a disposition to emigrate. When, therefore, a real infringement of the Privilegium was perpetrated upon them, and in a particularly sensitive area at that, the preparedness to depart the country was of massive proportions, though it was not untinged by accumulated personal disillusionments and disappointments with life in Mexico.

In May of 1935, without prior announcement, an inspector toured the colonies in Chihuahua. He visited all schools, taking notes on the buildings, equipment, and quality and kind of instruc-

34. Caught up in these restrictions was a sizeable group of late-coming Altkolonier from the Hague–Osler district of Saskatchewan, who wished to emigrate to the Hague colony in Durango. In November of 1931 there were four families in El Paso awaiting permission to enter Mexico, more than twenty families in Ojinaga, and over forty in Laredo. Most of those in Laredo and Ojinaga were probably new emigrants on their way to Durango, because both places had good rail connections to Durango via Torreón. Rev. Johann P. Wall of the Hague colony went to Mexico City where he succeeded in obtaining entry permits for those of his Gemeinde.

35. The rate of exchange in 1932 was 3.20 pesos to the U.S. dollar.

tion.[36] The schools were found not to conform to Mexican law and were placed under interdiction pending regularization of their status. The Hague colony, though also subjected to inspection, escaped having its schools closed, perhaps because it was small as compared to the Chihuahua colonies (approximately 1,000 inhabitants as against 8,000), perhaps because it was situated in a politically less agitated part of the country.

This action caused immediate and grave alarm in the colonies. It was feared that Mexican teachers and Spanish instruction were to be imposed upon them. Rev. Abraham Dyck and Vorsteher Gerhard J. Rempel were dispatched at once from the Manitoba colony to Cd. Chihuahua to seek a reversal from the governor, failing which they were to proceed to Mexico City on the same matter.[37]

The delegates engaged Daniel Salas López, with whom the Mennonites had had dealings since their first exploratory mission to Mexico in 1921, to help them in laying their case before the government. They also turned—perhaps, initially, mainly for assistance in overcoming language difficulties—to the Consulate of the Federal Republic of Germany. After several weeks of fruitless waiting to gain an audience with the president, they drafted a complaint (amparo) to President Cárdenas in the hope that they might thus reach him. The complaint vigorously protested the infringement of the Privilegium implicit in the closing of the schools and asked for permission to reopen them. Failing that, the Mennonites stated that they would be "caused to seek another place of refuge."

As the matter dragged on without any positive indications as to the government's intentions, concern mounted. On September 9 the Chancellor of the German Consulate, Hugo Natus, reported to the representatives of the Mennonite colonies that the Ministry of the Interior had dispatched a special representative to the colonies

36. Instruction in the Altkolonier and Sommerfelder schools in Mexico was (and is) strictly limited to reading, penmanship, recitation, and arithmetic. Permissible reading material consists of a fourteen-page primer, the catechism, the Scriptures, and the Hymnary, all in German.

37. David Harder, "Chronik," and readers' reports to the Steinbach Post, June 12 and June 19, 1935.

in Chihuahua to determine the basis of persistent reports that the Mennonites were planning to leave Mexico en masse and return to Canada. Where difficulties existed between the colonies and the administration, they were to be resolved. However, he was also instructed to inform the Mennonites that, although they were regarded as useful elements in Mexico, "no hindrance would be placed in the way of an emigration in the event that the difficulties rested solely therein that the colonists were not in agreement with the Mexican education laws: for the primary thing which must be required was respect for the laws of the Mexican Republic, which must be obeyed by aliens as well as by Mexicans." [38] To this disheartening news was added notification of the passage, on August 26, 1935, by the government of President Cárdenas of a law under which all land and building whose ownership was vested in churches and other religious cults were declared confiscated to the state. Because of the sectarian nature of the Mennonites' schools and Waisenämter, it was feared that these too, as well as the lands in the names of the latter, would be subject to confiscation. Moreover, it was stipulated that where conflicts existed between the new law and prior covenants or legislation, the new law was to prevail. It appeared, therefore, that the entire Privilegium might be subject to capricious unilateral abrogation by the government.[39]

In his discussions with the colony authorities in Chihuahua, however, the government representative took a conciliatory approach. The Mennonites took some heart from this development, but inquiries were begun to determine the possibilities of emigrating to some other country. In view of what he considered the slender possibilities that the matter would be resolved to the Mennonites' satisfaction, Natus too counseled for emigration.[40] In the

38. Hugo Natus to Abraham Dyck, Gerhard J. Rempel, Abraham P. Friesen, Johann Dueck, Johann P. Wall, and Gerhard P. Kroeker, representatives of the Altkolonier and Sommerfelder colonies in Chihuahua and Durango, September 9, 1935, from the files of Gerhard J. Rempel.

39. *Ibid.*

40. Hugo Natus to Johann P. Wall, Hague colony, Gerhard J. Rempel, Manitoba colony, and Johann Dueck, Santa Clara colony, October 28, 1935, from the files of Gerhard J. Rempel.

colonies no firm position on the question of emigration had as yet (autumn, 1935) evolved. The subject was, however, everywhere under serious consideration, although the sentiment for departing the country was stronger in the Chihuahua colonies than in Durango. The dominant feeling, in spite of the forcefully expressed disapproval of their leaders, was for a return to Canada. A return to Canada, in their leaders' opinion, would represent abdication of all the principles for whose maintenance they had endured the difficulties, privations, and hardships of over a decade of pioneering in Mexico. Popular pressure, nevertheless, was so strong that it could not be effectively countered. At conferences held by the Altkolonier in Chihuahua, it was decided to send delegates to Canada to investigate the nature of settlement opportunities there.

The Altkolonier church leaders continued to contest the "Back to Canada" movement, as it came to be known, stating that "if in its time it was right that we should leave Canada, then it cannot today be right also that we should return there." The next few months were punctuated by considerable infighting. However, when it became evident that the "Back to Canada" party would persist in its designs with or without Gemeinde support, the church leaders capitulated and agreed to send a delegation.[41]

Meanwhile, the Reverends Johann P. Wall, Peter H. Klassen, and Abraham Dyck returned to Mexico City in the admittedly forlorn hope of obtaining an audience with President Cárdenas and attaining a full reinstatement of the Privilegium. The German Consulate employed its good offices on their behalf, but Chancellor Natus held out little hope of the Mennonites achieving their ends. Through an intermediary, he discovered Cárdenas' position in the matter. It was simply this: although it was painful for him to have to imply that his still much-revered predecessor, Alvaro Obregón, had acted unconstitutionally in granting the Privilegium, in the prevailing political climate and in view of his own strongly stated position on Mexican nationalism and socialist education, it was im-

41. David Harder, "Chronik," *passim*, and reports by A. W. Peters and Johann V. Wolf, *Steinbach Post*, October 2 and December 4, 1935.

possible for him to grant the Mennonites special rights.[42] Reverends Klassen and Dyck returned to their homes, leaving Reverend Wall to press the issue.

While awaiting the opportunity to present his case to the president, Wall established contact with the British consul-general in a tentative move to discover, if possible, what the reaction of the Canadian government would be to a Mennonite appeal for admission. The consul's opinion was that "it does not really enter the question, whether or not the colonists who left Canada have occasion to anticipate a friendly reception. If, upon request of the Canadian Mennonites who emigrated to Mexico, the Dominion Government issues them passports or recognizes them as Canadian subjects, then it is not for love of its prodigal offspring but only due to the fact that insofar as they are still Canadians in law the issuance of these documents cannot be denied them." [43] He advised them, moreover, not to anticipate the reinstatement of their former exemption from military service nor to expect to escape the secular schools.

Somewhat surprisingly, Wall was granted an audience with the president. He received assurance that the Privilegium, in its entirety, would be honored by the government, and President Cárdenas ordered the Ministry of Education to so advise the regional authorities:

Decree No. 6-330 of 19 December 1935.
   On decision of the President of the Republic you will kindly direct the Inspectors of Schools in Chihuahua and Durango to permit the resumption of instruction in the schools of the Mennonite colonies of those Federal states, for the reason that the aforementioned highest office of the Republic has commanded that the agreement which the Government of General Obregón entered into with the parties in question must be given due regard.

The local authorities did not at first comply with the instructions; they refused to permit the reopening of the schools and attempted

42. Hugo Natus to Vorsteher Johann Dueck, Santa Clara colony, December 3, 1935 (carbon copy to Gerhard J. Rempel).
43. Contained in a memorandum from Hugo Natus to Gerhard J. Rempel.

to have the order rescinded. Categorical instructions were thereupon issued from Mexico City, and in January of 1936 the Mennonite schools resumed operation.[44]

Although there was general relief at the full reinstatement of the Privilegium, confidence was not restored. Remission of the recent incursions was regarded by many, including the Mennonite leadership, not as being permanent but as merely offering time during which affairs might be so ordered that in the event of a recurrence of infringements an orderly departure, minimizing losses, might be undertaken. During the eight months of 1935 when the status of the Privilegium hung in the balance, the sentiment for departing the country had gained so much momentum that the presidential decree of December 19, 1935, did not alter thinking in the colonies.[45] Steps preliminary to a general exodus continued. At a conference held in Sommerfeld, Santa Clara, in January 1936, a decision was reached by the Sommerfelder to emigrate to Paraguay, inasmuch as it was agreed that there was no possibility that the Privilegium concessions would be granted by Canada.[46]

The Altkolonier delegation to Canada left in February. They engaged the assistance of the member of parliament for the constituency of Lisgar, which included the entire Mennonite West Reserve in Manitoba, to assist them in working out permission for a

44. From the files of Gerhard J. Rempel. Translation by the author. Although frequently threatened, the schools in the Hague colony were, in fact, never closed by the inspectors, as was the case in Chihuahua. However, the representatives of the Hague colony, and particularly Rev. Johann P. Wall, were involved in all the representations made to the government.

45. The Mennonites' suspicions were, to a degree, justified, for, although the schools were permitted to reopen, local officials promised to make certain that no religious instruction was carried out in them. This, of course, was inimical to the nature of the Mennonite schools, most of whose teaching material was of a religious nature.

46. It appears likely that in reaching the decision to emigrate to Paraguay, the Santa Clara Sommerfelder were influenced by Hugo Natus' letter of October 28, 1935, to Vorsteher Johann Dueck of Santa Clara and Wall and Rempel of the Altkolonier in which he praised very highly the concessions the Paraguayan government had made to settlers and dwelt at length on the fruitfulness and agricultural potential of the land. However, one must also take into consideration the fact that there already was a substantial Sommerfelder colony, Menno, in the Gran Chaco, which dated from 1926–1927.

reentry into Canada. As a result, many in Mexico, who now regarded an imminent mass return to Canada as certain, began to sell off their property and chattels. The attitude of the Canadian government, however, was not encouraging. The government of the province of Quebec, which was still assisting settlement in the Abitibi region, was also approached. It appeared at first that Quebec might extend the sought-for concessions in regard to education, but no commitment was immediately forthcoming.

While the delegates were in Canada, offers were received in Mexico of land in the United States and Paraguay. There ensued then, among those desirous of emigrating, the same sort of divisions as those which characterized the period prior to the migration from Canada to Mexico, with different groups pushing for emigration to different destinations.

The attitude of the local authorities, particularly in Durango, continued to be that, although the Mennonite schools might remain in operation, religious teaching, being expressly proscribed by law, must not be given. Inquiry to the British consul-general in Mexico City brought the reply that to all appearances instruction in the Mennonite schools would be required to be altogether of a non-religious nature. Subsequently another amparo was drafted, reiterating the Mennonites' grievances and asking for a clear statement guaranteeing future observance of the entire Privilegium or, failing that, a period of grace to wind up their affairs in Mexico. Three days later President Cárdenas assured them in writing that he had instructed all levels of the civil and military authorities to abide by the terms of the Privilegium.

As no further direct threats to the Privilegium ensued, the urgency to emigrate diminished. Nevertheless, the colony authorities, concerned about keeping their people together, continued to take tentative steps toward emigration. On the advice of the chancellor of the German Consulate, statistics were gradually compiled as to the acreage, buildings, and other property owned by the colonists. It might be possible, it was reasoned, to sell the entire colonies as going concerns to the Mexican government in one block, to be used for the resettlement of some of the many nationals being repatriated from the United States. They had been accustomed to a relatively high standard of living and would be more content to move into ready-made properties such as those of the Mennonites than to be settled in *ejidos* (collectives) on uncultivated former hacienda lands. Such a sale would, of course, set in train a wholesale emigration of the Mennonites. In that event, Canada would almost certainly be excluded as a possible destination, and Paraguay would be the logical choice—a situation much more to their leaders' liking.[47]

There remained, however, a substantial minority—mainly in Chihuahua—who were more immediately bent on leaving Mexico, under Gemeinde auspices if possible, alone if not.[48] The group agitating for a general return to Canada gathered lists of signatures to convince their unwilling leaders of the weight of opinion in favor of such a move. Repeated attempts at obtaining a commitment from either the Dominion government or that of Quebec, however, brought no firm reply.[49] Appeals to the province of Alberta, although initially greeted with little enthusiasm, finally culminated, in the spring of 1938, in permission being granted to Mennonites who were entitled to enter Canada to homestead in the Peace River district.[50]

About the same time, however, two men purporting to be officials of the government of South Dakota appeared in the Chihua-

47. An inquiry directed to the government of Australia, regarding settlement opportunities and the possibility of obtaining a Privilegium, elicited a negative reply, and the matter was pursued no further. The Chancellor of the German Embassy, Natus, offered to arrange German citizenship for all the Mennonites in Mexico in the event that a migration to Paraguay materialized, arguing that under such circumstances the retention of Canadian citizenship could no longer have the least value for any of them. The Mennonites showed little interest in the offer, and very few—it was possible to authenticate only one case—availed themselves of the opportunity.

48. An Altkolonier who left Mexico under other than Gemeinde auspices was automatically excommunicated. This ban was recognized by the Altkolonier churches in Canada, who were themselves under ban from the mother church in Mexico, so that the only possibility of reinstatement for the individual was for him to return to Mexico.

49. David Harder, "Chronik."

50. Report by Chester Bloom, Ottawa, reprinted in the *Steinbach Post* of May 4, 1938. The Alberta government did not at first want to entertain the Mennonites' petition. The matter was, however, pursued by R. J. McKinnon, M.P. for Edmonton, who was aware of their possible value as pioneers in the developing Peace River district.

hua colonies. South Dakota, they said, had two million acres of public lands for disposal. Prospects were held out for the granting of the desired concessions with respect to schools and military service.[51] There arose then a "South Dakota Party" which, failing to win Gemeinde recognition, carried forward its particular ambitions for emigration independently.[52] Indeed, for some time there was optimism that something might come of this plan. Finally, early in January of 1939, several delegates of the "South Dakota Party" had an audience with the United States consul in Cd. Chihuahua. Precisely what transpired between the Altkolonier and the consul is not known, but the matter of emigration to South Dakota was abruptly dropped.

Although no organized migration back to Canada developed either, substantial numbers of both Altkolonier and Sommerfelder returned there during the late 1930's, many of them to the districts where they had formerly had their homes. Others took advantage of the Alberta government's provision permitting them to homestead in the Peace River District. As a result, quite a community of Altkolonier came into being in the Fort Vermilion area.

Conclusion

The return to Canada was arrested by the onset of World War II in the late summer of 1939, which brought the question of military exemption once more to the fore.[53] Concerned about their status in that regard, many returned once more to Mexico.

51. Johann V. Wolf, Springfeld, Campo 41, Chihuahua, report of March 14, 1938, appearing in the *Steinbach Post* of March 30, 1938. It seems hardly credible that South Dakota would have extended any concessions. The Hutterian Mennonites in the James Valley, who practice a form of Christian communism, were harshly treated there during World War I. There was also considerable resentment against acquisitions of land by them.

52. David Harder, "Chronik."

53. A few families continued to return to Canada until the summer of 1940, when Canada undertook another national manpower registration as part of its wartime mobilization. By that time it was apparent that some form of service would be required of conscientious objectors. The border, however, was not closed to draft-age men until some time later.

Actually, such a countermovement had existed practically from the first, not infrequently prompted by recurring difficulties over the requirements of the provincial Schools Acts. Following the implementation of stricter immigration laws in 1931, such returnees had great difficulty in reentering Mexico or were simply turned back.[54] If they did manage to get into Mexico, they were often destitute when they arrived in the colonies. Since the colonies themselves were still struggling for survival, and since employment opportunities were few, such persons were forced to seek their livelihoods on ranches, in the irrigation districts of southern Chihuahua and elsewhere.[55]

Once the reinstatement of the Privilegium late in 1935 came to be accepted as genuine, there appears, in fact, never to have been a general sentiment for emigration. By 1936 the colonies were beginning to recover from the depths of the depression and were moving slowly toward solvency. Since that time the probability of a total dissolution of the Mennonite colonies in Mexico has become progressively more remote.

54. One way of circumventing the immigration laws was to obtain a visitor's visa good for a specified period, then simply vanish into the colonies and not return. In 1939 Mexico once more relaxed its immigration regulations. Persons who were in the country on six-month visas were permitted to remain if they came forward to regularize their status.

55. These persons faced another complication. In leaving Mexico, they had incurred the ban and were thus subject to shunning until such time as they obtained reinstatement in the church.

Chapter 7

Land Hunger, Expansion, and Other Developments

During the time that the fortunes of the colonies appeared to be marching from crisis to crisis, and their continued existence remained a matter of conjecture, the majority of the colonists, were, of course, occupied from day to day with the business of making a living. Despite the numerical attrition caused by numerous departures during the better part of the first two decades, the population of the colonies had, in fact, been holding its own almost from the beginning. An early expansion of the area they occupied, in view of the Mennonites' firmly rooted agrarian tradition, was therefore inevitable.

The Altkolonier Manitoba and Swift Current colonies, having made allowance for future expansion in their initial acquisitions, did not need to seek an enlargement of their holdings for many years. Indeed, as has been shown, they had for some time an embarrassing excess of land. However, the Sommerfelder at Santa Clara and Halbstadt and the Altkolonier of the Hague colony at Nuevo Ideal had provided more or less only for their immediate requirements at the time of settlement. Thus, over the years these groups have made several acquisitions of land.

Santa Clara's first new acquisition of land represented no expansion of its area. In 1928 or 1929, 3,000 acres of stony land without water at the eastern edge of the colony were traded back to the Russek interests for an equal acreage—less stony and with a spring—that now forms part of the lands of the villages of Weidenfeld and Schoenthal. With the acquisition of this land, the small village of Waldeck, situated approximately one-half mile east of the south end of the present site of Weidenfeld, gradually broke up. Most of the people moved to Weidenfeld to be nearer the newly acquired source of water.[1] Over the years the relinquished land, and more besides, along the eastern margin of the colony was purchased privately, on a piecemeal basis, from the Russeks.

During the 1940's a few Sommerfelder began gradually to acquire land some fifteen miles to the southwest of Santa Clara, and eventually a small dispersed village, Campo 51T, Edenthal, took form there. In 1956, the 4,090 hectares (10,200 acres) for Campos 75 and 76 were added. Most of a four-kilometer-square block southwest of Weidenfeld, locally known as the Redekop ranch, has been privately acquired by Santa Clara farmers over the years. The land was made over to Altkolonier depositors by the Russek interests in 1923, following the bank failure. Because of its remoteness, however, the owners did not go to reside there. In time Santa Clara farmers bought parcels of it and either farmed them from their home villages or went to live there. Eventually a Russländer Mennonite businessman of Cd. Cuauhtémoc acquired the unsold portions.[2] Following its original transfer to the Altkolonier, however, the land had never been surveyed. The Sommerfelder who then purchased parcels of it had no deeds and could not substantiate ownership. Fearful of becoming involved in a situation not unlike that on the Swift Current colony following the foreclosures there, they abandoned their investments and withdrew. Since that time most of the property has once more passed into Sommerfelder and Altkolonier hands. By 1930 the Sommerfelder at Halbstadt, Campo 55, were beginning to acquire land on the present site of Bergthal and Springfeld, Campos 40 and 41, by private purchase from María Zuloaga de Muñoz. Today these two villages extend over 2,718 hectares (6,750 acres).

The first expansion beyond the boundaries of the Altkolonier mother colonies in Chihuahua came about not as a result of land

1. The site of Waldeck is still recognizable from its graveyard and the remnants of a small orchard.

2. Jacob Loewen, Campo 76, Santa Clara colony, personal communication.

shortage but in the wake of the foreclosures on the Swift Current colony between 1932 and 1936. Some of the dispossessed families, by settling on as-yet-unoccupied lands of the Manitoba colony, aided internal expansion there. Others took up 2,500 hectares (6,250 acres) at Saucito (Altenau), Campo 35, which was part of the Rancho San Carlos owned by María Zuloaga de Muñoz; this land was privately acquired in 1933 by a consortium of Altkolonier investors.[3] Purchases outside the Manitoba colony continued to be a source of embarrassment to it for some years until its own original territory was fully occupied. Whereas it was committed to the retirement of its land debt at the rate of $9 per acre, nearby land could be had from Mexican owners at prices which during the 1930's went as low as 2.40 pesos ($1 U.S.) per acre.[4] During the time of severest economic stress, the Manitoba colony reduced the price of its still-vacant land to 14 pesos (approximately $4.40 U.S.) per acre. It was also made possible for buyers to retire mortgages entirely through crop-share payments. Despite these inducements, some 34,000 acres of the Manitoba colony still remained unsold at the end of 1937.[5] So keenly was this burden of excess land felt that, at the time, it could have been purchased from the Gemeinde for the outstanding taxes.[6]

By 1938, however, the more desirable portions of the Manitoba colony, from the point of view of accessible water supplies, were filled up and, indeed, were experiencing considerable population pressure.[7] With accumulated experience in the drilling of deep wells, it became possible to obtain sufficient water for household and farmyard use in the area south of the right-of-way of the North-

3. They were Johann J. Giesbrecht, Jacob S. Thiessen, and Herman Bueckert.

4. The price of 2.40 pesos per acre was paid for some of the Russek land purchased privately by Santa Clara colonists. Some of the foreclosed land on the Swift Current colony is said to have been bought back from the Zuloagas for as little as 2 pesos (about $.60 U.S. at the then prevailing rate of exchange) per acre.

5. David Harder, "Chronik".

6. Such price reductions, of course, merely meant that the difference between the price received and that contracted to the Zuloagas had to be met through general levies on the entire colony.

7. The population of the Manitoba colony at the end of 1937 was 5,437 according to Gemeinde records. This was approximately equal to the number which, all told, emigrated from Manitoba.

western Railway. In 1938 Kronsgart, Campo 27, was laid out. By the spring of 1939, however, there were again more than 150 families without land.[8] The following year (1940) Campos 26 and 28, Silberfeld and Weidenfeld, were surveyed.[9] Other previously vacant or sparsely settled portions of the colony, along its western and eastern margins, also filled up. Whereas a few years before land had been in surplus to the point of constituting a burden, the situation was suddenly reversed. Since that time the Altkolonier colonies in Chihuahua have been continually in the market for additional suitable land.

Additional land has been acquired by the Altkolonier, as well as by the Sommerfelder, in two ways. One—historically the first—has been for private investors to acquire tracts of land which they either farmed themselves or made available for rental or purchase by their fellow colonists. Another has been for the mother colonies themselves to delegate agents for purposes of negotiating the purchase of large tracts for the establishment of daughter colonies. In either case such lands are brought under colony administration. Chronologically, Altkolonier expansion beyond the boundaries of the original colonies began in 1933 with the private purchase of Altenau, Campo 35. Thereafter, they progressively advanced northward until their boundaries abutted on those of the Santa Clara colony.

The Altkolonier of the Hague colony in Durango, who originally bought only some 3,000 acres, were more or less forced to extend their holdings at an early date. The first purchase was a low-lying tract, subject to flooding during the summer rainy season and so saline as to be unsuited for tillage. Land for the accommodation of five villages—Gruenfeld, Blumenort, Neuanlage, Reinland, and Hochfeld—was added at an early date (about 1928–1930). Despite the continuing arrival of new colonists from Canada into the 1930's, further major new acquisitions of land were not required

8. Report by A. W. Peters, April 23, 1939, carried in the *Steinbach Post* of May 10, 1939.

9. The new villages were laid out on the customary basis of approximately 160 acres to a full Wirtschaft, of which about one-quarter was in the communal pasture.

for some years. A substantial number of new immigrants found employment on the large irrigated farm and cattle-raising enterprise of Dr. Harry Grey, a Durango physician who also served as British Consul for the state, and who reputedly hailed from Saskatoon, Saskatchewan. Others, usually in groups, were able to rent from large landholders.[10]

The history of land acquisitions is less well documented for the Hague colony than is the case in Chihuahua, but it appears that the next substantial purchase of land took place late in 1934, when 6,500 acres on which the village of Schoenthal is now located were acquired from Dr. Grey. The price was 11,000 pesos ($3,050 U.S.), including stock and equipment.[11]

Beginning in 1932 and continuing into the 1940's, considerable areal expansion was accomplished through rentals and rental-purchases of tracts of land contiguous with, or very close to, the colony proper. Schoenfeld and Hochstaedt were begun in this way, at a rental of 15 percent of the crop for five years, after which they had a contract option to purchase. Land for the future village of Hamburg was bought in 1938 from Dr. Grey for one ton of corn per acre, to be paid on the basis of one-half of the crop.[12] Since that time a number of larger and smaller purchases have established the colony's present boundaries. Since one of the prime requisites set by the Altkolonier is that new land acquisitions must be contiguous, or very nearly so, with the existing colony, very little suitable land has become available to the Hague colony in the last twenty years. This is particularly so because to the east the colony already extends well into low, saline ground on the approaches to the laguna. To the south all land is in the hands of ejidos. The only possible

10. Confiscations of land from large holdings, for award to agraristas, did not commence on a large scale until the mid-1930's.

11. The sale may be partly accounted for by Dr. Grey's fear of expropriation in favor of the agraristas. Land prices such as those paid to Dr. Grey served as a stimulus to numerous Altkolonier in Chihuahua to abandon insecure tenure (as in the Swift Current colony) or heavy colony debt (as in the Manitoba colony) and to make a fresh beginning in Durango.

12. Jakob Bartsch, Gruenthal, Campo 9, Hague colony, personal communication.

direction of expansion locally therefore has been to the north and west, and then only in competition with the claims of ejidatarios.

Since the attempt to alleviate land shortages through the purchase of adjacent or nearby tracts which could be administered from the established colonies showed inadequate results, increasing effort has been devoted to the creation of daughter colonies, often at considerable distances from the parent colony. In all, thirteen colonization attempts at locations remote from the mother colonies have been made over the years, most of them since 1950.[13] Ten of these have been in Mexico, in the states of Coahuila, Chihuahua, Durango, Zacatecas, and Tamaulipas, and three in British Honduras. Some have been under Gemeinde auspices, while others have been private group ventures. Two other colonies, Ojo de la Yegua and Santa Rita, have been established in the Bustillos and Santa Clara valleys.

The Saltillo Venture

The first of the daughter colonies was founded in 1944 at Estación Agua Nueva near Saltillo, in the state of Coahuila, following a four-year search for a suitable location. On March 4, 1944, some twenty Altkolonier families from Chihuahua entrained for Agua Nueva. Initial reports were encouraging: the pasture was superior to that in the Chihuahua colonies, and land seekers who had inspected the region in 1943 had described in glowing terms the results obtainable with corn and alfalfa. However, the colonists' own attempts with these crops, under irrigation, were failures. They reported that whereas sprouting and early growth were satisfactory, the plants shortly died, and irrigating merely caused them

13. This number does not include the small group of Holdemann Mennonites from Oklahoma who settled at Cordovana, Campo 45, at no great distance from the Altkolonier and Sommerfelder in Chihuahua in 1927. In 1945 they moved to Estación Agua Nueva, Coahuila. Some years later those who were left of the group returned to Chihuahua, to the vicinity of La Junta, west of Cd. Cuauhtémoc. The unsuccessful colonization attempts of the Amish and Old Mennonites from the United States, in San Luis Potosí, are also not included in this figure.

to die the more quickly. The cause was laid to one or more of several factors, such as too thin a layer of topsoil, "saltpeter," and "chalk." [14] The colonization effort began shortly to disintegrate, as one member and another, despairing of attaining a viable adjustment to this difficult environment, gave up and returned to Chihuahua. By June of 1944 the Vorsteher of the colony was back in the Manitoba colony, and only a small group, under the leadership of Rev. Franz Loewen, remained, determined that the colony could yet be made to succeed. With the sudden death of Loewen on June 19, however, this determination dissolved in a general breakup of the colony.[15] Fortunately it was later possible to dispose of the Agua Nueva property at a price which very substantially reduced the losses of the colonists.[16]

Ojo de la Yegua

In 1948 Campos 30 to 50 (excluding the Sommerfelder villages of Halbstadt, Bergthal, and Springfeld, Campos 55, 40, and 41, and Cordovana, Campo 45) were incorporated with Campos 59 to 71 on the former Rancho Ojo de la Yegua; together these became the Ojo de la Yegua colony [17]—colloquially referred to as the

14. Their evaluation of the grass cover appears to have been a subjective one which did not take into account the potential sustained carrying capacity of the range. The communal pastures of the Mennonite villages were chronically overgrazed. The land at Agua Nueva, on the other hand, had apparently not been in use for some time, and hence the superior grass cover. Their disappointing results with irrigation also appear to reflect a lack of understanding of the environment. Saltillo is on the eastern edge of the northern interior desert of Mexico. Valley soils under arid conditions characteristically have a high salinity content. Careful management is necessary if such soils are to be productive. The Mennonites were almost totally ignorant of irrigation technology. Application of water prior to planting would dilute the salinity of the soil solution and, to a degree, carry salts downward beyond the root zone of young plants. Water at Agua Nueva, however, was not in abundant supply, and conservative applications of water were probably made, with the ultimate result that moisture moving upward through the soil profile by capillary action carried an excess of salts. This would be sufficient to cause physiological stress resulting in the death of the plants.

15. David Harder, "Chronik".

16. Gerhard J. Rempel, Blumenort, Campo 22, Manitoba colony, personal communication.

17. Its official designation is "Colonia Menonita en Riva Palacio," referring to the municipio in which the colony lies.

Nordkolonie—with its own separate church and secular organizations. The fact that the area developed so rapidly as to warrant its becoming a separate colony only two years after the Rancho Ojo de la Yegua was thrown open to settlement is an indication of the land hunger which, ever since the "old" colonies were fully occupied, has been a chronic problem. There was therefore no relaxation of the search for additional suitable land.

Yermo

In 1949 Gerhard J. Rempel and Jacob Wiebe of the Manitoba colony were delegated to seek a new and substantial land complex for the establishment of another colony. Numerous offers were received from the region of Torreón and Jiménez, in the tri-state area of Chihuahua–Coahuila–Durango, but the great depth to reliable ground-water supplies and the high down payments asked made them unattractive to the Altkolonier.

Then Wiebe was informed of the availability of some 41,000 acres (16,500 hectares) fronting on the Mexican National Railway and Highway 45 between Yermo and Ceballos in the state of Durango, property of the brothers Celso and Rómulo Garza Gonzales of Torreón, Coahuila. The Garza Gonzales brothers offered the land to the Mennonites for an initial five-year term at a rental equal only to the taxes. A contract was entered into on this basis, and the Mennonites were also accorded first refusal to purchase at the end of the contract period. The specified purchase price, reckoned in U.S. dollars, was 25 pesos per hectare of *lomas* or low hill lands not suited to irrigation, and 50 pesos per hectare for irrigable flat lands. All improvements made during the term of the agreement, except movable structures, were to devolve upon the owners in the event that no purchase ensued.

The Yermo colony lies in the Bolsón de Mapimí, a large *cuenca cerrada* (basin of enclosed drainage) in the Chihuahua–Durango–Coahuila tri-state area, near the western edge of the northern interior desert. Rainfall since 1950 has been from four to eight inches annually, with a late-summer maximum, usually in September.

Very rarely rain or snow may fall in winter. The soils are water-laid grey mineral desert soils of a relatively high clay content, extremely powdery when dry, yet slightly pebbly and of moderate porosity and, consequently, of fairly high hydraulic conductivity and absorptive capacity. In the western portion of the colony's lands there is some caliche (soil rich in calcium carbonate and gypsum), occasionally occurring at the surface. The soils support a natural vegetation including sagebrush, *candelilla (Euphorbia antisyphilitica)*, mesquite, and *savaneta (Muhlenbergia* sp.).[18]

Work on the Yermo colony was begun in 1949. The easternmost portion was surveyed into holdings of 50 hectares (125 acres) each, and some of the necessary buildings constructed. In 1950 about twenty-five families came out from Chihuahua. There was mixed success with the first wells. Some found no water, while others obtained a yield sufficient for a six-inch pump at depths of 250 to 300 feet. Cotton, which is the dominant crop of the region but with which the Mennonites had had no experience whatsoever, was the first crop planted. There were some excellent results with it in the first few years, but then insect pests became a serious problem. By 1953 the originally good wells began to fail. Wells of greater depth were drilled, some to 800 feet or more, again with mixed success. A few gave a good yield of water initially, at pumping depths of 60 to 100 feet. However, wells such as these are extremely costly, running to 140,000 pesos ($11,200 U.S.) and more. The frequent failures to obtain water sapped the economic strength of the colonists, and one by one they began to leave. The first village, Reinland, was abandoned except for one farm as the wells failed,[19] and a random settlement pattern, oriented to the producing wells, evolved.

By the time the original rental contract expired, the group at

18. The writer is indebted to Dr. Robert Frenkel of the University of California, Berkeley, and to Dr. Beecher Crampton of the University of California, Davis, for their assistance in identifying the *Muhlenbergia*.

19. The one remaining farmer on the Reinland site is irrigating only some ten hectares, planted mostly in melons which have a short irrigation season and for which the one remaining well in that part of the colony has, until now, had sufficient water.

Yermo had shrunk to about twenty families. The original contract had included a clause providing for possible renewal of the agreement. All structures and wells, however, were to become the property of the owners, and they were to receive a stated percentage of all future income of all kinds. In view of the very substantial investment already at stake, it was thought best to buy the land if the necessary funds could be raised. Up to this point the colonization attempt at Yermo, although enjoying the moral support of the parent Altkolonier Gemeinde in Chihuahua, was not under its financial auspices. However, it was hoped that the parent colony in Chihuahua would adopt the project.

Some time before the initial rental agreement expired, John Martin, one of the Amishmen who had spent some time in Chihuahua prior to the abortive colonization ventures in San Luis Potosí, visited the Chihuahua colonies. He became interested in the Yermo venture and visited the colony. While there, he offered to aid in the raising of funds for the purchase and to use his good offices with well-to-do Amishmen of his acquaintance in the United States, who might lend the Yermo colonists the money. Eventually, thirty-odd of his brethren in Iowa and Ohio offered to lend sums of up to a few thousand dollars each. Since there appeared to be a good chance that the parent Gemeinde in Chihuahua might still adopt the Yermo venture and aid it in retiring its debts, it was decided to go ahead with the purchase and to accept the Amish offer of funds. During the term of the original contract, however, the Mexican currency had been devalued from 6.87 to 12.50 pesos to the U.S. dollar. Since the contract stipulated payment at the exchange rate current at the time of its initiation, this meant that the price of the land in pesos was now practically double that originally asked and agreed upon. Finally, the Mennonites agreed to absorb the devaluations and they borrowed $57,000 (U.S.) from the Amish lenders at 6 percent interest. However, when the parent Gemeinde in Chihuahua failed to adopt the colony as anticipated, it became impossible to retire the debt to the Amish. Furthermore, to minimize the risk of possible foreclosure, it became necessary to first pay off the former owners, to whom was still owed a residual amount of some 185,000 pesos ($14,800 U.S.). An amount in excess of 80,000 pesos ($6,400 U.S.) was paid out privately by Gerhard J. Rempel, Bernhard B. Penner, and Rev. Abraham Dyck of the Manitoba colony to satisfy the former owners. Since the Yermo colonists continued to be unable to pay off their debt to the Amish, the latter came voluntarily to Chihuahua to renegotiate the entire matter. They initially offered to drop $11,000 (U.S.) of the original debt and all of the interest. In 1964, Rempel, Penner, and Dyck privately paid out $6,500 (U.S.) to the Amish lenders, leaving a residual indebtedness of $27,800 (U.S.). At that time, only thirteen families remained at Yermo, and of those, only five had access to sufficient water for any irrigation of field crops. Only a little over 250 acres were ever placed under irrigation, and by 1965 this had shrunk to 150 acres. The other families make their living primarily by hiring out, often with power equipment, to Mexican irrigation farmers in the Yermo–Ceballos area. It is hoped by some that the entire Yermo land complex may at some future date be given in trade on some other land deal.[20]

Considerable bitterness has been engendered, particularly among the men initially charged by the Gemeinde to seek new lands, by the refusal of the parent colony in Chihuahua to take responsibility for the Yermo debt. As a result, the Yermo colonists have been left to discharge it out of their private means.[21]

Conejos

In 1950, the Hague colony also began to cast about for land in the region between Torreón and Jiménez. For a while the purchase of a tract of land at Zavalza, Durango, some twenty-five miles north of Yermo, was contemplated, but nothing came of it. The following year, however, a colony was founded at Conejos,

20. Details obtained from Gerhard J. Rempel, Blumenort, Campo 22, and Isaak I. Dyck, Osterwick, Campo 18, Manitoba colony, and from Johann Bartsch, Jakob Enns, Peter Penner, and David Wall of the Yermo colony, personal communication.

21. A contributing factor which has prompted Dyck, Penner, and Rempel to pay off much of the Yermo debt privately is the fact that they have children living there who would be dispossessed if the colony were to dissolve.

about fifteen miles south of Yermo, under conditions of soils and climate more or less identical to those prevailing at Yermo. Despite glowing reports of the agricultural possibilities of the land when placed under irrigation, and although the venture had the approval of the parent colony, people were reluctant to move to irrigation land,[22] and only some eleven families ever participated in the venture.

The Conejos property was bought by a land-seeking party from the Hague colony without any knowledge of the local ground-water situation; the price was approximately 25 pesos ($3.65 U.S.) per hectare ($1.45 per acre). A substantial amount of land was immediately cleared of brush, leveled and dammed in preparation for cropping. Several wells were drilled simultaneously. Some of the colonists had brought considerable capital into the venture, and preparations for irrigation were made on the basis of the anticipated use of eight- and ten-inch pumps. However, not one good well resulted, the best producing a flow equal to the capacity of a two- or three-inch pump.

By the end of 1952 the colony at Conejos had been abandoned. The family which owned the only producing well was prepared to stay, but when all the rest left they too departed. No crops were ever raised. Four families—all interrelated—joined the colony at nearby Yermo. The rest returned to the Hague colony. As in the case of Yermo, the parent colony declined to assume financial responsibility for the Conejos venture, and private individuals ultimately had to absorb a substantial part of the debts incurred.[23]

In the cases of both Conejos and Yermo, an excess of individualism among the colonists is held, even by themselves, to be at the root of a large part of the economic reverses that ensued. All wells were drilled on individual, not group, initiative. In addition, wells were spaced much too closely together to permit a realistic assessment of the water-yield potential of the underlying aquifer. Nor were the people of the Department of Water Resources consulted.

22. Report by Johann Bartsch, Conejos, Durango, September 2, 1951, carried in the *Steinbach Post* of October 10, 1951.
23. Johann Bartsch, Yermo colony, Ceballos, Durango, personal communication.

The Mennonites thought of themselves as better farmers than their ejidatario and colono counterparts in the valleys of Bustillos and Guatimapé, and this sentiment carried over into the desert Bolsón de Mapimí. As a result, they were loath to seek the advice of their Mexican neighbors, and the learning of the technologically exacting techniques of cotton culture and irrigation farming was therefore protracted much beyond what it need have been.

Another Durango Venture

Another small colonization venture, involving only eight families, was undertaken from the Hague colony in 1952, at a location about midway between Canatlán and Cd. Durango. It, too, shortly disbanded. The area is one of very sandy soils. Moreover, 1952 and 1953 were drouth years, and the crops on these soils were a total failure. Even in the event that more favorable conditions of precipitation might prevail in the future, it was feared the light soils would not stand up to sustained agricultural use. Furthermore, the area available to the Mennonites was small and was surrounded by and dotted with Mexican settlement. It would therefore have been impossible to establish the type of occupancy that is regarded as imperative to permanent colonization. Another important psychological and physical factor militating against a permanent settlement stemmed from the natural environment. The sandy soils were readily whipped into intense local dust storms by the temperature-induced high winds which characterize the daylight hours in this region during most of the year. To the otherwise bleak prospects of the place there was thus added frequent and intense discomfort. In 1954 the last of the eight families returned to the Hague colony. Because of the drouth of several years' duration in the region, and the resulting near-failures of crops, land prices in the parent colony had fallen temporarily to about 200 pesos ($16 U.S.) per acre. This served as an added attraction to those who had not yet committed everything to the doomed venture to return to the Hague colony.

The lack of success of these attempts by the Mennonites to establish daughter colonies remote from the original colonies may be attributed to several factors. Not the least of these was the fact that the areas selected reflected the nature of the type of land most readily available to them; such land was either of the most marginal kind or of unproven potential, and its colonization thus represented a terrific gamble which would at best require a great deal of capital. The physical environment was in most cases radically different from that to which the Mennonites had been accustomed, and their adaptation to it was hindered by their unwillingness, and failure, to seek competent advice. A sense of being isolated in strange surroundings and the refusal of the parent colonies to provide financial assistance were the final elements of discouragement for many.[24]

The "Land Bank"

The colonization efforts represented by the ill-fated settlements near Saltillo, Cd. Durango, and Conejos, and by the slowly wasting cluster of colonists at Yermo, served essentially no useful function in alleviating the Altkolonier's pervasive and intensifying problem of land hunger. Efforts to expand the land base have therefore continued. In 1956 an attempt to systematize the process of land acquisition was instituted through the establishment of a sinking fund which was to be accumulated out of voluntary contributions by all Altkolonier colonists in Chihuahua of 1 percent of their income. These contributions, it was reasoned, would quickly grow into a respectable sum which would enable

24. Underlying the latter factor was a substantial element of disapproval brought to bear upon the colonists by the church authorities of the parent colonies. In striving for economic viability under conditions very different from those prevailing in their former home areas, and partly because supervision from a distance was less effective, the colonists ultimately resorted to innovations not countenanced by the parent Gemeinde and, therefore, incurred the ban. This same situation prevails today in Yermo, where colonists are unwilling to relinquish technological innovations in their equipment, holding them to be essential to their economic survival. The parent Gemeinde thereupon simply does not provide its religious offices for the colonists. (About 1962 the Kleine Gemeinde of the Quellenkolonie in Chihuahua began sending a circuit preacher to Yermo at intervals of a few weeks, and it has also been providing a school teacher.)

the colonists to take immediate advantage of any suitable future land offers that might come their way. Poor or landless persons might be permitted to purchase land on credit and repay the fund as they were able, so that eventually it should become self-sustaining. The plan, however, never attained more than 50 percent participation from the colonists. In view of this grudging cooperation, the voluntary levy was reduced to one-half of 1 percent in 1958, in the hope that full participation—and, consequently, the same level of revenues as had accrued when the levy was 1 percent— might thus be gained.[25] Results, however, were disappointing.

When, subsequently, several attractive land offers came to hand more or less simultaneously, pressure groups developed, each insisting that the amount in the sinking fund be diverted to the purchase in which it was interested, and threatening to withdraw financial support from the fund unless its wishes were met. Nevertheless, by 1962 the fund had participated in three land deals, with a total disbursement of 331,000 pesos ($26,480 U.S.). Then, because of dissatisfaction and diminishing participation and because of the internal political implications involved, the fund was dissolved.[26]

Buenos Aires

Early in 1958 the Altkolonier in Chihuahua were approached with an offer of a property known as Buenos Aires, which consisted of 2,792 hectares (6,935 acres) of land in the Llanos de Carretas, just north of the Río de Janos. This property is situated some forty miles northwest of Nuevo Casas Grandes in the municipio of Janos. Included were some wells and 743 hectares of cultivated land leveled and ditched for irrigation. The balance was rangeland. The price was 550 pesos ($44 U.S.) per hectare ($17.60 per acre) for the irrigated portion and 420 pesos ($33.60) per hectare ($13.50 per acre) for the rest.

25. General colony bulletins prepared jointly by Elder Isaak M. Dyck, Vorsteher Gerhard J. Rempel, and Vice-Vorsteher Johann Fehr, Manitoba colony, August 25, 1955, and July 1, 1958.

26. Heinrich J. Martens, Neuenburg, Campo 21, Manitoba colony, personal communication.

A decision to buy the property was quickly reached. The existing wells appeared to have ample water for eight- and ten-inch pumps at a depth of less than 200 feet.[27] The soils were of a quality at least comparable to those of the colonies tribuary to Cd. Cuauhtémoc, and furthermore were largely free of stones.

The purchase itself proved to be much beset with legal complications. The property was heavily mortgaged and was, in fact, in the process of being foreclosed by the creditors. The owner, trying to salvage something, had sent a representative to the Altkolonier in the hope of making a private transaction and paying off the bank. All legal papers pertaining to the property were, however, already in the bank's possession, and ultimately the transaction had to be completed with it as vendor. The property changed hands during the first half of April 1958.

When the Mennonites proceeded to survey the property in preparation for settlement, it was found that the deed included almost seventy-five acres (thirty hectares) more than were actually enclosed by the property's fence. The vendors authorized them to draw the boundary so that the area stated in the deed was enclosed. This, however, led to conflict with another title, 240 years old, pertaining to the property immediately to the east of Buenos Aires. The boundary was resurveyed by an engineer and the Mennonites were found to be correct. Nevertheless, ultimately the old boundary was allowed to stand. The Altkolonier were accorded a reduction prorated on the price of the entire property, but were required to absorb the cost of the official survey, amounting to 8,000 pesos ($640 U.S.).[28] Because the western and eastern boundaries were no longer parallel, considerable extra work and inconvenience resulted in subdividing the property into holdings of uniform size.

27. The wells on the property at the time of purchase, together with related structures and equipment and some buildings, were sold within the colony on January 1, 1963. The amount realized made possible a rebate of 100 pesos per hectare to the colonists, which was credited to the balance of their land debt.

28. Heinrich J. Martens, Neuenburg, Campo 21, Manitoba colony, personal communication. Mr. Martens has been for many years the unofficial land surveyor for all of the Altkolonier colonies in Chihuahua. The amount of land in question was 29.8274 hectares.

Although the Llanos de Carretas are only some 200 miles north-west of the Valle de Bustillos, the natural conditions prevailing there, owing mainly to lower elevation and less rainfall, are more comparable to those in the Bolsón de Mapimí. Total annual precipitation is on the order of ten inches, with pronounced maximums in July and September and a lesser winter maximum in December–January. The elevation at Buenos Aires is roughly 1,500 meters (about 4,900 feet) above sea level, some 600 meters (2,000 feet) less than the elevation of the colonies tributary to Cd. Cuauhtémoc. Because the region is open to the north, toward the continental interior, frequent outbreaks of polar air are experienced during the winter. Summers are long and hot, with a frost-free period well in excess of 200 days.[29] Potential annual evapotranspiration is approximately ten times the annual rainfall, being in excess of 2,500 millimeters or 100 inches.[30]

Climatically, the Llanos de Carretas are on the desert fringe. The soils are characteristically chestnut brown to grey, varying in texture from fine adobe clays to gravelly loams. On Buenos Aires the dominant portion, which is somewhat lower-lying and was already under cultivation when the Altkolonier made the purchase, has a considerable proportion of dark-brown to black soils strongly resembling chernozems. These soils supported a natural vegetation of mesquite (*Prosopis juliflora*), acacias, screw bean (*Prosopis pubescens*), cassias (a legume), mimosa (a legume), chamisa (*Atriplex canescens*), and bunch grass (*Sporobulus*). Under a grazing economy, their sustained capacity was approximately one animal to thirteen hectares (thirty-two acres).

The Buenos Aires property was subdivided to accommodate four villages, Reinfeld, Neustaedt, Eigenhof, and Neuendorf. Initially the Mennonites continued the land-use practices of the former owners, concentrating on cattle but also producing corn and milo maize under irrigation to supplement the natural pasture.

29. Mean temperatures for the warmest months are, approximately: April, 67° F; May, 69° F; June, 77.5° F; July, 76° F; August, 78° F; September, 71.5° F; and October, 64° F. See *Boletín Meteorológico*, p. 16 (the data are based on values for Nuevo Casas Grandes).

30. *Ibid.*

Gradually, however, interest developed in the growing of cotton, substantial amounts of which are raised by small holders—ejidatarios and colonos—in the region. By 1965 better than half the cultivated acreage was being planted in cotton, with much of the balance devoted to milo maize. Although as a result some individuals have reduced the livestock sector of their farming operations, there has been no general decline in the number of animals owing to the increased emphasis on cotton. This is partly a reflection of progressive increases in the area under irrigation as new wells are drilled, and partly a deliberate hedge against natural calamity, to which an undiversified economy is extremely vulnerable. One drawback to the expansion of irrigation on Buenos Aires, however, is the fact that the depth to which wells must be drilled if they are to have adequate potential for irrigation increases sharply to northward, rising to 700 feet at Neuendorf, Campo 4. Since the costs both of the well and of raising the water rise sharply with increasing depth, the economic viability of irrigation farming under such conditions is seriously impaired.

British Honduras

In 1958, the year that the Altkolonier acquired Buenos Aires, another avenue of areal expansion opened up to the Mennonites in Mexico. Sometime in the spring of 1955, Peter H. W. Wiebe, an Altkolonier, had been in conversation with the U.S. vice-consul in Ciudad Juárez while awaiting clearance to enter the United States. During the course of their chat, the matter of land shortage in the Mennonites' Chihuahua colonies was mentioned. The vice-consul, who had connections in British Honduras, suggested that the Mennonites investigate settlement opportunities in that country, as there was much land to be had. Back in Chihuahua, Wiebe's account aroused sufficient interest to ultimately prompt the colony leaders to approach the government of British Honduras with a proposal to settle there, subject, of course, to guarantees of a Privilegium patterned after that granted by Alvaro Obregón in 1921 and embodying the same elements with respect to language, schools, and military service. This British Honduras—at that time still a Crown Colony—granted. The Gemeinde consequently supported the venture. The delegates sent were enthusiastic about the prospects of the region,[31] and land was readily available. By early spring of 1958, a migration was under way, by rail and truck. Ultimately over 130,000 acres of land were acquired in British Honduras by the Altkolonier, at Shipyard, Blue Creek, and Richmond Hill. Over 200 families have gone there from Mexico in a continuing trickle of migration. By the end of 1966, the Altkolonier in British Honduras numbered over 2,700.[32]

The Kleine Gemeinde at Los Jagueyes also became quickly involved in the migration. That colony had recently undergone an internal split resulting out of differences of attitude with respect to the conducting of schools, liberalism in secular matters, and involvement in mission work. This created the climate for emigration. When glowing descriptions of British Honduras reached Los Jagueyes, there was immediate interest, which was heightened by that country's British administration. Between March of 1958 and July 1962, 66 families, consisting of 402 persons, left the Quellenkolonie in 30 groups for British Honduras, where they established a colony at Spanish Lookout. A few families have followed since then. Although there has been a trickle of returnees from among both the Altkolonier and Kleine Gemeinde, the majority of those who migrated to British Honduras have remained there.[33] The details of this venture are presented in the Appendix.

Capulín

In 1962 the Altkolonier received another offer of land in northwestern Chihuahua; this time it was a property known as Capulín, comprising 5,280 hectares (13,000 acres). It lies thirty-two

31. The delegates were greatly impressed with the lush vegetation, which contrasted sharply with the normally sere brown landscape of Chihuahua, and regarded it as evidence of high soil fertility.

32. Information concerning British Honduras was supplied by Elder Peter B. Loewen, Los Jagueyes; Deacon Diedrich Friesen, Steinreich, Campo 38, and Johann J. Giesbrecht, Altenau, Campo 35, Ojo de la Yegua; and Johann Reimer, Campo 6A, Rosenthal, Manitoba colony.

33. Elder Peter B. Loewen, Los Jagueyes, personal communication.

kilometers (twenty miles) due east of the southeast corner of Buenos Aires, astride the Río Casas Grandes, in the municipio of Nuevo Casas Grandes. The seller was an American resident in Mexico who was concerned about agrarista agitation for expropriation of his land and who preferred to sell before the matter became earnest. The price was 450 pesos ($36 U.S.) per hectare ($14.40 per acre) for 4,667 hectares (11,670 acres), with another 613 hectares (1,530 acres) of hilly rangeland in the extreme western portion being included in the deal free of charge by the vendor, except for the cost of transferring title.

Since the elevation of Capulín is very nearly the same as that of Buenos Aires (approximately 1,500 meters or 4,900 feet), essentially the same climatic conditions prevail. The soils, however, are of a slightly different character. West of the Río Casas Grandes the ground is generally saline. East of the river fine-textured grey to red calcium-rich soils—sierozems—of high clay content prevail. The present natural vegetation is similar to that on Buenos Aires, but there is a higher incidence of mesquite, and, in the western portion, cacti are numerous.[34] The broad *galeria* of the Río Casas Grandes is dominated by magnificent poplars.

Six villages—Neuenburg, Blumenheim, Rosengart, Rosenthal, Blumenhof, and Blumenthal—were laid out on Capulín. The lots were so oriented as to take advantage of the natural slope of the land for future irrigation. Capulín, however, is much less well endowed with water than Buenos Aires. Although water from a two-inch pump can be obtained anywhere east of the river at depths of from twenty to forty feet, this is insufficient for irrigating large acreages. Furthermore, the dominant avenue of recharge of this shallow aquifer is, to all appearances, from the bed of the Río Casas Grandes. Deep wells have not encountered any other promising water-bearing strata to 400 feet. Given adequate water, the nonsaline soils on Capulín are very productive.[35] Emphasis has been on

34. Since both Buenos Aires and Capulín have had a long history of use as cattle ranges, no doubt significant changes in the natural vegetation have occurred.

35. A high level of soil fertility would have been expectable on Capulín, since there is a high natural incidence of mesquite, which is leguminous and has the faculty of fixing atmospheric nitrogen in the soil. Mimosas, which also occur naturally, have the same property.

the production of fodder crops from the very limited areas which it is possible to irrigate under present conditions of water availability. However, cotton, which is attractive as a cash crop, is making inroads on this adjustment to land-use possibilities, and is also spurring a level of irrigation development which the presently accessible shallow aquifer cannot possibly sustain.

La Batea

The Altkolonier in Durango have also had substantial success in recent years in acquiring land for the creation of daughter colonies. In 1961 a group of seventy-five Altkolonier from the Hague colony, together with a group of five from the Chihuahua colonies, completed a deal with Angel Mier, owner of the Hacienda La Batea, some ninety kilometers northwest of Fresnillo in the state of Zacatecas. The initial transaction was for 3,000 hectares (7,500 acres) of cultivated land at a price of 900 pesos ($72 U.S.) per hectare ($28 per acre), with no down payment, the principal to be retired in five years at 12 percent interest on the unpaid balance. Once the deal was completed, the Hague colony Gemeinde accorded the venture its approval and moral support, although it took no responsibility for its financial commitments. During 1962 three villages—Grünfeld, Blumenhof, and Blumenheim—were established, each on 1,000 hectares (2,500 acres). Two years later an adjoining 1,500 hectares (3,750 acres) were bought from Mier by nine families from the Hague colony at 1,500 pesos per hectare ($48 per acre), payable in three years at 12 percent. Here the village of Neureinland was laid out. In 1964 Grünfeld, Blumenhof, and Blumenheim jointly purchased an additional 185 hectares of pastureland at an average price of 870 pesos ($69.60 U.S.) per hectare. This brought the colony to its present size of 4,685 hectares (11,700 acres). The majority of farms in Grünfeld, Blumenhof, and Blumenheim are 50 hectares (125 acres) in extent. In Neureinland they are substantially larger.

Physiographically the La Batea colony lies within the border zone between the upland and basin province flanking the Sierra Madre Occidental, and the Zacatecan highland, the Meseta Central. The elevation is approximately 2,600 meters (8,600 feet). Except for the elevation, which exceeds that of the parent colonies in Chihuahua and Durango by 300 to 600 meters (1,000–2,000 feet), the physical setting is very comparable. Soils and vegetation, too, are not fundamentally different. The soils of the alluvial fans flanking the surrounding hills of volcanic andesites and tuffs are calcium-rich adobes of varying texture, ranging in color, within the colony, from light brown on the higher elevations to near-black and with a chernozem-like appearance in the area adjacent to the lagunas. The natural vegetation, where remaining, runs to open live-oak forest (*Quercus mexicanus*), with a sprinkling of western yellow pine (*Pinus ponderosa*) and a fairly close sod of grama (*Bouteloua*) and bunch grasses (*Sporobulus*).

The precipitation regime is also very similar to that prevailing in the mother colonies. Annual amounts, however, are somewhat higher and, owing to the greater elevation and consequent lower temperatures, of considerably higher effectiveness. There is appreciably more rainfall in winter, which is of great benefit to the livestock sector of the economy in that it helps maintain the carrying capacity of the pasture lands.

The high elevation thrusts this location, although situated almost directly on the Tropic of Cancer, into a zone critical for agriculture. Owing to the cool summers, corn does poorly, even for fodder. Beans do tolerably well. Cereals—wheat, oats, and barley —appear to be most satisfactorily adapted to the region. Residues from these crops also work in fairly well with the livestock sector of the Mennonites' agriculture. Rust, however, which attacks cereals and beans, poses a serious threat to their successful cultivation.

Fortunately for agriculture the rainy season here begins some two to three weeks earlier than in the mother colonies, thus permitting utilization of a greater segment of the reliably frost-free season, which begins with the onset of the summer rains. In early fall, however, under once more predominantly clear skies, the hazard of radiation- and air-drainage frosts returns, often before crops are properly mature.

With them, to La Batea, the Altkolonier brought their dairying and cheese-making practices. However, this sector is still under-developed. Behind this lack of emphasis on dairying lies the fact that almost all the land purchased for the colony was under cultivation.[36] Its high price and the short repayment terms have forced the colonists to gamble on cash crops,[37] for few have the capital to enlarge their herds and meet their land payments simultaneously. Cattle, however, do well in the temperate climate. Water supply, too, presents no serious problems, as adequate amounts, requiring a haul of no more than a few kilometers for anyone, are available from two lagunas and from springs. Drilled wells with good yields are readily obtained at depths of from 60 to 150 feet. No doubt more will be put down as capital becomes available.

La Honda

Another land purchase which the Altkolonier of the Hague colony have recently completed—and which has, for the time being, largely eliminated landlessness in their Gemeinde—was the acquisition, in 1964, of 17,000 hectares of the Hacienda La Honda, which is situated approximately midway between Río Grande and Juan Aldama in the state of Zacatecas. Negotiations for this purchase were originally begun some ten or twelve years earlier by Rev. Johann P. Wall. The matter fell into abeyance, however, because Wall believed the soils to be of inadequate quality. In 1964, with some 200 landless families in the Hague colony, action became necessary, and since no other large tract of land was available, it was decided to go through with the purchase.

The original intention was to buy the entire La Honda property, comprising 29,000 hectares (72,500 acres). Owing to agrarista

36. Because of the agrarista agitation, Mier was anxious to sell all the land he had under cultivation. Since crop production changes the classification of land and reduces the extent of property which one person may legally hold, his position against expropriation would probably have been weak. He needed the remaining range land, however, for his own livestock operation (he raised Brown Swiss stock as replacements for a large dairy enterprise near Irapuato), and, as the price paid by the Altkolonier for 185 hectares of range (870 pesos per hectare) indicates, he was not eager to sell uncultivated land.

37. In 1965 most of the crop at La Batea was destroyed by early frosts.

inveighings against a sale to the Mennonites, however, 12,000 hectares (30,000 acres) were released from the deal. The price paid to the owners was 200 pesos ($16 U.S.) per hectare ($6.40 per acre). Additional costs, resulting mainly from the purchase of 4,000 hectares for award to agraristas as a goodwill gesture, have raised the price to the colonists by one-third to 267 pesos ($8.50 per acre). The down payment was to be raised by a levy of 10 centavos per liter of milk delivered to cheese factories in the Hague colony, but this was met by much the same response as the 1 percent land-fund levy in Chihuahua from 1956 to 1962.

La Honda is situated near the western edge of the Meseta Central, at an elevation of approximately 2,300 meters (7,600 feet). It lies in a structural basin floored with the alluvial deposits of coalescing fans issuing from hills flanking the colony to the west. Physiographically, therefore, it has much in common with La Batea and with the mother colony in Durango.

The soils are predominantly red adobes, rich in calcium and frequently underlain at no great depth by an indurated stratum of caliche. Indeed, in some parts of the colony the caliche layer is so near the surface as to interfere with and even prevent tillage. The caliche lands, which were a type unfamiliar to the Mennonites and which Wall wished to avoid buying, have already proven, to the surprise of the colonists, to be more productive than those soils in which the caliche horizon is absent. Within the existing climatic framework, oats, beans, and corn appear to be the crops most suited to this locale.

Climatically the region in which La Honda lies bears a close similarity to La Batea. Late spring and early fall frosts are a serious hazard. Indications are, however, that precipitation is substantially less, equal perhaps to the thirteen-inch annual average for the Valle de Bustillos. Owing to lower elevation and, consequently, somewhat higher mean temperatures, precipitation effectiveness is also appreciably below what it is at La Batea. There is evidence to this effect in the natural vegetation, which under range-land conditions was dominated by mesquite, huisache, yellow-blossom sagebrush, and prickly pear cactus, with gramas and bunch grasses. In parts of the western and northern portions of the colony lands, the prickly pear cactus is the dominant vegetation form.

Settlement commenced in 1964. The property was surveyed and platted for eleven villages. Individual farm units range from 20 hectares (50 acres) each to 50 (125 acres) and more. Approximately one-half of the land is potentially arable. Since the entire hacienda headquarters complex of storehouses, stables, and dwellings, together with the workers' village about two kilometers to the northeast, was included in the purchase, there was adequate accommodation for the colonists until such time as they were able to complete essential structures and move onto their own land.

Water supply would not appear to present a serious challenge to the future development of the colony. Three deep wells with wind motors and large stock tanks, as well as a dam which impounds approximately thirty acre-feet of water (an acre-foot is the amount of water which will cover an acre to a depth of one foot), were included with the land. Indications are that wells of adequate yield for domestic and farmyard use may be obtained anywhere on the colony at depths of less than 200 feet.

From the short-term point of view at least, the La Honda colonists appear considerably better off than those at La Batea. The cost of the land was much lower, whereas the land does not appear to be potentially less productive. It should therefore be substantially less difficult to retire the outstanding debt. Furthermore, the mother colony has taken financial responsibility. This has made it possible for 176 landless families to take up minimum holdings of 20 hectares (50 acres) on La Honda with no down payment and with long-term credit from the Gemeinde.

Sommerfelder Expansion

The Sommerfelder in Mexico have made few endeavors to found daughter colonies, having mainly contented themselves with such land acquisitions as it has been possible to make adjacent to their original settlements at Halbstadt, Campo 55, and at Santa

Clara. The few ventures that have been undertaken to establish themselves elsewhere have been on the basis of private initiative.

Motivated by land shortage, a Sommerfelder family by the name of Falk moved to the irrigation district of Villa Aldama, northwest of Cd. Chihuahua, in 1946 or 1947. There they rented land and began to grow cereals and truck crops. They expected eventually to buy a farm of their own there and hoped that others would join them so that a Mennonite community would develop. This did not happen, however, and, failing to realize the economic progress they had hoped for, the Falks left the area.[38]

Tamaulipas

The only other Sommerfelder attempt at settlement away from their home area in Chihuahua has been in the state of Tamaulipas, in the vicinity of Gonzales and Estación Manuel, on the gulf coastal plain midway between Tampico and Cd. Mante.

In 1951 a few Sommerfelder came from Chihuahua to the Gonzales area in response to an offer of land some twenty kilometers west of the present settlement. They made a deposit of $1,000 (U.S.) on a tract which was to their liking, only to discover later that the person with whom they had made the transaction was not the owner and had, of course, vanished.

Two years later a group of seven Sommerfelder families from Chihuahua came to the area and rented land in the vicinity of the present settlement, at San José de las Norias. The minister who had come with them left after only a few days, and three families followed him back to Chihuahua. The following year, however, four more Sommerfelder families from Chihuahua came to the area, with the intention of remaining if prospects warranted it. They were impressed with the economic progress made by the group which had come there in 1953. Three of them remained and rented partially wild land at Chicolar, fifteen kilometers southeast of San

38. From a report by Mrs. Elizabeth P. Falk carried in the *Steinbach Post* of April 2, 1947; and Jakob Loewen, Campo 76, Santa Clara colony, personal communication.

José de las Norias, which they placed under cultivation, growing corn, beans, and small acreages of truck crops.

In 1956 ten more Sommerfelder families came to Chicolar from Chihuahua. The settlement was shortly joined by three men, brothers, from the Altkolonier Hague colony.[39] Then, the following year, twelve Altkolonier families from Durango came to the area. They had been on their way to take up residence in Spanish Honduras. However, when informed by Honduran representatives in Mexico City that, although they would be admitted to the country, no Privilegium would be forthcoming, they terminated that venture. Knowing of the three men from their colony already at Chicolar, they came there to investigate settlement possibilities.[40] The following year one group of four families bought approximately 160 hectares some eight kilometers northeast of the present site of the colony and founded a village, Blumenfeld. They appointed one of their number to handle the land transactions. This person, however, apparently did not meet his obligations, and in 1960 the land was repossessed. He left for Canada. The rest of this group, except for one family, returned to the Hague colony. Another group, consisting of five families, purchased 300 hectares

39. The Penner brothers from the Hague colony had been on their way to Spanish Honduras as forerunners of a larger group which had notions of emigrating to that country. When the Honduran Consulate in Mexico City refused them visas, they came to Chicolar.

40. The Hague colony had completed a deal for a substantial tract of land in the Gonzales area of Tamaulipas in 1957, at 300 pesos per hectare. Then it decided to discontinue proceedings. There was considerable trepidation about moving into the tropical gulf coastal region. Whereas numerous people wished to buy land there—on speculation, it is said—only two families expressed a firm intention of going there to live. Furthermore, in view of the growing Sommerfelder settlement there, the Hague colony Gemeinde was fearful that, since the Sommerfelder take a much more permissive approach toward innovation and luxuries than do the Altkolonier, any colony established there would be shortly lost to them. The vendor, for his part, having realized meanwhile that the area was rapidly becoming a major cotton-producing center and that land values were rising, was content to terminate the deal and refund the 132,000 pesos which had been advanced as earnest money and part payment. (Peter S. Peters, Neuenburg, Estación Manuel, Tamaulipas, Franz Penner, Blumenhof, Campo 2, La Batea [one of the three brothers referred to in note 39 above], and Jakob Bartsch, Grünfeld, Hague colony, personal communication.)

(750 acres) on which they founded the village of Neuendorf.[41] They were later joined by the remaining family from the defunct Blumenfeld venture.

In 1957 also, in view of the termination of their rental contract at Chicolar, the Sommerfelder there, together with those at San José de las Norias—nineteen families in all—purchased 685 hectares (1,700 acres) of brush land some three kilometers north of Neuendorf, nearer Gonzales, where in 1958, after camping in temporary shelters at Neuendorf while their land was being surveyed, they founded the village of Hoffnungsfeld. Since that time a further 570 hectares (1,425 acres) have been added to the village, and ten more families from Chihuahua have joined it (April 1965).[42] Interest in the settlement continues to be keen among the Sommerfelder in Chihuahua.[43]

A few Altkolonier families from Chihuahua and Durango have settled at Neuendorf since its founding. Of particular significance has been the effect which an Altkolonier family from Yermo has had on Mennonite agriculture in the area. Peter S. Peters had lived at Yermo since 1950. In 1958 he visited the Neuendorf–Hoffnungsfeld settlement and was an occasional visitor there until he bought 300 hectares of raw land at Neuendorf in 1960.[44] Until Peters' arrival, the Mennonites in the area had continued the agricultural practices brought from Chihuahua and Durango, which were predicated on beans and corn. The only obvious change they had undertaken was to occasionally grow small plots of tomatoes, onions, or peppers for the Tampico market. They grew no cotton, although it was a crop of increasing importance in the area. Peters, however, was familiar with cotton culture,

41. The land, mostly cleared and arable, was bought at 575 pesos per hectare. The buyers were Isaak Martens, Peter Unger, Jakob Giesbrecht, Johann Giesbrecht, and Gerhard Klassen.

42. The initial 685 hectares were bought at 158 pesos per hectare. 250 hectares of raw land purchased in 1964 cost 1,500 pesos per hectare. In 1965, 320 hectares—half raw, half arable—were bought at 2,000 pesos per hectare.

43. Except for two families who have gone to Canada, all the Sommerfelder who settled in the Gonzales area are still there.

44. The price paid was 100,000 pesos ($8,000 U.S.).

having grown it under irrigation at Yermo. He recognized the possibility of cultivating it under natural rainfall conditions in the Tamaulipas settlement. In 1960, before he took up residence at Neuendorf, he persuaded another Mennonite at the then not-yet-defunct settlement at Blumenfeld to try it. Five hectares were planted and successfully harvested. Since that time emphasis in land-use practices among both Altkolonier and Sommerfelder has shifted progressively to cotton.

The region in which the Mennonites in Tamaulipas have settled is, by the Köppen classification, Aw; that is, it is tropical with a relatively dry winter. The precipitation regime is fundamentally the same as that which prevails in the parent colonies in Chihuahua and Durango, differing only in amount and frequency of incidence. The rainy season of high summer, which is preceded by several weeks of high humidity and great heat, usually begins during the second or third week of June. It lasts until October, with two distinct maximums separated by a relatively dry period in August. Annual precipitation approximates forty inches but, since 1958, has been as high as sixty and as low as twenty inches. Occasional outbreaks of continental polar air—*nortes*—during the period from November to March bring a danger of air-drainage frosts to low-lying areas. They are normally followed by light, drizzly rains associated with the meeting of the nortes and warm air from the Gulf of Mexico. Cool, clear periods following such rains, because of high residual atmospheric moisture content, bring little danger of frost.

The surface deposits are markedly different from the leached soils of low fertility normally associated with the tropics. The entire tract now occupied by the Mennonites in the Gonzales–Manuel area is situated on the eastern flank of an extinct volcano, Pico Bernal, from whose weathered ejecta—to all appearances exclusively volcanic ash—the local soils are derived. These are dark, calcium-rich clays, high in humus, varying in color and often black in moister depressions. When fairly dry, the surface- or A-horizon—two to five feet in vertical cross-section—exhibits a columnar

to nutty structure, but it becomes mucky when wet.[45] It is underlain by from six inches to five feet of friable yellow clay subsoil,
which is in turn succeeded by a regolith of compacted clays. In
their physical characteristics and moisture-retention capacity, these
soils bear a strong resemblance to chernozems and black prairie
soils.[46] Their natural fertility is high.

The natural vegetation cover consists of scrub forest—ebony,
mesquite, and occasional chacate (*Krameria grayi*), lianas, and
thorn bush of various kinds. None of these species have any particular commercial value although they may be rendered into char-
coal during clearing operations. Where undisturbed, the scrub
forest shelters a rich wildlife that includes deer, peccaries, tejón
(badger), and wild turkeys and parrots.

Bolivia

The gradual disappearance from the land market of
tracts suitable for the establishment of new daughter colonies has
driven the Mennonites to look beyond Mexico. The first such venture was in British Honduras. In the mid-1960's another minor
exodus, by now involving some 2,000 persons mostly from the Chihuahua Altkolonier colonies, was set in train. This time the destination was the Santa Cruz region of eastern Bolivia. For some
years prior, Mennonites had been entering this region via an overland route from their home colonies in the Paraguayan Chaco. It
was from these Mennonites that word of the opportunities in Bolivia reached Mexico.

45. The soils on the flanks of Pico Bernal appear to include a high bentonite
fraction. They exhibit the high rates of expansion and contraction with changing
moisture conditions which are typical of such soils.

46. Chernozem-like soils, given suitable parent materials, are not rare under conditions of relatively light rainfall in the tropics, since chemical weathering and
elluviation (downward displacement of colloidal materials) are arrested during the
dry season which extends over some seven months of the year. Dr. George Beishlag,
Department of Geography, Towson College, Baltimore, Maryland, has described
(in a personal communication to the author) chernozems in areas of Puerto Rico
which have climatic conditions similar to those of the Gonzales–Manuel region in
Tamaulipas.

Interested parties from Mexico returned satisfied not only that the Bolivian government was willing to extend the Privilegium, but that the Santa Cruz region, which lies at approximately 4,000 feet elevation, offered a subtropical environment with usually reliable rainfall in which they would be able to continue their accustomed farming methods. The migration, which is not under official Gemeinde sponsorship, has consisted mainly of small groups, usually families, who, having sent their heavy freight ahead by ship, have then gone by air to La Paz and thence to Santa Cruz. As in the British Honduras venture, a few families from Canada have also been attracted. Recently (1969) there have been indications of serious intent among the Sommerfelder at Santa Clara to also seek their fortunes on this new frontier, where they would once more be in contact with the Chaco brethren from whom they have been separated since the migration from Canada in the 1920's.

The experience of the Chaco Mennonites, if it diffuses through the new immigrant groups from Mexico and Canada, should serve the venture well. Major obstacles to rapid economic growth, however, will be the limited capacity of eastern Bolivia to absorb their growing agricultural surpluses, the high cost of trans-Andean transport, and the consequent difficulty of maintaining a commercially oriented and mechanized agriculture. The Canadians (among whom a few have already returned) will probably be the most disappointed. Given a stable state of civil order in the country, the Mennonites from Mexico, like those from the Chaco, toughened by nearly half a century of life in environments substantially harsher than this, will probably, by their own standards, make a very good success of the venture indeed.

Their departure from Mexico in such numbers has, to some degree, alleviated the land shortage in the Chihuahua colonies. However, it has once more driven home a major truth which those who contemplate emigration must face. Would-be emigrants need substantial liquid capital to engage in ventures such as a move to Bolivia. Both emigrants and those who would buy up their properties in Mexico must therefore be reasonably well situated financially. So limited is purchasing power that, despite the overriding land hunger, the price of a full *Wirtschaft* of sixty-five hectares fell by as much as one-half in the period 1966 to 1968 in colonies such as Ojo de la Yegua which lost substantial numbers to the Bolivian venture.

Off-Colony Farming

Another avenue of expansion of the land base, in addition to the purchase of large tracts for the formation of new colonies, is the purchase by individuals of isolated smaller blocks of land, ranging to a few hundred hectares, outside the colony boundaries but near enough to permit their operation from the old base of residence. Until now, this has been resorted to only in the Manitoba colony in Chihuahua and only since about 1960. A major attraction of this type of expansion is the price of land, which has been on the order of one-third that of equivalent colony lands. A further attraction is availability. Land shortage has reached such a pitch within the colony, and parcelization and fragmentation have proceeded to such a degree that single, economically viable units are seldom available, even if the price could be met.[47] "Mexican" land, on the other hand, in units small enough to be managed by one or a few families and possibly representing investments by businessmen of Cd. Cuauhtémoc, comes on the market fairly regularly. To the present time, the maximum distance to which such

47. Such purchases are also particularly attractive to individuals who are under excommunication. Since such persons are, under the meaning of Article 4 of the act of incorporation of the holding companies in which title to the Manitoba colony is vested, no longer members of the "company," they may not buy land within the colony. They are not, however, divested of property already owned. The purchase of land outside the colony is thus one of the few avenues of expansion open to them. They almost invariably prefer to continue residing in their village and to commute to their off-colony farm. The fact that until now—to the best of the writer's knowledge—only Manitoba colony residents have bought isolated "Mexican" farms is large explainable by the fact that it alone of the Altkolonier colonies takes a stand on technological innovation which is sufficiently permissive to tolerate, although not officially permit, pneumatic tires on tractors. Forty kilometers with such a tractor represents approximately a two-hour journey which, during busy times, is made only at the beginning and end of the week. The alternative to pneumatic-tired tractors would be the maintaining of two sets of equipment, one for home use, the other for the distant farm, but this is usually not economically feasible.

farms are removed from the colony has been on the order of forty kilometers (twenty-five miles). Normally a local colono or ejidatario is engaged to live on the property and keep an eye on things during the absence of the Mennonite owner.

Another, much more common method of overcoming land shortages within the colonies has been to rent small tracts from ejidatarios and colonos in nearby settlements or, occasionally, larger acreages from absentee landowners. This method avoids the large investment that the outright acquisition of a "Mexican" farm entails. The renting of small ejidatario and colono holdings—as a practice distinct from rental prior to purchase—dates back several decades. In Durango it had its origins about 1935, when Mennonite farmers began breaking new land for their Mexican neighbors with tractor plows in return for the first three years' crop. Mennonite renting quickly came to include cultivated land as well. For many years, into the 1960's, the combined area rented in the vicinity of the Hague colony by Mennonite farmers amounted to as much as half the area of the colony.

In Chihuahua the renting of nearby small holdings from Mexican farmers appears to date from about 1944. There, it came into being as the result of failure, owing to early-season drouth, of the Mexicans' corn and bean crops. The ejidatarios and colonos were not equipped to take advantage of alternative land-use possibilities and under such circumstances left their fields fallow until the ensuing year. This presented the Mennonites, who by the mid-1940's were experiencing considerable land hunger but were also increasingly replacing draft animals with tractors, with an opportunity to rent the land and put it into oats. The practice grew rapidly, soon becoming a straight business proposition unrelated to crop failure. By the late 1950's and early 1960's several thousand hectares were annually being rented from the Mexican settlements adjacent to the colonies. Indeed, for a time, in some villages of the Manitoba colony, it represented as much as half of the total acreage under cultivation.

In the years since 1960 a combination of circumstances has served to greatly reduce the incidence of this type of renting, particularly of ejido lands. Under ejido tenure, ownership remains vested in the state. The farmer is expected to till the land assigned to him himself. If the ejidatario rents out his land for more than two successive years, his rights may be forfeited. Local *caciques* and *jefes vecinales* (influential persons) have been campaigning among their people against the practice of renting ejido land to the Mennonites, threatening to invoke the law against those who persist. To a pronounced degree their campaign has been successful. Moreover, combined with this influence is competition from a growing number of colonos—and, occasionally, an ejidatario—who have improved their economic condition to the point where they, too, have acquired power equipment. Desiring to expand their own farming operations, they are bidding against the Mennonites in the rental market. The net effect has been to sharply reduce the amount, particularly of ejido land, being farmed by them. At the Hague colony it is down to some 500 hectares (1,250 acres). In Chihuahua, particularly in the Manitoba and Swift Current colonies, the practice is still much more prevalent.[48] However, whereas less than a decade ago the common rental was 15 percent of the crop, this has risen until it is no longer unusual for the renter to pay one-half the crop or as much as 200 pesos ($16 U.S.) per hectare (over $6 per acre) cash in advance. These high rentals may be attributed in part to the Mexican farmers' shrewd assessment of Mennonite land hunger and what the market will bear, and in part to the bidding up of rentals by the Mennonites themselves, in competition with each other.

The only other avenue of renting extra-colonial land open to the Mennonites has been the occasional opportunity to take over

48. Manitoba Colony residents in 1965 were renting approximately 8,000 hectares (20,000 acres) from Mexicans. Another 2,000 hectares were similarly under cultivation by Swift Current colonists. A partial explanation of the difference between the situation at Nuevo Ideal and that prevailing around Cd. Cuauhtémoc is that a considerable amount of land at the latter location is owned by colonos, and they do as they see fit with their property. Furthermore, the ejidatarios in the Cd. Cuauhtémoc region have discovered a way of circumventing the regulations against renting by "hiring" a Mennonite to farm their land for an agreed share of the crop. They frequently claim that they would rather rent to Mennonites because they farm with tractors, which unlike draft animals do not consume part of the crop, they are generally scrupulous about paying the agreed rental, and there is no danger that they will invoke the law to dispossess an ejidatario who is renting out his land contrary to regulations.

larger blocks—several hundred hectares and more—from absentee landowners, usually at some considerable distance from the colonies. However, because of the amount of equipment and short-term risk capital involved in this sort of operation, it is not possible for Anwohner and small proprietors to take advantage of such opportunities. Nonetheless, in contrast to the renting of small holdings, the renting of these larger tracts is on the increase; some Altkolonier and Sommerfelder farmers are now operating blocks of up to 600 hectares at distances as great as sixty miles from their villages in the colonies, at Pedernales and up toward La Junta and Guerrero, along the line of the Northwestern Railroad. In sum, it has been the lack of availability of small holdings to Anwohner and small proprietors which has played a major role in decision-making in the Mennonite colonies. Loss of this avenue of expansion has materially influenced the nature of the recent massive, and to a significant degree successful, Mennonite drive for the acquisition of more land.

Despite the continuing passage of ejidatario and colono small-holdings into Mennonite hands since 1935, there has been, at the same time, almost continuous agitation from the same segment of the Mexican rural population against further acquisitions of land by them. The first encounter the Mennonites had with agrarista resentment has been related in detail in Chapter III. The Hague colony had no such experience initially. Possibly this was only because its first acquisitions were in an area of heavy black clays which the agraristas had avoided because they lacked the equipment to break the difficult sod. Once mellowed by tillage, however, these soils presented few problems that are not also encountered in the zones of coarser brown adobes nearer the valley walls. Under cultivation their high capacity for moisture retention gave them particular virtues for the planting of corn.

Other Aspects of Competition for Land

In the late summer of 1935 agraristas, urged on by political agitators, began moving onto a 6,500-acre tract acquired by the Hague colony Mennonites the year before, on which the village of Schönthal had been founded. Early the next spring they moved on Grünfeld, Rosenfeld, Neuanlage, Blumenort, and Reinland, measuring out fields for themselves and planting their crops. Whether there was any connection between this development and the banditry to which the Hague colonists were victim in those years, and which necessitated the stationing of troops in the colony, cannot be established. The colonists, for their part, vigorously protested the invasion of their property to the government and ultimately received assurance from President Lázaro Cárdenas that their rights would be respected. The agrarista problem, however, dragged on for another year before it was resolved in the Mennonites' favor.

During 1936 and 1937 expropriations against large landowners were being carried out at a rapid pace in Durango, partly to accommodate Mexican nationals being repatriated from the United States. Title to the Hague colony, in the manner customary among the Altkolonier, rested in a few deeds, with individuals having ownership only in right of scrip issued by the colony authorities. The colony therefore could be assailed as representing a latifundio, subject to expropriation. In the spring of 1937, the presidente of the municipio of Canatlán came to the colony and advised the Mennonites not to make any further improvements on their land inasmuch as it was to be expropriated and given over to agraristas. Indeed, it appeared for a time that it would be. Early that summer, agraristas were once more planting their crops on colony land. Then, quite abruptly, about the end of June, the agraristas vacated, and the governor of the state, apparently on instructions from Mexico City, informed the Mennonites that the matter had been decided in their favor.[49]

Then, in 1941, the Hague colony bought 2,000 hectares (5,000 acres) out of the Rancho Tobosa. Once more a conflict of interest

---

49. From a series of reports from the Hague colony, appearing in the *Steinbach Post* of November 6, 1935, June 10, 1936, April 28, 1937, July 28, 1937, and June 25, 1941, written by Bernhard Penner, A. B. Schmitt, and Heinrich J. Fehr, all of the Hague colony, and verified by persons involved in the events described.

between Altkolonier and agraristas had to be resolved. Previously the problem had been one of agrarista encroachment upon colony lands. In this case, however, there were settlements of agrarista squatters already on the Tobosa land, creating a situation similar to that which prevailed in the Valle de Bustillos in the 1920's. Eventually they were more or less gently dislodged by the former owners, and the Altkolonier took possession.

Except for a brief flurry in the early stages of the founding of the Quellenkolonie at Los Jagueyes in 1947, there were no serious clashes between Mennonite and agrarista interests during the twenty years following the Tobosa incident. The tracts acquired during that period, however, were relatively small, or they were so situated that they were outside the immediate sphere of interest of the rural Mexican population. More recently four situations of varying degrees of seriousness, three of them related to land transactions in Zacatecas and Chihuahua, have had to be resolved.

At La Batea a spirited confrontation between Mennonites and a segment of the local population developed in 1962. Squatters had formed a settlement some little distance outside the northeast boundary of the new colony, grouping around a spot where water had been piped in for cattle. Trouble developed when they began planting on the Mennonites' fields. When this was reported to the owner of the hacienda, he had the pipes torn up, thereby cutting off the squatters' water supply. When they failed to disperse, he called in soldiers, who wrecked their buildings.[50]

At La Honda, as has been described, agrarista interjections against the purchase of the land by the Altkolonier were stilled when the latter made them a gift of 4,000 hectares (10,000 acres).

Agrarista inveighings against the purchase of Santa Rita, which borders the Ojo de la Yegua colony on its northern flank, were stilled when, in 1963, 13,500 hectares (33,750 acres)—one-third of the entire property—were made over to them.

In Durango, in 1962, local ejidatarios, under the urging of political agitators, once more laid claim for the expropriation of the

50. The squatters were, however, provided with an alternative location in a favored south-facing valley, one of the few places in the area where corn will mature.

Traditional *Wohnstallhaus,*
balloon-frame lumber construction,
built in 1922 or 1923 at Neuenburg,
Campo 21, Manitoba Colony.

Detached barn and house
of stuccoed adobe, Gnadenfeld, Campo 2-B,
Manitoba Colony. Note the *corredor*
at front of the house.

Farmstead, Capulín Colony north of Nuevo Casas Grandes.
The barn is sheetmetal over balloon frame,
the house of adobe because of its
superior insulating qualities.

Wohnstallhaus of adobe construction,
Campo 3-B, Steinbach, Manitoba Colony.

Bedroom in an *Altkolonier* home. Note the Dutch curtains.
Pictures and paintings are forbidden, but calendars,
being functional, are permitted. The great chest has come on the treks
from Danzig to the Dnieper before 1800, to Canada in the 1870s, and to
Mexico in the 1920s.

Kitchen in well-to-do *Altkolonier* home in Rosengart,
Campo 7-B, Manitoba Colony.

Threshing beans with a home-made thresher,
Manitoba Colony.

These *Altkolonier* girls
are carrying home pails of dough
which they will bake into *Zwieback* for
an engagement celebration to be held on the following day.

Mexican *agrarista*
threshing beans by treading
with animals.

Pebbly alluvial adobe soil
underlain by a heavy stratum of cobbles,
Ojo de la Yegua (*Nordkolonie*). The bulk
of the arable soils of the
Mennonite colonies in highland Mexico
is of comparable type.

Lichtfeld, Campo 67, Ojo de la Yegua Colony.
Note erosion on sloping roadway and adjacent fields.
Windmotors pump water from deep wells.

Dibble-planted first crop of corn
on new clearing, Spanish Lookout, British Honduras.
Following harvest of the crop, bush may be allowed to grow back in
for a year or two. Resultant light growth may then be slashed
and burned, thereby consuming also the bulk of old
heavy deadwood remaining from initial clearing.

"Coppiced" cornfield, Manitoba Colony.
The upper parts of the plants are harvested green,
after ears are set. After the ripe ears are snapped
the remaining portions of the plants
are also harvested for fodder.

Statute labor, hauling road-surfacing materials,
Shipyard. *Altkolonier* doctrine forbids pneumatic tires on tractors.
Horses, with little or no high-energy feed such as grain available to them,
have a low work capacity in the heat and humidity of British Honduras.

Detail from a painting in a Ciudad Cuauhtémoc hotel lobby depicting dour Mennonites digging gold from the soil, leaving it rock-strewn and devastated, while above the whirlwind and holocaust are poised to engulf them.

Hague colony. The governor of the state had the matter secretly studied. When it was found that more than one-third of the land of the ejidos involved was under rental to Mennonites, he informed them that, such being the case, they already had an excess of land. The matter ended there.[51]

Such incidents, although they do not appear to have impaired the day-to-day relations between the Mennonite community and the surrounding Mexican world, nevertheless point to a situation which serious-minded Mexicans, ambitious for the advancement of their countrymen, regard with concern. It is simply that Mennonite ambition and initiative, combined with their land hunger which drives them to seek, through rental, to appropriate to themselves a portion of the productive lands of their Mexican neighbors, tend to encourage indolence in the latter. The ejidatario or colono can, in view of the high rentals obtainable, frequently secure a larger revenue by turning over his land to a tractor-farming Mennonite than by cultivating it himself. By the same token, agitation by Mexican farmers for awards of more land are not always connected with a desire to expand their own agricultural endeavors. This was illustrated by a situation which developed in the Santa Rita and Ojo de la Yegua colonies in 1964. That year there was, for some time, a persistent rumor that a substantial portion of the Rancho Tepejuanes would be expropriated for the benefit of ejidatarios. That summer Mennonite colonists in the area adjacent to the ranch received numerous offers from expectant ejidatarios—often with the request for a cash advance—to rent their land once it was awarded to them.

Land Hunger

Despite concerted efforts by the colonies to compensate, through the purchase of new and substantial tracts of land, for the present trend toward diminution of rental opportunities among Mexican proprietors in nearby areas, and notwithstanding some substantial successes in these endeavors, land hunger among the

51. Jakob Bartsch and Jacob B. Wiebe, Hague colony, personal communication.

Mennonites in Mexico is intensifying. This is particularly so in Chihuahua, where, in proportion to colony populations, the resolution of the land shortage problem has met with markedly less success in recent years than has been enjoyed by the Hague colony. Nonetheless, although 176 Hague colony families acquired at least a minimum holding of 20 hectares (50 acres) at La Honda in 1964,[52] some 50 landless families still remained in the parent colony. In Chihuahua, despite the fact that the acquisition of Santa Rita in 1962 permitted the creation of 348 new farms, 305 of which are full units of 65 hectares (160 acres), there continued to be in 1965 some 700 families of Anwohner in the Manitoba, Swift Current, and Ojo de la Yegua colonies.[53] Although movement between the Altkolonier colonies is normally unrestricted, a realization of the magnitude of the problem of landlessness in Chihuahua prompted the Hague colony decision to restrict the sale of land at La Honda to bona fide residents of the Hague colony.

In the Sommerfelder colony of Santa Clara the problem of landlessness has also become acute. In 1965, 61 of 159 families—over 38 percent—were Anwohner. At Halbstadt and Bergthal, 16 families out of 70 were similarly landless.

One Workable Solution

The Kleine Gemeinde of the Quellenkolonie at Los Jagueyes, although also confronted with a land shortage, has nevertheless avoided the Anwohner problem. Here, the situation has been greatly aided by the emigration to British Honduras and Canada of persons approximately equal in number to those still remaining. The colony authorities, however, play a major role in forestalling landlessness. The price of land—subject to revision—

52. The total area acquired by former Anwohner at La Honda is 5,790 hectares, or 34 percent of the colony.

53. This is an estimate based on a known total of 591. Whereas there was full participation in the writer's survey on the part of the Swift Current and Ojo de la Yegua colonies, only thirty-two of the forty-three villages in the Manitoba colony agreed to provide this information. The numbers of Anwohner families in each colony in 1965 were: Swift Current—100; Ojo de la Yegua—95; and in thirty-two of the forty-three villages of the Manitoba colony—396.

is fixed at \$30 (U.S.) per acre, and the colony reserves the right to determine, on the basis of need, who may buy land which comes on the market. Purchases by persons who are not members of the Kleine Gemeinde, in keeping with the practice of Sommerfelder and Altkolonier Gemeinden, are prohibited.

Why the Land-Fund Idea Foundered

Financing, either to permit the discharging of contracted obligations as they fall due or to make possible the completion of purchase arrangements for desirable tracts of land, has been a source of continual difficulty to the Altkolonier colonies.[54] Attempts to establish a permanent land fund, such as those in Chihuahua from 1956 to 1962 and in Durango to raise the down payment on the La Honda property in 1964, have met with truculent participation and outright opposition. The failure of these funds to become established in the institutional fabric of the colonies may be largely ascribed to the colonists' lack of comprehension of the continuing common benefits that possession of their own land bank could bring. However, the basic cause of the poor reception accorded such ventures is a lack of confidence that stems from a single set of events in colony history.

During the late 1920's, after the influx of immigrant capital had ceased, new wealth was not being created at a rate sufficient to permit the retirement of the debt to the Zuloagas. As we have seen, leaders of the Manitoba colony prevailed upon persons who still possessed dollar reserves to lend them to the colony, and trust funds in the Waisenamt were diverted to the same purpose. At the time these loans were made, the dollar stood at 2.15 pesos. By the time they were retired in 1957, the Mexican currency had passed through several devaluations, and the value of the dollar was 12.50 pesos. However, it was unilaterally decided—without prior con-

54. The Santa Clara colony, where deeds are registered in the individual owners' names, does not take collective responsibility for land acquisitions, although colony officers may be delegated to act for groups of persons. The Quellenkolonie has not yet had occasion to expand its boundaries.

sultation with the lenders—to pay off these loans at the exchange rate which applied at the time they were made, that is, at 2.15 pesos for every dollar originally borrowed. This procedure and the manner in which it was carried out, with the debtors in effect voting themselves the remission of all interest and approximately five-sixths of the principal, generated disillusionment and resentment among the former lenders. For this reason many persons who could be influential in fostering the establishment of a permanent land fund will not now support such a venture.

Another reason for resistance to the land-fund concept stems from the provision, originally made in 1924, whereby vacant lands of the Manitoba colony could be purchased on time, with no down payment, at one-fifth crop shares. Many persons who acquired land in this way, however, later attempted to renege on their obligations. The colonies' position in respect to collection of such debts has always been weak. A person threatened with foreclosure can, if he chooses, rather effectively abdicate his responsibilities by intimating that if dispossessed he will permit his family to become a public charge.[55] A parallel situation, it is feared even by colony leaders, would develop out of any financing or lending organization which might be brought into being, however desirable and plausible such a venture might appear in theory and before the event.

Land Financing

Because they lack a sinking fund to cover at least the down payments on new land acquisitions, colony authorities are commonly compelled to resort to expedients which have decidedly negative aspects. When new tracts are acquired, impecunious Anwohner are customarily given an opportunity to take up minimum holdings on credit, with no down payment. In order to bring to hand the initial sum needed, it has become necessary, in the ab-

55. The same type of experience is recorded with respect to some who emigrated to Mexico with "public" assistance, then later made no effort to discharge their obligations.

sence of willing lenders among the wealthier colonists, to encourage persons of capital to buy outright a portion of the new lands sufficient to cover the contingency. These persons pay the actual initial acquisition price. Such lands are then frequently given into rental to less well-to-do colonists for the first five to ten years. By that time, according to past experience, their market value will have at least trebled or quadrupled. They are then commonly sold for a capital gain. In Chihuahua, land purchased speculatively in this fashion has been sold to the renter for more than seven times its first cost, at 12 percent annual interest, seven years after purchase.[56] At La Honda, land bought by persons in the parent Hague colony for cash at the acquisition cost of 267 pesos per hectare has been resold without development of any kind for as much as 1,000 pesos per hectare on a five-year term at interest up to 12 percent per annum.

Where provision has been made in newly founded colonies for Anwohner to take up minimum holdings on long-term credit, the results have not always been as hoped for. On Ojo de la Yegua each village was originally platted with two or three twenty-acre properties reserved for appropriation on credit by Anwohner. All but a few of these plots have since been absorbed into larger farms simply because it was impossible to make a living on them. There is, indeed, little incentive to buy so small a farm, because in accordance with custom in most villages, as an Anwohner, an individual can obtain a pasturing privilege approximately equal in value to a twenty-acre holding without incurring any financial obligations. At La Honda the same process of relinquishment by Anwohner of small holdings assumed on credit began during the first year of colonization. Other Anwohner from the Hague colony, entitled to reserve twenty hectares on La Honda on extended repayment terms but incapable of raising funds to cover the costs of moving, of bringing the land into production, and of subsisting

56. An extreme case may be cited from Campo 74, Weidenthal, where some land which was bought in 1956 at $13 (U.S.) per acre was rented out for seven years and then sold to the renter on time, at 12 percent interest on the unpaid balance, for 1,200 pesos ($96 U.S.) per acre.

until a first crop could be produced, have on occasion sold out their parcels for a small quick gain without ever going to the new colony. This, however, is regarded as rascally behavior by the more well-to-do and generates sentiment against the creation of similar opportunities in the future.

The inability to pay out quickly the principal involved in land acquisitions has, on occasion, where the price was stipulated in U.S. dollars, worked to the substantial disadvantage of the colonists. A major example is manifest in the contract with the Zuloagas. By the time the residuum of that debt was retired in 1948, the peso had fallen in value from 2.15 to 6.87 to the U.S. dollar. Similarly, before the debt incurred for the purchase of the land for Rosenheim, Springstein, and Ebenfeld, Campos 43, 44, and 46 of the Ojo de la Yegua colony, was discharged, the peso fell from 6.87 to 12.50 to the dollar. The same thing happened at Yermo during the initial rental-with-option-to-purchase contract. Although partly compensated by rises in prices of farm commodities in the wake of devaluations, these occurrences have nevertheless sharply increased the burden of debt retirement to the people involved.

The Constant Shadow

Over the years Mennonite landholding practices have repeatedly been subjected to criticism and, occasionally, outright challenge from Mexican interests. Most common have been assertions that blanket deeds, under which individual colonists hold real property only in right of scrip issued by the colony, represent latifundia which, under the Código Agrario (Agrarian Code), should be subject to expropriation. The nearest approach to success of such challenges came in Durango in the 1930's. In every instance, however, the Mennonites' interests have ultimately been upheld by the government, which is apprised of their practices with respect to landholding and recognizes them under the terms of the Privilegium. The colonies, for their part, have made adjustments calculated to obviate the possibility of some day having deeds to large tracts declared ultra vires. This has been done, however, without basically changing the character of their internal landholding customs, that is, without enlarging the sector of individual initiative or, conversely, diminishing colony control over colony lands.

The Hague colony, which because of its piecemeal growth was never under a single deed, has progressively redeeded its lands in smaller blocks which legally constitute individual holdings. Although there has been some attempt to draw new deeds in such a way that the lands they represent are owned by family ar clan groups, in fact it is only fortuitously that their bounds coincide with property lines as they exist within the colony.

In Chihuahua no basic alterations have been undertaken in the title structure of the Manitoba and Swift Current colonies. In the latter, titles reflect the original division of the colony into village blocks or, where foreclosures occurred, the changes that were wrought at that time. Title to the Manitoba colony continues to repose in the two holding companies originally formed to take possession of the land. In recent years government officials have been pressing for a change to individual deeds. The reason given is that agraristas cannot or will not understand that the colony does not simply consist of two haciendas. However, each new deed would cost at least 1,000 pesos ($80 U.S.), most of which would be absorbed by legal fees and surveys to resolve the tangles among property lines which have developed over the years through parcelization and fragmentation. The colony hopes to avoid this expense by compiling and presenting detailed villages plans showing actual ownership boundaries.

In more recent land transactions, the Mennonites in Chihuahua have taken care to assume title in such a way as to meet the requirements of Mexican law with respect to the area which may be deeded to any one person. The Ojo de la Yegua ranch was deeded to seventy-five persons after its purchase in 1946. The entire Los Jagueyes property acquired by the Canadian Kleine Gemeinde and Altkolonier in 1947 was similarly deeded, in seventy-four tracts. Buenos Aires in northwestern Chihuahua is registered in eight names, and Capulín in fourteen. Nowhere, except fortuitously, do the legal bounds of these titles coincide with the actual village plans or individually owned properties. The persons in whose names the separate blocks are registered need not live on those blocks or even in that colony. Only one of the titleholders to Buenos Aires, for instance, was living there in 1965. Indeed, some of the titleholders to the several colonies are no longer living.

The Old Ways Hold

Such subdivisions of large tracts into individually deeded blocks have not broadened the scope of individual initiative with respect to the disposition of property deeded in their names. Only one "irregularity" has arisen out of this system of vesting land ownership in persons who have no real proprietary interest in it. The case in question was one in which a person in whose name one of the blocks of the Ojo de la Yegua colony was registered attempted to assume actual proprietorship. The matter was quickly regulated, with the understanding of Mexican officials. Since that time, however, a *carta poder,* or caveat, has been filed against each of these properties, so that titleholders can take no action with respect to them without the initiative coming from colony authorities. Placing the land in private titles registered to the actual owners would of course make possible developments not unlike those which disrupted the Altkolonier way of life in Canada; of particular importance and concern are the implications inherent in the passage of colony lands into the lands of excommunicants or outsiders.

Conclusion

It appears that significant changes in the character and distribution of future colonization ventures in Mexico may be in the offing. Where Mennonites reside in large numbers, as in Chihuahua, there has been a growing objection, often appearing in the form of polemical attacks in tabloid-type periodicals, to the exclusiveness of their way of life. Coupled with this is an increasing level of protest against further areal expansion by them, of a kind very similar to that experienced by the Hutterian Brethren (Hutterites) in South Dakota, Montana, and the Prairie Provinces of Canada. Other states, in which they are less numerous or have not hitherto established themselves, are still prepared to welcome Mennonite colonization, regarding it as an asset to the agricultural development of the areas in which their colonies are founded.

However, large contiguous blocks of land suitable for agricultural colonization are coming on the market with increasing rarity. When they do, the rural Mexican population is speaking with increasing assurance for reservation of available lands to themselves. Mennonites born in Mexico, however, have the same rights of acquisition and proprietorship in land as the native population.[57] It appears probable that future colonization ventures will involve relatively small blocks of land, as at La Batea in Zacatecas, Neuendorf–Hoffnungsfeld in Tamaulipas, and Buenos Aires and Capulín in northwestern Chihuahua. In such small colonies outside contacts are much more frequent. Traditional insularity and exclusiveness, undermined by the need to accommodate to new and usually difficult environments, are already showing marked evidence of diminution. Indeed, it appears possible that Mexican-born Mennonites might one day invoke the law and petition—in the same way as their ejidatario and colono neighbors—for awards of land to form either ejidos or colonias.[58]

57. In Tamaulipas one large (15,000 hectares) American landowner has taken advantage of this fact by deeding some 1,400 hectares to Mexican-born Mennonites in what appears on the surface to be a legitimate colonization project. His express understanding with them is that if his property is nevertheless expropriated, they are to receive the land deeded to them, free of charge.

58. In the face of the Mennonites' long tradition of land ownership, the colonia appears to be the more probable development. However, since many today do not aspire to fee-simple ownership of property, the freehold tenure of the ejidatario would possibly also be acceptable to them. Such developments are not unique in Mennonite history. The entire Fürstenland colony of the Altkolonier in Russia was held under a quitrent system (see Chapter I).

One development which could set such events in train in Mexico is an expedient proposed in Chihuahua with respect to the Rancho Tepejuanes, adjacent to the Ojo de la Yegua and Santa Rita colonies. Agraristas have been campaigning for expropriation of the ranch, much of which is potentially arable. The proposal is

A massive Mennonite emigration from Mexico in response to land hunger is hardly to be contemplated as long as the Privilegium continues inviolable to them. In this day of waxing nationalism in the underdeveloped countries—and these are the only ones which can provide the frontier conditions necessary to large-scale exclusive-group settlement—few are willing to contemplate the issuance of Privilegia to alien colonists. This is not to say that individuals would not consider going to live in a country which extended them no special privileges and immunities; the substantial numbers who have come to Canada attest to that. It is feared by Mennonite leaders in Mexico, however, that organized group departures for such a country under Gemeinde auspices would suggest to the Mexican government that they collectively no longer lay great weight on the maintenance of the Privilegium, and that it might then be tempted to abrogate it.

---

to rent the land to the Mennonites for a term of five years at a fixed annual rate. All accruing rentals would be paid to the present owners as compensation. At the end of the five-year term the Mennonites would vacate the property, and it would be given over to the agraristas free of encumbrance. It is a certainty, however, that should such a plan be executed, in the five years during which they would be allowed to rent the Tepejuanes property the Mennonites would become dependent upon the land and would not readily be induced to give it up. In such circumstances they might well invoke the law in their own interests, as suggested above.

Chapter 8

The Gradual Economic Transformation

Mennonite agrarian economies, through the several centuries of their history in Prussia, Russia, Canada, and now Mexico, have characteristically been predicated upon the commercial production of plant and animal products. Only in the earliest stages of the development of pioneer frontiers have the subsistence elements of their agriculture outweighed the commercial. In the main, however, they have depended on outside entrepreneurs to provide the facilities whereby they could dispose of their surplus products. Even in the most conservative groups, though, notwithstanding the usual official church attitude toward such endeavors, individual and even group action from within the community has occasionally been applied to the creation of new markets and opportunities.

Whereas the colonies in Chihuahua were large enough to attract the development of marketing facilities geared almost solely to the profitable disposal of the Mennonites' products, such was not the case with the much smaller Hague colony. By 1933 Mennonites there, acting singly or in groups, were taking the initiative in shipping corn by the carload to outside markets. About the same time Mennonite entrepreneurs in the Chihuahua colonies were shipping substantial quantities of butter and meat products, particularly hams, to market in Mexico City. By 1934 live hogs were being shipped by train to packing houses in Chihuahua and Monterrey.[1] As these products became known and an active demand de-

1. Active in the development of the markets for butter, meat, and hogs were Peter Blatz and Abram Martens, the same two men who provided financing for the first cheese factory in the Manitoba colony.

veloped for them, Mexican business concerns gradually took over the marketing function. In this the motor truck has assumed an important role. The colonies, with their populations concentrated in villages, offer good opportunities for the "collecting" buyer of farm products. Indeed, this method of disposing of their surpluses is preferred by most Altkolonier, who have no motor vehicles but whose more remote villages are as many as seventy miles from Cd. Cuauhtémoc. Considerable specialization and time-scheduling have gradually developed. Buyers of hogs and calves, particularly, make regular rounds of the villages throughout the year. Meat packers from Chihuahua and Monterrey maintain trucks which regularly canvass the colonies from Cd. Cuauhtémoc to Los Jagueyes for hogs. Buyers from the cities of Durango and Torreón are active in the Hague colony. Most of the calves appear to find their way into the replacement market for range animals among Mexican ranchers, and occasionally into dairy operations.[2]

The commodity market in corn, beans, and oats, despite the entry of increasing numbers of buyers into the business over the years, continued in a very unsatisfactory state until about 1938. The distribution facilities were inadequate. A crop bountiful enough to create a local surplus automatically heralded a flooded market and disastrous declines in prices. Buyers also appear to have taken advantage of the captive nature of suppliers. Prices paid in Cd. Cuauhtémoc, for instance, were normally not more than two-thirds the Chihuahua price. Those paid on the farmyard in the colonies were lower still, usually, owing in large measure to the colonists' lack of knowledge of the true state of the market.

By the late 1930's the Mexican economy, owing to stabilization of the civil state of the country and the gradual waning of the depression, and, possibly, to reorganization of the market and improvements in transportation, was showing marked improvement. Since that time the Mennonite colonies have experienced little difficulty in disposing of their commodity surpluses. Prices, how-

2. The generally good grade of Holstein–Frisian cattle in the Hague colony makes selected calves from that area particularly desirable as replacements in dairy operations.

ever, have continued to exhibit the annual cycle of fluctuations typical of commodity markets which are not stabilized by state intervention, finding their lowest level during and just after local harvesttime, when, because short-term obligations incurred by farmers have to be discharged, the bulk of the crop enters market channels.

Developments in the market situation were, predictably, more favorable with respect to beans and corn, which are staples of the Mexican diet, than with respect to oats, of which the Mennonites were essentially the only major producers in the regions where they had settled. Since oats was a staple product of Mennonite agriculture, its production rose markedly during the late 1930's and early 1940's in response to the progressive expansion of areas under cultivation.

Initiatives in Contract Marketing

Reliance upon the initiative of Mexican buyers left the market situation for oats in a chronically shaky state. About 1942 a decision was reached by the authorities of the Manitoba colony to attempt to stimulate the interest of buyers and processors. Two men were delegated to the task. Results of their efforts appeared sufficiently promising to warrant an expansion of this line of activity. In 1944 a committee was delegated to continue efforts at stabilizing the market for oats. The committee established contact with processors in Mexico City (Quaker) and in the United States.[3] Later, buyers and processors from Mérida, Yucatán (Avena Rivero), Cd. Chihuahua (Avena Número Uno, Juan Henríquez, and Arturo Wisbrun), and Cd. Cuauhtémoc (Baltazar Meléndez) also were brought into the scheme.

Following a survey of the colonies—the Sommerfelder of Santa Clara also participated—to establish the approximate tonnage of oats available, sales were made on a contract basis, with the Ge-

3. There was a good market potential in the United States during World War II. Exports, however, were permitted only after Mexican processors had had an opportunity to fill their own needs.

meinden acting as surety for commitments made by the committee. Buyers from the United States, although permitted to contract only for surplus amounts remaining after Mexican processors had been afforded an opportunity to fill their anticipated needs, exerted a very salutary influence. Because of their activities, the prices arrived at closely reflected those prevailing in the United States.

In order to meet contract commitments, fairly elaborate arrangements were made to facilitate delivery to buyers and payment to farmer-suppliers. The committee purchased scales and rented a large storehouse in Cd. Cuauhtémoc. They ordered boxcars and notified farmers when to make delivery. Arrangements were made with buyers to release money for payment of deliveries as they came in, after proof of lading had been furnished to a local bank. Because of the war, however, boxcars were not always available, and incoming deliveries frequently had to be placed in storage. Farmers nevertheless demanded cash to meet their commitments. To avoid diversion of the grain to other buyers, credit arrangements were made with the Banco Comercial, using oats in store as collateral pending shipment and payment by the buyers. Costs of all these services were prorated and levied against the price paid to farmers. The overall effect was to stabilize prices at a level approximately 60 percent above that prevailing immediately prior to the establishment of the "marketing board" and contract selling.[4]

Despite its promising beginnings, the contract system of marketing oats was short-lived. Problems arose when buyers wanted amounts beyond those for which they had contracted, and when noncontract buyers attempted to bid on available supplies. Not infrequently farmers making deliveries in fulfillment of contracts were intercepted and offered a premium to divert their grain to these buyers. Then one of the major processors built its own warehouse in Cd. Cuauhtémoc and began to bypass the contract system.

4. The price of oats early in 1944, prior to contract selling, was 180 to 190 pesos per ton. Contract prices arrived at later that year were at 300 and 310 pesos per ton. A worthwhile side benefit accrued to the colonies when one of the major buyers, Avena Rivero of Mérida, Yucatán, assisted them in obtaining binder twine cheaply. (Hénequen, from whose fibers binder twine is made, is a major crop in Yucatán agriculture.)

A further difficulty arose in the maintenance of the quality promised in contracts when farmers attempted to meet their commitments with low-grade oats, retaining their best grain for independent sale to the highest bidder. This type of subversion made it very difficult for the Gemeinde committee to meet contract obligations. Although because of these factors the system of contract selling lost most of its effectiveness in the first year, it was carried on, under increasing difficulties and with diminishing results, for four more years, after which, its stabilizing function thoroughly undermined, it was dissolved.[5]

The Government and the Private Trader

Over the years the Mexican government has taken some action toward stabilizing prices and assuring consistent markets. This influence, however, insofar as the Mennonite colonies have been concerned, has applied mainly to the staples of the Mexican food economy, beans and corn. The earliest of the government agencies to operate in the market was the CEIMSA,[6] whose activities extended over a considerable range of agricultural commodities. It was superseded by the Almacenes Nacionales (National Storehouses), which, in the regions where the Mennonite colonies are located, operates only in the purchase and distribution of the *primeras necesidades*, beans, corn, and wheat. Almacenes Nacionales (A.N.) does not monopolize the market but operates along with the private sector of trade in these commodities. However, at buying points where only relatively small volumes of beans and corn are marketed, the presence of A.N. has been sufficient to discourage private buyers, even though, to assure low moisture content and consequent prime storage condition of its purchases, it does not normally begin buying operations until some weeks after

5. During the last two years in which the contract marketing system functioned, the colonies' interests were represented by the several colony Vorsteher together with two other representatives. Details obtained from David B. Penner, Gnadenfeld, Campo 2-B, Manitoba colony, and Jacob F. Enns, Yermo colony, Ceballos, Durango.

6. Compañía Exportadora e Importadora, Sociedad Anónima.

the end of harvest, usually about mid-December. By that time independent buyers have had ample opportunity to bid on available supplies.[7] In the Chihuahua colonies the bulk of the Mennonites' crops of beans, corn, and wheat are sold through private agencies, although prices realized are normally somewhat lower than those paid by A. N. There are two main reasons for this. First, the government agency commences buying too late for farmers to meet due dates of short-term—often, three-month—credit arrangements made during the summer. Second, A. N. handling procedures are primitive and inefficient, and frequently involve waiting periods at buying depots of as much as a week or more. Private buyers, on the other hand, often provide haulage service directly from the farmyard, and also provide relatively speedy unloading service at their buying depots for those who do their own hauling. At Nuevo Ideal, Durango, however, most of the beans and corn which enter the market from the Hague colony are sold through A. N. This is primarily because the volumes marketed are too small to attract much activity from private buyers in competition with the government agency. Because the majority of Mexican small proprietors—ejidatarios and colonos—sell to A. N., and because handling procedures in Nuevo Ideal are just as inefficient as at Cd. Cuauhtémoc, the Altkolonier farmers, to avoid lengthy periods of waiting to unload, generally prefer to wait until the rush is over before making their own deliveries. This delay has sometimes led to serious consequences, for A. N. has occasionally closed its buying depot in Nuevo Ideal early and without prior announcement. This happened in the spring of 1965, with the result that much of the Hague colony's 1964 bean and corn crops remained unsold; the colony authorities then had to appeal to the governor of the state to use his influence in having its operations resume. In the meantime it became possible to sell part of the corn crop to a firm based in Monterrey.

The very loosely knit marketing system, together with a lack of accurate information in the colonies with respect to the state

7. By law Almacenes Nacionales may buy only from primary producers, not from speculators and middlemen.

of the market owing to the absence of newspapers and radios which might carry such reports, stimulates the entry of individuals, frequently fly-by-night operators, known everywhere as *coyotes*, into the commodity market, often with considerable loss to producers. A coyote's common mode of operation is to tour the colonies by truck and buy for cash—frequently at slightly above the current price—small quantities of grain, hogs, cheese, or other commodities. Word of this, as in any rural community, quickly gets around. On a subsequent trip payment is made by check. When the banks honor the checks, confidence is established. The coyote then buys as large a quantity as possible in a short time, pays with worthless checks, and vanishes. Over the years many individual farmers have been duped out of much of a year's saleable crop in this way. Cheese factories, too, are a favorite object of attention by coyotes. In the spring of 1965 one such operator, using a semitrailer, managed to dupe factories in the Santa Rita, Ojo de la Yegua, Swift Current, Manitoba, and Hague colonies out of some 600,000 pesos worth of cheese. Even when the coyotes' methods are aboveboard, there is a serious element of hazard in selling to them. Many of them, lacking funds for immediate payment, buy on speculation, making purchases on consignment and undertaking to make payment as soon as they effect delivery to organizations buying from them. In order to make certain that payment is indeed made as promised, it is usually necessary for the Vorsteher or some other colony official to accompany the coyote to the destination to which he is shipping and to collect on the spot for the colonists.

On a few occasions groups of Mennonite colonists have contracted to grow barley for the brewing industry. The advantage in such arrangements is that seed is usually furnished at reasonable cost by the brewer and is charged against the crop. On occasion such contracts have made possible the planting of considerable acreage for which no seed—or the money to buy it—was otherwise available.[8]

In the new colonies where cotton culture is dominant, the crop

8. As far as can be established, the production of barley under contract to brewers has been undertaken only in the Hague and La Batea colonies.

is usually delivered to the ginner with whom credit arrangements for seed, fertilizer, and insecticides have been made. Yermo colony farmers sell mainly in Torreón. Cotton grown by Mennonites in Tamaulipas is sold to local ginners in Gonzales. Buenos Aires and Capulín deliver theirs to various gins in Nuevo Casas Grandes, Villa Ahumada, and Ascensión.

The perishable crops produced by the Mennonites in the several colonies—generally small amounts of potatoes, tomatoes, melons, and orchard produce—are absorbed to some extent by the local internal market. Surpluses are usually sold in the nearest large urban center, although in the case of melons grown at Yermo and apples grown in the Manitoba and Swift Current colonies, the best market is in Mexico City.

Intercolony trade in commodities is limited. However, because of chronic severe rusting of its oat crops, the Hague colony has periodically turned to its sister colonies in Chihuahua for seed supplies. More recently La Batea has been supplying this market. The advent of "Cleanland" and other new rust-resistant varieties of Texas oats will probably result in a phasing-out of this inter-colony trade in seed stocks.

The new colonies in the Zacatecan highland, La Batea and La Honda, have encountered particular difficulties with respect to markets, similar to those which beset the parent colonies during the first fifteen years or so of their existence. Fresnillo is the nearest market and supply center for La Batea, and Río Grande and Juan Aldama are the nearest centers for La Honda. These are small centers, however, quite incapable of absorbing the colonies' agricultural surpluses and very easily flooded. Placing produce in more reliable markets in Tampico, Aguascalientes, and Mexico City involves high truck and rail charges. La Batea particularly, since it lies more than ninety kilometers from the railroad, over bad roads and trails, has to contend with high haulage costs. La Honda is somewhat more fortunately situated in this respect, since it is located only some eighteen kilometers from Highway 45, the main route from Cd. Juárez to Mexico City.

The Land-Use Mosaic

Although the land-use pattern in the colonies located in the upland and basin country along the eastern edge of the Sierra Madre Occidental is basically that which evolved during the first decade of settlement, some significant local patterns based on soil capabilities and microclimate have developed.

The belt of sandy soils in the northeastern portions of the Manitoba and Swift Current colonies, although of mediocre quality for agriculture, has proven to be best suited to corn, but other crops are also grown there. The high west and southwest winds which persist into late spring normally cause soil drifting sufficient to create a surface dust mulch which retards moisture loss. Corn planted into subsoil moisture in late April or early May can usually survive until the onset of the summer rains. Being less sensitive to moisture stress than beans and oats, corn is also better able to mature in these drouthy soils.

In the belt of heavy black soils developed upon the clay botton of the ancestral Laguna Bustillos there is also considerable concentration on corn. The same holds true for the black-soil area of the Hague colony. These gypsiferous soils are highly moisture-retentive. They do not, however, yield up water readily, resulting in conditions of moisture stress which give corn a relative advantage in relation to other crops common to the region. Moreover, the sturdy root systems of deep-planted corn are better able to survive the "heaving" of the soil that takes place with changing moisture conditions than are more shallow-rooted crops.[9] Over much of their area, particularly where ground water is high or where occasional ponding of runoff occurs, these soils exhibit varying degrees of salinity. It is only in wet years, therefore, when there is sufficient moisture to dilute the soil solution to salinity levels easily tolerated by cultivated plants, that yields superior to those

9. These clay soils expand and contract greatly with changes in moisture content. Before they were placed under cultivation, they commonly cracked so badly at the surface that it was not unusual for cattle to become trapped by getting their legs caught in the fissures.

on the adobe soils are obtained from them. Because of this salinity factor, and because of a low hydraulic conductivity which reduces water loss into the subsoil beyond the root zone, these soils are more responsive to irrigation than the sandy soils and adobes which represent the other major soil classes. In the areas of high soil salinity on the approaches to the lagunas of Bustillos and Santiaguillo in the Manitoba and Hague colonies, land use is dominated by mixed dairy- and beef-cattle enterprise.

In the adobe and chocolate loam soil zones of the Manitoba and Swift Current colonies, cultivated acreage is approximately equally divided among beans, oats, and corn. Much the same holds true for the brown adobe zone of the Hague colony, except that there beans have only recently assumed an importance equal to that of oats and corn.[10] In the Ojo de la Yegua and Santa Rita colonies and on Los Jagueyes, because of generally low levels of soil fertility and moisture retentiveness, little corn is grown. At La Batea, cereals—wheat, barley, and oats—appear to hold the most promise. At La Honda, beans and oats will probably dominate the cropping picture, with corn and possibly wheat in minor roles.

A Resurgence of Wheat

The interest in wheat culture which strongly influenced the rate of adaptation of the Mennonites' accustomed land-use practices to crops better suited to the Mexican environment, although much diminished over the years, has never completely disappeared. This persistent interest in wheat cannot be explained solely by a desire to assure themselves of a reliable supply of breadstuffs, since flour has been in adequate supply during all but the first years. Rather, the interest stems in large part from the Mennonites' wheat-farming tradition, which harks back to the prairies of Canada and the steppes of Russia.

10. The reason for the increased interest in beans is a realization of their value, as a nitrogen-fixing legume, in crop rotations. Stabilization of prices under Almacenes Nacionales has also tended to focus greater attention on beans, as contrasted to oats, the price of which is not government supported. Because of the relatively small bulk of the harvest, beans are also a favored crop on distant rented lands.

In the Mennonite colonies in Mexico, there has been a succession of attempts, with varying but usually minimal success, to grow rust-resistant Canadian varieties of wheat. In recent years, in part owing to the stabilization of wheat prices by the A. N., interest in wheat culture has once more intensified.[11] This is so notwithstanding chronically recurring fodder shortages and despite the fact that residues—straw and chaff—from beans, oats, and corn are much superior in palatability and feed value to those from wheat. Attempts to grow Canadian varieties, which continued sporadically until about 1960, have ceased. It has been discovered that winter-wheat varieties developed for the irrigation districts of the Mexican Pacific slope—notably Humantla, Lerma Rojo, and Sonora 64—can be grown successfully as summer crops under natural rainfall conditions in the highland valleys of the Sierra Madre.

The Approach to the Land Resource

The Mennonite approach to resource management has been governed, with few exceptions, by the traditions and techniques brought with them from Canada, and substantially reflects the institutional rigidity which characterizes much of the fabric and structure of colony life. An element basic to resource management is the structure of the village Streifenfluren, on which the Koerls are laid out. By custom the orientation, as well as the distribution of the several Koerls which together compose the individual homestead, is such as to assure as nearly as possible an equitable division of soil quality found on the village *Flur*. On the Canadian prairie—and before that on the steppes of the Ukraine—where gradients were gentle and soil quality was more or less uniform over large areas, these considerations were perhaps less weighty than drainage and the equalization of the combined distance from the Hauskoerl to the other Koerls of the individual farm unit. In the zones of brown adobe soils of the colonies in the Bustillos,

11. The price paid for wheat by Almacenes Nacionales has for several years been stabilized at approximately 900 pesos per metric ton, whereas that of oats, in which A.N. does not deal, has fluctuated between 400 and 1,200 pesos.

Santa Clara, and Guatimapé valleys, and in the chocolate loam zones of the Manitoba and Swift Current colonies, however, slopes are on the order of 30 to 200 feet per mile. On a localized scale, slopes ranging to gradients of 10 percent are cultivated. The first subjective evaluation of the land prior to the formation of the individual village Streifenfluren revealed the most notable variations in soil characteristics to occur in the direction of slope. On that basis the orientation of the Koerls was determined.

In Canada, and in Russia too, Mennonite agriculture had been predicated on cereals and flax, broadcast-seeded crops which, at least during the growing season, offered considerable impediment to potential runoff. In the older colonies in the upland and basin country on the eastern flank of the Sierra Madre in Chihuahua and Durango, some two-thirds of the cultivated land is normally devoted to beans and corn, intertilled crops which provide ready-made channels for potential runoff. Disc plowing, practised almost to the exclusion of other methods of after-harvest tillage, leaves no protective trash on the surface to retard the work of wind or water. Furthermore, plowing to the same depth each year has resulted in the formation of a plow pan, at furrow depth, which is almost impervious to water. The soil is particularly vulnerable at the time of the onset of the summer rains, when there is no protective cover of vegetation. In contrast to the friable chernozems, rich in humus, of the Mennonites' former homelands, the clayey mineral soils on the most pronounced slopes—adobes and chocolate loams—puddle readily at the surface under the impact of the convectional showers which are characteristic of summer precipitation in this region. With gentler rain, runoff commences when the soil is saturated to plow-pan depth. The net result is a high incidence of sheet erosion and, because of the rapid gathering of runoff waters, severe gullying of slopes and the occasional inundation of substantial areas in the lower-lying terrain on the approaches to the lagunas. The cumulative effect over the years has been, through soil loss and gullying, to seriously impair the agricultural potential of the land. Indeed, on the alluvial fans there are occasional Koerls on which sheetwash has stripped the soil down to hardpan or bedrock.

The communal pasture, a traditional feature of the village Flur which normally occupies a quarter or more of the land, has also shown manifest weaknesses in terms of resource management. Since winters are mild and open, without frozen ground or snow cover, cattle are taken out to pasture throughout the year. Horses also are frequently set out to forage when they are not needed for farm work. The grass cover is therefore kept continuously cropped down almost to ground level, and fails to reseed, giving a relative survival advantage to woody plants and inedible forbs. Over the years the problem of overgrazing has been compounded by the increasing number of Anwohner—occasionally equal to the number of landowners in a village—all of whom are by tradition entitled to a grazing right.

As suggested above, during the growing season erosion on land planted to intertilled crops is more severe than on that seeded to small grains. Runoff water moving downslope between the rows carries with it much soil. Measures to arrest the serious attrition of the soil resource on which the agrarian economies of the colonies rest have been minimal. The predominantly narrow Koerls make mechanized cultivation at right angles to the direction of slope almost impossible. Where contour cultivation has been tried, the methods used have been imprecise, and experience has shown that runoff accumulates until the water breaks through the confining crop rows. This normally results in the formation of one or more gullies of major proportions on the field in question, with attendant serious tillage problems and outright loss of land. When plantings are run up and down the slopes there is loss of soil too, but the size of gullies thus created is determined by the somewhat limited capacity of the runoff from the space between two rows to carry the soil with it. These are therefore rarely too large to be filled in with the plow. Because of the relatively unspectacular magnitude of the overall rate of erosion and visible year-to-year manifestations of soil destruction, there is little comprehension of its long-term implications. Even if there were, a thorough reorientation of the Streifenfluren, keyed to soil conservation, is hardly to be contemplated. Since little of the cultivated land is in slopes greater than 4 percent, a more practical, but partial, solution to the problem of soil attrition might be gained through adoption of the lister, an implement which can be used to throw up small dams at short intervals between the rows of intertilled crops. Potential runoff would thus be contained until it could be absorbed by the soil. Implementation of this technique should also make a positive contribution to the chronic problem of moisture inadequacy at intervals during the cropping season.

Certainly slopes on the cultivated portions of the colonies in the upland and basin country are nowhere so great as to preclude sustained mechanized tillage. Indeed, the destructive potential of runoff under the present system of land management may be attributed mainly to the predominantly long, smooth fan slopes, which permit the attainment of high water velocities and a consequently high capacity for erosion. The rigidity of the Mennonites in laying out their village Fluren, together with the inadequacy or outright unsuitability to the environment of their techniques of land management and a general lack of comprehension of the implications of past and present trends, prevents any effective dealing with the overall problem of soil erosion.

The problems of water control which the colonies face are compounded by the large volumes of freshet waters draining across the colonies from the valleys which penetrate the enclosing hills. These are the basic cause of the inundations to which low-lying areas of the colonies are sporadically subjected. The problem is, however, magnified by the colonies' approach to it. In Manitoba particularly, in the Agassiz Lake Basin in which the Mennonite West Reserve is located, drainage was almost a prerequisite to agricultural settlement. Indeed it was out of considerations of drainage that the Altkolonier, who were first in the West Reserve, settled solidly in its western portion, above a pronounced beach ridge to the east of which the country was less well drained. Drains were necessary also to dispose of local spring meltwaters, as well as those pouring off the Manitoba Escarpment immediately to the west of the reserve, at a time of year when the ground was still frozen and consequently unable to absorb much moisture. Under the conditions with which they have to contend in Mexico, the indicated approach to temporary surpluses of moisture accruing from precipitation falling within the colonies would be to invoke measures that would cause it to be absorbed where it falls, thereby withdrawing that amount from the total runoff and leaving essentially only runoff from the surrounding hills to be disposed of. Such measures, effectively applied, not only should appreciably diminish the problems of erosion and flooding, but would also contribute to the recharging of aquifers. The approach taken, however, has reflected a preoccupation with drainage; the effect of this has been for the Mennonites to permit potential runoff to accrue and then to dispose of it, as they did in Canada, as efficiently as possible through the expansion of drainage works. Destruction of the original grass cover, further mineralization of the soil under continuous cropping, and the gradual formation of plow pan have all contributed to a progressive increase in the volume of runoff. Older stream valley villages such as Campos 41 and 42, Springfeld and Blumstein, in Chihuahua, which formerly had no serious problems with excess water, have been experiencing progressively more severe flooding since the acquisition of Rancho Ojo de la Yegua and the ensuing cultivation of the long fan slope leading to Campo 59, Hochtal. In the Hague colony, similarly, the cultivation, because of land hunger, of slope lands on the northeast flank of the colony, which were formerly used only for pasture, has resulted not only in severe local erosion but also in periodic flood damage in adjacent downslope areas.

In general, however, because slopes over most of the Hague colony are less pronounced than is the case in the colonies in the Bustillos and Santa Clara valleys, erosion has taken less of a toll. At La Batea, where slopes are more pronounced, the emphasis on cereals, which impede runoff, tends to inhibit erosion. At La Honda it is likely to become severe, particularly on the potentially arable portions of the caliche lands, once these are broken up. The shallow depth to the caliche horizon suggests a history of sheet erosion. There is little doubt that the rate of soil loss will be greatly increased once the land is placed under cultivation.

The lack of the colonists' comprehension of the implications of these trends, or of the measures which might be applied to halt and reverse them, is indicated by the fact that in the more recently established colonies, under conditions of precipitation and terrain comparable to those prevailing in the parent colonies, fields have once more been predominantly laid out in the direction of most pronounced slope.

Trash-cover tillage, which uses the chisel plow and which leaves crop residues on the surface to protect the soil, was known to the Kleine Gemeinde Mennonites at the time of their migration from Canada to Los Jagueyes in the late 1940's and has been practised to some degree. It has also found limited favor among the Altkolonier and Sommerfelder. In view of prevailingly light crop stands, however, and of the fact that most crop residues are used as fodder, little trash is left on the land. The light cover obtained with chisel-plow tillage affords considerable protection from wind, but wind erosion, despite the almost daily storms which punctuate the winter months, is of little consequence on the predominantly coarse-textured soils. Chisel-plowing does break up plow pan and prevents its further formation, significantly increasing the absorption rate and moisture capacity of the soil, and is to be recommended for this reason. Other factors, however, also influence the climate of opinion with respect to trash-cover tillage. The residues left on fields cultivated in this way attract the unwanted attention of free-ranging Mexican cattle during the long winter drouth. A fire hazard is also involved. Mexican horsemen often dismount to gather grass and stubble for small fires at which to warm themselves on rides across the colonies. These are usually left to burn themselves out, but such fires frequently spread over substantial areas, burning over fields and pastures and presenting hazards to the villages.

The nature of rental agreements entered into by the Mennonites, both on and off their colonies, also militates again the implementation of soil-conserving practices. Customary rentals, reflecting the intensity of land hunger, are high, yet, since most agreements are made on a one-year basis, security of rental tenure is low. The effect is to direct the efforts of renters to a maximization of returns in ways which can only be defined as *Raubwirtschaft* (robber economy). This is not to suggest that the Mennonites alone resort to exploitative land-use practices. Their Mexican neighbors generally also show a notable lack of concern in matters of soil conservation, and their crop yields are not superior to those of the Mennonites. In general, the Mennonites' land-use and cultural practices are not in fact inferior to those which characterized the first two generations of agriculture on the Western Great Plains.

Mennonites have a reputation of long standing as being good husbandmen devoted to their land. Their ability to achieve permanent settlements in regions which, not infrequently, have discouraged or defeated other attempts at agricultural occupation has gained widespread acknowlegement. On the steppes of the Ukraine they developed techniques of land utilization which, fortuitously and to their great advantage, proved applicable to the subduing of the prairie sod of the Great Plains as well. These techniques have been perpetuated, almost without change, in Mexico. However, they were and are techniques not of conservation but of exploitation! The generously endowed soils of their former homelands, recognized as being among the finest anywhere, were able to absorb the importunings of the plow and cereal monoculture until such a time as methods more saving and protective of the soil resources were found acceptable. Nonetheless, much of the land vacated by the Altkolonier and Sommerfelder in Canada was seriously impaired. Wind erosion, a particular hazard to the fine-textured prairie loams, had in many cases piled the topsoil into high ridges along the boundaries between the Koerls. Occasionally these ridges were so high that men working in adjacent fields could not see each other. It took many years to restore such land to its former productivity.[12] The shallower, more modestly endowed soils of their colonies in the highland valleys of the Sierra Madre have sustained exploitation less well, and its effects, particularly

12. These windblown ridges of soil were a particular nuisance following the breakup of the Streifenfluren of the Altkolonier villages in the wake of the Mennonite exodus. Several decades after the Altkolonier departure, farmers were still working them down, occasionally with the help of bulldozers. In some places they are still visible. Aerial photographs show them distinctly.

since considerable outright soil removal and destruction are involved, promise to be more permanent. Under cultivation the limited accumulations of plant nutrients which they possessed in their virgin state were withdrawn within a few years. Since that time yields, given a bare adequacy of precipitation, have been almost constant, being to all appearances dependent on the year-to-year release of plant nutrients through mineral decomposition in the soil.[13] A crop of 450 to 600 pounds per acre—equal to approximately eight bushels of beans, fifteen of oats, or ten of corn—is regarded as a good yield over most of the areas of adobe and chocolate loam soils.

There is another aspect of the Mennonites' attitude toward their resource environment—deeply rooted in their religious philosophy and their folk psychology—which has bearing on their approach to the serious question of sustained productivity of their land. Among the ultraconservative Mennonite groups represented in Mexico, who have a history of migration every few generations in response to unwelcome impositions by secular governments, there has grown the belief, fostered by their religious leaders and particularly evident among the Altkolonier in Chihuahua, that it is part of the divine plan for them that they should be forced from time to time to forsake their homes and seek another Heimat.[14] Objections to their Privilegium, the exclusiveness of their way of life, and their generally superior economic condition relative to their Mexican neighbors are increasingly voiced in articles, some responsibly written, others merely polemical, in newspapers and periodicals, with the result that the Mennonites have been brought increasingly under public scrutiny. Simultaneously there has once

13. The nonsaline portions of the black-soil areas of the Manitoba, Swift Current, and Hague colonies are an exception; given sufficient moisture, they are still highly productive. Owing to pressure of population, fallowing of a portion of the arable land each year, as was customary in Canada and Russia, has been all but abandoned. Considerable criticism tends to be focused upon persons who do resort to this practice, by Anwohner and the near-landless, who regard it as wrong that badly needed land should be thus withdrawn from cultivation and feel that anyone with such an obvious surplus should relinquish it to those less fortunate.

14. Frequent comparisons are drawn between their migrations and the wanderings of the people of Israel.

more come into being an increasing apprehension of an imminent abrogation of part or all of the Privilegium. Such an eventuality would of course trigger another migration. In the face of such a likelihood, why then leave behind a flourishing land for the benefit of one's persecutors? This is not to suggest that such a consideration has a serious bearing on day-to-day decision-making by individuals. In the long run, however, it impinges significantly on the man-resource relationship. Certainly the entire panorama, viewed in historical perspective, suggests that the farmer of a conservative European peasant culture, availing himself of mechanized tillage and operating in a commercial economy, rather than fitting the image of the inherent conservationist, is by nature an exploiter who ultimately reduces his resource base to that lowest common denominator which permits of few fluctuations.

Adjustment in the Newer Colonies

In their colonies outside of the upland and basin country—at Yermo, Capulín, and Buenos Aires, where irrigation is mandatory, and in Tamaulipas—the Mennonites have, for the present at least, achieved a reasonable adjustment within the framework of available resources. It appears that in these regions, where their traditional concepts of land use and crop culture were not readily applicable, adaptation to the environment and attainment of at least a minimum level of economic viability, following initial difficulties and reverses, have been more quickly achieved than was the case, for instance, in the parent colonies in Chihuahua and Durango following the migration from Canada.

Of the irrigation-dependent colonies, Buenos Aires appears the most favored in terms of water resources. Water from a Mexican reservoir, approximately equal in flow to the capacity of a ten-inch pump, may be had, although not reliably, at a cost of 5 pesos per hour of flow. It augments pumping from the Mennonites' own wells, which runs to as much as six times the cost of water from the reservoir. The cost of water is, indeed, partly responsible for the growing emphasis on the production of cotton, since, although it takes more water to produce it, the returns can be much higher than those from corn or sorghum. Yields as high as 1,600 kilograms per hectare (1,400 pounds per acre) have been achieved at Buenos Aires and Capulín. The average yield, however, is nearer 1,000 kilograms per hectare (880 pounds per acre).[15]

At Yermo, on the fertile desert soils of the Bolsón de Mapimí, cotton has yielded as much as four metric tons per hectare (3,500 pounds per acre). Three tons, however, is regarded as an average crop, and yields of half that amount have occasionally been experienced. One reason for the high yields has been that, in view of the shortage of water and the fact that only fifty-odd hectares are planted by the four colonists who are still irrigating, land is rotated in and out of production, with substantial fallow periods between.

In 1964 a first attempt was made to utilize, for irrigation, run-off waters which sporadically flood flats several hundred acres in extent along the course of the intermittent stream which crosses the colony.[16] Flooding normally occurs each summer, following the few heavy showers which deliver most of the annual precipitation. Sorghum is capable of withstanding both drouth and excess moisture, which are inevitable with flood irrigation, better than corn, and therefore produces higher yields which offset its normally somewhat lower price. Unfortunately the characteristic late-summer precipitation maximum tends to encourage "suckering" (new stalks sprouting from the base of the plant), with attendant losses owing to uneven ripening and delays in harvesting. Initial yields of sorghum on 100-odd acres in production have been on the order of 650 pounds per acre. However, it is hoped that with increasing experience in flood irrigation, better results will be obtained. Mexican farmers in the area, from whom the Yermo colonists

15. These figures are based on the raw weight of the unginned cotton. Approximately two-thirds of this is represented by the seed, one-third by the fiber. The higher yield would be almost a bale per acre, which is regarded as satisfactory also in neighboring areas of Texas and New Mexico.

16. All rights to the waters from this stream belonged to the former owners, Celso and Rómulo Garza Gonzales, and devolved upon the Mennonites when they purchased the land.

learned the technique, occasionally achieve yields as high as 3,500 pounds per acre.[17]

If more successful in the future, this method of sorghum culture should contribute significantly to a broadening of the Yermo colony's economic base and thereby materially aid its survival. Families now without facilities for irrigating may be able to get back into farming, thus reducing the prospects of a further numerical attrition of the already much-reduced colony. Sorghum has particularly important implications for the livestock sector of the colonists' economy. Residues from the crop, unlike those from cotton, are a valuable source of fodder and should foster an increased interest in livestock-rearing and cheese production. In 1965 the cattle population of the colony was less than 200 animals. Supplementary fodder requirements were being met from a few acres of irrigated oats, but there was never enough water to permit much development in that direction. Much of the colony, particularly those areas subject to sporadic flooding, is, however, covered with a more or less sparse growth of a native grass, savaneta (*Muhlenbergia*). Although a few colonists have jointly hired a Mexican herdsman and are pasturing some animals in the western portion of the colony, the grazing potential of the range has been underutilized. If supplementary feed production could be suitably expanded, as now seems possible with flood-irrigated sorghum, it is estimated that a five-fold expansion of dairy and beef production should be possible.[18]

17. Sorghum was introduced in the Yermo-Ceballos area about 1959 by a Texan named Beckman, who was attracted by the region's isolation from other sorghum-growing ventures and planned to produce hybrid seed there.

18. Klaas Heide, Vorsteher, Yermo colony, personal communication. Cheese production in 1965 was approximately 30 kilograms per day (which required 300 liters of milk), much too small for efficiency.

Although parasites are few, the screwworm fly (*Callitroga americana*) does constitute a problem to cattle-raising in all the areas of Mennonite colonization in Mexico. *Callitroga americana* lays its eggs on any open wound. The maggots feed on the flesh of the living animal and prevent healing. The government of the United States has been assisting in combatting this menace by releasing large numbers of sterilized male *Callitroga*. Mating between females and these males results in infertile eggs, which effectively interrupts the insect's reproductive cycle.

In Tamaulipas, at Neuendorf and Hoffnungsfeld, almost all cropping is carried on under temporal (natural rainfall) conditions. Although no crop failures have been experienced during the history of the colonization venture there, the rather high fluctuations in annual precipitation, which ranges from twenty to sixty inches per year, have resulted in large variations in yields. Cotton, which does not need to be irrigated, has become the crop of first importance to the colonists. Since it was first grown by the Tamaulipas Mennonites a few years ago, its yields have averaged approximately 2,750 pounds per hectare, raw weight (1,100 pounds per acre, or two-thirds of a bale, ginned), although yields as high as 7,700 pounds per hectare (3,100 pounds raw, or two bales per acre, ginned) have been realized under favorable rainfall conditions. As a cash crop with an assured market, cotton holds particular attractions for the retirement of land debt.[19] It appears unlikely, however, that a concentration on cotton such as has developed in the irrigating colonies of Buenos Aires, Capulín, and Yermo will occur here, since alternative land-use possibilities are also attractive. The relatively long rainy season permits double-cropping of corn, and total yields as high as three metric tons per hectare (approximately forty-five bushels per acre) have been realized in this way. A planting of beans following corn, or vice versa, is also possible. The preferable procedure is for beans to follow corn, since the latter is better able to withstand the heat of high summer. Grain sorghum planted in June or July is harvested in October and under favorable moisture conditions will yield a ratoon crop which matures in February. On the other hand, cotton, which requires 200 days or more to mature, cannot be double-cropped. Because the postharvest season from December onward is normally too dry for cotton, continuous cropping cannot be implemented either. Wells put down to date have not penetrated any aquifer of adequate yield for irrigation. Impounding of runoff for small-scale irrigation has, however, been successfully attempted and appears

19. The price of cotton has been relatively stable in recent years: 280 to 300 pesos per quintal (100 pounds) for the "strict middling" grade which constitutes the bulk of production.

to offer substantial scope for expansion. Supplementary irrigation could significantly broaden the scope of land-use possibilities; in particular, it could lead to an expanded cultivation of citrus, bananas, papayas, grapes, tomatoes, peanuts, and other tropical and subtropical crops, all of which do well and are already grown in small amounts. Market conditions, however, have been too erratic to encourage concentration upon them.

Neuendorf–Hoffnungsfeld, unlike any of the other Mennonite colonies, has very little livestock. None of the land acquired to date was in grass. Arable land was put in crop at once, and scrub-forest land has been cleared and put under cultivation as quickly as the financial resources of the colonists have permitted. The cattle breeds to which they were accustomed in their former homes in Durango and Chihuahua do not thrive there, while the locally dominant Zebú and Brahma strains are poor milk producers. There is some interest in these breeds, however. Seeded pastures of pangola (*Digitaria decumbens*) and guinea grass have been tried, and pangola particularly appears to hold promise for an amplification of cattle enterprise. Under irrigation, pastures seeded to it can support ten or more animals per hectare (two to three per acre) on a year-round basis. It is highly palatable to cattle, who graze it selectively in the presence of other forage grasses, and is highly digestible.[20] Future expansion of livestock enterprise may be anticipated, particularly as new wealth is released from the retirement of land debt, making it possible for the colonists to engage in endeavors whose potential returns are not realized as soon as those from cash crops.

In this small settlement the Mennonites, for the first time in their Mexican experience, are situated in an environment in which none of the aspects of soil fertility, slope, and amount and distribution of precipitation is so critical as to require sensitive adjustments—such as they have heretofore shown themselves to be largely incapable of devising or unwilling to adopt—if destructive inroads upon the soil resources are to be forestalled. There has

20. R. Milford, "The Nutritive Value of Pasture Plants," in *Some Concepts and Methods in Sub-Tropical Pasture Research* (Oxford: The Alden Press, 1964).

been less delay in the achievement of economic viability than in any of their other colonization ventures in Mexico. The rapid economic progress being made, together with a general lack of opposition to Mennonite land acquisitions in the region, has made this settlement the object of a good deal of interest and attention in the other colonies.[21]

The Forces for Innovation and Change

The gradually increasing readiness which the Mennonites have evinced to avail themselves of innovations has manifested itself most pronouncedly in the acceptance of new crop varieties and, in regions whose environmental characteristics differ sharply from those in the parent colonies, the adoption of new crop types and, where necessary, the implementation of irrigation-dependent agriculture. The overall level of sophistication of techniques employed in the application of factor inputs, and the precision of management in the utilization of resources, however, remain low. Moreover, substantial opportunities to expand the economic base of the colonies, which do not entail a concomitant necessity to broaden the land base, remain underdeveloped or neglected. The causes repose in a lack of capital, a lack of awareness of opportunities inherent in the intensification of inputs to production, and the obstacles presented by the physical and climatic environment. There continues also a traditional preference for extensive rather than intensive farming methods which is rooted, in part at least, in official ecclesiastical discouragement of innovation and technological change. Moreover, effective intensification of land-use practices, to be economically rewarding, requires a knowledgeable approach to fertilizers, irrigation, control of weeds and insects, and the adoption of improved strains of seed stocks. In the irrigation-dependent colonies and in Tamaulipas, where fertile soils

21. Serious attempts, particularly by the Altkolonier in Chihuahua, were being made in 1966 to acquire a substantial tract of land in the Gonzales–Manuel area of Tamaulipas for the establishment of a new colony.

have so far required little specialized management, considerable progress has been made along these lines. Elsewhere, however, less headway is evident.

Yields can be significantly increased through the use of fertilizers and manure. Of the latter, however, there is very little available, despite the substantial emphasis on dairying. Owing to the mild winters, it is seldom necessary to confine the animals. What little manure does accumulate, rather than being placed on the land, is frequently diverted to use as a binding material, replacing straw, in the manufacture of adobe brick. Indeed, so precarious is the situation of some colonists that straw cannot be spared for brick-making because it must be used as fodder. Nor does the economic condition of many permit the use of commercial mineral fertilizers, even if they should desire to do so, the cost—1,500 pesos ($120 U.S.) or more per metric ton—being prohibitive.

Irrigation

Under the highly variable and erratic precipitation regime which characterizes the upland and basin country in which most of the colonies are located, the use of commercial fertilizers, since they represent a considerable capital outlay, requires the implementation of irrigation. However, in this physiographic region, irrigation on any substantial scale is feasible only in portions of the Manitoba, Swift Current, and Hague colonies. At Los Jagueyes, although some wells yield water in quantities sufficient for a moderate scale of irrigation, the soil structure is generally too porous, and water loss into the subsoil consequently too great, to permit its implementation. Elsewhere, as in the Santa Clara, Santa Rita, and Ojo de la Yegua colonies, scarcity of water and the depths from which it must be pumped preclude development of irrigation on any scale.

Irrigation has in fact been practised in the Altkolonier parent colonies from the time the first deep wells were put down in the mid-1920's. Until about 1950 its extent was limited almost entirely to the watering of kitchen orchards and gardens. Without irrigation, orchard trees do not survive. In the Hague colony, where pumping depths are as little as sixty feet, small foreyard plots of alfalfa, an acre or so in extent and watered from the household well, became widely popular as a supplementary fodder source for dairy cattle following its introduction there in 1941. In the Manitoba, Swift Current, and Hague colonies, the total land under irrigation, per farmstead, has not usually been above two acres, this being the approximate maximum area which can be supplied by a wind-motor-driven pump.

The period 1948–1956 in this region was one of almost unrelenting drouth. In only three of those years did annual precipitation approach or exceed the long-term average of fourteen inches.[22] As one crop failure or near-failure followed another, some colonists whose economic condition permitted drilled new wells, installed large motor-driven pumps, and resorted to irrigation on a substantial scale. The expansion of irrigation to include field crops met with some token resistance from Altkolonier church leaders, who took the attitude that the bounty of the harvest should be left to divine discretion, and that indeed attemps at coaxing an "undeserved" yield from the land might invite divine displeasure. Although such factors appear to have exerted little influence on the magnitude of development, the maximum increment to irrigated acreage attained during this time was small. It is doubtful if it ever amounted to much more than 1,000 acres. Shortage of capital no

---

22. Annual precipitation at Grossweide, Campo 112, Swift Current colony, for the period 1948–1956 (in inches) was: 1948—10.8; 1949—16.3; 1950—9.8; 1951—6.5; 1952—9.8; 1953—8.4; 1954—13.8; 1955—13.1; 1956—9.1. (Compiled from records kept by Peter G. Froese.) The Hague colony also experienced severe drouth during the same period.

During the great drouth many of the colonists were reduced to very poor circumstances. When the colonies found themselves incapable of coping with the problems arising out of this situation, appeals for assistance were made to the Mennonites of the United States and Canada. The Hague colony borrowed $5,000 (U.S.) from Manitoba Mennonites to be used for the purchase of fodder so that the hardest-hit of the colonists might be spared from having to dispose of their dairy cattle, since these were regarded as being absolutely essential to eventual economic recovery. The Comité Menonita de Servicios, which is sponsored by the General Conference of Mennonites in the United States and Canada, assisted with seed and provisions, particularly in the colonies in Chihuahua.

doubt was an inhibiting factor. However, even had it not been, it appears doubtful that irrigation development would have much exceeded that which actually did occur. The Mennonites in Mexico, with few exceptions, have consistently evinced a preference for dry farming wherever economic survival has not been absolutely dependent upon irrigation.

Initially, emhasis in the raising of irrigated field crops was focussed on winter wheat and corn, together with small acreages of potatoes for local and regional markets. Under favorable conditions, winter wheat seeded in December produced growth sufficient for supplementary winter pasture. With luck it could be harvested before the onset of the summer rains and then followed by an unirrigated crop of beans, oats, or corn. Over the years, however, experience with irrigation proved less than encouraging. Not infrequently the summer rains interfered with the harvest; on occasion, they came on so strongly and persistently that the crop was lost. Initial yields of irrigated wheat on the black soils were as high as 3,000 pounds (fifty bushels) per acre. It sapped the soil, however, and there was a rapid diminution in the yield of subsequent crops, particularly under double-cropping. Ultimately, in the early 1960's, spring wheats, which were seeded in February or March and hence were subject to a much shorter irrigation season, consequently entailing lower costs because of smaller water demand, replaced winter wheats. Under favorable conditions, they too could be followed by beans, oats, or corn in the same year. However, the levying of a special tax of 35 pesos per hectare on irrigated land, together with imposts on the transport of unprocessed commodities,[23] made attempted expansion of production through the unsophisticated and imprecise methods on which the Mennonites based their irrigation practices economically precarious. In the absence of an integrated technological approach involving carefully calculated applications of water together with fertilization

23. This levy, imposed on unprocessed agricultural and forestry products, is collected by the *forestales* (officers of the Forestry Department) at intervals along all major roads in Mexico. From Cd. Cuauhtémoc to Chihuahua it has been 30 pesos per ton in recent years; from Nuevo Ideal to Durango it has been 40 pesos per ton.

and control of weeds and insects, it proved often impossible to sustain economically rewarding levels of production. The viability of irrigation was further diminished during the period 1959–1961 by progressive increases in the prices for motor fuel charged by the Mexican government petroleum monopoly. Fuel prices more than doubled.[24] As a result pumping costs became prohibitive, and there resulted a rapid diminution of the irrigated acreage within the colonies.

A few growers, mainly in the areas of moisture-retentive black soils, have nonetheless persisted in irrigating field crops. Emphasis has shifted almost entirely to supplementary irrigation of corn during the normal growing period for this crop. Some individuals, particularly in the Hague colony where pumping depths are much less, who have otherwise ceased to irrigate will occasionally apply supplementary water to small acreages in years when a fodder crisis threatens. The total area of field crops remaining under irrigation in the Manitoba, Swift Current, and Hague colonies in a normal year is probably not over 250 acres. In addition there is approximately an equal area, also varying from year to year, of irrigated potatoes. These do most satisfactorily in the lighter soils. In the black-soil zones and in the gravelly adobes there tends to be a high percentage of misshapen tubers, while the more friable sandy soils have a high hydraulic conductivity, water loss into the subsoil beyond the root zone is substantial, and irrigation costs are consequently high. Furthermore, the market, as is typical for perishable crops, is erratic. The Mexican public is not a large consumer of potatoes, and the bulk of the crop must therefore be sold locally. In Chihuahua much of the market potential lies in those colonies—Ojo de la Yegua, Santa Rita, and Santa Clara—in which little or no irrigation water, even for garden plots, is available. Owing to spring frost hazard, which delays planting, the demand from the general market has usually declined by the time the crop can be harvested.

24. Low-octane tractor fuel for the distillate-burning engines predominantly in use in the colonies increased in price from 17 centavos to 37 centavos per liter. Regular-grade gasoline of about eighty octane rose from approximately 40 centavos per liter to 80 centavos. The Mexican government offers no tax concession on fuel used in primary production, as is the case in Canada and the United States.

Orchard Crops

Irrigated land use is expanding, although only in the Manitoba and Swift Current colonies, in the raising of orchard crops, particularly apples, among which Red Delicious and Golden Delicious varieties predominate. Although in the parent colonies apple, pear, quince, and stone fruit trees were incorporated in the kitchen garden almost from the beginning of settlement, and although surpluses from these were sold in the colonies and adjacent market centers, it was not until the 1940's that the first commercial orchards made their appearance. Despite the fact that the valley of Bachíniva, just west of the Swift Current colony, and the region between Canatlán and Santiago Papasquiaro, which includes the Llanos de Guatimapé in which the Hague colony lies, have a long history of orchard farming, this line of endeavor has expanded very slowly among the Mennonites. By 1965 fruit trees in commercial orchards, all of them in the Manitoba and Swift Current colonies, numbered only approximately 12,000. There are several reasons for this low rate of expansion in the face of the predominantly good—even enviable—market and price situation which prevails. It is not unusual for producers to receive 35 to 40 pesos per twenty-kilogram crate of apples. At such prices a mature orchard may annually gross 400 pesos per tree. However, establishment of an orchard involves considerable capital which is tied up for several years before any returns are realized. The resources of many colonists—and their avenues of access to credit—are inadequate for such a commitment. Nor could many easily relinquish the land occupied by a young orchard for the several years that are required to bring it into production.[25] Moreover, there are appreciable natural hazards, particularly from frost and hail, to be reckoned with, and these make it desirable that an orchard form no more than a portion of the economic mainstay of a farm. Basically, however, the reasons for the slow rate of growth in this line of economic endeavor lie in the folk character of the colonists themselves. This

25. Attempts to retain in use land occupied by a young orchard by interplanting with potatoes or other crops until the trees come into production have not generally yielded satisfactory results.

has perhaps been best expressed by one of the colonists: "We are a farming folk, not gardeners." Curiously, in the Hague colony, where innovations in agriculture have met with less official discouragement than has been the case in the Chihuahua Altkolonier colonies, and where the climatic hazards, particularly from frost, are significantly less, and irrigation costs, especially those of pumping, are substantially lower owing to the higher water table, there was not in 1965 a single orchard of a size which can be classed as commercial. This is so despite the fact that thriving orchards belonging to Mexican proprietors abut the colony boundary at several places. Moreover, before the motor truck came into widespread use, Hague colonists used to find autumn employment teaming apples to the railroad for Mexican orchard owners,[26] a situation which surely must have enhanced their awareness of the possibilities inherent in orchard farming.

Interest in orchard farming, following in the wake of the substantial success of earlier ventures and indicated by a high percentage of immature orchards, has nevertheless increased markedly in the past few years. In 1965 and 1966 new orchards totalling several thousand trees were planted in the Manitoba and Swift Current colonies, and a lesser number were planted on Buenos Aires in northwestern Chihuahua.

The same unsophisticated and imprecise practices which have characterized the Mennonites' approach to irrigation of field crops have generally been applied also to orchard management. Soils in the Bustillos basin are boron-deficient, a condition which in apples manifests itself in a "corkiness" of the flesh (*manzana granizada*). With skillful irrigation, applied at the right time and in the correct amount, this can be largely overcome.[27] Mexican nurserymen also point to the lack of proper pruning practices among the Mennonites, which results in trees of poor configuration and branching characteristics. However, a few forward-looking individuals have

26. Report by A. P. W. Klassen in the *Steinbach Post* of October 1, 1947. A man with his own team and wagon received wages of 14 pesos (approximately $2.90 U.S.) per day, plus one box of apples.

27. Victor M. Mendoza, Department of Agriculture, State of Chihuahua, personal communication. Mendoza is in charge of the horticultural division.

recently been seeking the advice of these nurserymen and are consequently improving their management practices.[28]

Peaches, English walnuts, pears, plums, and quinces can be grown with a predictability of success at least equal to that which attends apple production.[29] While the market for peaches and pears has been generally favorable in recent years,[30] as soft fruits they present special problems in storage and shipping. The construction of a large cold-storage plant at Cd. Cuauhtémoc in 1966 should contribute a great deal toward the overcoming of short-term seasonal surpluses of orchard crops and can be expected, almost inevitably, to spur a considerable expansion of horticultural land use in the Bustillos region.

Some Implications for the Future

The limited extent to which irrigation has been developed in those colonies where, although water can be obtained, agriculture without irrigation is possible, has certainly, albeit fortuitously, conserved ground-water resources. Available evidence such as the drying-up of shallower wells owing to draw-down of the water table during periods of sustained pumping from nearby deeper wells, points to the likelihood that no impervious sub-surface strata, separating a series of aquifers, exist. Inasmuch as both the bolsones of Bustillos and Santiaguillo are of enclosed drainage, the volume of water which can be withdrawn without depleting aquifers is limited to the amount of recharge accruing

28. Unfortunately for the dissemination of innovational ideas, those who adopt new techniques are often persons who already are under the ban for other acts of "radicalism" related to economic activities which, under Altkolonier church regulations, are forbidden. Inasmuch as such persons are somewhat in disrepute and subject to shunning, their influence in disseminating new ideas is much diminished from what it might otherwise be.

29. Frosts during blossom time are perhaps the biggest single threat to the orchard farmer in these regions. High adobe walls which have been built around some of the smaller orchards to discourage pilfering also give considerable protection against air-drainage frosts.

30. Plums and quinces are produced in such small quantities that there is no established market for them.

from moisture falling within the basin limits.[31] Certainly in these semiarid regions depletion of ground-water reserves, either totally or to depths uneconomic for large-scale recovery, would appear to be inevitable under any major development of irrigation.

The Mennonites are not now skillful irrigators. Their technology in this sphere is limited, to all intents and purposes, to the pouring of water on the soil. If present practices of water application are long continued in the irrigation-dependent colonies of Yermo, Buenos Aires, and Capulín, the ultimate accumulation of harmful levels of soil salinity would appear to be inevitable. In the basins of Bustillos and Santiaguillo, in view of the high evapotranspiration rates prevailing there, a similar result might be anticipated on lands irrigated for a protracted span of years. In the interests of forestalling soil deterioration and of conserving limited ground-water resources, therefore, it would appear that a small-scale development of irrigation, with emphasis on crops of high potential return but exacting management requirements, could offer an enduring and profitable adjustment to environmental limitations.

The Cheese Industry Today

Another area in which the achievement of greater efficiency in the utilization of material resources could substantially enhance economic returns is the cheese industry. The fact that the Altkolonier prohibit ownership and operation of motor vehicles as a fundamental tenet of ecclesiastical policy has directly influenced

31. CECHISA (Celulosa de Chihuahua, Sociedad Anónima), which operates a large pulp, paper, and viscose mill at Anáhuac on the southeastern limits of the Laguna Bustillos, and which also depends on deep wells for water to conduct its operations, has shown considerable concern regarding the extent of exploitable water reserves in the basin and the possibility of their depletion through expanded use by the Mennonites for irrigation. The company has retained William F. Guyton and Associates, ground-water hydrologists of Austin, Texas, to run well logs in an effort to establish the probable magnitude of the basin's reserves. Estimates are that at present rates of use the recoverable ground water reserves of the Bolsón de Bustillos are capable of sustaining 50 to 100 years' exploitation, taking into account anticipated rates of recharge. (Luis R. Lafon, CECHISA, Anáhuac, Chihuahua, personal communication.)

the distribution and proliferation of cheese factories. Because of the limited distance that milk can be carried by team and wagon without spoiling, it is necessary that at least one cheese factory be located more or less centrally to each three or four villages. The degree of decentralization thus incurred has resulted in many of these enterprises being simply too small—some process as little as 300 kilograms of milk per day—to achieve efficiency. Overhead, particularly for labor, despite prevailingly low wage levels, is therefore inordinately high. According to one private processor with more than thirty years of experience, it is doubtful if any of the factories make a gross profit of as much as 10 percent.[32]

Since only cheddar and, in a few factories, small amounts of process cheese are made, much of the cream could be diverted into the manufacture of butter.[33] However, such a multiproduct approach has been resisted by farmers, who are suspicious of it. The butterfat test, as the basis of determining milk value, was introduced in 1942 or 1943, but it met with serious opposition from the colonists, who refused to believe in its accuracy or validity.[34] Greater precision in the utilization of milk, it is believed, could add more than five million pesos annually to gross revenues from dairying.

Because no bacteria count is taken, there is little incentive toward the implementation of good sanitation practices. By the time

32. In his own business, which appeared better organized than many, two weeks' operation revealed the following details: the cost of milk was 55,156.84 pesos; the cost of milk haulage was 3,635.15 pesos; and the cost of materials was 4,200 pesos, for a total expenditure of 62,991.99 pesos. Through the sale of 5,993 kilograms of cheese at 11.50 pesos per kilogram, he received 68,919.50 pesos in revenues; this figure minus his expenses of 62,991.99 left him with a gross profit of 5,927.51 pesos. To arrive at his net profit, one must deduct the maintenance costs and depreciation of the plant, as well as any wages which the owner, who managed his factory, paid himself.

33. A butterfat content of 2.6 percent, compared to the 3.5 percent or more normally contained, is ample for the production of cheddar-type cheeses of adequate quality. A few factories do make small amounts of butter from cream left over in the manufacture of process cheese. Only three of the thirty-eight factories in the colonies make butterfat content the basis of their milk purchases.

34. Since farmers were (and are) in the habit of taking the top from the previous evening's milking before it is hauled to the cheese factory in the morning, implementation of the butterfat test to determine value would have forced cessation of this practice or meant an appreciable reduction in the price received for the milk.

it is delivered to the cheese factories, much of the milk is sour, particularly in summer. Animals are not tested for diseases such as brucellosis (Bang's), tuberculosis, and undulant fever. Since there are no legal requirements as to the aging of cheese prior to marketing, most of it is sold within two weeks of manufacture. Inasmuch as humans are susceptible to all three of the above-mentioned diseases, the cheese becomes a potentially fertile vehicle for their transmission.[35]

Insect Pests and Weeds

Insect and disease problems in the orchards of the Mennonite parent colonies in Chihuahua and Durango have not been serious. There is some incidence of woolly aphid, coddling moth, rose chafer and nematodes, powdery mildew, San José scale, fire blight, crown gall, and mosaic. While it is to be anticipated that a heightened incidence of pests and diseases would naturally ensue upon any substantial increase in horticultural land use, there is evidence also of a growing awareness of the proper cultural practices for overcoming them.

Insect pests constitute a moderate to severe problem to agriculture in most years. Damage tends to be greatest in dry years when vegetation is not only relatively scarcer but less able to resist the inroads made by pests. Except in the growing of cotton, where the financial commitment is such as to make the use of the best available measures for insect control mandatory,[36] relatively little progress is evident. Effective control would also be very difficult to

35. Typhoid can also be transmitted to humans through inadequately aged cheese. In Canada, three months' aging is required by law, that being regarded as the maximum length of time that the disease organisms retain viability.

36. The most troublesome pests in cotton are the measuring worm (*Alabama argillacea*), pink boll worm (*Pectinophora gossypiella*), corn ear worm (*Heliothis zea*), and boll weevil (*Anthonomus grandis*). Young plants are vulnerable to the cotton aphid (*Aphis gossypii*). The boll weevil is most easily controlled by dusting in the early morning when it is feeding in the flowers. The cotton aphid is vulnerable only to contact poisons. The ear worm can best be combatted with contact poisons at night when the adult moth is attracted to the lights of machinery and is thus brought into the range of the toxic spray. The pink boll worm, because it lives inside the immature bolls, is almost completely invulnerable to both alimentary and contact poisons.

achieve, even with the best available methods, for the most frequently recurring insect threats to crops stem from borer and ear worms and pod worm in corn and beans. Since they attack from inside the plant tissues, they are practically impossible to reach with either alimentary or contact poisons during the larval stage when they are feeding voraciously. In 1964 the Mexican government began distribution of a new corn variety, Cafime, which is less plagued by ear worm than are other varieties. It found immediate acceptance in the Hague colony.[37]

Weeds constitute a serious agricultural problem but are better controlled in the intertilled crops which are characteristic of the irrigation-dependent colonies. Where cropping is precipitation-dependent, the weed problem is often compounded by the haste with which planting is pursued following the onset of the rainy season. The result frequently is poor seedbed preparation, with a high rate of survival of weeds which therefore have a head start and consequent competitive advantage over planted crops. Particularly troublesome under dry-farming conditions are wild sunflower (*Helianthus annuus*), redroot pigweed (*Amaranthus retroflexus*), spiny pigweed (*Amaranthus spinosus*), spiny cocklebur (*Xanthium spinosum*), and Canada thistle (*Cersium arvense*). All

37. Cafime has also been grown in the Manitoba colony under experimental conditions by the Comité Menonita de Servicios, which is sponsored and staffed by the Mennonite General Conference of the United States and Canada. It matures about two weeks later than presently common varieties, which may make it too frost-susceptible to attain general acceptance in the Bustillos and Santa Clara valleys. Under 12.7 inches of rainfall, it has yielded twenty-six bushels per acre on the test plots in the vicinity of Cd. Cuauhtémoc with fertilization at the rate of fifty-three pounds per acre of ammonium nitrate and thirty-eight pounds of superphosphate. Another Mexican variety, Colorado General Cepeda Brecoz, a purple hybrid, has yielded twenty-eight bushels per acre under similar conditions. Its color and hybrid character are against it attaining acceptance, however. (Mr. Philip Dyck, Comité Menonita de Servicios, Cd. Cuauhtémoc, Chihuahua, personal communication.) Non-hybrid varieties such as Cafime, which breed true to type, are much superior to hybrids in a country like Mexico, where the majority of farmers might not be expected to understand the limitations of hybrids as seed stocks beyond the first generation or might not be able to afford fresh seed each year.

Cafime was developed at the Centro Agrícola Francisco Madero northwest of Cd. Durango by the Instituto Nacional de Investigaciones Agrícolas with aid from the Rockefeller Foundation. (Dr. Richard G. Milk, Agricultural Technologist of the Methodist Church, Cd. Durango, personal communication.)

of the foregoing are controllable with the broadleaf-selective herbicide 2-4-D. The use of chemical weed control to date, however, is very limited. In part this is owing to the high cost (15 pesos per acre in 1966 in the Manitoba colony), and in part to a lack of knowledge of proper dosages and methods of application and, in the case of many, a lack of confidence in its efficacy.

Under dry farming wild oats (*Avena fatua*) and wild mustard (*Brassica kaber*) do not constitute a problem. Wild oats, whose moisture content must be reduced to approximately 10 percent (from the 35 percent or so which it contains at the time it drops from the parent plant) before it breaks dormancy, desiccates quickly in the dry months following the rainy season. With the small amounts of precipitation which normally occur in January and February, it rapidly germinates in the warm daytime temperatures already prevailing at that season. It is then either exhausted by the repeated night frosts which persist well into spring or, if it survives these, expires from moisture deficiency long before the summer rains. For these reasons it rarely goes to seed. Under irrigation, however, dormancy may persist through to late winter because of the higher moisture content of the soil, so that germination is delayed until irrigation commences. It is aggressive and produces seed prolifically. Plowing may bury much of the seed below the depth of penetration of the normally light winter rains, thus further contributing to a build-up of seed reserve in the soil.

Wild mustard, which also responds to winter precipitation, normally suffers the same fate of death by frost or drouth, so that although small numbers of plants may go to seed from year to year, its presence does not assume problem proportions. It also seeds prolifically, so that under the impact of irrigation it rapidly becomes a serious problem. It is easily controlled in cereals or corn by the application of as little as two ounces of 2-4-D per acre. This method of weed control cannot be implemented in orchard crops, however, because these are themselves susceptible to the chemical.

A new problem emerging in the Hague colony is an invasion by Johnson grass (*Sorghum halepense*) from irrigating ejidos which adjoin it along its southern boundary. Although Johnson grass has considerable value as cattle feed, it is also a particularly aggressive weed, and although the problem is not yet one of serious proportions, it is feared that it could shortly become so.

The problems encountered with weeds are, in general, intensified by the layout of the Streifenfluren. Whereas originally the Koerl boundaries were represented only by a furrow line, the advent of the binder, which requires a clear span to the right if grain is not to be trod into the ground upon opening of a field, was already causing the lines to be widened in the western Canadian settlements before the Mennonites' departure for Mexico. In Mexico, under the same field system but with the almost universal use of tractors for agricultural draft purposes, boundary width has almost invariably increased to the five or so feet necessary to accommodate their passage. These stripes become weed-infested and serve as starting points for their distribution over the adjacent cropland. Another consideration, of course, in view of prevailing land hunger, is the amount of land uneconomically tied up in Koerl boundaries. In some villages it amounts to as much as 5 percent of the total, or the equivalent of a full homestead.

Incomes and the Creation of Wealth

With the exception of returns to the limited acreages devoted to such land- and capital-intensive crops as tree fruits and cotton, returns to the individual Mennonite farmer's agricultural endeavors, which reflect cultural practices, land capability, climate, and market conditions, are generally not impressive. Although no statistics are kept by any of the colonies which could yield accurate details on returns to labor and investment, information which it was possible to obtain suggests that in an average year the Mennonite colonies produce agricultural commodities to the value of about 95 million pesos (between $7 and $8 million U.S., or about $1,600 per family). This amount breaks down approximately as follows: all field and orchard crops, 60 million pesos; all livestock sold, 10 million pesos; and dairying, 25 million pesos. To this total derived from agriculture must be added approximately 10 million pesos, about equally divided between the cheese industry and other manufacturing pursuits, which accrues as value added through the processing of either local agricultural commodities or imported materials. The total of new wealth created in the colonies would therefore appear to be on the order of about 105 million pesos per year. Approximately one-half of this amount, in the opinion of informed persons, may be regarded as net disposable income. It may be assumed that most individuals utilize subsistence benefits to the value of several hundred pesos annually. Furthermore, a portion of the difference between gross and net income enters the internal economy of the colonies through the provision of goods and services. Per capita income of the 30,000 Mennonites in Mexico[38] therefore would appear to be on the order of 2,500 pesos ($200 U.S.) annually. This amount is of course subject to considerable variation from year to year, depending upon the harvest; at best it represents a close approximation to average conditions and compares with a gross per capita income of approximately 4,500 pesos ($360 U.S.) for Mexico as a whole, and $100 to $125 (U.S.) in rural areas of the country.[39]

There are also considerable differences in per capita income between the several colonies; these are derived mainly from differences in soil quality and water availability. Whereas in a normal year a 160-acre (65 hectare) farm, supporting a family of seven or eight, in the Manitoba, Swift Current, and Hague colonies will produce a net cash income from all sources of approximately 20,000 pesos ($1,600 U.S.), a comparable Ojo de la Yegua farm will produce an income closer to 15,000 pesos ($1,200 U.S.), and a Santa Rita income will be closer to 11,000 pesos.[40] On Los Jagueyes revenues are similar to those realized on Ojo de la Yegua. On Santa Clara, however, where the dairy sector is much less developed, the

38. Church records at the end of 1964 revealed a total population of 30,611. This is subject to slight inaccuracies because of movement between the colonies and imperfect record-keeping. Also, persons under the ban are omitted. Any error would not likely be in excess of a few hundreds, however, since a census was taken in 1962.

39. Information provided by Oficina Federal de Hacienda, Cd. Cuauhtémoc, Chihuahua.

40. The difference between Santa Rita and Ojo de la Yegua incomes can be largely accounted for by the fact that the former colony is still very young, and its cattle population and the related important dairy sector are not yet built up to the desired level. Once this is accomplished, incomes on Santa Rita should approximate those on Ojo de la Yegua.

average net income per 160 acres is probably not above 10,000 pesos per year. Individual incomes of course vary substantially from these amounts, even on farms of similar size. Those of the landless are usually very small indeed.

At La Batea and La Honda, despite environmental drawbacks, present levels of soil fertility on cultivated land are such that revenues from land utilization hold promise of equaling those attained under the existing dairy and field-crop economy of the parent Hague colony.

At Yermo and Buenos Aires irrigators are making some progress in capital accumulation, but debt charges and the high cost of credit, of irrigating, and of combatting insects and diseases tend to keep individual net incomes low on the prevalently small acreages in crop.[41] At Capulín the development of land use is such that many of the colonists still have to live partly off the capital they brought with them.

Only one-third or about 1,400 of approximately 4,070 families in the colonies in Chihuahua and Durango, which are predominantly dependent on dry farming, possess at least a full Wirtschaft of 160 acres.[42] It follows that the majority of the rest—of whom

41. Gross revenues from cotton commonly reach 2,500 pesos per acre at Yermo and 800 pesos per acre at Buenos Aires, based on a price of 280 to 300 pesos per 100 pounds of fiber. At Yermo this can mean a net revenue of 1,200 pesos per acre. The limitation there is shortage of water. Since fixed costs in cotton culture are high, the figure cited for Buenos Aires, while more than covering the expenditures incurred, does not result in attractive net revenues.

42. This statement is based on statistics from the Quellenkolonie, Santa Clara, Santa Rita, Ojo de la Yegua, Hague, and Swift Current colonies, and on an estimate for the Manitoba colony derived from known totals for thirty-two of forty-three villages. The sizes of farms in selected colonies are as follows:

Colony	160 Acres and More	80–159 Acres	Less than 80 Acres	Number of Anwohner
Santa Clara	46	38	13	61
Santa Rita	305	43	0	0
Ojo de la Yegua	295	159	83	95
Quellenkolonie [a]	57	21	46	2
Hague	111	145	186	50[b]
Swift Current	160	141	101	100
Manitoba [c]	462	640	156	532
Totals	1436	1247	585	844

(Notes to table are on p. 246).

over 1,200 families hold from 80 to 159 acres, nearly 600 hold less than 80 acres, and over 800 are Anwohner—normally have less than the estimated income of a full Wirtschaft at their disposal.

Mechanization and Manufacture

Noteworthy under such circumstances of income realization have been the Mennonites' preoccupation with agricultural mechanization and the degree to which this has been accomplished. Although substantial quantities of machinery and implements were brought from Canada by the original colonists or were acquired by them in the United States before they entered Mexico, there were serious shortages almost from the start. Some implements such as moldboard plows did not work well and had to be replaced with equipment more suited to the tillage of the difficult Mexican soils. Major equipment items such as threshing machines and binders have been in short supply throughout the colonies' history, largely because of the investment they represent. Lacking specialized equipment and the capital to purchase it, some colonists early turned to the manufacture of these items. By 1932, bean threshers were being built in numerous smithies in Chihuahua and

---

[a] Includes a number of farms whose owners have left the colony for Canada or British Honduras.

[b] Excludes the 176 Anwohner who reserved land at La Honda.

[c] The Manitoba colony figures are estimates based on known totals of 344 farm units of 160 acres or more, 460 units of 80 to 159 acres, and 116 units of less than 80 acres, as well as 396 Anwohner families; these figures represent complete totals as of the beginning of 1965 for thirty-two of the forty-three Manitoba colony villages. Estimates were arrived at by simple arithmetical extrapolation.

La Honda and La Batea are excluded from the above table. In both colonies the size of a full Wirtschaft has been reduced to 50 hectares (124 acres). Of the 79 families at La Batea early in 1965, 29 held less than 50 hectares. At La Honda the situation in 1965 was too fluid for accurate data to be obtained, inasmuch as there was a heavy flow of migration from the parent Hague colony at the time, and there was also considerable trade in land. However, it can be stated that of the 176 Anwohner families who reserved land there, 126 took from 20 to 25 hectares (50 to 62 acres).

Durango.[43] Improvements made over the years as builders gained experience have resulted in the development of very satisfactory and durable machines. A well-constructed new bean thresher of colony manufacture can be had for 5,000 pesos or less, while a used grain-threshing machine imported from the United States will cost 15,000 pesos or more.

Another piece of equipment which the Mennonites have turned to manufacturing themselves is the hammer mill. The coarse crop residues which must almost everywhere be utilized as fodder are more palatable to animals when finely chopped. This also reduces wastage and helps to stretch often limited fodder supplies.[44] Because of the high speeds at which these machines must run, and the consequent problems of dynamic balance involved, their construction presents more technical difficulties than does that of the slow-running bean threshers. Their manufacture therefore has tended to become concentrated in a few shops which have the necessary equipment and skills at their disposal, although a number of persons have constructed one or a few machines. In 1965 there was a small factory producing hammer mills at Campo 4½, Neureinland, Manitoba colony, another at Campo 67, Lichtfeld, Ojo de la Yegua, and one at Campo 4, Reinland, Hague colony. In addition, a smithy at La Batea was producing about twenty machines per year. Total annual production is about 300 machines. After considerable trial-and-error experimentation, the three major builders are succeeding in producing machines, patterned after popular U.S. makes, which will bear any comparison of functionality and durability. The prices at which they can be placed on the market

43. Report by a correspondent from Campo 35, Altenau (Saucito), Chihuahua, in the *Steinbach Post* of October 20, 1932. Grain threshers can be used for threshing beans if the cylinder speed is reduced to between 500 and 600 r.p.m. from the normal 1,000 to 1,100. Since beans grow close to the ground, they are harvested by being pulled up by the roots or by cutting the stems below the surface with a disc implement. Threshing of beans occasionally results in damage to the cylinder and concaves from stones which adhere to the plants, a risk which owners of the scarce and expensive grain threshers were unwilling to take.

44. In 1965 the colonists at Capulín in northwestern Chihuahua were eking out fodder supplies with hammer-milled tumbleweed harvested from the surrounding semidesert.

are as much as 2,000 pesos below the cost of equivalent U.S.-built machines.[45] The manufacturers are gradually extending their businesses to include customers in the Mexican market outside the colonies. A significant step was taken by both factory owners in the Chihuahua colonies late in 1965 when they exhibited their products under registered trademarks—Estrella Blanca and F.M. (Fábrica de Molinos)—and maintained order offices at a regional industrial fair held in Cd. Cuauhtémoc.

Another area of endeavor which has absorbed considerable effort has been that of answering the colonists' need of vehicles for local transportation. By the early 1930's, the wagons brought from Canada were beginning to wear out. The only replacements readily available on the Mexican market were heavy four- and six-horse *remolques* descended from the ore wagons of the Spaniards. Imported wagon gears cost as much as 500 pesos (over $150 U.S.). Then a much less expensive and in may ways superior type of farm vehicle came into existence. The source of the new vehicles was the numerous Mexican nationals who, by 1933, were being repatriated from the United States. Many of them arrived in automobiles, but once in Mexico they quickly found themselves in much reduced circumstances and unable to continue operating their vehicles. The Mennonites quickly began acquiring these cars, at prices ranging from 150 to 200 pesos ($45 to $65 U.S.). They were stripped down to the bare chassis and a horse pole was attached. The result was a light-draft, well-sprung, pneumatic-tired running gear with a load capacity at least equal to that of the heavier, more cumbersome North American farm wagon; it was useful as a heavy-duty buggy but could be pulled by a light team. Variously fitted with grain tanks, bundle racks, seats, or closed coach bodies reminiscent of the Bennett wagons of the depression days on the Prairies, they answered most of the Mennonites' local transportation needs.[46]

45. Popular makes by U.S. farm-equipment manufacturers normally sell in the price range of 5,000 to 6,000 pesos, while those produced in the colonies cost from 3,000 to 4,000 pesos at retail. Steel is obtained from mills in Monterrey, Nuevo León.

46. The Bennett wagon was named after Prime Minister R. B. Bennett, who headed the Conservative Party whose policies were blamed for much of the severe impact that the depression of the 1930's had upon western Canada. It appears, in-

The engines were frequently put to use as stationary power plants to drive threshers, crushers, and other machinery.

Conversion of automobile chassis into the now ubiquitous *Karrenwagen* (auto-wagons) has continued to supply the bulk of the vehicle market in the colonies. Tandem hitches of as many as four pulled by one tractor are particularly convenient for transporting crops from distant rented lands. They have also become popular among the ejidatarios and colonos of the Bustillos, Santa Clara, Santiaguillo, and adjacent valleys,[47] among whom ownership of such a vehicle has come to convey a certain element of prestige. There is therefore a lively market for superannuated automobiles in these regions. Truck chassis, too, are favored among the Altkolonier, to whom ownership of motor vehicles is forbidden, for conversion into tractor trailers. The price of a well-built Karrenwagen runs from 2,000 to 3,000 pesos ($160 to $240 U.S.), while a heavy gear fashioned from a truck chassis will fetch from 4,000 to 6,000 pesos.

The buggy continues in favor for personal transportation among those who can afford it in addition to the heavier Karrenwagen. Some of those originally brought from Canada are still in use. Since the end of World War II many more have been brought from the former homeland, where they had been displaced by the automobile and could for some years be had very cheaply. The high-wheeled buggy has fallen into disuse among all but the most conservative of the Altkolonier, however. Steel wheels with pneu-

---

deed, on the basis of the best evidence obtainable, that the idea of building wagons out of old automobiles was brought to Mexico by late-arriving Altkolonier from Canada, or possibly by others who returned from visits to their former homes. The Altkolonier continue to be the greatest users of *Karrenwagen*. While permitted to hire motor vehicles, they are forbidden by church ordinance from owning and operating them. The Sommerfelder and Kleine Gemeinde have no ecclesiastical regulation governing ownership and operation of motor vehicles, and commonly have them.

47. There is a considerable trade in Karrenwagen between Mennonites and Mexicans. The latter, who usually lack the shop equipment needed to make the conversion from auto to wagon, continue to obtain them almost exclusively from the Mennonites. In lieu of cash, the sale of a Karrenwagen by a Mennonite to a Mexican not infrequently involves transfer of cropping rights to the latter's land for a specified period of time.

matic tires have displaced iron-tired wooden spoked wheels, which were hard to maintain in the dry climate, and the short-travel leaf-type cross springs formerly used have given way to four-wheel independent suspensions, supported by coil springs or torsion bars, which give an exceedingly comfortable ride under light loads. These light buggy gears are constructed in several smithies in the Altkolonier colonies.

The founders of the Hague colony, who brought much less equipment with them than did their brethren who settled in Chihuahua, had few vehicles besides the absolutely necessary farm wagons. Karrenwagen later became popular there, but many people desired a lighter, one-horse vehicle for personal transportation. Ultimately a light, well-sprung rubber-tired vehicle, smaller than but similar in appearance to the Karrenwagen and taking the place of the buggy, was evolved.

Public Transportation

Public transportation has also made a considerable response to the needs of the Mennonites. This has been particularly so in Chihuahua, where the Altkolonier colonies, which constitute much of the economic hinterland of Cd. Cuauhtémoc, and in which private motor vehicles are all but absent, extend northward for over 100 kilometers from this regional market center. Transportes de Noroeste, a bus company based in Cd. Cuauhtémoc, traverses these colonies with two lines, one across the Manitoba and Swift Current colonies and the other terminating at Campo 82, Steinthal, Santa Rita colony, which offer daily round-trip service to Cd. Cuauhtémoc. In addition, *rápidos*—half-ton panel trucks with seating for nine or ten persons—travel the new highway (completed in 1965) from Cd. Cuauhtémoc to Bachíniva, west of the Swift Current colony, on an hourly basis throughout the day, picking up and depositing passengers and goods at any point along the road. In 1964 the Santa Rita and Santa Clara colonies together completed a one-lane road through the Sierra del Nido to connect with Highway 45 (which runs from Juárez to Mexico City); this eliminated use of the old canyon road by means of which the Sommerfelder originally had access to Santa Clara and shortened the distance to Chihuahua by some forty kilometers. Since that time a daily passenger and package service has operated from Namiquipa, west of Los Jagueyes, via the Quellenkolonie, Santa Clara, and Santa Rita, to Chihuahua. The fact that from Santa Rita the trip is only two and one-half hours, as against six hours for the bus journey to Cd. Cuauhtémoc, has resulted in much of the traffic from Campo 72, Rotfeld, northward being diverted to Chihuahua, which also offers wider selections of merchandise.

In response to a substantial incidence of intervillage travel over distances too great to be quickly negotiated by horse-drawn vehicle, Mexican taxi operators have established themselves in more or less strategic locations. Several automobiles operate out of Campo 107, Burwalde, Swift Current colony, and several more out of Campo 67, Lichtfeld, Ojo de la Yegua colony. It is common also for persons—either on business or for social reasons—to take a bus or rápido to Cd. Cuauhtémoc and then hire a taxi there to complete their journey to a specific destination.

Elsewhere, Mennonite settlement has not elicited a similar response from Mexican entrepreneurs in terms of catering to the demand for public and personal transportation. The Sommerfelder and Kleine Gemeinde Mennonites of course have their own motor vehicles. The other Altkolonier colonies, such as the Hague colony, are either situated near enough to a market center to make the journey with horse-drawn vehicles, or, like the daughter colonies in northwestern Chihuahua and in Zacatecas, they are making use of regional transportation facilities that were already in existence at the time of the colonies' founding.

Agricultural Machinery

The maintenance of machinery and equipment has presented a continuing challenge to the colonists. Most replacement parts have been both chronically difficult to obtain and, relative to agricultural returns, high in price. In response to these conditions, common replacement items have come to be manufactured locally. In 1936 a small foundry was set up in Schoendorf, Campo 115, Swift Current colony, where replacement parts for the generally uncomplicated equipment then in use were produced. This operation has subsequently been expanded to include the manufacture of plow discs and cultivator shovels—for which, owing to rapid wear in the predominantly coarse soils, there is a good replacement market—as well as other durable goods which are fabricated from sheet steel brought from Monterrey. As in the case of the manufacturers of hammer mills, this small industry has been exerting itself to extend its market beyond the immediate region of the Mennonite colonies. Plow discs and cultivator shovels are now manufactured to replacement-part specifications for all common makes and sell at 30 to 40 percent below the cost of comparable articles imported from the United States.

Of greater significance than any other development in the field of mechanization, notwithstanding the important contributions to the material progress of the colonies that the foregoing endeavors have made, has been the almost total replacement of horses by tractors in tillage and field operations. Only a very few tractors were brought to Mexico on the initial migration, and these were used mainly as threshing engines. The changeover to tractors for draft purposes first gained momentum about 1937 and was in response to several simultaneously operative factors. Foremost among these appears to have been concern over chronically recurring shortages of fodder, which often made it difficult to maintain horses in good physical condition. Moreover, at the elevation of the Bustillos, Santa Clara, and Santiaguillo valleys, their stamina, and consequently their work potential, is much diminished. Furthermore, the cheese industry was convincingly proving its importance to the economic viability of Mennonite agriculture. This argued for an expansion of dairying operations which, in view of the precarious fodder situation, could be best achieved through a diminution of the horse population. By 1937 the depression was waning and economic conditions generally were improving. Following the express recognition of the Privilegium by President Lázaro Cárdenas in 1936, the sentiment for an exodus from Mexico began to die out and was slowly replaced by a determination to remain. Elsewhere in the country, however, expropriations against foreign-owned assets were being energetically prosecuted. Among them were American corporate irrigation farms in the region of Torreón, Coahuila. The owners were consequently forced to dispose of their machinery and equipment at whatever prices they could obtain. Mennonites from the colonies in Chihuahua and Durango seized this opportunity to acquire tractors and plows in particular.[48] Meanwhile, also in 1937, individuals from the Chihuahua colonies began to import farm equipment, both new and used, from the United States.[49] This activity continued for several years, into the early 1940's, when, owing to the completion of expropriation proceedings in the Torreón area on the one hand and the diversion of resources in the United States to war production on the other, farm equipment became very scarce.

After World War II, Mennonites from the Chihuahua colonies began once more to comb the used-equipment market in adjoining areas of the United States, occasionally extending their activities into Canada. Since much of Canadian and U.S. agriculture was undergoing something of a revolution in terms of its mechanical equipment in the postwar years, the market in those items which the Mennonites from Mexico particularly wanted—distillate-burning tractors, threshing machines, binders, windmotors, and older implements of almost every description—was very favorable. Despite the effects of the severe drouth which persisted almost uninterrupted from 1948 to 1956, considerable headway continued

48. Irrigated agriculture in the Torreón region was (and is) heavily predicated on the growing of cotton. Except for tractors and plows, therefore, little of the equipment being offered was suited to the Mennonites' farming practices. One side effect of the Mennonites' activities in Torreón appears to have been the entry of buyers from that city into the commodity and produce market of the Hague colony. Another has been the development of a favorable prejudice toward Torreón as a center where a good selection of equipment and repair items is reliably available. From the time of their first equipment acquisitions there, the Hague colonists, although they have to travel via Cd. Durango, have made their major purchases in Torreón.

49. In 1937 one Mennonite also imported a carload of new disc plows and wagon gears from Canada (John Deere, Brantford, Ontario).

to be made in agricultural mechanization. In part it was progress forced by an epidemic of equine encephalitis (sleeping sickness), which decimated the remaining horse population in 1952. By 1954, some 75 percent of all agricultural field operations were being carried out with tractors.[50] Ten years later the figure had risen to almost 100 percent.

In view of prevailing levels of income, the cost of mechanization has been high. That it has been achieved at all may be ascribed in large measure to the frugality—the lack of conspicuous consumption—which is basic to the conservative Mennonite way of life and permits diversion of surprisingly large percentages of income to purposes of capital creation. Freight, middlemen's profits, and various levies and charges involved in the importation procedure frequently bring the final price of equipment to three or more times the cost at the point of purchase.[51]

Special permits which allow a low entry tariff are available on an individual basis when farm equipment is imported by—or directly for—the final user. The Quellenkolonie (Kleine Gemeinde at Los Jagueyes) has created a cooperative which maintains a truck and personnel to shop the used-equipment market in the United States for machinery ordered by the colonists. Tariffs, costs of haulage, and a surcharge of approximately 15 percent to cover miscellaneous costs and wages are added to the basic acquisition cost to arrive at the price charged to the colonist.[52] Any residual profits are paid into the colony treasury. As a result of this arrangement, the price of used farm equipment imported from the United States

50. Dr. Walter Quiring, "Wir Erleben Mexiko," *Steinbach Post,* January 20, 1954. Dr. Quiring has published several books on Mennonite colonization in Russia and South America.

51. In 1966 a power binder in excellent condition which cost $150 in the United States sold for 8,000 pesos ($640) in the Manitoba colony. Older distillate-burning tractors (mainly John Deere), which can be had very cheaply in the U.S., normally sell for 7,000 to 15,000 pesos ($560 to $1,200 U.S.), depending on model, condition, and size, in the Mennonite colonies.

52. Permits covering a few extra pieces of equipment are commonly drawn to allow the colony to take advantage of bargain opportunities which may arise and to reduce unit haulage and personnel costs by assuring a full load on each trip. Equipment thus acquired is sold on the same basis as that imported strictly to order.

has been reduced to little more than half that charged by private importers. No similar organization exists or has been attempted in any of the other colonies. There, import permits covering anticipated need are commonly drawn by the Vorsteher, who turn them over to individuals on request. Private entrepreneurs have taken on the function served by the Quellenkolonie cooperative. Prices charged for equipment imported on this basis are considerably higher than those which farmers in the Quellenkolonie commonly pay. So attractive has this trade in machinery become that there are now several small groups of Mennonite entrepreneurs who specialize in canvassing the market in the United States and expediting importations into Mexico. A number of equipment dealers in Texas and New Mexico have informal arrangements with these groups and try to cater to the demand emanating from the Mennonite colonies south of the border, a demand which for economic reasons is largely focussed upon a class of equipment which cannot readily be disposed of at other than sacrifice prices in the United States. A few Altkolonier have taken up residence in Texas and California to further expedite the acquisition and movement of desired equipment items. The range of these items has broadened substantially in recent years to include tools and machines for the few small industries in the colonies, electric generator sets, irrigation pumps, and diesel engines; much of this equipment either comes from U.S. Armed Forces surpluses or has been retired from oil-field service. One of the Altkolonier now living in the United States and engaged in this business estimated that the value of the imports of machinery, implements, and related equipment for the Mennonite colonies in Chihuahua has been in excess of 5,000,000 pesos annually in recent years, based on the delivery price in Mexico.

The completion of the Chihuahua–Pacific Railway (Ferrocarril Chihuahua al Pacífico) in 1961 has opened up another source of farm equipment to the colonies in Chihuahua. This railway runs from Eagle Pass, Texas, via Chihuahua and Cd. Cuauhtémoc, across the Sierra Madre Occidental; it then follows the valley of the Rio Fuerte in descending the Pacific slope to its western terminus at Los Mochis in the state of Sinaloa. It thus provides easy access from Chihuahua to the regions of intensive irrigated commercial agriculture upon which the economies of the cities of the Pacific coastal plain—Los Mochis, Fuerte, Navojoa, Cd. Obregón, and others—are based. Because of its intensive agriculture, this region is a good source of used agricultural equipment. Moreover, it is now actually more accessible to most of the colonies in Chihuahua than are the adjoining American states, and buying equipment there does not involve any of the particulars that importation from the U.S. involves. It is therefore relatively easy for an individual to go to the Pacific coast, inspect and purchase the equipment he wishes, and return with it to Cd. Cuauhtémoc by rail, all in the space of a few days.[53] Since no middlemen need be involved, the savings over importation of the equivalent article from the United States can be substantial.

The Hague colony in Durango, although able to tap the equipment market in Torreón, has been less fortunately situated with respect to accessibility to sources of farm equipment which is within the colonists' economic reach. There are noticeably fewer major equipment items—tractors, binders, threshing machines—in the Hague colony than in its sister Manitoba and Swift Current colonies. Moreover, what equipment there is tends to be older than that in the Chihuahua colonies. Indeed, it is not unusual for machines traded in on newer models by colonists in Chihuahua to find their next owners in the Hague colony.

Characteristically, the effective demand for tractors in the Mennonite colonies has concentrated on used machines of older, relatively uncomplicated design and of proven durability (two-cylinder John Deeres and four-cylinder Farmalls are most favored),

---

53. Particularly attractive bargains can occasionally be obtained as a result of the liquidation of assets of communally run irrigation ejidos to reduce heavy commitments to the Banco Ejidal, through which ejidos obtain financing. Not infrequently these ejidos invest in expensive machinery which, because of lack of properly trained personnel to operate and maintain it, deteriorates quickly in use or is cannibalized for repairs to other machines. The Mennonites have learned to look for such disabled equipment, which can as a rule be bought cheaply, and then to carry out the necessary repairs, often with parts obtained from the United States.

which are designed to burn inexpensive low-grade petroleum distillates ("Tractolene") and for which replacement parts can be most readily obtained. Since their manufacturers ceased production of such models at least ten years ago, it is becoming increasingly difficult to obtain them in reasonably good condition on the used-equipment market in the United States. Gasoline models are readily available, but the cost of fuel for them—80 centavos per liter as against 37 centavos for "Tractolene"—is prohibitive. They can be altered to burn distillates, but only at considerable expense. Propane- and butane-burning tractors are also in good supply in nearby states of the U.S. Fuel for them is readily available in Mexico, at a cost comparable to that of distillates. However, the highly volatile nature of propane and butane makes sophisticated (and expensive) refueling equipment mandatory. A change to diesel-powered tractors, which efficiently consume cheap (34 centavos per liter) fuel oil, is regarded as the most desirable transition. It is only in recent years that they have become really numerous in U.S. agriculture, however. Their cost when new is considerably higher than that of equivalent gasoline models, and this fact is reflected in their price on the "used" market as well. Although durable if properly serviced, they are more expensive to repair. New models in the power range capable of handling a four- to six-disc plow cost upward of 50,000 pesos, a price which is beyond contemplation for all but a few of the most wealthy of the colonists. The situation can be expected to improve in a few years' time, however. Since the majority of agricultural tractors sold in the United States during recent years have been diesels, increasing numbers of older models, at a price which is within the means of the colonists, can be expected on the market before long. For a few more years, though, in view of the fact that most colonists are interested in older machines designed for specific types of fuel, some difficulties can be anticipated in meeting their particular demands.[54]

54. One effect of this situation has been to maintain the price of distillate-burning tractors at a high level. Such a tractor, purchased second-hand four or five years earlier and maintained in good condition, would sell in 1966 for at least as much as the price initially paid.

Agricultural and Other Credit

A continuing impediment to progress in agricultural mechanization and in other aspects of life in the Mennonite colonies is the lack of adequate avenues of credit. Although the Waisenämter control capital, representing estates held in trust for widows and orphans, which may be lent at 6 percent interest, this is greatly inadequate for the needs of the community. Because the majority of the colonists enjoy possession of their land only in right of scrip issued by colony authorities, its use as collateral in extra-colonial transactions is impossible. In order to forestall the possibility of foreclosures and the passing of lands into the owner-ship of outsiders—or, conversely, of the colonies being forced into the position of having to redeem mortgaged lands to prevent such eventualities [55]—colony leaders have consistently refused to permit land to function as collateral to outside lenders. Only persons who hold private title to land—those, for instance, who own off-colony "Mexican" farms—are therefore in a position to avail themselves of this avenue of credit. Long- and medium-term credit is practically inaccessible to the vast majority of the colonists. Short-term chattel bank loans to cover crop-production expenses and minor capital acquisitions are therefore the most common form of credit utilization. The conventional term for loans of this type is ninety days, with interest at 1 percent per thirty-day period. Since it is not often possible to produce and market a crop in so short a term, renewals are commonly necessary; in this case the rate of interest rises to 1.5 percent per thirty days, or to roughly 18 percent per annum.[56] Considerable pressure was brought to bear on Vorsteher

55. When a person nevertheless gets himself too deeply into debt, the policy is to declare the debtor bankrupt and sell off his land to persons qualified to acquire colony lands under the terms of charter of the original holding companies and then pay off his creditors. Any residue is paid to the dispossessed person. Not only is ownership of colony lands by outsiders thus effectively prevented, but lenders are limited to principal plus interest in the amounts they can collect. Persons who are colony members in good standing are not, of course, limited in this way; as lenders they may freely foreclose on property for arrears of debt.

56. Such high interest rates, of course, tend to force the sale of crops as soon as they are harvested in order to retire loans; this is at a time when the market

and other influential persons in the colonies in 1965, when the Alliance for Progress (Alianza para el Progreso), acting through the Banco de México, offered development loans to Mennonite colonists for terms of up to five years at 6 percent annual interest, subject to the proviso, however, that their land stand as surety. A considerable number of persons appealed to colony leaders for a relaxation of policy to make borrowing of Alliance for Progress funds possible. No such concession was made.[57] Quite a number of persons who own land off the colonies have, however, availed themselves of such loans, letting their land stand as surety.[58]

---

is normally at its lowest point for the year. Other credit arrangements which the colonist-farmers can make are even more expensive. Advances of seed from grain merchants normally bear interest at the rate of 25 percent of value given for each three-month period. Cotton against which advances have been made by ginners is paid for at the rate of 10 pesos per quintal (about 3.5 percent) below the market price; in addition, there is a 1 percent per month interest charge on the principal amount of the advance.

57. According to one of the Vorsteher involved, two reasons were basic to their refusal to make possible the borrowing of Alliance for Progress funds. One was a feeling that the creation of such an opportunity would result in a flood of irresponsible borrowing. The colony authorities would then ultimately find themselves forced to redeem mortgaged properties in order to maintain the colonies' "territorial integrity." The other reason was a suspicion that the Alliance for Progress offer was somehow part of a strategem by bankers and businessmen to eventually break down the colonies' aloofness by creating conditions under which their lands would become a common commodity.

The Alliance for Progress was created under the auspices of the late U.S. President John F. Kennedy to provide development funds free of interest to Latin American countries. In Mexico it operates through the agency of the Banco de México, which investigates loan applications, supervises the disbursal of funds, and administers repayment. For these services it applies a charge of 6 percent against the unpaid balance of loans.

58. The relatively long repayment period on Alliance for Progress loans permits their use for development of delayed-return ventures such as the establishment of new orchards. However, although repayment terms can be arranged under which the heaviest payments fall due in the terminal years of a loan, a substantial retirement of principal—15 percent or more on a five-year loan and commensurately more on those made for shorter terms—plus accrued interest is required to be made even in the first year. Unless a person commands substantial additional productive capital with which to retire the initial installments, therefore, no long-term investment with delayed returns can really be chanced. Alliance for Progress loans are not available for purposes of land acquisition, since it is reasoned that permitting their use for such a purpose would merely tend to inflate land prices without serving any basic productive function. (They can, however, serve to release other capital, which may then be devoted to land acquisitions.)

The Kleine Gemeinde of the Quellenkolonie has to a large extent forestalled the severe shortage of credit with which the other Mennonite colonies are plagued. From Canada they brought with them a familiarity with the nature and function of credit unions. In Mexico they have established an aid society (Hilfsverein) which was initially endowed with 1 to 1.5 percent of each member's estate —the lesser amount from the poorer colonists, the higher from the more well-to-do. In practice, this society functions as a non-profit depository and lending institution, paying interest at 4 percent per annum to depositors and charging the same rate to borrowers. To strengthen the capital fund, a new endowment is levied each ten years, with persons who have sustained net financial reverses during the preceding decade being exempted.

Another avenue of credit which the Kleine Gemeinde has opened to its members is provided by their cooperative cheese factory. Farmers desirous of enlarging their dairy herds can have the Quesera Jagueyes pay for the animals; it will then deduct their cost in regular installments from payments for milk deliveries. This is of particular benefit to young farmers whose capital is often too limited to establish a dairy herd. A goodwill fund (Gemeindespeicher) is also maintained; those whose crops have been a near or total failure, yielding three bushels or less per acre, may in the succeeding year draw seed from the fund free of charge. These provisions, by extending assistance in critical areas, have done much to spare the Kleine Gemeinde the kind of destitution into which numerous Altkolonier and Sommerfelder families tend to pass either because they cannot muster the capital necessary to establish economic viability or because their crops have failed.

Business and industry in the colonies—represented by some forty general stores, fifteen machinery and implement suppliers and associated repair facilities, five dealers in lumber and building materials, two sawmills, two foundries (one of which also manufactures plow discs and cultivator shovels), four feed mills, a rolled-oats factory, two furniture factories, three hammer mill factories, and thirty-eight cheese factories—also have chronic difficulties both in obtaining adequate credit and in meeting the high cost of borrowing. Commercial properties situated on land to which private ownership is vested only in right of scrip issued by the colonies cannot, as is the case with colony real estate generally, be used as collateral. The only common avenue of borrowing for businesses therefore is through chattel loans secured by movable property.[59] General stores, however, can normally obtain at least short-term credit from suppliers.[60]

Their own inadequate access to avenues of borrowing in turn makes it difficult for business to extend credit to their customers [61] or to expand their operations. In the absence of individuals capable of obtaining adequate financing, recognized needs have frequently been answered through the pooling of capital. Thus, fourteen of the thirty-eight cheese factories are now owned and operated either as producer cooperatives or extended partnerships. A rolled-oats factory and associated feed mill were founded in Gnadenfeld, Campo 2-B, Manitoba colony, in 1959 as a limited stock company, Elaboradora de Avena, S. de R. L.[62]

59. One strategem which is being employed by a few of the larger businesses in the colonies, and which is contrary to the intent if not the letter of colony regulations, is to obtain operating and expansion capital by taking in Mexican investors as silent partners.

60. This is not so at La Batea, La Honda, Buenos Aires, and Capulín. The small general stores which have been established there had no wholesale connections in 1965. They simply purchased their stock, usually at a discount of 10 percent, from retail establishments in Fresnillo (La Batea), Río Grande (La Honda), or Nuevo Casas Grandes (Buenos Aires and Capulín).

61. The cheese industry is a case in point. Because of the coarse quality of much of the available fodder, coupled with the heavy overall dependence of farmers on milk sales, the feeding of supplements such as cottonseed meal has become quite general. As a convenience to farmers, most of the cheese factories have taken to stocking the meal, permitting it to be taken on credit against forthcoming deliveries of milk. As a further service, and because it is a reliably fast-moving item, many of them also stock flour, which may be taken on the same basis as cottonseed meal. The result has been that many milk suppliers chronically draw more meal and flour than their deliveries of milk will cover, and are therefore constantly in arrears. The cheese factories find it hard to carry these delinquent accounts, but they must face the prospect of a cessation of deliveries from suppliers like these if further credit is refused.

62. S. de R. L. (Sociedad de Responsibilidad Limitada) is the equivalent of "Co. Ltd."

Nonagrarian Functions and Ideological Position

In view of the large distances and the time involved in getting to urban centers, village general stores, as their numbers suggest, have come to dot the colonies, particularly in the Bustillos and Santa Clara valleys of Chihuahua. Unlike other lines of business, the store is a traditional feature of the Mennonite village and was common in Canada and South Russia before the Mennonite groups now in Mexico left those countries. There has therefore been little if any opposition to them from religious leaders, despite the fear that engaging in commercial activity might be regarded as a breach of the Privilegium which could be seized upon by Mexican authorities as cause for its abrogation.[63] Some of them have developed certain specialty lines, such as medical supplies or yard goods, for which they have come to be known throughout the surrounding region. The village stores also serve as outlets for local products such as cheese and beef sausage,[64] which enjoy a good market in the colonies as well as outside.

Industries—the hammer mill factories, the rolled-oats factory, and the sawmills, whose main product is pre-cut materials for the manufacture of crates for the regional orchard industry and the fruit and vegetable producers of the Pacific slope—much of whose potential market lies outside the colonies, have been subjected to considerable ecclesiastical discouragement. This is directed more toward the nature of some of the adaptations and input factors considered by their owners to be necessary to these endeavors than toward industry per se, although there is some concern also that their existence might be construed to constitute a breach of the Privilegium. Unlike the cheese factories, whose market situation

63. Partly to protect the colonies against such an eventuality, their own authorities, who collect all taxes on farm income and land, refrain from performing the same function with respect to businesses, thus making the point that these are operating outside colony jurisdiction.

64. Two small private abattoirs—one at Campo 6-B, Rosenort, and the other at Campo 18, Osterwick—in the Manitoba colony produce this sausage, Salchicha Menonita, which is sold both in the colonies and in Mexican market centers of the region.

generally is such that they have little need to actively promote their products, these others must do so. To their operations the owners tend to consider the use of electricity, the motor truck, and the telephone essential. Although the generating of electricity by small engine-driven private plants is now permitted,[65] connection to the state power grid, even where this would be convenient, is forbidden. Ownership and operation of motor vehicles [66] and the installation of telephones are also strictly prohibited to all Altkolonier. Such considerations have on occasion had serious repercussions upon extended partnerships or companies; there have been cases where one faction of associates has chosen to implement innovations, while another faction, more mindful of ecclesiastical ordinances, has held back and has ultimately withdrawn its capital to avoid conflict with both its partners and the Gemeinde. The effect to date has been that the majority of the most progressive and inventive among the Altkolonier have been subjected to excommunication. They do not believe, however, that they can afford to relinquish the innovations for which they were placed under the ban, a necessary step before they can sue for reinstatement. In the hope of avoiding further discord and, at the same time, of improving their locational position, three of the largest manufacturing concerns in the Altkolonier colonies in Chihuahua have formulated tentative plans to relocate outside colony boundaries at Quinta Lupita, some four kilometers northwest of Cd. Cuauhtémoc. If such a development actually occurs, more than twenty men presently employed by them will also have to move or give up their jobs.[67] In view of the limited alternative employment opportunities available and the anticipated small likelihood that much of the present labor force could (or would) remove to the

65. In the Chihuahua Altkolonier colonies the domestic use of electricity for illumination and other amenity purposes is now also permitted. In the Hague colony it is still restricted to utilitarian use in machine shops and the like.

66. Some storekeepers and others who felt the use of a private business vehicle to be imperative to their economic interests have avoided church discipline by registering it in the name of a Mexican employee whom they then retain as driver.

67. It is of interest to note that the three villages in which they were located in 1965 had thirty-three families of Anwohner, many of whom derived their livelihoods from these industries.

263

proposed new location, the economic and social problems of the villages affected would be intensified. Since the present official attitude toward the innovations held to be indispensable to the growth of manufacturing industries (as distinguished from processors of locally produced commodities, such as the cheese industry) shows little likelihood of substantial modification in the near future, it appears probable that the Altkolonier colonies may derive little benefit from such nonagrarian economic development as may occur.

Chapter 9

Institutions and Forms

Central to the life of the Mennonite colonies is the concept of the Gemeinde. Among Mennonites in the United States and Canada, this term refers to the church community alone, but in Mexico, because of the exclusive nature of the colonies under the Privilegium, it signifies both the church and the secular community since in terms of their populations these are essentially the same. In keeping with the concept of segregation of church and "state," ecclesiastical and secular functions are performed by separate bodies of officials. In practice, however, secular affairs are conducted in accordance with church policy.

The Central Role of the Church

The basic areal units of church administration are the individual colonies, each of which has its own Elder and lay ministers who normally serve only that colony.[1] Among the Altkolonier a new colony will normally form a separate Gemeinde, with its own Elder and ministers, within two years or so after its founding.[2] As a rule, at least one minister takes part in any new colonization venture. Experience—as at Saltillo and elsewhere—has shown the presence of a representative of the church to be essential in stimulating a solid commitment on the part of participants to

1. Both the Kleine Gemeinde and the Sommerfelder have small "dependencies"—the former has the small colony at Yermo and the latter has the settlement in Tamaulipas—which are served either regularly (Yermo) or occasionally (Neuendorf–Hoffnungsfeld) by visiting ministers.

2. Buenos Aires and Capulín in northwestern Chihuahua, partly because of their small numerical strength and partly because of their relatively close proximity to each other, have formed a joint Gemeinde.

make a new colonization venture an enduring one. The Elder of such a new Gemeinde is selected for his proven adherence and devotion to traditionalism in both ecclesiastical and secular affairs. In consequence, although new colonies are settled predominantly by younger people who might be expected to be relatively open to new and different ideas, the rate of social change there cannot be said to be greater than in the parent colonies. A substantial level of communication within and between the several Altkolonier Gemeinden is maintained.[3] Local church matters are dealt with at a general meeting (Bruderschaft) of the men of the Gemeinde concerned. Matters of general concern are discussed at joint meetings of the Gemeinden affected. The uniformity of custom and adminstrative forms prevailing in the several colonies, which emerges from this substantial communication, has a great deal of bearing on the intercolony mobility of the Mennonite population. Because an essentially similar social milieu is encountered in every colony, little adjustment is necessary, and people move freely, and frequently without prior investigation, to other colonies.

The Maintenance of Orthodoxy

The Altkolonier church, as has been frequently suggested in foregoing chapters, has very considerable powers in the formulation and implementation of its policies, many of which impinge directly upon the secular life of the individual and the community. Each village has an appointed summoner (vernacular: *Kroagha*) whose duty is to detect and ascertain the particulars of behavior or innovations which are at variance with the official church position and to report such matters to the clergy. The latter then visit the alleged offender and, if the infraction is slight, remonstrate with him in the hope that he will mend the dispute, renounce the unorthodox practice, or dispose of the luxury or

3. Official contact between the original founding Manitoba, Swift Current, and Hague colonies is normally much less close than that between parent and daughter colonies. However, on matters of general concern, particularly threatened incursions upon the Privilegium, all the Altkolonier Gemeinden act together, even if all of the colonies are not directly affected.

other "worldly" innovation which brought him to their attention. If the offence is serious or is repeated, the individual is instructed to appear at one of the periodic open Thursday hearings (vernacular: *Donnadagh*) [4] held by the Elder and clergy to deal with such matters. At the Donnadagh the particulars of the case are reviewed, and if the charges originally brought by the Kroagha are substantiated, the accused is instructed to abjure the forbidden practice or face excommunication. If the ban is applied, reinstatement can then be obtained only after the accused has set right the matter in question and begged the pardon of the Gemeinde. The Sommerfelder and Kleine Gemeinde have equivalent provisions for the maintenance of orthodoxy in the religious and secular life of their communities, but, since they have fewer proscriptions pertaining to secular matters, the incidence of this type of disciplining is much lower among them than among the Altkolonier.

Secular Administration

The administration of secular affairs is also based upon the individual colony and is conducted by elected officials. Heading each colony is the Vorsteher, equivalent to a general superintendent, whose function is to integrate its "municipal" affairs; he is concerned with levying and collecting taxes, the construction and maintenance of roads and drains, overseeing the operation of the Waisenamt, keeping records of land ownership, and dealing with the "world" (government or individuals) in colony matters such as land acquisitions, the formulation of tax agreements, and the like. He also acts as arbitrator and, if necessary, judge in disputes over property between colonists. Although elective, the office of Vorsteher tends to be semipermanent, with the incumbent normally retaining the position until retirement from active participation in colony affairs.[5] He has an assistant, also elected, whose function

4. The word also means, literally, "day of thunder" and is occasionally so used in a rather nervously joking manner, particularly by persons who have undergone a summoning before this essentially ecclesiastical court.

5. The former Vorsteher of the Manitoba colony, now retired, held the office for seventeen years.

may be described as that of vice-Vorsteher; he serves to reduce the Vorsteher's very considerable work load and also insures the presence of a person thoroughly informed on colony affairs in the event of the Vorsteher's absence.

An integral element of colony operations is the mutual fire insurance (*Brandordnung*) program, first implemented in Russia, under which buildings and chattels may be insured against damage or loss by fire only.[6] Presiding over the Brandordnung is a fire marshal and general manager (*Brandschulze*). He is represented in each village by a person delegated to write coverage, collect premiums, and investigate claims. Daughter colonies normally participate in the Brandordnung of the parent colony for the first several years of their existence before establishing their own.[7]

The basic unit in the administrative hierarchy of the colonies (except in the Kleine Gemeinde's Quellenkolonie, which has only a central administration) is the individual village. It is headed by an elected *Schulze* (vernacular: *Schult*), whose office is roughly equivalent to that of mayor.[8] In council (vernacular: *Schultenbott* or *t'Schulten*) with the landowners (*Wirte*), he conducts the internal business of the village: he hires the herdsmen, establishes and collects local school and other levies, collects "colony" taxes for delivery to the Vorsteher, sets the statute labor for the village's share of work on roads and drains, delegates persons to plow protective firebreaks after harvest, and the like.

6. Buildings and movable property are insured for two-thirds of their value. Most losses appear to result from fires caused by lightning, which also kills numerous farm animals each year. Since most buildings are constructed almost entirely of noninflammable materials, major fire losses are rare, a fact that the prevailing low premium rates of 10 centavos per 100 pesos of coverage reflect. (The Quellenkolonie Brandordnung rate, however, is 20 centavos per 100 pesos.)

7. Ojo de la Yegua, for instance, established its own Brandordnung in 1949, three years after its founding. In 1965 La Honda and La Batea continued to participate in the Brandordnung of the parent Hague colony. The total amount insured in 1965, in buildings and chattels, in all of the colonies was approximately 170 million pesos ($13,600,000 U.S.). Despite the uncompromising attitude taken toward excommunicants in other matters, they are freely permitted to continue subscribing to the Brandordnung.

8. The position of *Schulze*, unlike that of the Vorsteher, rotates on a regular—usually two-year—basis, and normally each *Wirt* is expected to take a turn at these duties.

The Altkolonier village enjoys considerable autonomy in the planning and management of its affairs. Aside from the matters mentioned above, the village council determines the conditions under which the landless (Anwohner) are permitted to live in the village; that is, it determines who is eligible, whether or not some form of rental will be charged for the yard place and grazing right in the pasture (*Anwohnerstelle*) alloted an Anwohner, and the assessment to be made against them to help defray school costs. It also determines on what basis partial sales of farm units may be made,[9] decides whether a person who wishes to take up residence in the village on rented property may do so,[10] and, through the Schulze, administers the provision of welfare to the indigent.

This relative independence of initiative has resulted in several innovations upon the structure of the Strassendorf and its Flur. The increasing incidence of landlessness, particularly in the parent colonies, has resulted in the development of large Anwohner "suburbs" in the communal pastures, either in a line with the orientation of the village or at right angles to it. Resentment against this phenomenon has been growing among the farm proprietors (Wirte) of many such villages. Not only are they relinquishing their rights to land, often without compensation, in the communal pasture to accommodate the Anwohner's building lots, even though they are often unable to provide land for their own children, but the Anwohner's cattle also have first access to the already inevitably overcrowded pasture and keep the adjacent area thoroughly grazed down. The animals belonging to the Wirte must therefore travel to the remotest portions of the pasture—often a journey of two miles or more—to graze. Because of this, some Wirte, claiming the cattle need more fodder to get to and from the grazing area than they can pick up there all day, no longer send their cattle out. There is therefore a considerable and growing inclination on the part of Wirte in many villages whose pasture lands

9. Some villages permit sales of individual Koerls, while in others any sale of land must involve equal fractions of all Koerls, including the Hauskoerl.

10. The authority vested in the village with respect to renting is most frequently invoked against excommunicated individuals who under colony regulations are barred from purchasing land.

are potentially arable to set aside a block for the existing Anwohner population and turn the rest into cropland. Since many of the pastures are in very bad condition owing to overgrazing, with heavy infestations of unpalatable weeds and woody shrubs, it can be forcefully argued that the land would then be much more economically productive than at present. Moreover, it would forestall further encroachment by Anwohner, who might well be left altogether destitute by such a development, however. One village, Campo 20, Schoenwiese, Manitoba colony, anticipated the Anwohner problem before land scarcity became severe. One-half of its pasture was converted into cropland, and the stipulation was made that no Anwohner would be accommodated on the remaining portion.[11]

Up to the present, majority Wirte opinion in other villages of the Chihuahua colonies has favored maintaining the status quo, and no breakup of communal pastures has as yet been undertaken. In several areas, however, in new colonies or where new villages have been founded, although grazing land may now be in communal use, individual pasture Koerls were created at the time of the founding, with provision for the assumption of private use at such time as the majority of Wirte opt for it. Campo 5, Gruenthal, Manitoba colony, which although platted in 1923 was not occupied until about 1940, appears to have been the first newly created village to adopt private pastures, apparently in emulation of nearby villages of the Swift Current colony whose Fluren were reconstituted following the foreclosures of the early 1930's. Whether deliberately so planned in every case or not, the effect attendant upon abandonment of the concept of the communal pasture is not only to remove the question of Anwohner admissibility from the jurisdiction of the Schultenbott but to dismiss altogether the possibility of the village developing an Anwohner appendage. Landless families in such villages are usually limited to the married children of Wirte living with their parents.

11. In 1965 the village had two landless families; these consisted of married children living at the homes of their parents. Much of Schoenwiese's potential problem of landlessness has simply devolved upon neighboring villages, particularly in cases where its residents have married there. If of the Anwohner class, they naturally gravitate to villages where they have some claim to being admitted.

Voting rights are based almost solely upon a property franchise. However, since one-half of the school assessment is usually raised by a head tax on each pupil, the Anwohner who pay this are accorded a voice in school matters. In other secular affairs they have no power to affect village or colony policy decisions.

In the Hague colony the same aspects of the Anwohner problem that are apparent in Chihuahua resulted in 1965 in the breaking up of the communal pastures of two villages, Campo 9, Gruenthal, and Campo 6, Hochfeld. A substantial number of the arable Koerls thus created are in the process of being occupied by the otherwise landless children of the Wirte. On the daughter colony at La Batea no communal pastures have been created. At La Honda, on the other hand, cattle are being communally pastured during the first stages of settlement. There is no indication that any change is contemplated, and this arrangement will no doubt prevail until private wells are much more numerous than at present.[12] The cost of fencing private pastures also militates against their establishment under a chronically capital-deficient economy until serious Anwohner pressure develops.

Several other innovational features have been incorporated in a number of the most recently created villages of the Chihuahua colonies. One of the most obvious is in the form of the Strassendorf. All villages on Santa Rita except one and several on Ojo de la Yegua are laid out with Hauskoerls on only one side of the street, so that the rear of each farmyard opens onto the communal pasture. This appears to be a modified form of an innovation which originated in the "Kansan" villages, Campos 30 and 31; there, since the Hauskoerls are on both sides, half of the village has a direct approach to the pasture, while access corridors are provided for the farmsteads on the far side of the street. The villages which have as-

12. There were three watering stations with deep wells on La Honda at the time of the purchase. The fact that large tracts on the colony, totaling approximately one-half its area, are not potentially arable suggests that communal pasturing will be maintained. The same consideration holds true also for the Ojo de la Yegua and Santa Rita colonies, where rough land suitable only for grazing ranges from 25 percent (Campos 43, 44, and 46) to 80 percent (Campos 30, 31, 32, and 35) of the total. Fifty percent of the former Ojo de la Yegua ranch and 65 percent of Santa Rita are unsuited to tillage.

sumed this new form, like those which have adopted the private pasture, gain several advantages of economy and convenience over the traditional form of the Strassendorf.[13] The village is spared the expense of hiring a herdsman, and cattle have only a short distance, which is the same from all farmsteads, to go to pasture. Breeding of the animals can also be much more closely supervised. Moreover, each Hauskoerl faces an arable field of considerable extent immediately across the village street. This, together with one other field so situated on the village lands as to equalize the distance all farmers must travel to their several fields, normally constitutes the entire arable portion of a farm holding. The time spent in journeying to and from work is therefore much diminished from that so expended in the extensively parcelized and more traditionally arranged villages of the parent colonies.

Architectural Styles

Although in the overall sense the avenues of innovational initiative and self-expression open to the individual colonist are limited, in the structuring of his farmstead and the design of his buildings he has, short of ostentation and within his means, free rein.[14] The architecture of the earliest Mennonite villages in

13. Those which have adopted the private pasture, however, incur the added expense of fencing each plot.

14. This has not always been so. After 1817, under the supervision of Johann Cornies (1789–1848), a Mennonite of the Molotschna colony in whom, because of his foresight and progressiveness, Czar Alexander I and his successors vested almost dictatorial authority over the internal affairs of the Mennonite colonies in Russia, the form of the Mennonite Strassendorf, the layout of the farmyard, and the design of buildings became rigidly standardized along functional lines. Although the Bergthaler (later, also Sommerfelder) in Manitoba made many innovations, particularly in building plans, early in the history of their settlements, the Altkolonier held almost exclusively to the by then traditional style, in which the joined house and barn (the Wohnstallhaus), placed with its long axis at right angles to the village street, was the main structure.

The Wohnstallhaus is a structural form of great antiquity in northwestern Europe and was known to the Mennonites in Flanders and Holland. In the polder lands of the Vistula region the heavy timbered ceiling characteristic of the Slavic *Speicherhaus* was added to the dwelling, and the garret space was made to serve as a granary. This compact building (a suitable name would be *Wohnstallspeicherhaus*), incorporating all the major functions of shelter and storage related to the farmyard,

Mexico was very much along traditional lines. The material used was lumber, either brought on the migration or obtained from sawmills nearby or up the line of the Northwestern Railway. Farmyards and buildings were like those of the villages left behind in western Canada. Within the first few years, however, the advantages of adobe brick as a construction material came to be appreciated. Where suitable, it was shortly to replace other building materials almost entirely. Adobe was cheap and universally available. It was fireproof, and it had insulating qualities, against both heat and cold, much superior to those of wood. Stone, although readily available, never gained a vogue in construction. As far as is known, only one building, a dwelling in Kleefeld, Campo 1A, Manitoba colony, was ever built of stone, and it had adobe gables. For roofing, galvanized corrugated-iron sheeting replaced wooden shingles.

Architectural changes were also introduced. Among the first of the traditional structural features to be modified was the joining of house and barn in the form of the *Wohnstallhaus* (literal translation: dwelling-stable-building). In the predominantly dry Mexican climate with its mild winters, there was no particular advantage in having house and barn joined. Separating them, on the other hand, diminished the fly problem, which varies from acute to merely bothersome throughout the entire year. During the settlement of the original parent colonies, many colonists began to build dwellings and barns as individual units, some separated by only a few feet, others by a considerable span. Other colonists inserted a summer kitchen as a connecting link between house and barn; the summer kitchen was an innovation common among the Bergthaler and Sommerfelder in Canada, which in the mild Mexican climate quickly came to be utilized throughout the year. The great Russian

---

was particularly suited to the polder lands. Because of the danger of spring flooding from a combination of high tides, onshore winds on the shallowly shelving Baltic coast, ice jams on the lower Vistula and Nogat rivers, and the consequent backing-up of river-borne melt waters, it was necessary to raise earthen mounds upon which to set the buildings. The compact Wohnstallhaus required the least possible labor in accomplishing this objective. The building type was adhered to on the steppes of the Ukraine and the plains of western Canada largely because of the convenience it offered in the performance of necessary farmyard functions during the long winters.

stove, common in Canada, was installed in very few of even the earliest houses built in Mexico.

Over the years there have been numerous adaptations of Mexican building styles as concessions to the Mexican environment. In their architectural expression they often reflect the adoption of individual components in a variety of combinations which have been incorporated with traditional Mennonite forms. There are those too, however, whose buildings reflect no concessions of form or function to the Mexican environment beyond the utilization of adobe brick as a structural material.

Perhaps the first adoption of form from the Spanish-American world was the attaching of a *corredor* or covered gallery (such as is typical also of the American Southwest) to the front of the dwelling, below the eaves, its roof projecting outward at a low angle for five to six feet and supported at the outer edge by widely set pillars. It is now frequently, although by no means universally, encountered. Another early—and basic—structural change adopted was a reduction in the pitch of the roof. In Canada the roofs of the Mennonites' buildings commonly had a pitch of at least 1:1 (an angle of 45°)—a legacy from the days of thatch—so that snow would not accumulate excessively upon them. No such consideration was called for in the Mexican colonies, where snow is a relative rarity. Corrugated iron shed rainwater effectively at much lower angles, and new construction gradually began to exhibit a much shallower slope in the roof line.[15] Nowadays a pitch of 1:4 is common. Latterly this reduction in roof angle may be ascribed to a growing appreciation of the possibilities of roofing with a widely occurring calcareous, gypsiferous earth much used by the Mexican population and colloquially referred to as caliche, which puddles readily at the surface and thus forms a good seal against moisture. An ordinary truss-frame understructure is simply overlaid with boards, then covered to a depth of several inches with caliche. A final layer

15. Although a few examples of it exist, the Mediterranean tiled roof has never gained popularity among the Mennonites. This is so largely because of the greater cost of tile relative to other readily available roofing materials and the heavy understructure necessary to support its great weight.

of pebbles may be laid over this to keep the material from blowing away during the dry season. Such a roof, if wet down occasionally, will sprout a growth of small weeds which further helps to retain the caliche in place. Because it has excellent qualities of insulation, the caliche roof has come to be preferred above all other types in house construction.[16] Nowadays, in new construction, it is relatively rare for buildings other than dwellings to have this type of roof installed. Those used for animal housing or storage are not generally considered to require the insulating properties associated with caliche. In them a light truss-frame understructure of lumber is usually covered with corrugated sheet iron—or even, more recently, aluminum—or a cheaper though hail-vulnerable and generally less durable corrugated, tar-impregnated fiberboard. Because they build their adobe structures on a foundation of fieldstone or concrete, the Mennonites have adopted neither projecting rainspouts nor wide eaves to protect the base of walls from water shed by the roof.

Another structural modification which has recently made a scattered appearance, in new outbuilding construction, mainly in the Swift Current and Manitoba colonies, is the clear-span, arched, truss-frame roof covered in sheet metal or fiberboard. This building technique was learned a few years ago by a Mennonite who took on a contract to close in a small movie theater in the nearby Mexican hamlet of Rubio (Colonia Obregón), in which the plans called for such a roof.

A modification applied to adobe structures in recent years in the Chihuahua colonies has been to crown the walls with a six- or eight-inch course of reinforced concrete. The Mennonites' buildings, being generally less squat than those of Mexican con-

16. A comparable but superior, although more expensive, roof type has found some favor in the Hague colony in recent years. Over a substructure similar to that needed for the caliche roof are laid three courses of flat, fired tile (obtained from a small brick-making enterprise at Nuevo Ideal) separated by one-and-one-half-inch layers of *mezcla* (a mortar of coarse sand and cement). The weather surface is finished with a coat of mezcla. Such a roof, besides presenting a neater and more attractive appearance, possesses insulating qualities as good as those of caliche and has the added advantage, because of its lighter color, of being more reflective and thus keeps the interior of the house cooler in summer.

struction, are subject to considerable buffeting by high winds. As a result, the gable ends are prone to crack, with consequent serious structural weakening and attendant problems of repair. Setting the concrete course at the eave line greatly strengthens and stabilizes the structure. The technique is also useful in imparting greater rigidity to buildings such as granaries in which there is a certain amount of lateral loading on the walls. Spacing-in one or more courses of reinforced concrete permits a wall of much thinner cross section than is otherwise necessary, while ensuring against lateral displacement and collapse.

Over the years experience has shown an adobe wall of approximately fourteen inches in thickness to be most satisfactory for dwellings under the climatic conditions prevailing in the basin and range country on the eastern flank of the Sierra Madre Occidental, in which most of the colonies are located. A wall of this cross section does not heat through until late in the day, but then it warms the interior throughout most of the night. Window openings are flared to the outside to permit greater entry of light. Sashes are mounted near the outer edge of the opening. The traditional shutters, though still common, are gradually passing out of use since the thick walls permit direct entry of sunlight only during the early and late hours of the day.

In the Hague colony, in the wake of the depredations of the early 1930's, it became customary to bar the windows of dwellings with iron gratings set in the walls from the inside. The practice is now gradually being abandoned, reflecting an improved state of civil order in recent years. In the Chihuahua colonies very few houses have ever had barred windows, although stores and cheese factories may.

The building habits of the Sommerfelder have closely paralleled those of the Altkolonier except that to a substantial degree they had already abandoned the Wohnstallhaus in Canada and do not appear to have recreated it at all in Mexico. However, the architectural changes apparent in their earlier structures are largely confined to the physical separation of the components of the Wohnstallhaus, with the occasional addition of a lean-to to the house to serve as summer kitchen in place of the passage which formerly among them often connected house and barn. Together with the Altkolonier, they represent the only groups in Mexico who brought with them traditional Mennonite building styles. The architecture of the others—the "Kansans," Russländer, and Kleine Gemeinde—reflects almost wholly the influence of their various past host societies.

The "Kansans" brought with them building styles common to the American middle west: the rambling one-and-and-one-half-story farmhouse with its several chimneys to serve kitchen and space-heating requirements, and the barn with hay sling and hoist to fill the capacious loft. There are only a few examples of this type of construction to commemorate the tiny group from Meade.

The architectural influence of the Russländer is confined to the Santa Clara colony and is traceable to one person, the man who built the first cheese factory there. He built an adobe house in the style common to the Russian *khutor* (isolated farmstead of the well-to-do peasant). Although he constructed only the one house in this style, it has since been copied in three other dwellings in the villages of Weidenfeld, Silberfeld, and Blumenthal.

The structural forms employed by the Kleine Gemeinde people who settled the Quellenkolonie in 1947 and succeeding years reflect styles in vogue on the Canadian prairies during the 1940's, but they are executed in adobe, which these colonists adopted at the outset. The only obvious innovation which they have introduced is a circular adobe brooder house which prevents crowding in corners, one of the most common causes of chick mortality.

In Tamaulipas, the Mennonites accepted at the outset both the style and the materials of construction common to the region. Most dwellings are constructed with the corredor or covered gallery extending around the entire building as an integral part of a four-slope roof (*a cuatros aguas*). Mud-and-wattle walls and palm-leaf thatching are giving way now to concrete-block construction and sheet-metal roofs.[17] The Mennonites do not like thatch, which

17. Concrete-block buildings were the only structures at Neuendorf–Hoffnungsfeld that successfully withstood the force of Hurricane Iñez in the summer of 1966.

harbors insects and vermin. Aluminum is a roofing material well suited to the region. Being highly reflective, it minimizes heat transfer to the interior of the house. A few buildings have been constructed of lumber. They are, however, vulnerable to attack by termites. Adobe, although employed to some extent, is not well suited to the relatively moist conditions, with frequent long spells of dampness, which characterize the climate of the region.

A recent development in the Chihuahua colonies is a growing interest in metal-clad outbuildings—barns and sheds. The metal components, which are produced in "kit" form in the steel center of Monterrey, Nuevo León, may be erected over a light balloon frame of steel or lumber. In the last few years, in view of rising labor costs in the manufacture and laying of adobe brick, metal buildings have become competitive in cost with adobe structures. Dwellings, however, because of a greater concern with interior environmental conditions, continue to be constructed exclusively of adobe.

The Altkolonier in Canada did not customarily paint their buildings. Although not exactly proscribed, the practice was frowned upon as evidence of unseemly pride in appearance and worldly possessions. In Mexico, similarly, most of the wooden buildings erected by them have not been painted and have weathered to the not unpleasant brownish-grey characteristic of exposed wood in dry climates. Among the Sommerfelder, too, wooden buildings have generally remained unpainted, perhaps a reflection as much of poverty as of attitudes.

Most of the Mennonites' adobe structures are likewise innocent of adornment. However, since adobe walls gradually wear away under the influence of wind and weather, it is of practical interest to protect them from the elements. This can be accomplished with relative ease through the application of a stucco coating of *mezcla*. If a building is to be stuccoed, jagged pebbles are set in the mortar between courses in such a way as to protrude an inch or so beyond the face of the wall; these serve to anchor the mezcla. Subsequent spalling of the stucco is thus greatly inhibited. A building finished in this fashion is easily whitewashed or painted. Although known to the Mennonites in all their colonies, mezcla stuccoing is most in evidence in the Hague colony. In sum, however, the vast majority of the Mennonites' buildings are unadorned and blend in color with the soils from which they were raised.

Functional Organization of the Farmyard

Along with structural changes in the Mennonites' architecture, there have come functional modifications that reflect economic conditions, relative cost and availability of materials, and further adaptation to the environment. In the mild Mexican climate and under the prevailingly dry conditions, there is little need to store fodder under shelter. In addition, animals—horses and cattle—can be kept outside throughout the year. The number of horses, which were stabled during seasons of heavy work, is now much reduced, and the need for loft and stabling space has greatly diminished. In the younger colonies, therefore, and wherever new farmyards have been laid out, the tendency has been to build barns much smaller than was customary in the past. Indeed, at La Honda in Zacatecas indications are that some of the colonists will build no barns at all, and that cattle will be milked in the open. In general, then, physical appearance—the quality of construction and maintenance—rather than the size and number of outbuildings, is the better indicator of a family's economic position.

Conclusion

The community as embodied in the church organization of the Gemeinde assumes a dominating role in guiding the conduct of the individual Mennonite colonist with respect to standards of orthodoxy in many aspects of life. To a pronounced degree this inhibits initiative and tends to leave the individual with a low capacity for well-reasoned self-assertion and self-determination. On the other hand, it also inhibits conspicuous consumption and the pursuit of innovation for its own sake, while still leaving significant if narrow avenues for self-expression and the testing of new ideas. Whether conservative Mennonite society is sufficiently flexible to be able to continue to assert itself in an era of rapid change is a theme which will be developed more fully in Chapter X.

The Quality of Living

Within the Mennonites' dwellings there is also much evidence of structural change. The Altkolonier and Sommerfelder patriarchs built their houses in keeping with the traditional floor plan; this called basically for a one-story edifice in which the living space could be expanded by utilizing the large garret above the heavy-beamed ceiling, where in times past the grain was stored. The structural changes involved in the adoption of the caliche-covered roof left little room in the garret and reduced the living space to a single floor. Over the years the tendency has been for the floor plan to be reduced to two or three rooms, and the outside dimensions, too, have been as a rule substantially diminished.[1] These changes may be regarded in part as a reflection of the greater extent to which living in Mexico is carried on outdoors as compared to the former Canadian homeland, and in part as a reflection of the limited, often meagre means at the colonists' disposal. The houses of Anwohner are often even more modest, sometimes consisting of a single room. Among the Anwohner, too, it is not unusual to find examples of the Wohnstallhaus, but this often consists of a single room opening directly into the quarters in which the animals—a cow or two and possibly a few chickens and a pig—are sheltered.

Although some of the poorest homes have dirt floors and walls of bare adobe, they are few in number. In older homes the architectural expression is traditional: there are ceilings with exposed

---

1. Although there were no standard dimensions, the floor area of the traditional house was generally at least twenty-eight by thirty-six or more feet. More recently it has become quite common for dwellings to be smaller than twenty by thirty feet.

beams, varnished or painted; walls are plastered and whitewashed or painted, but often they are paneled with boards or plywood to a height of four feet or so; and there are wooden floors, also varnished or painted. Gradually, beginning in the kitchen, wooden floors have been displaced by concrete and occasionally by tile. Nowadays new houses, even those of the well-to-do, often have concrete floors throughout.

Furnishings are severely simple. In the homes of older colonists they often consist in large part of items brought from Canada at the time of the migration. Among them are many articles of considerable antiquity: goose-down pillows from Russia; great chests, some of which made the trek from Danzig to the Dnieper before 1800, and others made in Russia; pendulum clocks (the so-called Kroegeruhren, but many predating this familiar make) also dating back to Russia and Danzig; and *Schlafbänke*, sofa-like benches of wood with a folding trundle bed inside, capable of accommodating two people. Many other items—chairs, benches, cupboards, lamps, and utensils—date back to Canada. New furniture, the bulk of which is manufactured in the colonies, mainly copies the traditional styles. In recent years upholstered chairs and sofas of simple design, usually covered in leatherette or plastic, have gained a certain popularity and are also being manufactured.

Decorative plants and herbs are permitted, but most other kinds of ornamentation in the home are proscribed. Pictures and paintings, which are classed with graven images and therefore considered to be in violation of the Second Commandment, are forbidden. Calendars, however, being functional, are permitted. In most homes they are evident in a profusion explainable only in terms of the absence of other decorative touches. One functional yet decorative item of furniture which is found in almost every home that can afford it is the *Glasschaap*; this is a bureau with several drawers, in which linens and the like are kept, topped by a glass-doored hutch in which items of china—among them often heirlooms of considerable beauty—and knicknacks are displayed.

By North American standards, the luxuries and work-saving amenities in the Mennonite household are few. Despite the chilly temperatures—often below 50° F even during the day—which characterize the winter months, many homes have no space-heating facilities. Wood is expensive [2] and coal a rarity. A small wagonload of deadfall wood, amounting to about a quarter of a cord, fetches 60 pesos ($4.80 U.S.) or more in the Mennonite villages.[3] In the majority of homes, heating is restricted to that which is incidental to cooking. Although, since animals are seldom stabled, little manure accumulates—and none of it is pressed for fuel as was customary in Canada and Russia—it is not unusual, particularly for poor families, to gather cow chips for fuel. Garden residues, such as sunflower stalks and the like, and corn cobs [4] are also commonly used to stoke the kitchen stove. In recent years, most of those who can afford it have been using liquid petroleum gas (butane) for cooking purposes. At 40 centavos per liter ($.12 U.S. per gallon) delivered in the villages, it is easily the cheapest and most readily obtained fuel available. However, a stove, regulator, and other necessary accoutrements will cost anywhere from something under 1,000 pesos to several thousand, an investment beyond the reach of many.

The installation of butane gear immediately suggests to the Mennonite hausfrau the acquisition of another highly prized appliance: an *Eisschaap* or butane-fired refrigerator. Since these cost

2. The Mexican Department of Forestry strictly prohibits the cutting of live wood for fuel. Deadfall, roots, and stumps scavenged from the hills by Mexican woodcutters therefore constitute the bulk of wood fuel available to the colonists in Chihuahua, Durango, and Zacatecas. Ojo de la Yegua and Santa Rita colonies had considerable areas of open oak wood at the time of their acquisition. Clearing permits were obtained and, in their hurry to render the land fit for cultivation, the Mennonites gave away most of the wood to Mexican woodcutters who sold it off the colonies. Only a few villages have maintained a wood lot. Campo 68, Silberthal, permits the cutting of five cords of green wood per year to each Wirtschaft of 160 acres and proportional amounts to other Wirte. Deadfall, roots, and stumps may be taken in any amount by any resident of the village, including Anwohner.

3. In Mexican cities and towns of the region, fuel wood is customarily sold by weight, a few sticks at a time, at 60 centavos or more per kilogram, a price that works out to between $40 and $50 (U.S.) per ton for, usually, weathered wood of mediocre heating value.

4. Corn, however, is usually sold on the cob, and that used on the farm for animal feed is hammer-milled, cobs and all. As a result, very few corn cobs become available for fuel.

anywhere from 4,000 pesos for one in good used condition, to 8,000 pesos or more for a new one, they are out of reach of all but the more well-to-do. The majority of households, however, have a refrigerator substitute which the Mennonites apparently learned to utilize within the first few years of the founding of their Mexican colonies. Essentially it is simply an evaporation cooler which takes advantage of the substantial air movement and high potential evaporation rates characteristic of highland Mexico. Originally a box, fitted with a roof to provide shade and fly-screen walls to keep out insects, was simply mounted five feet or so off the ground in a breezy location. Inside it were placed the food items which the colonists wished to keep cool, together with a container of water which was replenished as needed. A cloth, one end of it dangling in the water, was draped over the contents of the box. Drawing water wick-like, it encouraged a high rate of evaporation and, consequently, pronounced cooling. Dairy products and meats could be kept for days in such an enclosure without spoiling.[5] It is claimed that under near-ideal conditions of evaporation temperatures as low as 38° F are possible in summer with such a contraption. Not long after the initial implementation of this technique, the colonists began to incorporate it as an integral part of their dwellings, as a cold pantry. A small windowless room provided with louvered wall openings which permitted free passage of air was added off the kitchen or in back of the pantry. An open container of water placed in the cold pantry, along with the eggs, dairy products, vegetables, fruit, and meats which the colonists desire to maintain in fresh condition, enhances the cooling effect, which can be regulated by partially opening or closing the louvers. Placed in the cold pantry, fresh meat quickly develops a glaze of its natural juices which seals the surface and inhibits further moisture loss. Lightly cured meats such as pork sausage will readily keep without spoiling for a month or six weeks under similar conditions. By then, however, moisture loss begins substantially to affect palatibility.

5. This technique of keeping foodstuffs is, of course, known to campers everywhere. It does not appear, however, that the Mennonites utilized it in Canada, where wells and to some extent icehouses were used.

Water

Fortunate indeed is the household which, either individually or jointly with one or two neighbors, possesses a well, for having one at close proximity to the buildings makes possible the piping of water, at low cost,[6] to strategic parts of the farmyard. An above-ground concrete cistern is usually constructed, from which house and barnyard can be served by gravity flow. Although frost is a problem in winter, it is not so great as to threaten bursting of cisterns. Pipes will not freeze if buried to a depth of half a foot provided the taps are left slightly "cracked" during the coldest nights. Pumping is accomplished by wind motor or fuel engine. To a depth of 250 feet or so, a wind-motor pump will bring to the surface enough water for domestic and barnyard use and the irrigation of a kitchen orchard and garden. Beyond that depth, to approximately 500 feet, an auxiliary engine is really necessary. Much beyond 500 feet the wind motor is of little use, and all water must be raised by engine power. Even if the initial investment in the well is ignored, the cost of water rises rapidly once favorable depths for free-energy wind-motor pumping are exceeded. Then the amenity use of water falls off sharply. The same holds true where water must be hauled from a distance, either from surface sources or wells, as is the case over much of Ojo de la Yegua and Santa Clara, and, for the time being, until the necessary wells are drilled, at La Batea and La Honda.

Among the first to fall victim then are ornamental plants—the flowers which traditionally adorned the foreyard of the Mennonite Wirtschaft. The avenues of shade trees which traditionally lined both sides of a village thoroughfare were never fully recreated in Mexico except in the Hague colony, where depths to ground water are relatively shallow and trees, once brought along to maturity, can often tap the water table. As in Chihuahua, the native poplar is most in evidence in Durango, but there is a sprinkling of eucalyptus. In part, though, trees have been supplanted there by maguey (Century plant) and, occasionally, by hedges of prickly pear

6. Nowadays polyethylene pipe is much used for transporting domestic water supplies over distances of up to a few hundred yards.

cactus.[7] In the Manitoba colony the shaded street is only fragmentally represented, and in the Swift Current colony it is represented hardly at all.[8] Elsewhere, on Ojo de la Yegua, Santa Rita,[9] Santa Clara, and Los Jagueyes, shade trees are almost totally absent. There are no indications that amenity tree-planting is contemplated in the young colonies of Buenos Aires, Capulín, La Batea, or La Honda. Neither have shade plantings been undertaken at Yermo. In Tamaulipas the practice has been to remove practically all trees as part of agricultural clearing operations, even in areas set aside for farmyards.

After amenity planting, the next of the traditional aspects of the Mennonite farmyard to be abandoned in the face of dearth of water is the kitchen orchard, which requires substantial irrigation if it is to bear. Depending on the labor and expense involved in obtaining water, the kitchen garden also becomes circumscribed, occasionally to the point where only the growing of the dietary staple, potatoes, continues under a dependence upon rainfall augmented by household wash water. The culinary variety in the Mennonite kitchen, never large in the first place, thus becomes narrower still. Although the beans, peppers, and tortillas characteristic of Mexico have long since been accepted, the Mennonite diet continues to be heavily predicated upon potatoes and white bread, together with pork for those whose means permit.[10]

7. It could not be established that the Mennonites utilize *agua miel,* the sweet sap of the maguey, for the manufacture of *pulque,* the mildly intoxicating national beverage of Mexico. Nor does it appear that the fruit of the prickly pear cactus is rendered by the Mennonites into the popular Mexican confection, *queso de tuna.*

8. This can be explained at least in part by the fact that trees grew well in the West Reserve in Manitoba. In the drier Swift Current region of Saskatchewan this was not so, and the Mennonites there had become used to doing without the benefit of shade trees during the two or three decades they resided there prior to the exodus to Mexico.

9. In a few of the villages on the eastern edge of Ojo de la Yegua and in the northeast part of Santa Rita, some of the naturally occurring oak and ponderosa pine have been spared for ornamental and shade purposes.

10. There is little concern with vegetables, although roots such as carrots and turnips can be had fresh even in winter if covered with straw and simply left in the ground until needed. Completion of the Ferrocarril Chihuahua al Pacífico has resulted in great reductions in the price of fruit from the Pacific coast in the Chihuahua region. Although the Mennonites are buying more fruit than formerly, it is still considered a luxury not to be regularly included in the diet.

What Is "Humble"?

Other elements of living which suffer early attrition in the face of dearth of water or the necessity of expending considerable labor or material resources in making it available to the household are cleanliness about the home and personal hygiene. Like any European peasant people, the Mennonites have never made a fetish of spotlessness. They were, by and large, soberly clean about their persons and tidy about their homes and buildings, but labor was considered honorable. Thus, soiled clothes and dirty hands were the badge of the industrious farmer to whom his labors were his way of life, and they were therefore above reproach. Permitting the condition to persist beyond the necessity for it, however, was looked upon with disfavor as an indication of holding a mean opinion of oneself. To a pronounced extent these standards have been abandoned. Particularly, although by no means solely or universally, is this so of the Altkolonier in Chihuahua, and it is not restricted to areas where shortage of water is a real and pervasive problem. The situation, then, speaks of cultural attrition and impoverishment among a people living, over a period now approaching half a century, in a world narrowly circumscribed and largely innocent of positive outside cultural contacts, in the presence, often, of economic hardship and under the control and subject to the indoctrination of a largely unlettered and reactionary-conservative leadership. In brief, humility has become confused with self-abasement.

There are other aspects in the mode of living of many Mennonites which also speak of ignorance and apathy. Despite frequent outbreaks over the years of virulent communicable diseases such as diphtheria and the so-called "children's diseases" (mumps, scarlet fever, measles, and various digestive-tract infections), which often threaten to assume epidemic proportions, there is widespread neglect or ignorance of elementary quarantine procedures. Moreover, although the purpose of immunization is known, it is mistrusted and there is much opposition to it. It is common in many homes for persons to spit indiscriminately on the floors. Often concrete floors are strewn with sawdust and dampened at intervals throughout the day to keep down dust. The potential for the spread of infection, particularly to toddlers and small children, inherent in these practices is obvious. Many know little or nothing of proper nutrition. Among poorer families it is not unusual for children to have to forego the drinking of milk so that more may be sold for cash to purchase the "indispensable" white flour. Children of poor families often go barefoot throughout the winter. Characteristically many of them develop a hacking cough in November, which persists until the following spring. Many children and teenagers look "peaked," a condition described by Mexican doctors as being largely owing to improper diet. The consensus of opinion from them is that if these youngsters would be fed more milk, oatmeal, and beans instead of white bread and coffee it would represent a great dietary improvement. Infant mortality is high. In three colonies—Ojo de la Yegua, Hague, and Swift Current—it averaged 9.7 percent from 1950 to 1964.

The Visual Impact of the Village

The adobe fence that fronts the street in the Mennonites' older Mexican villages differentiates them from the villages they left in Canada. In Canada, and in Russia, the fronting fence commonly consisted of vertical posts set eight to ten feet apart and connected by three horizontal, evenly spaced ribs consisting of one-inch boards, four inches or so in width; a six-inch piece of lumber spanned the top (set at an upward angle of 15° or so, to shed water). Often the fence was extended to line the driveway as well as the fore- and backyard boundaries of adjacent Hauskoerls, to which access was provided by small gates. Among the Altkolonier it was usually left unpainted. There are a few examples of this type of fence in the Manitoba, Swift Current, and Hague colonies. In these older colonies it has, however, in the main, been replaced by the adobe fence, possibly in imitation of the dry-masonry fieldstone fences much utilized to mark property boundaries in the basin and range country of Mexico.

The adobe yard fence is usually built over a fieldstone-and-mortar base course. The top course may be capped with an inch or so of mezcla to shed water, inhibit weathering, and improve the appearance.[11] An adobe-walled cattle pen, often running the full width of a Hauskoerl and enclosed to a height of five feet or so, may extend rearward from the far end of the barn. Where air-drainage frosts have proven to constitute a particular hazard to the kitchen orchard and garden, the walled enclosure may be raised to eight feet or more, but such examples are rare. In contrast to the traditional board fence, the most notable impact, outside of the visual one, made by the adobe fence is the impression of privacy, of an identity apart from the *whole* village, which it imparts to the farmyard.

Nowadays the adobe fence is being gradually abandoned as a feature of the Mennonite farmyard. During the dry, windy winter season, unsightly banks of trash and dust tend to pile up against them and have to be hauled away. Such trash accumulations become a particular nuisance on the west side of north-south-oriented villages, where rear yards, stock pens, and feed stacks—sources of such material—are situated in the upwind direction. Moreover, as with other structures in adobe, increasing costs have in recent years tended to discourage the building of new adobe fences and even the keeping in good repair of old ones. It is not unusual nowadays to see sections of barbed wire replacing ruined parts or even to see an entire adobe fence replaced by a few strands of barbed wire. Aesthetically, the effect of this change is decidedly negative. Yet in the younger colonies only a few adobe yard enclosures have been built, and barbed wire was used in place of adobe from the outset.

The Rhythm of Life

To the outside observer, life in a Mennonite village has an almost other-worldly quality of rustic unhurriedness. Shortly before 8 A.M. on weekdays, the high-pitched note of the milk haul-

---

11. Weathering on the upper surface of an adobe fence not protected by a capping of mezcla takes place at the approximate rate of one course (four inches) every twenty years.

er's pipe announces that it is time for last night's and the morning's milk to be trundled to the street and set on its journey to the cheese factory. Almost simultaneously the herdsman passes by, ringing a cowbell to signal that animals which are to be taken out must be in the street by the time he returns. There follows then the jostling mêlée of the herd moving slowly up the adobe-walled and sometimes tree-lined street, growing in numbers occasionally to several hundred head before the pasture gate is reached. Shortly after, for half the year, except on Saturdays, the little Old World urchins—miniature *Oomtjes* and *Mumtjes*—go trooping by to school.

As the morning breeze rises, the wind motors begin to creak about their rounds. Gradually the tempo of activity increases as here and there a tractor coughs to life, a hammer mill hums, a one-lung diesel labors to irrigate the garden. As people go about their tasks, there is time to "neighbor" across the back fence, or to saunter over to the village store for tobacco—perhaps the *Steinbach Post*, the vehicle of communication between Mennonites of two continents, has arrived—and pass the time of day with others on like errands. On the farmyard the day's labors may be punctuated by the visit of a cattle-buyer, various pedlars hawking fruit, tortillas, and other goods in a patois of Plattdeutsch and Spanish, perhaps by a beggar, an agrarista seeking work, or a rider asking permission to water his horse, each of whom hopes to satisfy his weakness for wheaten bread and butter with zwieback and *mantequilla menonita.*

The working day is interrupted at noon by dinner, the day's main meal, and again at 3 P.M. by *Vesper,* a lighter meal usually of coffee, bread, butter, and jam. About 6 P.M. the herdsman brings the cattle back down the street, each animal unerringly finding its own gate. Chores and supper are tended to, and the working day ends.

If it is Wednesday and the Wirt has occasion to see the Vorsteher, he may take his buggy, the jitney bus, or a rápido to town, where the colony leaders of the whole region meet each week to thrash out matters of mutual concern. There one is also likely to meet friends and relatives from remote parts of the colonies, who because of distance can seldom otherwise be visited.

Like any other day, Sunday begins with chores, but work is restricted to the necessary tending of the animals. By 8 o'clock, if they are going to church, the Wirt and his wife are on their way. The children seldom go, and there is no Sunday school. Since the Scriptures, catechisms, and hymnals are the only literature in the schools, children are considered to be getting an adequate exposure to religious education during the week. For a short while on Sunday the roads are dotted with buggies and Karrenwagen of every description, some drawn by inelegant working nags, other by horses whose gait and form belie care and breeding that violate the orthodox concepts of humility and pridelessness.

Men and women enter the church by separate doors. They sit apart, women to the left, men to the right. A song is announced by one of the six *Vorsänger* who sit on the raised platform to the right of the pulpit. All singing is in unison. The preacher, in black frock coat, vest, collarless black shirt, and trousers tucked into leather knee boots [12]—a garb that has remained unchanged since the Mennonites left the Frisian Waterkant four centuries ago—reads from a laboriously copied book of sermons first composed in Danzig and Russia, speaking in a singsong tone in archaic German with occasional ad-lib commentary in Plattdeutsch. The service, interspersed with singing and prayer, may continue sonorously until noon. Among the men there is a considerable coming and going to see to the horses or, using that as a pretext, to enjoy a quick smoke.

When church is out, invitations may be extended, particularly to those from other villages, to come to dinner and stay the afternoon to visit (*spazieren*). The visitors' horses are always unharnessed and put up and fed in the barn. After dinner and possibly a nap, host and guests retire to the parlor (*grosze Stube*). Bowls of

12. The leather knee boots are regarded as having been ordained by the Apostle Paul in his epistle to the Ephesians. Ephesians 6:15, in Luther's German translation, states: ". . . und an den Beinen gestiefelt, als fertig, zu treiben das Evangelium des Friedens," which translates, ". . . and wearing boots, as though prepared to promulgate the gospel of peace." The King James version has: "And your feet shod with the preparation of the gospel of peace."

roasted sunflower seeds are handed around, the men may light cigarettes, and soon the room is littered with hulls and redolent of smoke. Neighbors, if they drop in, enter without knocking and join in the visit. Later the men may be offered a schnapps by their host. Vesper is served, and soon the guests make their way homeward.

The young people, meanwhile, have been congregating in groups, more or less by age—boys and girls apart—along the village street. Sports are not permitted. Radios and musical instruments are also forbidden, but almost invariably one appears from somewhere, and the groups draw closer together to hear a broadcast or listen to a village troubador give forth with a song, usually a cowboy love song in Spanish learned from the radio in stolen moments.

Kinship ties are strong. At Christmas, Easter, and Pentecost—the great holidays of the year—three days, each accorded the status of a Sunday, are set aside. The first two days are devoted to family reunions, at which all members who possibly can do so gather at the parental home, one day at "his," the other at "hers." It is not unusual for more than a hundred individuals, representing three or four generations, to congregate for these occasions. The third day is given over to visiting among friends and the like. Family members living in a remote colony, or in Canada or British Honduras, are likely to come for a visit when time and finances permit.

Other, more general occasions for meeting are engagement celebrations, weddings, and funerals; for such occasions it is customary to send around letters of invitation which are forwarded by each recipient to the next person on the list. Engagements are celebrated on Saturday, at the home of the bride-to-be. The young couple is seated in the *grosze Stube*, surrounded by their elders. Songs suitable to the occasion are selected from the old hymnal (*Gesangbuch*) and are sung to sonorous melodies handed down unwritten through six or more generations.[13] The event begins at noon and lasts well into the evening. In good weather tables may be set up outside and the entire company served a banquet whose sumptuousness, although in some measure possibly reflecting the host's

13. Charles Burkhart, "Music of the Old Colony Mennonites," *Mennonite Life* (January 1952), gives a detailed analysis of Altkolonier music.

means, generally leaves little room for complaint. Although, as the invitation states, it is "a Christian and solemn occasion," a few high jinks, aimed at the engaged couple, may erupt. That these are in part anticipated may be inferred from the response elicited when, for instance, a shotgun, its stock resting on the window sill behind the guests of honor, is discharged into the air.

During the ensuing week the engaged couple visits among relatives, and on the following Sunday the wedding is solemnized. After the ceremony, which takes place as part of the morning church service, a reception very similar to that which followed the engagement is held at the bride's house. Among the Altkolonier and Kleine Gemeinde there are no further festivities, but the Sommerfelder customarily hold a dance. There is no honeymoon. The newlyweds move directly into their own Wirtschaft—nowadays a rare event—or set up housekeeping in the home of either the bride's or the groom's parents, where they may reside until they manage to obtain a place of their own or, as is not infrequently the case, they assume an Anwohnerstelle at the end of the village.

Funerals are a simple and solemn occasion, held from the church or the home. Following the eulogy, the assemblage moves to the cemetery, where a plain coffin is lowered and the grave is filled to the accompaniment of prayer and singing. Then the mourners go to the home of the deceased for a simple repast of zwieback and coffee. Altkolonier graves are not mounded, there are no ornamental plants, and no marker to the dead is ever raised.[14]

Mutual Assistance

Communal ownership does not enter into the traditional agrarian philosophy of the Mennonites. Only one communal enterprise (as distinct fom the cheese cooperatives, which are really extended partnerships from which individuals may recover their

14. This may be a carry-over from their experiences in Danzig (see Chapter I, note 4), before the migration to Russia, where, it appears, in response to certain religious disabilities invoked against them, private—and possibly secret—burial was resorted to by the Mennonites. The Kleine Gemeinde and Sommerfelder customarily raise simple headstones.

capital), a sheep-raising venture by the Kleine Gemeinde in the hilly western one-third of the tract originally purchased from Estrada and Luna, has ever been attempted in Mexico. The endeavor enjoyed considerable success until it became necessary to dispose of it and the hill lands in order to raise capital to buy the land of those departing for British Honduras, thus maintaining the territorial integrity of the colony. The principle of mutual assistance, on the other hand, which perhaps more than any other single factor has guaranteed the survival of Mennonite colonization efforts on a succession of difficult and unproven agricultural frontiers, is thoroughly a part of the social fabric. Although there is some exchange of labor, mutual interdependence is represented today more by the lending and hiring back and forth of the chronically inadequate number of machines—mowers, binders, threshers, and the like. The colonist struggling to become established on his own farm benefits greatly from such assistance since it permits him to defer the purchase of essential equipment until he can better afford it.

Mutual assistance takes a less economically oriented form in working "bees." [15] One prominent surviving form of this type of shared labor is the slaughtering bee.[16] It is largely restricted to the slaughtering of hogs, which, because of the large variety of products rendered—hams, bacon, sausage, liverwurst, lard, spare ribs, cracklings, several kinds of pickled and brined meats, and head cheese—involves a great deal of work in comparison to the killing

15. Although it is a form of labor exchange, the bee is different in that assistance is given in response to invitation and does not carry the direct obligation of repayment on the part of the recipient.

16. Another is the digging of graves, at which assistance is rendered by invitation. No member of the family of the deceased ever assists in this task.

The performance of *Scharwerk,* the statute labor imposed by the colony on each Wirt in relation to the size of his holding, although it bears a considerable similarity to the bee, differs in that a direct pecuniary value is attached to the work, and in that statute labor or an equivalent payment in cash is compulsory.

Another form of mutual assistance is the village baking in preparation for major occasions such as engagements, weddings, and funerals; at these times dough is taken to each house to be made into zwieback for the meal which always accompanies such gatherings. Again this differs from the bee, since the work is performed separately in the homes.

of beef.[17] In Mexico, because of the limits on the keeping of fresh and lightly cured meats imposed by the climate, this bee tends to be smaller than was the case in Canada, involving usually only one or two hogs, with perhaps three or four invited couples to assist with the slaughtering. It is common, though, for neighbors to get together and hold a joint killing, in which case a greater number of people is involved.

On the day appointed for the slaughtering, the invited working guests arrive for breakfast. During the course of the day the men are wont to interrupt their work for a "measuring of the bacon" (*Speck messen*)—the passing around of something to ward off the chill. It is altogether a sociable occasion, punctuated by a big dinner and Vesper which usually suggest that the women of the house have tried to outdo the achievements of their neighborhood counterparts on similar occasions. Late in the afternoon, when all is tidied up, when the hams have been salted down and the sausage has been hung in the smokehouse (hams will not be smoked for some weeks yet), everybody goes in to supper. Then there is a spell of visiting in the grosze Stube, and the guests depart, each with a liverwurst and a chunk of spare ribs, a token payment for his services.

Economic Disparity and Social Tension

The foregoing descriptions of colony life are valid primarily for people who are comfortably well off. In the main these

17. The parasite trichina, which may infest the tissue of hogs and which may be transmitted to human beings through the consumption of raw or improperly cooked pork, is apparently unknown among the reasonably well-fed, penned hogs of the Mennonites. In neighboring Mexican settlements, however, where hogs often survive mainly by scavenging, its incidence is quite common. It is not unusual, therefore, when Mennonites buy slaughter hogs from these sources, to find that they have trichinosis. The parasites tend to congregate in the lymphatic nodes of the neck region. Since the first butchering operation the Mennonites perform on a hog is the removal of the head, it becomes at once apparent if the carcass is trichina-infested. If the condition is serious, the carcass is destroyed, or it is thoroughly cooked and used for animal feed. If the infestation appears light, the meat may be retained for human consumption, but extra care is taken in cooking. No case of trichinosis could be established as ever having occurred among the Mennonites in Mexico.

are the Wirte, who, although even few of them are well-to-do by Canadian or United States family-farm standards, generally enjoy more security and a higher standard of living than do the Anwohner. This disparity in material well-being is the root cause of considerable mutual recrimination between Wirte and Anwohner.

The Anwohner, for their part, feel that the colonies' failure to acquire new lands at a rate adequate to meet the needs of a rapidly expanding population is to a pronounced degree the fault of the propertied class—the Wirte; they assert that the Wirte wish to assure the perpetuation of a substantial pool of cheap, docile, and to some extent "captive" labor.[18] They further point to the fact that although opportunities for employment are inadequate, Wirte show a preference for hiring Mexicans as farm laborers.[19] The Wirte, in turn, feel that, in view of the nominal quitrent charged for Anwohnerstellen and the included right to pasturage, in view of the fact that no statute labor is required of Anwohner, and in view of the substantial cost to colony treasuries of aid to the indigent, most of whom are Anwohner, they are being well done by indeed.[20]

18. The situation between Anwohner and Wirte in Mexico today is very comparable to that which prevailed in Russia a hundred years ago. A case is cited from 1864, when the Anwohner in the Molotschna region, despairing of the colony authorities taking positive steps to relieve their landless situation, addressed an appeal to the Inspector of Colonies of the Fürsorgekomitee and to their own Vorsteher and Agricultural Superintendent. The latter two indicated that nothing would be done to provide land for the Anwohner, since "then the landowners would have to pay too much for laborers." (J. J. Hildebrand, *Hildebrand's Zeittafel* [North Kildonan, Manitoba: J. Regehr, 1945], p. 220, entry of February 1, 1864.)

19. The Wirte give several reasons for their preference for hiring Mexican laborers. They claim that if they do not give at least some of the jobs they have to offer to the Mexican population, the latter will be driven by extremity to beg or steal. Moreover, by and large the Mexican laborer is recognized as a willing worker who not only will take on almost any task but is undemanding and recognizes the complete authority of the employer or anyone in charge. Mennonite employees, on the other hand, tend to consider themselves the social equals of the employer and expect to be treated accordingly. Furthermore, in the absence of the Wirt, they tend to balk at taking orders from children or women delegated to supervise the work, a situation the Mexican is considered not to mind.

20. It is also not unusual for Wirte who either have few or no children, or whose families are still very young, to take in the teen-aged children of Anwohner at a nominal wage (up to 200 pesos [$16 U.S.] per month for boys, less for girls). Although their earnings are small, they gain experience in domestic and agricultural pursuits which they could not otherwise have had.

Considerable social tension ensues out of this situation. The solidly agrarian philosophy of Mennonite leadership offers deliberate discouragement to any broadening of the economic base. Inherent in the interdiction against technological change is not only a negative effect on the number and variety of opportunities alternative to farming, but a resulting situation of un- and underemployment which affects all economic levels of the society. Moreover, because of the narrow range of opportunities in existence, many persons whose natural bent might be in the direction of altogether different lines of endeavor are now farming, albeit badly. These, together with the Anwohner who are not fortunate enough to escape their condition, tend to gravitate toward the lowest levels of the economic ladder. Generally they are regarded by those who have prospered as the undeserving poor who have been too unenterprising to make something of themselves.

Economic Attrition Despite Frugality

Even those who by prevailing standards have prospered cannot as a rule divert much of their income to consumption purposes. Within the framework of traditional Mennonite society, one of the prime functions of the homestead is to serve as a nucleus for capital creation in order to provide for the needs of the rising generation. Children as a rule remain at home until they marry. Until that time they contribute their labor and most or all of any outside earnings to the parents, who in turn later assist them to become established on farms of their own. To this end, the homestead may stand as collateral; surpluses and savings are also diverted to it. In this, and in matters of inheritance, all children are by custom to receive equal and impartial treatment. In the commonly prevailing situation of large families, this system generally prevents the accumulation of much wealth by any individual family, and it remains necessary to continue to live frugally even in the presence of considerable material success. Moreover, the functioning of this traditional system is contingent upon a continuing supply of land at prices which make possible its acquisition. In large measure these prime requisites have not been met. Not only has land become scarce and dear, but many Wirte can no longer manage to accumulate sufficient capital to assist their children onto Wirtschaften of their own. Indeed, this process of attrition in personal fortunes has been operative for a long time. Many of the Anwohner of today are themselves the children of Anwohner.

Population Problems

The problems of encroaching impoverishment are compounded by the high rate of natural increase characteristic of the Mennonite population. In the forty-odd years since the founding of the colonies in Mexico, the Mennonite population has grown from approximately 6,000 to over 30,000. This rate of growth represents a doubling each eighteen years. The growth rate is particularly high in the more recently founded colonies, which have a predominantly youthful population. They begin therefore to experience intense population pressure even in the early years of their existence. In the face of these levels of population increase, the Mennonites have managed to acquire additional land approximately equal in area to that originally purchased in 1922. They have not, however, greatly altered their land-use technology to compensate for the growing disparity between population growth and the agricultural resources upon which they predominantly depend.[21]

21. It is recognized that there was vacant land in the Manitoba colony until about 1940. This, however, reflected not so much an absolute surplus of land as the inability of the colonists, primarily because of water shortage and lack of finances, to place it under cultivation.

According to church records, the populations of the several colonies, representing some 4,000 family units, were as follows as of January 1, 1965:

Manitoba colony	10,987	
Swift Current colony	3,559	
Ojo de la Yegua colony	5,080	
Santa Rita	1,576	
Santa Clara (plus outliers)	1,873	
Quellenkolonie	578	
Buenos Aires and Capulín	900	
Hague colony	4,112	
Yermo colony	104	(head count)
La Batea	612	
La Honda	1,030	
Neuendorf–Hoffnungsfeld	200	(estimated; no records)
Total	30,611	

The frustrations associated with the press of numbers is, if any-thing, heightened by the frequent necessity for children, when they marry, to continue to live in the parental home of either the hus-band or the wife. There are situations in which as many as three families of married children share a single dwelling with their elders and younger siblings. The tensions resulting can be readily imagined.

Other Aspects of Tension
Stemming from "Orthodoxy"

Another, more pervasive source of social tension, particu-larly among the Altkolonier, emanates from the single-minded in-sistence upon orthodoxy in dress and speech, and from interdic-tions against technological innovations in farming or business. The Old Testament teaching that transgression will be surely fol-lowed by punishment is deeply ingrained in the Mennonite cul-ture. God punishes directly, although not necessarily for a precisely known cause, by withholding His blessing from or visiting mis-fortune upon the transgressor; such punishment may take the form of crop failure, lightning striking buildings or animals, personal accident, disease, and so forth. This belief, in its present-day expres-sion at any rate, appears to have been strengthened by the high incidence of greater or lesser natural calamities that have plagued the Mennonites and by the fact that in their last years of schooling, when their reading comprehension, limited as it may be, is at its peak, Mennonite children read almost exclusively from the Old Testament. The fatalism with which misfortune is borne and the docility with which sanctions such as the ban and shunning are en-dured are amazing.

The enforcement of orthodoxy through the proceedings related

For details of the life and problems of other "exclusive" or "utopian" societies, see Victor Peters, *All Things Common* (Oxford: The University Press, 1967), George M. Foster, *Traditional Cultures* (New York: Harper and Brothers, 1962), Henrik F. Infield, *Cooperative Communities at Work* (New York: The Dryden Press, 1945), and John W. Bennett, *Hutterian Brethren* (Stanford: Stanford University Press, 1967).

to the Donnadagh has the effect of encouraging spying and inform-
ing, activities which are not always untinged by motives of winning
favor with the leadership, of diverting attention away from the in-
former's own shortcomings, or, for that matter, of "getting one's
own back" in relation to personal differences. Since the possibilities
of falling short of the orthodox "ideal" are many, and since gadgets, creature comforts, and luxuries are coveted despite their interdiction, there is a great deal of watching one another and of
justifying one's own contravention of rules through the rationalization that it is no worse than the next person's. This mutual surveil-
lance is encouraged by the fact that practically the entire population is concentrated in villages.

Curiously, the rationalization of the veniality of one's own infractions of rules constitutes one of the few avenues of access to new
ideas and innovations in the conservative Mennonite culture. As
greater and greater attention comes to be focussed upon a certain
innovation and as its virtues become increasingly apparent—and,
for that matter, enhanced by the fact of interdiction—a few ultimately defy the rule forbidding it. They are duly called before the
Donnadagh and, if thought necessary, placed under the ban. However, if the innovation in question is, in a real or imagined way, indispensable or simply highly desirable, others too will risk excommunication and acquire it. Ultimately, when the tide can no longer
be stemmed, the church quietly ceases to apply the ban, but does
not withdraw its interdiction.

In the Altkolonier philosophy, conventions once decided upon
by the Bruderschaft and sealed with prayer constitute a covenant
with God which can never be altered. Although this is the source
of slavish traditionalism and doctrinal rigidity in church and society, it also ensures against the seeking and implementation of
innovation for its own sake. A case in point is the use of pneumatic
tires on tractors. Their use was placed under interdiction when
they first began to appear in the colonies on tractors brought from
the United States. Tractors with rubber tires, is was reasoned, since
they can travel twelve, fifteen, or more miles per hour, would
heighten the temptation of young people to visit the towns and

ranchos; there they would learn to mingle socially with the Mexican population and ultimately, perhaps, even intermarry with them. The advantages of fuel economy, of reduced repair bills (on steel-wheeled tractors radiators are particularly vulnerable to damage as the tractors jolt over the hard and often stony ground), of operator comfort, of greater mobility, and consequently of opportunities to work more distant lands which rubber-tired tractors present have resulted in particularly heavy pressure against the ecclesiastical regulation forbidding them. In many colonies it has been possible, through the liberal invocation of the ban, to exact compliance. In the Manitoba colony, however, from whose farthest villages the trip to the market center of Cd. Cuauhtémoc is only ninety minutes by tractor but generally too long for horse-drawn conveyances, and where Mexican lands to the south and west offer opportunities to rent or buy if these lands can be easily reached, the regulation against rubber-tired tractors came to be so widely disregarded that at one point the Elder threatened to excommunicate an entire village. When it was drawn to his attention that to do so would create a solid knot of dissidents within the colony, who would be unified by the common ban, he desisted. Since that time, the ban has no longer been invoked on this particular issue in the Manitoba colony,[22] although in the other Altkolonier colonies in Chihuahua it continues to be applied.

The Sommerfelder and Kleine Gemeinde, who do not forbid utilitarian innovations, have correspondingly fewer difficulties in maintaining orthodoxy among their members. An indication of the attraction which greater freedom for personal initiative holds for the Altkolonier is the fact that of the seventy family units in the Sommerfelder villages of Halbstadt and Bergthal, Campos 55 and 40, about one-half represent intermarriage with Altkolonier, all of whom have joined the Sommerfelder. On the other hand, there have been only two or three instances of Sommerfelder mar-

22. Rubber-tired tractors have been less of an issue in the Hague colony, all of which lies within relatively easy distances of Nuevo Ideal by horse-drawn conveyance. Indeed, in the black-soil portions of the colony, rubber tires have serious limitations in that they have poor traction and cause an undesirable degree of soil-packing when the ground is wet.

rying Altkolonier and then joining the latter.[23] Other cultural aspects would appear to have no bearing on the phenomenon, for in education and other matters Sommerfelder and Altkolonier doctrines are very similar.

The Sommerfelder and Kleine Gemeinde frequently receive requests from Altkolonier, including persons under the ban, for admission to membership. The Sommerfelder, however, do not admit to their Gemeinde persons who are under the Altkolonier ban; if they can get the ban rescinded, they may be considered. To be admitted, however, they must own property and reside in one of the Sommerfelder enclaves. The Kleine Gemeinde does not recognize the Altkolonier ban per se. It does, however, closely check an applicant's motives. Furthermore, to be admitted to the Kleine Gemeinde, persons must reside on Los Jagueyes.

An Emerging Class Structure?

Although it cannot be said that social class stratification exists as a deliberately created and sustained element of Mennonite society, nevertheless differences in economic status tend to be carried over into social relations. There is notably less visiting, which is practically the only form of recreation available to adults, between Wirte and Anwohner, for instance, than between Wirte and Wirte or Anwohner and Anwohner. Moreover, as was the case in Russia, there is a noticeable tendency for the more well-to-do families to intermarry, out of considerations, at least in part, of the accumulation and protection of wealth.

The large Anwohner appendages which have developed in some villages have resulted in overcrowding of existing school facilities to the extent that in a few cases a second school has been built at the Anwohner end of the village.[24] Although the facilities

23. In each of these cases, it was claimed, the reason for the person in question leaving the Sommerfelder was that he or she was landless, whereas the Altkolonier partner had a Wirtschaft of some kind.

24. In the Altkolonier villages enrollments of eighty or more pupils are common, even though the school-leaving age is twelve years. (In the Kleine Gemeinde schools children attend until the age of fourteen.)

provided in them are not inferior to those of the other schools, their separate existence tends to emphasize to children at an early age the social and economic differences between Anwohner and Wirt.

The Gradual Closing of Avenues of Opportunity

There was a time, until about 1946, before the parent colonies became crowded and before land became scarce and dear, when an enterprising and frugal Anwohner could, from an initial endowment of a few cows and possibly some pigs and a small flock of chickens, advance sufficiently within a relatively few years to acquire a modest farm and become a Wirt in his own right. Even nowadays the occasional Anwohner manages to acquire the status of Wirt, but the majority of them are unable to do this without organized intervention on their behalf. Where such intervention has been forthcoming, as at La Honda in Zacetecas from the parent Hague colony, the problems of removal to the new lands, of bringing them into production, and of subsistence until an economic return can be realized have been left to the individual. This, and the precariously small units which the erstwhile Anwohner can acquire on credit, can cause the venture to culminate for some in greater poverty and, possibly, destitution.

The majority of nonfarm employment opportunities are in the cheese industry, which provides part- or full-time employment to approximately 250 men. The hammer mill factories, oatmeal factory, feed mills, furniture makers, and the like employ some 60 to 75 more. In addition, there are job opportunities in a few of the village stores and smithies. Since the total number of landless families appears to be in excess of 800, this leaves some 450 men who are either entirely dependent on such incomes as they derive from their Anwohnerstellen, or who augment them with agricultural labor or through self-employment. In addition, there are many among the smaller landholders who do not derive an adequate subsistence from their farms, and, along with numerous young unmarried men, they are driven to compete with the landless in the narrow field of alternative economic opportunities open to the colonists.

Service functions offer several avenues of opportunity for self-employment which in general are open to the person who can command at least a small amount of captial. A few Anwohner, having acquired or built well-drilling machines, usually from scrap steel and machine parts, offer their services both in the colonies and nearby Mexican communities.[25] Others take up watch and clock repair. A few women help to augment family incomes by making pillows and other articles of bedding or the intricate black lace caps worn on Sundays by all Altkolonier matrons.

Catering to Mennonites and Mexicans, some colonists have apparently found bone-setting, doctoring, and dentistry and denture-making rewarding pursuits. Although the practitioners of these arts are not necessarily without some measure of competence and may have some notable successes to their credit in terms of suitable treatment bestowed, they are self-taught and therefore totally without formal training. Moreover, the "doctors" and "dentists" have no laboratory facilities at their disposal to aid in diagnoses, which are made on the basis of descriptions in "doctor books" and the past experience of the practitioner. The level of clinical hygiene maintained about their premises and their persons generally betrays a relative unawareness of and lack of concern for high standards of antisepsis. Moreover, their presence in the colonies frequently discourages ailing persons from seeking the advice and aid of properly qualified practitioners, who are generally consulted only as a last resort.

Not only are these persons untrained, but, in view of their cultural prejudices and the sophistication of modern techniques in

25. Although some feel that it represents an appeal to a dark power, water-divining is widely practised among the Mennonites. No doubt this reflects in part the near-desperation with which water is often sought. It is also common for Mexican ranchers to employ the services of one of the several Mennonite water diviners who have attained some notoriety by virtue of their successes in selecting productive well sites. Conversely, Mennonites are also known to avail themselves of the services of Mexican water diviners.

medicine and dentistry, they would also, in the main, be untrain-
able. The reasons for this are the Mennonites' suspicion of "book-
learning," which has been fostered to the degree that it has become essentially a part of their conservative folk character, and the
marginal level of literacy imparted by their existing school systems.

Education

Throughout their history the Mennonites have exhibited a relatively sincere interest in providing a good education
for their children. But the impact of the manner in which secular
schools were imposed upon them in Canada was traumatic, and
it led to a denigration of learning. The result of this, although the
basic thinking on education—to teach children what it is needful
to know—remains the same, has been a decline in standards of
secular learning over the past several decades. A realistic evaluation
of the situation now prevailing suggests that three-quarters or more
of that portion of the Mennonite population which has received
its education in Mexico—and by now that must be over 90 percent
of the entire population—is, by any meaningful standard, below
the level of functional literacy.[26] The schools do not impart to
them even a working knowledge of German, their "mother
tongue," and most women never learn enough Spanish to make
themselves understood even reasonably well. The majority of the
men learn only enough street vernacular to get along on their
necessary forays into the Spanish-speaking world. On balance, then,
most Mennonites experience little communication of ideas beyond
face-to-face exchanges in their own vernacular Plattdeutsch, and
they are thus effectively isolated from the more positive aspects of
the world about them. The reading of secular materials is not en-

26. By "functional literacy" the author here means specifically the ability to
convey ideas in writing beyond simple, elementary statements of fact and, likewise,
the ability to decipher writing whose idea content goes beyond the level of simple
fact. Since German, the language of instruction, is almost completely phonetic in
pronunciation, it is quite possible for a person to learn to read without understanding what he is reading. Indeed, in a number of ad hoc experiments made with young
people, this was found to be almost universally the case.

couraged, both because church authorities do not approve of it and because it is regarded as unproductive and a waste of time.[27] Moreover, since the unwritten dialect, Plattdeutsch, is the vernacular of everyday communication, the majority of colonists have no real occasion to use German and never develop a real working knowledge of it, although it is the language of the church and of instruction in the schools. Fewer still learn to read Spanish. As a result, most adults have very limited access to information of any kind.

School curricula are under the direct control of the clergy, who make periodic visits to the schools to ascertain that no aberrations from orthodox procedures and subject matter are introduced. Study material consists of a fourteen-page primer—the *Fibel*—the catechism, hymnary, and Scriptures, together with elementary arithmetic designed to teach the child what he needs to know to work simple problems dealing with weights, measures, areas, and volumes which he is likely to encounter as a farmer later on. Among the Altkolonier and Sommerfelder, school is normally in session from November to March and again in June.[28] The Kleine Gemeinde school year is somewhat longer—it runs a minimum of 140 days—and the curriculum is slightly broader; it includes a modicum of geography and elementary hygiene,[29] as well as very

27. Very little reading material enters the colonies. One of the few books approved of is the *Martyrerspiegel* or *Martyrs' Mirror*, which relates the persecutions to which the early Anabaptists were subjected. The *Mennonitische Rundschau*, a weekly published in Winnipeg, has a small circulation. The *Steinbach Post*, which was published in Manitoba and carried selections of secular literature and material on world affairs as well as direct reports from the various Mennonite settlements in North and South America, was acquired in 1966 by a publishing firm in Omaha, Nebraska. A change in style and content occurred, with the result that the formerly large readership in Mexico is falling off. Many, therefore, who until now read at least a little will in the future read practically nothing. There is a small number of individuals who receive journals published by various farm machinery companies, such as John Deere's *El Surco*, and illustrated periodicals in German or Spanish, such as *Der Stern* and *Life en Español*.

28. This arrangement of the school year harks back to Russia, where April and May were the time of spring work on the land, and school was let out so that children could remain at home to help.

29. The geography taught in Kleine Gemeinde schools relates mainly to the migrations of the forefathers of their group and to the journeys of the Biblical Patriarchs and of Christ and the Apostles. Instruction in hygiene emphasizes the

limited amounts of English and, recently, Spanish. There is, in general, no advancement of the child by grades from year to year. Much of the instruction is at the same level for all pupils. In reading, however, there is a sort of grading. The text for young pupils is the *Fibel*, that for the intermediate years the New Testament, and that for the final years the Old Testament, with the classes being sometimes referred to as *Fibler, Testamentler,* and *Bibler.* Luther's German translation of the Scriptures does not make easy reading. An analogous situation with respect to the learning of language could be imagined if the King James version of the Bible were substituted for all conventional types of reading material now available in elementary schools in the United States and Canada. Children normally commence school at the age of seven. Among the Altkolonier and Sommerfelder, girls normally leave at twelve, but boys may continue to the age of thirteen. In the Quellenkolonie school-leaving age is fourteen, with the proviso that boys must complete the year in which they reach that age, whereas girls may leave on their fourteenth birthday.

School attendance is nominally compulsory in all the Mennonite Gemeinden in Mexico and has traditionally been so. It is common, however, for children of all ages to be kept out of school sporadically, even for protracted periods, to assist with farm work. In Canada and Russia, where the main period of instruction also coincided with the winter months, there was less occasion for this than in Mexico, where the winters are open and the harvest itself often continues into the new year. Work is a way of life, and children are made to learn that at an early age. Smaller children, including preschoolers, may be set to gleaning beans or corn from the harvested fields. In the characteristically large families elder daughters must assume a good deal of responsibility for their younger siblings at an early age. Boys of twelve, ten, or even fewer years are often placed in sole charge of teams and take the place of men on tractors. For these and other reasons, then, absenteeism is high and does much to explain the low levels of erudition attained.

importance of cleanliness about the person and precautions to be taken to avoid the transmitting of communicable diseases.

The basic educational philosophy hinges on Romans 12:2 and 16: "And be not conformed to this world . . . Mind not high things, but condescend to men of low estate. Be not wise in your own conceits." It is fixed by the admonition contained in I Corinthians 7:20: "Let every man abide in the same calling wherein he was called." The latter passage is interpreted to mean that a person is born into the faith and calling of his forefathers, and must remain therein or risk divine retribution. For the Mennonite, then, it requires that he accept unquestioningly the religious rationale of his forebears and that he follow the traditional agrarian way of life. Within this framework, the learning imparted in the schools is regarded to be adequate. In the Danzig region and in South Russia before the exodus of the 1870's, at a time when few peasants learned to read, the marginal literacy of the Mennonites was adequate to the needs of their lives. In Canada, prior to the emigration to Mexico, the inadequacies of the traditional educational system within a more erudite host society were already apparent to some. The willingness of a significant section of the Altkolonier and Sommerfelder communities to comply with the law with respect to secular education proved a major hurdle to their leaders in getting the migration underway. Although it would be incorrect, in view of the alternatives to migration—in the case of the Altkolonier, excommunication—to say that all those who left Canada were of the ultra-conservative wing for whom the schools question was a critical issue, certainly the key religious and secular positions were held by members of that group, which consequently controlled the decision-making powers. Among the ultra-conservatives, there were those who would have done away with formal schooling entirely; they believed that children could be taught as well at home and that, in any case, God imparted knowledge and wisdom directly to persons deserving of them.

Under the influence of this type of thinking, teachers came to be chosen not for their erudition but for their orthodoxy. The academic qualifications of teachers had, moreover, declined in Canada during the pioneering period, while those who had obtained their education in Russia were already well on in years at the time of the founding of the colonies in Mexico.[30] Since the teachers are themselves products solely of the educational system they serve, receiving no professional training whatever, any attrition in standards of excellence tends to have a snow-balling, down-grading effect on the level of learning attained by each succeeding generation. Persons of superior intelligence and intellectual curiosity who persevere in extending their horizons are, if they become teachers, effectively prevented by ecclesiastical controls from imparting to their pupils knowledge relating to subjects other than those endorsed by the clergy.[31]

There is a general and growing awareness in the Mennonite community today of the inadequacy of the present educational system. People who themselves can read and write are seeing their children and grandchildren grow up illiterate, and they are becoming concerned about the implications for the future of such a state of affairs. This is not to suggest that there is much sentiment for the revolutionizing of education; there is not. Rather, the majority would probably like to see a raising of standards to approximately the level of those prevailing in the better—but still traditional,

30. In Russia, moreover, they had been forced to conform to the educational standards set by the more progressive majority, who did not participate in the migration to Canada.

31. The enforcement of orthodoxy in Altkolonier schools extends, for instance, to insistence upon use of archaic vowel inflections in the speaking of German. In the early 1940's a major ideological struggle erupted in the Manitoba colony when two villages, Blumenort and Blumenthal, began teaching the modern inflections in their schools. They were severely criticized by the Gemeinde. Finally, on October 8, 1942, at a Bruderschaft called for the purpose, they were called to account and categorically instructed to resume use of the archaic inflections. Upon their refusal to comply, they were threatened with wholesale excommunication, although this was never imposed. Gradually, as teachers who could or would teach the modern form became unavailable, the archaic inflections began to prevail once again in Blumenort and Blumenthal.

No grammar is taught in Altkolonier and Sommerfelder schools, nor would any such innovation be tolerated. In 1964 one teacher in the Manitoba colony, who had taught himself the fundamentals of German grammar, began to instruct his pupils in it too. When he failed to heed warnings to desist, he was placed under the ban.

Traditionally only male teachers are employed, but so acute has the shortage of persons who not only are willing to teach but also possess even the minimum level of literacy required become that in some instances women are doing the actual classroom teaching, although ostensibly their husbands are hired. In 1965 in the Hague colony one unmarried woman was also employed in one of the village schools.

orthodox, and German—Altkolonier and Sommerfelder schools in Canada prior to the migration. To such a step, however, the Altkolonier and Sommerfelder Elders, the majority of the clergy, and a substantial part of the community are still unalterably opposed. Nor is it likely that the colonies could effect a general raising of educational standards by themselves even in the event that overall agreement on the issue could be attained. The primary prerequisite of such a project would be an up-grading of teacher capabilities. The magnitude of such an undertaking is at least suggested by the fact that in recent years numerous schools have remained closed well beyond the customary November opening date simply because no person of sufficient literacy was available to teach in them.

The Kleine Gemeinde Quellenkolonie at Los Jagueyes has already confronted the problem of up-grading. During the early years of the colony, educational standards were deliberately neglected. There was always a minority, however, which, although opposed to the degree of secularization and to some of the curriculum content in Manitoba public schools at the time of their departure, would have liked to maintain their schools in such a state as to be capable of imparting a reasonable level of literary competence. Following the withdrawal of the ultra-conservative wing of the Kleine Gemeinde to British Honduras, the more liberal element became the majority in the Quellenkolonie, and a program of rehabilitating the schools was begun. This has proved extraordinarily difficult for two reasons. First, the persons who should be taking over the schools as older teachers withdraw attended these same schools during the years when a very low standard of education was maintained. Second, since the departure of the ultra-conservatives to British Honduras, many erstwhile Sommerfelder and Altkolonier have joined the Kleine Gemeinde and have taken up residence in Los Jagueyes. Although many of this group, which by now has a practical majority, came to the Quellenkolonie for the stated purpose of providing their children with the better education available in the Kleine Gemeinde schools, they are, by and large, blocking the up-grading attempts of the remainder of the original Kleine Gemeinde colonists. A substantial number of the latter, weary of internal ideological conflict over this problem and fearful of their own cultural and ethnic extinction if present trends are long permitted to continue, have during the past few years returned to Canada, where most of them are now participating with some of their Canadian brethren in the establishment of a minor but promising agricultural frontier in the region between lakes Manitoba and Winnipeg.[32]

Concessions to the Spanish-Speaking Umwelt

Of the Mennonite colonist groups in Mexico, only the Kleine Gemeinde has made any concession to the Spanish-speaking world. This has taken the form of adjusting its school curriculum to accommodate a very small amount of instruction in Spanish, the national language.[33] Not only is there no inclination among the Altkolonier and Sommerfelder to broaden into a secular curriculum and to commence the teaching of Spanish, but, even if there were, there is no acceptable personnel available to do it.

It is traditional among the Mennonites to have only Mennonite teachers. It was out of deference to this tradition and the tenacity with which it was adhered to that the government of Manitoba offered its assistance in improving the professional qualifications of Mennonite teachers when compulsory school attendance and the teaching of secular curriculum in the English language were first

32. In the autumn of 1965 delegates from the Quellenkolonie visited Ontario and Manitoba on a land-seeking mission. Their hope, in view of the anticipated problems of accommodating themselves to a former homeland which is much changed since the time they left it, was to find a tract of sufficient size to accommodate all those of the Kleine Gemeinde who were desirous of a return to Canada. No such block of land was found at the time. The trickle of families returning to Canada independently, however, continues.

33. The fact that the Kleine Gemeinde continues to teach more English than Spanish stems to some extent from a recognized uncertainty concerning their future in Mexico. The gradual withdrawal of friends and relatives to British Honduras and Canada diminishes the determination and commitment to carry on of those who remain. Since the national language of both Canada and British Honduras is English, it appears that the continued teaching of it in Mexico is owing to the possibility of a removal to one or the other of those countries.

instituted. Since in the Mennonites' Mexican colonies there are as yet no governmentally imposed requirements with respect to teachers' qualifications and curriculum content, these being exempt from such interference under the Privilegium, it does not appear, in view of prevailing ecclesiastical and community attitudes, that any concerted attempt to improve the quality of teaching or to broaden the curriculum can realistically be anticipated from the Altkolonier and Sommerfelder communities.

The situation which now prevails in Mexico does not represent the first instance in Mennonite experience of a deterioration in educational standards beyond the possibility of self-remedy within the colonies. A very comparable situation prevailed in the Chortitza mother colony in Russia in the 1830's and early 1840's. At that time the schools were under the supervision of the clergy, as they are in Mexico today. Since the founding of the colony half a century before, no steps had been taken to improve educational standards, which had badly deteriorated. In 1843 the Fürsorgekomitee (the Odessa-based Board of Guardians), which had authority over all colonial affairs, placed the management of all Mennonite school matters in the hands of the Agricultural Association headed by Johann Cornies.[34] Cornies set about raising educational standards partly through the importation of educators from Switzerland and Germany to train teachers, and partly through strictly enforced attendance.[35] In Mexico no such steps have been taken. There have been one or two Mennonites who, by virtue of their stature in the colonies and the confidence reposed in them by the government, might have been a "Johann Cornies." They have, however, failed to recognize the opportunity or have chosen not to seize it.

A Few Portents for the Future

There are, nonetheless, a few signs that point to the possibility that the process of cultural attrition and impoverishment

34. *Hildebrand's Zeittafel,* p. 192, entry of 1843.
35. "Education among the Mennonites of Russia," *The Mennonite Encyclopedia,* II, 154.

which has accompanied the deterioration of educational standards
might be ultimately arrested. In response to a small number of persons who desired a better education for their children than was
being provided in the village schools, yet who were unwilling to
place them in Mexican schools, the Mennonite General Conference
Board of Christian Service founded an elementary school on the
Redekop ranch south of Weidenfeld, Santa Clara colony, in 1951.
The ultimate Sommerfelder reaction was to buy the land and force
removal of the school. Later a similar elementary school was begun
in Cd. Cuauhtémoc, which was attended by children from a few
families in nearby Altkolonier villages and by those of the remaining Russländer in the town itself. This school has since been relocated just outside the boundary of the Manitoba colony, at
Quinta Lupita, some four kilometers northwest of Cd. Cuauhtémoc. Another elementary school has been functioning on a private farmstead at Campo 38½, Steinreich, Ojo de la Yegua colony,
for the past several years. Despite the fact that from the beginning
the Altkolonier have excommunicated those who permitted their
children to attend these schools and have exerted themselves
mightily to have them closed by government order, enrollments
have slowly increased until at the end of 1969 they stood at over
150.[36] The school at Quinta Lupita, named Escuela Alvaro Obregón in memory of the president under whose administration the
Mennonites came to Mexico, is staffed by qualified Mennonite personnel trained in Canada and Mexico, and has been accorded tacit
accreditation by the state authorities through the device of registering its students in the state school of Cd. Cuauhtémoc. At the present time, and for as long as the existing climate of opinion prevails,
there appears to be no justification for assuming that graduates of
Escuela Alvaro Obregón will be accepted for teaching positions in
the village schools of the colonies. The ecclesiastical attitude is
firmly entrenched and is not likely to be voluntarily modified. The
threat of excommunication would be used to exact compliance
with the official church stand from colonists who might be tempted

36. Miss Helen Ens, teacher in charge of Escuela Alvaro Obregón, personal
communication.

to engage such a teacher. Moreover, each individual village has powers of interdiction against the admission to residence of any person who is not a Wirt of that village and a member, in good standing, of the church. Even in the face of substantial support for the hiring of a qualified teacher, then, persons such as graduates of Escuela Alvaro Obregón, being the children of excommunicants and themselves not members of the Altkolonier or Sommerfelder church, would almost by definition be prevented from serving as teachers.[37]

In recent years, however, the Mennonite school system has been coming under the progressively closer scrutiny of the Mexican authorities. The Altkolonier in Chihuahua focussed attention upon their own educational system in particular as a result of their attempts to have the "renegade" schools closed. Investigators have been covertly evaluating Mennonite schools, and one team from Mexico City reported in the autumn of 1964 that in its judgment, if the present trends in cultural attrition among the Mennonites continue for another generation, the colonies will become a burden to the people of Mexico.[38] In November of 1969 Governor Oscar Flores of the state of Chihuahua went on record publicly to the effect that he intended to see Spanish taught in the Mennonite schools "very soon." Although no prediction can be made with certainty, it appears probable, in view of such investigations and such public statements, and in view of the Mexican government's sustained preoccupation with the campaign against analphabetism, that attidudinal changes at the highest levels, which may culminate in an infringement of the Privilegium in the area of education, have already been set in train.

If this be so, then the possibility of an ultimate wholesale Mennonite exodus from Mexico—possibly to Paraguay or Bolivia—

37. One student, a Sommerfelder from Santa Clara, has qualified for a teaching certificate by completing his training at the Colégio Palmore in Cd. Chihuahua and expects to return to teach at Escuela Alvaro Obregón.

38. The contents of the confidential report, sent by the central government to an official in Cd. Cuauhtémoc, were made available to the author through an intermediary, subject to the strict understanding that the identity of the persons involved would not be divulged.

must be reckoned with. Certainly the installation of native Mexican teachers in colony schools would trigger a major emigration, at whatever cost. If however at such a time there was already in existence a body of graduates of schools such as Alvaro Obregón, who were capable of effectively introducing educational changes which might be required, then, although a substantial portion of the Mennonite community might still be expected to depart the country, the majority would probably, with good will or ill, make their peace with the new conditions and remain.[39] It is well to note, however, that to the present time the enrollment of the "renegade" schools at Quinta Lupita and Steinreich is composed entirely of the children of families who have had considerable exposure to the world beyond the colonies and, almost invariably, beyond Mexico, particularly in Canada. None of those colonists whose experience has been limited essentially to the confines of the colonies has taken any overt steps either to affiliate his children with these two schools or to raise standards of achievement in the colonies' schools. Although, as has been stated, there is a general awareness of the inadequacy of the existing schools, this awareness has not extended to an appreciation of the magnitude of the inadequacy nor to the creation of a general positive determination to raise educational standards in the colonies.

The Ban

Because, when the church yields to public sentiment in matters of secular innovation, the interdiction is nevertheless not lifted, the stresses originally engendered remain to plague internal relations in the colonies. Such is the rigidity of doctrine that those

39. It seems unlikely that government encroachment upon the Privilegium in the area of education would call for the expunging of German from the curriculum in Mennonite schools. In remote parts of the country, where schools are only now being instituted for the first time and where the indigenous populations speak their Indian tongues almost to the exclusion of Spanish, up to one-half of the curriculum content is permitted to be in the native dialect. Such being the case, it would seem that this would constitute a good precedent for the Mennonites, as native-born Mexicans, to cite with respect to their paramount concern for the retention of German in their educational system.

once excommunicated for breaches of regulations under which the ban is now no longer invoked cannot be reinstated in the church without first "making their case"—begging the forgiveness of the Gemeinde. Few individuals who now see their erstwhile judges indulging with impunity in activities for which they endured the ban and ostracism are willing to humble and debase themselves to that degree. So firmly imbedded is the punitive concept, however, that there is little if any sentiment for freely reinstating such persons in order to expunge the matter once and for all. Neither is it possible to detect such a sentiment among the excommunicants themselves, who, having been banned and shunned for something now tacitly permitted, strongly feel that the interdiction should be revived and invoked as well against all who now transgress it.

The power of the ban in exacting compliance from the individual, although in general still substantial, is diminishing. In view of this and in recognition of the possibility that the existence of too large a body of excommunicants could lead to the formation of a new Mennonite group which might assume a role such as that of the Bergthaler, whose relative liberalism plagued and ultimately helped destroy Altkolonier solidarity in Manitoba, the ban is now invoked selectively and rarely upon more than one member of a family. Other family members, including the wife or husband,[40] are then admonished to shun the excommunicant. This technique, which places family members in the awkward position of having to choose between church and family, can cause anguish in well-meaning but baffled individuals. The usual result is that they appeal to the excommunicant to "make his case" at whatever cost in pride or dignity, to relieve them of the burden of decision.

The traditional closeness of the Mennonite "clan," with the high value it places on family ties, can also be seriously strained by the existence within it of banned individuals. Since others may not greet them, speak to them, worship with them, or sit down to eat

40. Menno Simon, the erstwhile Roman Catholic priest who assumed leadership of the Anabaptist wing which gave rise to the Mennonite Church, himself advocated shunning between man and wife where one or the other had incurred the ban. Later he recanted on this point, considering it too harsh.

with them, they cannot attend family reunions, engagement parties, weddings, or funerals without disrupting the proceedings.[41]

The clergy, too, can find themselves in a dilemma over the imposition of the ban when interdictions which are no longer strictly adhered to are not permitted to pass into abeyance simultaneously in all colonies.[42]

Quite a few individuals, troubled by their excommunicated status and unwilling to become reconciled with the church on its terms, have taken once more to "returning" to Canada. This is a curious phenomenon in its own right, for the majority of these are persons who, if they were not born in Mexico, at least grew up there. Moreover, they have been educated to the church's doctrine that the exodus from Canada was tantamount to expulsion; this is firmly believed by the clergy and is not therefore to be taken as promulgation of a deliberate falsehood. In view of these factors, the persistence of the "Canadian legend" and the care that is taken not to forfeit, by neglect, rights to Canadian citizenship are surprising. Another group of dissidents has created a new colony in British Honduras. In 1965 they had an Elder from a Mennonite Gemeinde in Manitoba come to ordain an Elder for them, thus creating a new Gemeinde for themselves, voiding their excommunicated status, and sundering any dependence on the former parent church in Chihuahua.

41. Often, nowadays, such persons are invited anyway (in defiance of church ordinance) to convey the point that there is no personal animosity involved. The excommunicant then responds by being "unable" to come. On private visits (also in defiance of rules) between friends the further provisions of the ban may be circumvented by verbal greetings, and the question of what to do about Vesper is settled by everyone eating fruit or other foods out of hand or by setting a place for the excommunicant at the table at a slight but symbolic remove from the rest.

42. The ultra-conservative Elder of the Manitoba colony, for instance, under whose tutelage the Elders of the daughter colonies developed their attitudes, himself came to be shunned by the latter for yielding to pressure on the question of rubber-tired tractors. Calvin W. Redekop, *The Old Colony Mennonites* (Baltimore: Johns Hopkins University Press, 1969), contains a number of case studies on stress situations in Altkolonier life.

Returnees to Canada

Others, too, not under the ban but often landless and responding to the hope of economic opportunity, have been returning to Canada ever since border regulations were relaxed after World War II. Originally the majority of these people were attracted to the West Reserve in Manitoba, where sugar-beet culture had been greatly expanded during the war and where consequently there was a considerable demand for unskilled labor to tend and harvest this and other crops in the early and late summer months. Since about 1955, although people continue to go to the West Reserve, other destinations have come to be preferred. In 1955, an agricultural settlement of Altkolonier from Mexico was begun at Matheson, Ontario. This has since dissolved, mainly as a result of internal dissensions. Some of the participants in this venture returned to Mexico, while others removed to other parts of Canada. A group of several hundred Mennonites from Mexico now lives in the area around Aylmer, Ontario, and another group is farming in the Rainy River region in the western part of the same province. Still others have established themselves in the Altkolonier community in the Peace River country of Alberta. In recent years, the Fort St. John area of British Columbia has been attracting a significant number of Mennonites from Mexico, largely because of the opportunities there to work in timber operations until a farm can be established. Others who are Canadian citizens and who are now of an age that makes them eligible for the Old Age Security pension return for that reason.

Few of these "returnees" make a clean break with Mexico. Rather, the common pattern has been for them initially to go to Canada for the summer, perhaps in conjunction with visits to relatives, to work until the ground freezes in the autumn, and to return to Mexico for the winter. Some do this year after year, living throughout the winter and spring months on money they have saved from the relatively high wages earned in Canada. Others remain in Canada for several years and save their money; then they return to Mexico and acquire farms of their own.

Many who would seem to have no hesitation about departing Mexico forever nevertheless return from their first forays into Canada. Cultural shock and the various problems they encounter in coping with life in a strange country, even though the majority gravitate toward Canadian Mennonite settlements where they can at least communicate in their Plattdeutsch vernacular, are the dominant causes. Some are also troubled by the disapproving attitude of the Altkolonier mother church in Mexico with respect to these activities and return there for the sake of remaining on good terms with the Gemeinde. However, the attraction of good wages and the personal freedom that exists outside of the orthodox milieu of the Mexican colonies lure many back to Canada. They may shuttle back and forth to Mexico several times, but each stay in Canada becomes longer than the previous one, and eventually they settle there permanently.

One of the main obstacles for many in a permanent return to Canada continues to be the thorny matter of schools. For almost half a century now the English-language public schools and the "injustices" associated with their implementation have been held up as the reason for the exodus—some would have it "expulsion"—from Canada. The average Altkolonier or Sommerfelder, having grown up with this belief, totally accepts it and harbors a very real if uncomprehending fear of the public schools in Canada. In the Peace River country some Altkolonier have always managed, more or less legally, to avoid sending their children to school through the expedient of homesteading beyond the three-mile radius of any school, thus removing themselves to a distance at which attendance is not compulsory. As an area in which Altkolonier lived developed and new schools were founded, the Mennonites would simply sell their farms and move once more beyond the settlement fringe and the jurisdiction of the public schools. However, now that schools have been provided for the entire region in which agriculture is feasible, this strategem is in general no longer workable, and some Altkolonier have in recent years responded by departing for British Honduras and Bolivia.

Other Mennonites keep their children out of Canadian schools by going from Mexico to Canada in the late spring. By the time they come to the attention of the authorities and action is taken to require attendance from their school-age children, the summer vacation has as a rule begun. In the autumn they similarly escape complying with the law for a month or two before action again is instituted. Then, when the issue can no longer be evaded, they return to Mexico. Gradually, however, usually after employing this strategem a few times, they begin to understand their Canadian surroundings better, and they learn to appreciate not only the earning opportunities that come with education but also the fact that Family Allowances are paid only on behalf of children actually attending school; as a result, they lose most of their apprehensions with respect to the schools and offer no further resistance to their children's attendance.

The bulk of the movement to Canada emanates from the colonies in Chihuahua, these being the most accessible to and therefore in continuing contact with the former homeland. In recent years, however, people from the more remote Durango region have also been participating in the movement to a considerable degree. Characteristically, those from Chihuahua have been attracted to Manitoba, where they gravitate toward the Plattdeutsch-speaking Mennonite communities and find employment in agriculture or the canning industry, or as common laborers. Ever since the settlement attempt at Matheson, Ontario, a considerable number have been proceeding directly to southern Ontario, where the cropping season is longer than in Manitoba and the concentration on labor-intensive crops higher. Those with capital may go to the Rainy River area and buy farms, or to Alberta, where after a year's residence they can exercise homestead rights in the Peace River region. From Durango the trend is to go to southern Ontario or to the Fort St. John area of British Columbia. Very few return to their old home areas in Saskatchewan, mainly because these are regions of extensive agriculture which offer few employment opportunities. The few who do return there to establish eligibility for the Old Age Security pension usually take up residence and live out their years in their former home communities.[43]

43. All that is required of Canadian citizens living abroad, in establishing eligibility for the Old Age Security pension, is that they return to Canada for one year

The Mennonites coming to Canada from Mexico appear to be universally aware of the Canadian government's Family Allowance program. As citizens, they can collect an amount ranging from $6 to $8 per month for each child under sixteen years of age from the time they enter Canada. Those who lack citizenship but come as landed immigrants are eligible for Family Assistance, which brings in an equivalent payment. Since large families are common, these monies can very significantly augment income.

Mexican–Canadian Mennonite Relations

Generally speaking, the "returnees" have a reputation as diligent workers. Since it is customary to put children to work at an early age, all but the very young generally find employment; it is not unusual for a family to work as a group in agricultural labor. Although most returnees are unobtrusive and go quietly about the business of earning a living, there are those who do not at first fit satisfactorily into the communities in which they locate. They then become the object of certain concerns and resentments on the part of the Canadians—Mennonites and others—among whom they live. In the main, their inability to adjust easily may be attributed to the cultural attrition among Mennonites in Mexico during the last half-century and their consequent backwardness relative to the Canadian host society. Their standards of personal cleanliness are often low and are viewed critically by their Canadian neighbors, particularly when close association, as among children in school, is involved. They have been known to bring communicable diseases such as dysentery from Mexico, whereupon the problems of quarantine and eradication devolve on Canadian health agencies. Employers who are accustomed to a high level of integrity on the part of Mennonite workmen complain that a substantial proportion of those from Mexico think nothing of breaking their word; this can have serious consequences if reliance is placed on them to

when they file their application and that they have lived a minimum of ten years in Canada during their lifetime. Once payment commences, the recipient may leave the country once more to live abroad. Persons who have lived forty years or more in Canada, but who are living abroad, need not return to Canada to establish eligibility for the pension.

perform urgent and necessary labors during the short Canadian summer. In their old home areas, such as the West Reserve in Manitoba, behavior of this type engenders resentment on the part of the Mennonite community at large. Many there have not forgotten the sometimes acrid terms in which they were censured in their time by those who joined the exodus for having abandoned their morality in making a pact with the "world" in relation to schools and other matters; moreover, they feel that their own integrity is somehow impugned when unfavorable comments about a few Mennonites are bruited about.

Those Mennonites who return each winter to Mexico are often criticized because they take most of their earnings with them, they spend practically nothing in the Canadian communities in which they work, and they pay essentially no taxes in support of the public services they enjoy while living there. Criticism is also leveled at the avidity and knowledgeableness with which they pursue all forms of public assistance available to them—notably Family Allowances, Family Assistance, and the Old Age Security pension, as well as welfare assistance from local municipal governments. Although their eligibility for these forms of assistance is not, in general, open to challenge in terms of the laws of Canada, many members of the community feel that if in its time it was "impossible" for these people to continue to live amidst the "evils" of Canadian society, then from the moral point of view they should not now look to Canada for a living; in addition, they are regarded as not having contributed to the creation of the wealth which they are now "undeservedly" sharing.

The Mennonite from Mexico does not see himself in these terms. He has grown up with a religion which teaches him not to feel a part of any secular kingdom or nation. His cultural horizons in Mexico have generally been limited to the traditional, largely autocratic, and paternalistic milieu of the colonies, together with superficial contacts, on a mundane level, with the Mexican world around him. He is a peasant. His conceptions of colony administrations and national governments are essentially the same. If the government is willing to pay him "child money" or an old age pension, it is a generous, paternalistic gesture which is not basically different—except in amount—from assistance he might receive from his Gemeinde in Mexico if he were indigent or ill. To him, Canada is a wealthy country which can well afford such largesse. If a bit of cunning should be involved in obtaining the maximum personal advantage from it, this too is a peasant trait. Within the slender frame of reference available to him, he well may not comprehend the effect his action has on others when he gives his word and then fails, without explanation, to keep it. In time, if he remains in Canada, he learns by experience to appreciate some of the subtleties that adjustment to life in a modern, as opposed to his heretofore largely medieval, community requires, and he also learns, very quickly, to appreciate the personal freedom he finds in his new community, as well as the gadgets and conveniences that are a part of it. In view of the many outside cultural contacts which nowadays are unavoidable in Canada, his children quickly adopt the prevailing values of the community and readily merge with it.

Relationship to the Mexican Umwelt

Much less positive than the adjustment which, as a rule, Mennonites make when they come to Canada has been their relationship with the host society in Mexico. Their position, however, within the Mexican Umwelt has changed markedly since the time the original colonies were founded. At that time, the Mennonites were the acknowledged superiors, culturally and in terms of material wealth, of the Mexican rural population, which was only then beginning to emerge from feudalism, in the regions in which they settled. This situation has changed, however, and is continuing to change, to the disadvantage, in qualitative terms, of the Mennonites, although they seem oblivious to it. While the Mennonites, in consequence of their ineffectual school system and the narrow range of experience afforded the individual in their closed colonies, have undergone a notable degree of cultural attrition since locating in Mexico, the country itself has for some years now, with telling effect, been waging a nationwide campaign against illiteracy. Almost all of the children in the regions in which the Mennonite colonies are located are now receiving at least an elementary school education. The Mexicans are eager for change and progress, and while they are willing to acknowledge the Mennonites as hard and diligent workers (*muy buenos trabajadores*), they are also recognizing them as very backward (*muy atrasado*). It is no longer difficult to find Mexican farmers who not only have learned all they could of Mennonite farming techniques, but who are now farming more scientifically and successfully than many Mennonites. Increasingly, too, the Mennonites' Mexican neighbors are becoming aware of the terms of the Privilegium (which are so much at variance with the ideals of the revolution which they learn in school and from many forms of propaganda) under which the alien Mennonites, who acknowledge no patriotic attachment to Mexico, are enjoying special immunities vis-à-vis their land. Mexican businessmen and government officials, while freely recognizing the economic benefits that Mennonite industry and thrift have brought to the regions in which they live, also do not approve of their special status. Political activists—particularly in the Chihuahua region where the Mennonites are most numerous—eagerly foster and exploit resentment and antagonism against them, stressing the point that they are Canadian or Russian or whatever, *not* Mexican, and making political capital out of the implied injustice and affront to the Mexican people inherent in the existence of the Privilegium.

Tabloid sheets such as Chihuahua's *La Jeringa* (The Syringe) and Cd. Cuauhtémoc's *Voz de Cuauhtémoc* (Voice of Cuauhtémoc) carry polemical attacks on the Mennonites almost daily. Illustrated magazines such as *Nosotros* (We), which has a national circulation, have also severely attacked them under headlines such as "La República Menonita de Chihuahua," [44] "Un Atentado contra México" [45] (A Transgression against Mexico), and "Feudalismo Menonita." [46] I have yet to see an article in any such periodical which presents an accurate picture of conditions in the Mennonite

44. *Nosotros*, May 17, 1965, pp. 20–24.
45. *Ibid.*, May 31, 1965, pp. 20–23.
46. *Ibid.*, June 14, 1965, pp. 24–29.

colonies. Rather they tend to concentrate upon manifestations of wealth, and contrast these with the manifestations of poverty among the Mexican population. Recently Chihuahua's moderate *El Heraldo* has also been publishing criticism, deploring the Mennonites' failure to participate in Seguro Social, the national social security and medical program,[47] and their grudging compliance in the continuing campaign against communicable diseases.

Many ejidatarios and colonos in the settlements near the colonies, as well as numerous business and professional people in the towns, would probably feel that the words of a Russian school teacher to a Mennonite boy some seventy years ago provide a good description of the Mennonites today (the appropriate Mexican terms have been substituted for their Russian equivalents):

That is the way you [Mennonite] colonists are. You regard the [Mexicans] as being beneath you. —— But you are the strangers here, are our guests, for this land is ours, the [Mexicans']! —— And would you look about you, look at the [Mennonite] villages, and then at those of the [Mexicans], only a short way from your own door. What a contrast! It seems as though our great landowners must disappear, if only to make way for you [Mennonites.] Their lands pass over into your hands, and our [agrarista]? He goes away empty-handed, remains poor, as he has always been. —— Your sons and daughters do not enter the service of others—not even that of other [Mennonites], let alone [Mexicans]. They remain properly at home in the full Wirtschaften, and when they marry they too have such a Wirtschaft, one with 65 [hectares] of

47. A subhead in an article in *El Heraldo* of April 13, 1966, dealing with a recently inaugurated study of the Mennonite colonies by a team from the Department of Health and Social Assistance of the federal government, reads, "La Ignorancia El Primer Obstáculo." The text states that a low level of culture prevails among all the Mennonites.

The Seguro Social, which is partly financed by funds from the Lotería Nacional, Mexico's national lottery, became a serious issue between Mexican authorities and the Mennonite colonies in the late 1950's, when the former attempted to require Mennonite participation. Such a requirement, however, was regarded as an infringement of the Privilegium and was vigorously opposed by the Mennonite leaders. Eventually an agreement was reached whereby participation on the part of self-employed individuals and their dependents would be on a voluntary basis, but all employees had to be provided with Seguro Social protection. Nonetheless, this issue is said to have been instrumental in the decision of a considerable number of persons to migrate to British Honduras.

land. The sons . . . of our farmers, however, must . . . work for you, as, when they were [peons], they worked for the [hacendado]. . . . It seems as though God Himself is for you [Mennonites] and against us [Mexicans].[48]

The Mennonites' Mexican neighbors, it may be noted, harbor no ethnically oriented antagonisms against them. Rather, they admire their tall stature and oftentimes blonde Nordic complexions, and they would gladly intermarry with them. The prevention of amalgamation with the local population, on the other hand, in Mexico as in Canada and Russia before, is one of the principal reasons for the Mennonites' insistence upon solidaristic settlement and closed communities. The desire to avoid incorporation into the host society is also at the root of the determination not to introduce Spanish in the schools, just as they refused to teach English in Canada, for this would open up new and inevitably interesting avenues of contact with the world around them. The Mennonite women in particular support the interdiction of Spanish. With it, they fear, would be imbibed certain cultural values and customs of the Mexican population, among them such "institutions" as the *casa chica* (the maintaining of a mistress in a separate establishment), which would inevitably diminish the stability of their society.

Although relations between Mennonites and Mexicans may be cordial and denote a considerable degree of mutual respect, few close friendships develop between them. There *is* a great contrast between the two peoples: the one is sober and somewhat dour in manner, the other is outgoing and hearty; the one is frugal, the other tends to prodigality.

Even though they do not identify in a patriotic sense with Mexico, the Mennonites do manifest a considerable sense of responsibility toward the government and toward the Mexican population in their immediate environs. Taxes, even in the most difficult years of drouth, have never been delinquent. Beggars— persons from the neighboring ranchos or Indians from the depths of

48. Arnold Dyck, *Verloren in Der Steppe* (Steinbach, Manitoba: Selbstverlag, 1944), p. 40. Translation from the German by the author.

the Sierra Madre—are not to be turned away but are to be given good food fit for the giver's own table.[49] Mexicans are always permitted to glean in the Mennonites' fields, even though this creates conflicts of interest when laborers are hired to harvest fields which they hope their families may glean. There is also an inclination—in the face of the alternatives of a high incidence of begging and commodity thefts—to give what employment they can to Mexican laborers. Although surely the Mennonites could own corn harvesters, they have desisted from acquiring them because the corn harvest is one of the major sources of employment to the rural population. Similarly, relatively few mechanical bean harvesters are employed, even though these can be manufactured in the colonies. Mexican cattle are permitted to forage freely over colony lands after harvest. In Chihuahua sheepmen are also permitted to pasture over the colonies on the annual late autumn drive from the Sierra Madre to market and wintering grounds.

The Mennonites also try to maintain good relations with local as well as higher levels of government. A good deal of work is done on colony roads to keep them fit for motor traffic. The Hague colony in particular has tried to build good relations through gestures of generosity. In about 1940 a gift of 5,000 pesos ($1,030 U.S.) was made to the town of Canatlán, seat of the municipio government, to improve its plaza. In about 1955 the colony made a gift of 18,000 pesos ($1,440 U.S.) to Nuevo Ideal to assist in the building of a new school. When the highway from Canatlán to Santiago Papasquiaro, which passes by the colony, was paved a few years ago, the Mennonites, since they own no motor vehicles, were exempted from the special levies laid on to pay for it. Nevertheless, they contributed 80,000 pesos ($6,400 U.S.). Similarly, when Nuevo Ideal was hooked up to the state power grid in 1964, the Hague colony donated 8,000 pesos ($640 U.S.) to help pay for the line, although it makes no use of it.

Local governments reciprocate in various ways. Herd law has been imposed, giving the Mennonites the right to impound bother-

49. The admonition not to turn away the traveler or beggar is based on the experience of the Patriarch Abraham, who unknowingly entertained God.

some free-ranging Mexican cattle; this applies all year in the Hague colony and from June to December in the Chihuahua region. In the Hague colony, too, when grazing land is converted to cropland, the assessor may fail to change its classification, even though cropland carries a substantially higher tax rate. When land was expropriated in the Manitoba and Swift Current colonies for the new highway from Cd. Cuauhtémoc to Bachíniva, the route was laid out in such a way as to inconvenience the Mennonites as little as possible.

Mexicans may be hired as village herdsmen. They are almost invariably employed for the making of adobe brick, a task which the Mennonites do not relish but which the Mexicans also are reputed to do better. Relationships reminiscent of the patrón-peón relationship that existed prior to the revolution not infrequently develop between Mennonite and Mexican. It usually comes about somewhat like this: A Mexican laborer will seek work with a Mennonite farmer. If he is fortunate and obtains work, he will complete it, take his wages, and depart. However, shortly thereafter he may be back, seeking a small loan which he undertakes to repay out of future earnings with the same farmer. Eventually a sort of regular arrangement emerges, with the laborer returning whenever needed, but gradually and deliberately increasing his indebtedness to the farmer. His reasoning is that: if he is in debt to the farmer, then the latter must, in his own interest, give what work he has to him or forfeit all hope of obtaining repayment. Moreover, if he is in debt to him, and if he or a member of his family becomes ill, he can, for the same reason, depend on at least some assistance from his employer. Characteristically such a relationship persists until the workman's indebtedness amounts to some 500 or 600 pesos, at which point he ceases to return, defaulting on his debt, which his erstwhile employer does not try very hard to collect. Before he takes the final step, however, the laborer will have tried to establish a similar relationship with another "patrón" in another village. Whether seen in that light or not, such arrangements are a form of "social security" and are as old as feudalism.

Although almost without exception the Mennonites treat Mexicans working for them fairly and feed them well, a considerable degree of social distance not evident in all-Mennonite employer-employee relationships is almost universally apparent. Mexican laborers are seldom asked to eat with the family of the Wirt but are fed separately, although usually as well. Children are discouraged from unnecessary fraternizing with them. This differs little from the relationship which will normally prevail in all-Mexican employer-employee relationships, except that in the former case the motivation is ethnic, while in the latter it is social in origin. There is no closeness in either case. Generally speaking, Mennonites get along well with Mexicans who work for them, and, as has been brought out, in certain situations prefer them to Mennonite laborers. There has been a growing number of instances in recent years, however, in which politically motivated persons have coached laborers to lodge complaints against Mennonite employers for alleged infractions of the labor code. The Mennonites do not understand the code but as a rule pay customary wages and furnish customary conditions of work. They are usually baffled by the threat of proceedings and pay the amount necessary to have the action withdrawn. This tactic is regarded by the Mennonites, with whatever justification, as another instance of "legal" pillage. Nowadays, when a project involving a substantial labor force is undertaken, it is usual for a Mennonite employer to let it out to a Mexican labor contractor, thus protecting himself against the possibility of any litigation arising out of the performance of the job.

Whereas Mexicans are frequently hired as common laborers, they also occupy an important niche at the opposite end of the labor scale. Because of the quality of the education they receive, the Mennonites generally lack ability in the reading and writing of Spanish, and in auditing, stock control, salesmanship, and other aspects of business life. Industries much of whose business is outside the colonies have therefore found it to their advantage to employ trained Mexican personnel. If a certain wariness that exists between Mennonites and Mexicans is to diminish, such mutually advantageous working arrangements would appear to be among the best ways of accomplishing that end.

Conclusion

Beyond attaining a level of material success which will make their economic survival possible, the ambitions of the Mennonites in Mexico are fundamentally these: linguistic, cultural, and ethnic survival, while avoiding absorption by the host society. In terms of these parameters the issues are clear and revolve around a calculated assessment of the potentialities of the environment followed by the raising of human capabilities to effect a rational, enduring adjustment to those potentialities. Inescapably this subsumes revision of the agrarian rationale and the reactionary-conservative philosophy which continue to dictate the nature and degree of the Mennonite response to the world around them. Just as inescapably, a reversal of the processes of cultural attrition and resource attrition now so much in evidence subsumes education, and secular education at that; this is a thorny question which can be approached only under the aegis of resolute coercive pressure or in the wake of a basic change in the governing attitude now prevailing. The fact that their Mexican neighbors are becoming ever more aware of and ever less willing to afford them the right to their aloof and privileged status, coupled with a diminishing capability on the part of the Mennonites to find a remedy for their own economic and social ills, lends urgency to these matters.

Appendix

Mennonite Colonization in British Honduras

The Mennonites, and particularly some of their more conservative branches, have had a history of repeated migration to remote frontiers in the attempt to maintain their traditional agrarian way of life. In response to unacceptable legislation and cultural incursions of the secular world, but always prompted also by land hunger, the Mennonite groups now in British Honduras have (with the exception of a small group of the Amish and Old Order persuasions) within the past century engaged in three such migrations—from South Russia to Canada in the 1870's, from Canada to Mexico in the wake of the two World Wars, and finally from Mexico to British Honduras. The immediate background of their colonies in British Honduras, then, is predominantly found in their Mexican experience, with further background in Canada.

Events Leading to the Migration to British Honduras

The sentiment for migration from Mexico developed in response to the threat of governmental imposition of unacceptable requirements, just as similar circumstances had prompted the movement from Canada to Mexico. In Canada compulsory secular education and the uncertainties surrounding the Mennonites' pacifist position, the latter of which had been subjected to considerable testing in the courts during the World Wars, led to exodus. In Mexico, in the mid-1950's, it was the unequivocally stated intention of the government to incorporate the Mennonites into its

331

social security system, Seguro Social, which ostensibly triggered migration sentiment. It must be understood, however, that economic and social stresses—the former relating primarily to land hunger, the latter to growing internal dissension—also figured importantly in the decision to migrate. That the ensuing movement came to be directed toward British Honduras was more a product of circumstance than design.

In the spring of 1955, Peter H. W. Wiebe, an Altkolonier Mennonite from the Manitoba colony in the Bustillos Valley of Chihuahua, went to El Paso, Texas on business. While waiting to have his visa application processed at the U.S. consulate in Cd. Juárez, Wiebe who had some knowledge of English, had occasion to assist other Mennonites in stating their business. This aroused the interest of U.S. Vice-Consul Peter S. Madison. Madison proved to be well informed on the Mennonites, largely, it seems, because of the traffic in used farm machinery to their Mexican colonies from the U.S. He was aware of their unwillingness to participate in the Seguro Social program and their prevailing land hunger. He was further aware that the Mennonites in Chihuahua were restless and were moving in small numbers to such widely separated places as the gulf state of Tamaulipas and Ontario in Canada. "Why not, then, move to British Honduras?" he suggested. He knew the nature of the Privilegium and felt confident that the government of that country would extend the immunities and guarantees which were the preferred preconditions to Mennonite migration to new lands. Madison himself, through his wife's family's commercial interests in British Honduras, knew the country at firsthand and also knew that its government was hopeful of attracting agricultural colonists. Wiebe began inquiry at the Office of Information and Communication in Belize. That led the authorities in Belize to issue an invitation for a delegation of Mennonites to visit British Honduras. For some months the Altkolonier considered the offer. In November of 1955, the Sommerfelder [1] of the Santa Clara colony

1. The Sommerfelder are a conservative offshoot of the Bergthaler, one of the church groups which came to Manitoba from South Russia in the 1870's. They split from the parent church in 1890 over qualifications of teachers in Mennonite schools. Their colony in 1955 was some twenty kilometers from the Altkolonier colonies in Chihuahua. The Altkolonier have since acquired the intervening land.

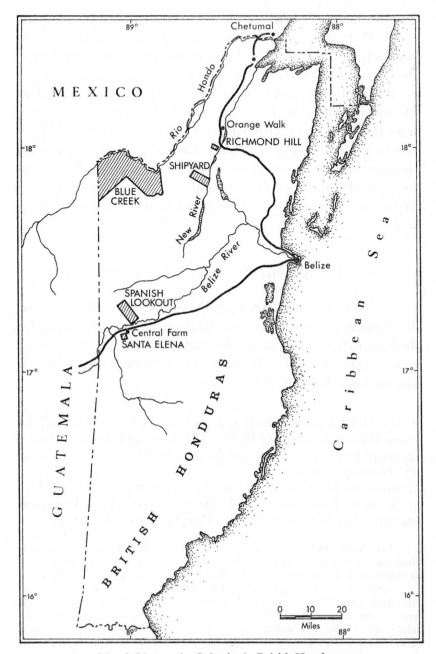

Map 2. Mennonite Colonies in British Honduras

sent two men with Wiebe to British Honduras. On the delegates' return their report of their trip aroused also the interest of the Kleine Gemeinde colony at Los Jagueyes on the western flank of the Santa Clara Valley. In January of 1956, a joint delegation representing all three groups went to Belize to pursue negotiations. Meanwhile, other Mennonite efforts were directed at obtaining from the Mexican government official exemption from participation in the Seguro Social program. Lack of progress in this direction heightened sentiment for emigration.[2] Further delegations were dispatched to British Honduras, and an inventory was taken to determine the amount of land which each of the several groups would require.

The Agreement with British Honduras

On December 18, 1957, the government of British Honduras finally extended to each of the three groups, the Altkolonier, the Sommerfelder, and the Kleine Gemeinde, a uniformly worded Privilegium [3] that was satisfactory to them in all respects. That issued to the Altkolonier read as follows:

THIS AGREEMENT made the 18th day of December, 1957 between the Government of British Honduras and the undersigned representatives of the Reinland Mennonite Church of Chihuahua and Durango, Mexico:
Whereas members of the aforesaid Mennonite Church (which members are hereinafter called "the Mennonites") are desirous of emigrating from Mexico and of settling in British Honduras:

2. Participation in Seguro Social has since been made voluntary for self-employed Mennonites. Employed persons must, however, be registered and contributions made on their behalf. The pressure to bring them into full participation continues.

3. Although it is quite possible—and common—for individuals and groups of Mennonites from Mexico to resettle in countries, such as Canada, that proffer no special status comparable to that provided by the Privilegium, their churches, for "diplomatic" reasons, can neither sanction nor support such activity. To do so would be to suggest to the Mexican government, which is under constant pressure from "patriotic" elements to accomplish the integration of the Mennonites, that they no longer lay great weight on the provisions of the Privilegium, and incursions upon it would then surely ensue.

And whereas such settlements will be to the mutual advantage of British Honduras and of the Mennonites:

And whereas it is desirable that there should be some Instrument setting forth in general terms the conditions under which the Mennonites will be permitted to settle in British Honduras:

Now Therefore This Agreement Witnesseth as follows—

1. The Government of British Honduras will grant to the Mennonites—
   (a) the right to run their own Churches and schools, with their own teachers, in their own German language, according to their own religion;
   (b) exemption from making the customary immigration deposits;
   (c) protection of life and property in Peace and War;
   (d) entire exemption from any military service;
   (e) the privilege of affirming with the simple "yes" or "no" instead of making oaths in or out of the Courts;
   (f) freedom of movement, according to law, to enter or leave the country with their money and property;
   (g) the right to administer and invest the estates of their people, especially those of widows and orphans, in their own "Trust System," called the "Waisenamt," according to their own rules and regulations;
   (h) the right to bring into British Honduras the old, infirm and invalid members of the Mennonite community provided that the individuals do not become a charge on the Government of British Honduras;
   (i) exemption from any social security or compulsory system of insurance.
2. The Mennonites will—
   (a) pay all costs and expenses incurred in establishing their settlement;
   (b) bring into British Honduras capital investment in cash and kind amounting to five hundred thousand dollars more or less British Honduras currency.
   (c) produce food not only for themselves but for local consumption and for the export market;
   (d) conduct themselves as good citizens, and subject to this agreement, observe and obey the laws of British Honduras;
   (e) pay all normal duties, taxes, fees and charges by law established, such as customs duty, land tax, estate duty, property tax and income tax.

3. It is understood and agreed that the privileges granted by the government shall be enjoyed by the Mennonites and their descendants for all time so long as the Mennonites observe and fulfill the conditions imposed upon them by this agreement.

In Witness Whereof the parties hereto have signed two identical copies of this Instrument this 18th day of December, 1957.

Signed for and on behalf of the
Government of British Honduras.

Witness: ——————————————   *Sir Colin H. Thornley*
                                                GOVERNOR

Signed for and on behalf of
the Reinland Mennonite Church.

Witness: ——————————————   *Franz D. Rempel*
                                                 Jacob J. Wiebe
                                                 H. W. Wiebe
                                               Johan C. Wolfe

Land Purchases

When the arrival of the Mennonite delegations in British Honduras made it apparent that the Mennonites were considering the founding of colonies, numerous offers of land, mostly of logged-over timber properties, were made to them. The Altkolonier finally settled on Blue Creek, a property of some 115,000 acres fronting the borders of Guatemala, Chiapas, and Quintana Roo. In early 1958, directly after the granting of the Privilegium, 45,000 acres were purchased for the sum of $100,000 (U.S.). Later that year, in anticipation of a large-scale movement from Mexico as promised by advance applications for over 80,000 acres, the remaining 70,000-odd acres of the Blue Creek property were acquired at a price of $3.00 (U.S.) per acre. There was disagreement among the Altkolonier delegates almost from the first, however, about the attractions of Blue Creek, and one faction entered into an agreement for the purchase of Shipyard, another timber property of 17,083 acres, situated about fifteen miles to the southeast of Blue Creek, at $3.00 (B.H.) per acre.

These acquisitions spurred the interest of Altkolonier elements in the Peace River country of northern Alberta. Since the second decade of this century, Mennonites had been trickling into that region, the last of Canadian agricultural frontiers. There the more conservative of them side-stepped outside influence by keeping to the margins of settlement, where the distance from schools legally exempted their children from attending. By the late 1950's, owing to the development of the region, in whose growth they had served a pioneering function, such "opportunities" were rapidly ceasing to exist. Numbers of them were from families who had joined the trek to Mexico in the 1920's, but owing to the hardships encountered they had returned to Canada and there sought nonparticipation in the affairs of the "world" in the manner just described. During the late 1950's and early 1960's, some two dozen families from the Peace River area took over 2,500 acres at Richmond Hill in British Honduras, about midway between Shipyard and Orange Walk Town, on a rental basis.

The Kleine Gemeinde, following inspection by its delegates of several proffered properties, elected to buy the former timber tract of Spanish Lookout, comprising 18,724 acres, in the west-central part of the country some twenty miles from the Guatemalan border. The price was $100,000 (U.S.). Sommerfelder interest appears to have been on the wane, possibly because of their small but relatively successful venture in Tamaulipas, and they never seriously attempted to settle in British Honduras. At the time the Mennonites acquired them, all these lands were inhabited by only a few Negro squatters and a few Maya Indians subsisting on small milpa (slash-and-burn) farms and on the gathering of chicle, wild pepper, and other natural products.

Migration

Settlement commenced in March of 1958. March is the beginning of the new crop year in Chihuahua and Durango, when early corn and potatoes are planted. It was, however, too near the rainy season in British Honduras for the colonists to be able to clear land in time to put in ground provisions. They were therefore faced at once with the prospect of having to live off their often meagre capital for a protracted period before even a minimum subsistence could be reaped.

Considerable difficulty was experienced in getting to their properties. Through April and May trucks could negotiate the logging roads, but with the onset of the rains these quickly became impassable. Colonists heading for Blue Creek were forced to go up the Río Hondo by boat from Chetumal, Quintana Roo, a water trip of some 100 miles which many could ill afford. Those Altkolonier heading for Shipyard had a logging road into the property from the town of Orange Walk, but it too was impassable to vehicles in the wet season. The Kleine Gemeinde colonists heading for Spanish Lookout encountered similar problems, but these were heightened by the fact that their property lay on the far side of the swollen Belize River, across which everything had to be carried by a crude and inadequate ferry.

The earliest arrivals were in each case essentially advance parties who were to erect shelters, cut trails, begin clearing the land, and the like. In this regard the Altkolonier going to Blue Creek had made perhaps the best arrangements. They had made the advance construction of ten houses by the vendor a part of their initial land transaction. Nonetheless, the rapid influx of colonists who, having sold their Mexican properties, had to vacate them, resulted in tremendous crowding. However, 70,000 board feet of sawn lumber had also been included in the purchase, and building went rapidly forward. Their second deal, which effected the transfer of the residual 70,000-odd acres of the property, included also a large sawmill and three crawler tractors, with which the colonists immediately set to work to meet the demand for building materials.

The first colonists bound for Shipyard arrived after the onset of the rainy season, when clearing and construction were very difficult. Consequently most of them were forced to obtain such shelter as they could in Orange Walk and Maskall, the two nearest centers of any size, and it was some months before all could locate on the colony.

The Kleine Gemeinde people at Spanish Lookout made perhaps the best overall initial adjustment to their new environment. Until their migration to Mexico in the late 1940's and early 1950's, most of them had lived in southeastern Manitoba, itself a wooded region. They therefore had a familiarity with land-clearing operations which their Altkolonier counterparts largely lacked. They brought with them, on the average, more capital, and their mutual-assistance institutions were better organized and articulated.

The Land

The lands selected by the three groups were in many ways comparable. The terrain, although of low relief, is rolling, with low areas indifferently to poorly drained. When the Mennonites acquired their lands, they were covered mainly by the "altered" [4] forest succession which follows the cutting of marketable timber, interspersed with swamp savanna and small areas of "wamil." [5] There was a scattering of valuable tree varieties— among them tropical cedar (Cedrela), sapodilla (Achras sapota), cabbage bark (Andira inermis), and mahogany (Swietenia mahogani) —which either had been overlooked by timber cruisers or judged too difficult of recovery by commercial operations.

The soils cleared and utilized as of 1967 on all colonies exhibit relatively little variation. Eight soil samples, selected with the help of colonists for observed differences (in texture, color, productivity, and so forth), range in texture from heavy clay loam to fine sandy clay loam. Except for a limited belt of alluvial soils adjacent to the Belize River on the Spanish Lookout colony, and possibly the sandy loams on Shipyard, all of the soils in the areas of Mennonite

4. The term "altered" is used here in preference to "second growth," since the desirable tropical timber species normally occur in highly dispersed fashion. Logged areas are not cut over in the way usual to temperate-forest operations. The culling of the relatively small number of valuable trees in a given tropical-forest area therefore normally results in less disturbance to the total vegetation complex, although the breaks occasioned in the forest canopy definitely affect the nature of the vegetative succession.

5. "Wamil"—derived from Maya huamil (in Nahua, coamitl)—is the term applied to old fields of cultivated land (normally, slash-and-burn milpa) which is in the process of reverting to forest.

Table A

ANALYSES OF SELECTED SOIL SAMPLES FROM THE
MENNONITE COLONIES IN BRITISH HONDURAS [a]

Description	Texture	CaCO₃	pH	NO₃-N ppm	Avail. P, ppm.	Avail. K, ppm.
Blue Creek upland	Clay	V. High	7.6	.46	10.0	335
Blue Creek bottom	Clay	High	7.5	39.90	4.4	304
Shipyard bottom	Clay	V. Low	7.8	.93	8.2	288
Shipyard west-central	Clay	High	6.0	69.00	5.6	284
Shipyard northwest	Fine sandy clay loam	V. Low	7.2	13.39	4.4	124
Spanish Lookout river alluvium	Heavy clay loam	High	6.1	32.86	6.6	618
Spanish Lookout central	Clay	Low	7.3	102.50	13.7	1582
Spanish Lookout north-central	Clay	V. High	7.6	26.93	5.9	386

[a] All tests were performed at Soil Testing Laboratory, University of Manitoba.

colonization appear to be residual and derived from calcareous materials. They vary from slightly acidic to slightly alkaline (pH 6.0 to 7.8). They are dark in color.[6] Although the samples tested exhibited marked variations in content of plant nutrients, most are seriously deficient in phosphorus. Potassium is in moderate to good supply in all cases, and so is nitrogen except in the case of an "upland" soil at Blue Creek and a "bottom" soil at Shipyard (see Table A). Except for the fine sandy clay loam, which occurs in the west-northwest portion of the Shipyard colony, the soils now under cultivation are "difficult," tacky and tough, with high draught requirements for satisfactory mechanical tillage.

Settlement and Adjustment

The Mennonites' approach to farming in British Honduras followed their former experience. Their initial assessment of

6. Although they contain varying amounts of humus, the dark color of these soils is probably owing primarily to the presence of oxides of manganese.

the verdant jungle growth which covered most of their land—which contrasted so sharply with the semiarid valleys of Chihuahua and Durango—was that it must spring from soils of exceptional fertility. By their own admission they knew nothing of the usually limited productivity of tropical forest soils. The Altkolonier at Shipyard, Richmond Hill, and Blue Creek had access to the Agricultural Station at Orange Walk, but, partly because of the language barrier and partly because of their pride in their own solid agrarian background and their characteristic distrust of "technology," they took few if any steps to avail themselves of its services.[7] They planted the corn and beans to which they were accustomed in Mexico; however, because beans showed little promise the first year, they also soon adopted rice and peanuts in a small way and gradually established subsistence plantings of the subtropical and tropical fruits (citrus, bananas, pineapple, papaya, and so on) common to the region.

In Mexico dairying and the production of cheese had been important, and one of the Mennonites' first concerns was to create pasture and reestablish their herds. The coarse savanna grasses and the volunteer grasses which sprang up on new clearing were, however, generally unpalatable to cattle. This, together with their failure to engage the services of the Agricultural Station in recommending suitable types, set the stage for a callous exploitation of their ignorance in 1960. It seems that a senior employee at a cattle ranch in the region had, in the absence of the owner, harvested, for private gain, seed from a pasture enclosure which had not been grazed in the customary rotation. This seed, which was mainly that of Johnson grass (*Sorghum halepense*), a most prolific and aggressive weed, was offered to the Altkolonier as a desirable pasture grass, which indeed it is when quite young. The farm demonstrator at the Orange Walk Agricultural Station, on being apprised of the fact that the colonists were planning to plant it, warned them

7. Altkolonier skepticism with regard to consulting the staff of the Agricultural Station may have been to a degree justified. The *Report of the Tripartite Economic Survey of the British Honduras* (May 1966), p. 13, paragraph 35, states that the farm demonstrators have, in the main, only an elementary education with a limited amount of informal in-service training.

against doing so.[8] However, possibly because of misunderstanding stemming from language difficulties, but apparently because of lack of faith in his advice, they went ahead, thereby setting in train a permanent weed problem which, to date, they simply are not equipped to combat effectively. The seeds are spread by birds and cattle and invade new land as fast as the forest is cleared.

Progress in the development of the colonies was slow. The enervating climate, disease—particularly malaria—the difficulty of clearing the dense forest, especially in the first two years, 1958 and 1959, which were inordinately wet, the perpetual and unequal battle with excess moisture, weeds, insects, rodents, and fungus, intra-group dissension,[9] and the attrition of their capital discouraged many. Of the approximately 275 Altkolonier families who originally emigrated to British Honduras, about 125 left within the first five years. Others, however, individually and in small groups, continued to replace them.

The Kleine Gemeinde colonists at Spanish Lookout, though numbering only some eighty families, took a more aggressive and calculated approach. They consulted the Central Farm Agricultural Station at Baking Pot on the Western Highway, across the Belize River from their colony, as to suitable crops and tillage practices. Since they had left Canada only a decade or less before, all the adult members of their community were at least conversant in English—a great advantage indeed as compared to the Altkolonier, few of whom spoke the national language at all. To husband their resources and avoid unnecessary duplication of effort, individuals whose interests and experience lay in those fields were delegated to engage in various crop and livestock pursuits. One man was appointed to maintain continuous contact with the Central Farm, so that communication and a flow of ideas might be maintained.

8. Peter H. W. Wiebe and Franz D. Rempel, Blue Creek, and Henry Clarence Bennett, Farm Demonstrator, Agricultural Station, Orange Walk, British Honduras, personal communications.

9. Although intra-group dissension among the Altkolonier can be said to have been at least in part owing to the stresses engendered by the difficulties of pioneering, the root causes went farther back in time and hinged on differences of attitude concerning technological innovation. The early separate purchase of Shipyard, despite the surplus of land at Blue Creek, reflected in part existing differences along ideological lines.

Despite the overall abundance of moisture—Spanish Lookout has averaged approximately eighty inches of precipitation per year over the past decade, and Shipyard and Blue Creek have averaged sixty inches—water supply was found from the first a serious problem. In Mexico most of the colonists had been accustomed to an abundance of high quality water from deep wells for domestic and livestock use. The geology here, however, was unfavorable, and drilling located no promising aquifers.[10] Shallow-dug wells also failed to solve the problem, for the clay soils yielded little or no water. The colonists were therefore reduced to utilizing surface runoff accumulated in depressions, which was often poor in quality and unpredictable in supply. Preoccupation with this problem led directly into the establishment of a minor industry, the manufacture of wooden and sheet-metal vats to store roof runoff for domestic use. While this source might also be adequate for small flocks of poultry, water supply for other livestock remained unprovided. Once more the Canadian experience of the Kleine Gemeinde colonists served them well. Some of them had lived west of the Red River in Manitoba, also a region of clay soils and inadequate yields of ground water. There they had been accustomed to excavating ponds or "dugouts" in natural depressions where meltwater and summer runoff would fill them, while the relatively impervious clay guaranteed against major seepage loss. In the absence of other sources of water they quickly turned to dugout ponds also in British Honduras.

In their approach to the tropical forest, the Mennonite colonists generally agree that grave errors in judgment were made. As clearing progressed, they culled the more easily worked timber, particularly cedar and mahogany, for their own building needs. But by their own admission, millions of board feet of desirable hardwoods, which might well have defrayed much of the initial cost of colonization until agriculture could be better established, were burned in the course of clearing because they were considered too

10. Over the last few years a few drilled wells have been successfully put down on the Shipyard colony, but the water is of marginal quality even for livestock, being high in dissolved minerals which adversely affect the taste. Although this water is drinkable, rain water is much preferred by the colonists.

hard to be worked. Had they but known their potential value and how to market them!

Among the first pursuits which proved economically worthwhile was the keeping of poultry. At the time the Mennonites arrived in British Honduras, practically all poultry products were imported. Eggs in the Belize City market were over $1.00 B.H. ($.70 U.S.) per dozen, and chicken was $.70 (B.H.) or more per pound. The Kleine Gemeinde colonists, therefore, most of whom were experienced chicken farmers in Canada and Mexico, imported live chicks from the United States and kept poultry almost from the start, even though the feed situation was precarious and most if it, including imported concentrates, had to be purchased for cash. The Altkolonier, too, soon got into poultry production. Rapid expansion of flocks, however, resulted in flooding of the market, and prices fell drastically, to as low as $.35 per dozen for eggs, which was less than the cost of production.

When some colonists sold off their birds to cut losses, they flooded the market for poultry as well, so that this venture became for many something of a disaster. One substantial long-term benefit, however, ensued. Before the Mennonites entered the market, many people seldom if ever bought poultry products. During the period of low prices, many who could afford them for the first time became regular consumers. As a result the demand rose sharply, and prices returned to a level at which modest profits could be made by efficient producers. A chick hatchery—the only one in the country to date—was established at Spanish Lookout. It provides farmers with a market for hatching eggs and supplies most of the replacement stock required not only by the Mennonite colonies but throughout the country as well.

The Market Center

As the amount and variety of surplus crop and livestock products increased, so did the problems of marketing. Dealers in the market centers to which the Mennonites brought their products, recognizing their frugal and toilsome nature, stalled in their buying, causing the colonists to waste time and money while chafing to get back to the imperative labors on their farms; this tactic effectively eroded the Mennonites' bargaining power to the point where they would accept the offered price simply to avoid spoilage or having to take their produce home again. In 1960, therefore, the Mennonite Central Committee, the relief arm of the Mennonite churches of North America, which had been taking an active interest in the British Honduras ventures, determined to assist the colonists by establishing a warehousing and market center in Belize City, where it undertook to market on consignment all surplus colony produce—meat, poultry, eggs, vegetables, and so on.

The Kleine Gemeinde colonists accepted these services at once and with few reservations. The Altkolonier did not. Since 1948 the M.C.C. had been active in Chihuahua, originally in response to a prolonged drought which had reduced many of the Mennonites there to a state of destitution. However, its assistance was, in the minds of the Altkolonier leadership, bound up with certain evangelizing functions which, it was felt, threatened to undermine religious solidarity in their colonies. In British Honduras, therefore, the Altkolonier harbored serious suspicions as to the M.C.C.'s motives, which were not allayed by M.C.C. offers of material aid directly to individuals. The Blue Creek and Shipyard colonists, under the influence of their religious leaders, almost completely ignored the proffered assistance and boycotted the market center.

Recognizing the futility of its position vis-à-vis the Altkolonier leaders while at the same time appreciating the fact that the individual condition of many of the colonists was becoming desperate, the M.C.C. in 1963 arranged for the Mennonite Eastern Conference Board of Missions of Lancaster, Pennsylvania, to assume the functions which it had been at pains to establish. Since that time the Altkolonier have been gradually drawn into availing themselves of the center's services.[11] Indeed, so much have relations improved that Altkolonier now not only market their produce

11. A basic reason for the improved relations appears to be the fact that the Eastern Conference represents the "Pennsylvania" Mennonites, with whom the Altkolonier share little common history. The Mennonite Central Committee, on the other hand, represents also those Mennonites—in Canada particularly—who were themselves Altkolonier and who are regarded as having "broken faith" by accepting secular influences and remaining behind while the faithful emigrated.

there but also regularly avail themselves of the center's provisions for lodging when they stay in Belize City overnight.

As the volume of Mennonite agricultural surpluses increased, and as confidence in the center broadened, its nature gradually changed, so that today it performs as a middleman, operating on a 10 percent markup to defray costs, and normally offers immediate cash settlement to farmers. It has also taken to selling noncompeting produce of "non-Mennonite" origin. Volume has expanded so that by 1967 the value of Mennonite produce handled by the center was approximately $350,000 (B.H.).

Equipment Imports

The center also functions as importer of implements and machinery for the Mennonite colonies. This service has its origins also in the initial attempts of the M.C.C. to render aid to the colonists by providing basic implements to needy individuals without charge, as gifts. This met with the Altkolonier opposition referred to above, with the atmosphere eventually becoming so acrimonious that their religious leaders resorted to excommunication of those who accepted M.C.C. assistance. This situation, too, has changed since the Eastern Conference took over from the M.C.C.

The Kleine Gemeinde people of Spanish Lookout at once appreciated the advantages provided by the M.C.C.'s proffered import service. From their colony in Chihuahua they had formerly ranged over the Great Plains states and even into Canada looking for the good secondhand machinery which could be acquired cheaply there. Being generally more well-to-do than the Altkolonier, they too insisted they needed no charity and wished the proffered service to be placed on a business basis. When the Eastern Conference took over from the M.C.C. in 1963, it was decided that assistance in obtaining capital equipment should be based on helping the colonists to help themselves by providing credit for acquisitions. This also met with a favorable response from Altkolonier leaders.

The service operates in an uncomplicated way. Individuals enter orders for equipment, specifying the amount they expect to be able to pay. These are relayed to a contact in Pennsylvania, who shops around to fill them at the best price.[12] Consignments are forwarded to Belize twice a year. As with the produce market, the service is provided on the basis of a 10 percent markup. Any colonist may make one purchase on credit, but he must discharge his indebtedness before he is permitted to make another. The program has functioned well overall, and as of July 1967 had effected the importation of implements and machinery to a value of over $50,000 (B.H.).[13]

The Canning-Crop Venture

Another venture, also sponsored by outside Mennonite interests and aimed at the involvement of the colonists, has proved less successful. In 1962 a food-processing concern, Peter Butland and Co. of Ontario, Canada, envisaging the possibility of drawing upon the colonies as suppliers of tropical products, proposed that they should produce, under contract, papaya, limes, peppers, and the like. These would be preprocessed in the colonies, then transshipped to Canada in bulk for final processing. Many of Butland's suppliers and employees in Ontario were Mennonites, and it was felt that their counterparts in British Honduras would respond with vigor to the market and job opportunities which this would provide. Although the type of production in which Butland's wanted them to engage was almost entirely outside the sphere of their previous experience, the colonists did respond, largely, it is admitted, because no adequate other sources of income had yet

12. Pennsylvania appears to be a good area in which to fill the equipment orders from British Honduras. Many Pennsylvania farms are small operations—comparable to those of the majority of the colonists—and hence surplus machinery from them tends to be of suitable size.

13. The volume of machinery imports, per year, has been: 1964—$6,882.11; 1965—$14,167.29; 1966—$20,572.49; to July 1967—$8,335.60 (B.H.). Information supplied by Mr. Paul Martin, Director, Mennonite Center, Belize City, personal communication.

been established. A small processing plant was built on each of the colonies to handle the first crops—peppers and papaya. The lack of success which attended these efforts may be ascribed at least in part to ignorance of proper techniques. There was, moreover, considerable reluctance to grow slow-maturing crops such as papaya and citrus fruits, even though Butland would extend financing. There was little confidence that such crops would be successful, and the colonists insisted that they would feel morally obligated to pay back advances against them even if the crops failed for causes beyond their control. Also, since the ultimate market was a distant foreign one, the prices payable to producers were of necessity low, and hence not really attractive in relation to those obtainable either for fresh produce of a like nature on the Belize market or for such less labor-intensive crops as corn and beans, with which promising results were by this time being attained, and this tended to divert interest from the more chancy canning crops.

Another factor which militated against success for the Butland venture but which had important positive implications for the colonists was Hurricane Hattie. On October 31, 1961, this storm destroyed much of Belize City and, indeed, caused much destruction throughout most of the country. The task of rebuilding created a market for goods and services of many kinds, some of which the Mennonites were in a position to provide. Throughout 1962 and beyond there was a great demand for lumber, and suddenly the supposedly worthless timber remaining on the colonies took on a new value. Spanish Lookout alone poured as much as a million board feet of lumber per year into this market, with the Altkolonier supplying lesser, unrecorded amounts. The effect of this together with such other opportunities—for sheet-metal work, the construction of water vats, and the like—which Hattie had provided, was to further divert energies from the canning enterprise. Although the issue is not altogether dead, little more has come of it to date. Only on Blue Creek, where some 10,000 papaya and 4,000 lime trees have been planted under Butland's auspices, is there any continuing involvement between the firm and the colonists.

Hurricane Hattie—
Opportunity Out of Disaster

Hurricane Hattie, although it also caused severe damage on the Mennonite colonies, is regarded by many, particularly at Spanish Lookout, as marking the turning point in their fortunes. Before then, although in retrospect the colonists feel that they were on the verge of becoming secure, no firm guidelines for the future had yet been laid. The opportunities which repair of the hurricane's destruction created had far-reaching effects.[14] The ready market for lumber made it possible to offer as yet unsold land to the landless and to those who wished to expand their holdings; those who took such land paid two cents per board foot on the timber harvested. This helped to greatly reduce the residual land debt on the Spanish Lookout colony, to increase the rate of clearing and expand the area under cultivation, to reduce the amount of taxes on unsold land which had to be met out of colony coffers, and generally to create a new atmosphere of optimism.

Yet another opportunity attended the aftermath of the storm. During the ensuing cleanup operations in Belize City, the army commandeered all tractors in dealers' hands. These were later sold, still practically new, on tender. Quite a few of the Spanish Lookout colonists obtained tractors on bids which they regard as having been much below the real value of the machines. That the Altkolonier did not generally respond to the same degree may be attributed in large part to their narrower horizons (a product of their more insular history and the language gap) and their greater individualism in economic matters.

The Character of the Colonies

The approach of the Mennonites to their several colonization ventures in British Honduras was characterized primarily by the transplantation of established institutions. The Altkolonier

14. To its credit it must also be mentioned that the Spanish Lookout colony sent teams of volunteers to Belize to assist in the cleanup operations.

laid out their colonies in Strassendörfer and Gewannfluren, along the lines of the medieval openfield village, wherein residence is in the village and each farmer's land, normally consisting of several plots or Koerls, is so situated on the Gewannflur as to achieve for all landowners a fair distribution of soil quality and an equal journey to work. One feature of this system, the communal pasture, is still lacking in British Honduras, apparently because the number of cattle kept to date by the Altkolonier is very small. The Kleine Gemeinde at Spanish Lookout have preferred to perpetuate the occupancy system employed by them in Mexico, with compact farms spaced along a network of main roads.

Since the colonies are self-administering, they render levies upon their members to meet real-estate taxes (which are delivered in a lump sum) and to pay for necessary internal functions such as the maintenance of schools and public works. In addition they exact statute labor for the maintenance of roads. Because of their strong tradition of engagement in commercial agriculture, market roads have always been—in Canada, in Mexico, and now in British Honduras—a prime concern of even the most conservative Mennonites, even though such roads tend to diminish the cultural isolation which they otherwise seek.

Property deeds to all colony lands are held in the name of the respective church groups, plus, usually, two named individuals who act as custodians. Individual ownership rests on colony registry only. Colony authorities can therefore specify who may own land (members only) and to whom it may be sold (members only, in good standing with the church). The system of land ownership is thus a powerful instrument not only for the maintenance of an exclusive society but also for the exaction of individual compliance with established rules of conformity.[15]

By the end of 1966 Blue Creek had 1,700-odd acres under cultivation and some 900 in pasture.[16] A further 354 acres were felled

---

15. For a detailed account of the administrative machinery of Mennonite colonies, see Chapter IX.

16. Of the approximately 4,100 acres which had been opened up at Blue Creek to the end of 1966, 1,439 acres remained as yet unprepared wamil and stump land, and 1,021 acres consisted of rough and stony ground unsuited to tillage. Colony records, courtesy of Isaak J. Wieler, Vorsteher (Superintendent), Blue Creek Colony.

Table B

GENERAL INFORMATION ON MENNONITE COLONIES

IN BRITISH HONDURAS

Colony	Date Established	Approximate Population 1966	Area in Acres	Arable Acreage Improved	Church Affiliation
Blue Creek	1958	750	115,000	2,600	Altkolonier
Shipyard	1958	1,950	17,100	3,700	Altkolonier
Richmond Hill	1958	90	2,500	200	Altkolonier
Spanish Lookout	1958	665	18,700	8,000	Kleine Gemeinde
Santa Elena	1965	100	4,000	300	Amish and Old Mennonite
Totals		3,555	157,300	14,800	

for 1967 clearing (firing), and 130 acres were cleaned up for cultivation (see Table B). Shipyard had 3,154 acres under cultivation, which was expanded by some 580 acres in 1967. Spanish Lookout at the same time had approximately 5,000 acres cultivated and a further 3,000 in seeded pasture. This represented, on a per capita basis, approximately two and one-half acres (exclusive of pasture) at Blue Creek, just under two acres at Shipyard, and nearly eight acres at Spanish Lookout.[17] The Altkolonier group at Richmond Hill appears to be breaking up. In 1967 only thirteen families, with approximately 200 acres under cultivation, remained. Most of the others have moved to Shipyard. There is ample evidence in all of the Mennonites' colonies of their capacity for toil. Obviously, however, the Kleine Gemeinde group has been considerably more successful in expanding its cultivated acreage than have its Altkolonier counterparts at Blue Creek and Shipyard. This cannot be explained on the basis of "easier" initial conditions at Spanish Lookout, for the conditions in all three locations were comparable. Rather, to all appearances, it reflects differences in the level of permissiveness—and, indeed, encouragement—with regard to ongoing adjustments, particularly those involving technology, as between the Altkolonier and the Kleine Gemeinde. These have been al-

17. Mennonite populations at the end of 1966 were: Blue Creek—744; Shipyard—1944; and Spanish Lookout—665. Taken from colony records.

luded to in the foregoing discussion but will emerge more clearly now.

Ideology vs. Necessity and Opportunity

That the Altkolonier have been less effective in rendering their lands tillable is owing not to lack of application to the task but rather to the severely restrictive stand which their leadership has taken on innovation ever since the technological revolution in agriculture began to assume major proportions in western Canada early in this century. Since the official church position— backed by the secular authorities of the colony—is that ordinances once made and standards of conformity once arrived at in church conclave and sealed with prayer can never be altered or rescinded, restrictions which may once have been uncomfortable yet tolerable to ambitious individuals can, in a changed or new environment, become grave disabilities. A case in point, which has become the crux of serious controversy among the Altkolonier, is the use of the modern rubber-tired tractor. The proscription against them has its roots back in 1916, when Altkolonier leaders in Manitoba and Saskatchewan agreed to ban the automobile forever and to arrest technological innovation in agricultural machinery at the then existing level. This meant that the farm tractor, which by then was fairly common, would be tolerated, but pneumatic tires are banned because, so the argument goes, they make the tractor equivalent to an automobile. Pneumatic tires, however, have considerable advantages of traction and flotation—and, consequently, of economy, fuel being $.60 (B.H.) a gallon—on the difficult soils in British Honduras. Moreover, they lend a tractor much greater versatility in field, bush, or roadwork than do steel wheels. Under marginal conditions of economic viability, considerations such as these can assume strategic importance. In consequence of such restrictions, many Altkolonier whose capital position originally was such that they could have afforded a tractor have attempted, instead, to use only horses for draught purposes. Horses, however, are severely limited in their capacity to work in the heat and humidity which prevail throughout most of the year, particularly since they can rarely if ever be given any high-energy ration such as grain.[18] As a result, then, much of the Altkolonier's arable land is in a very indifferent state of cultivation. Horses simply cannot compare in overall usefulness and versatility with the hydraulically equipped two- or three-plow tractors which have come to be most favored by those Mennonites who can afford them and are not kept by ideological considerations from having them.

This issue, of the permissible state of technology, is a direct legacy from Mexico, where it was already seriously affecting the solidarity of Altkolonier society at the time of the movement to British Honduras. Among the migrants were persons of all shades of conviction. Indeed, it is categorically stated by some that it was because a substantial number of known liberal-minded individuals planned to participate in the colonization of Blue Creek that the Shipyard purchase, by an arch-conservative faction, was made. In order to maintain practices consistent with the traditional view, Altkolonier religious leaders at Blue Creek invoked ostracism and excommunication against those who, because they were convinced that their economic survival was at stake, refused to conform. The effects have been highly divisive, both within the community and within family groups, and have culminated in the formulation of a new church organization of excommunicants who have discarded all proscriptions against useful innovations. From this have stemmed two further effects. Shorn of its former ideological disabilities, the radical group is, by and large, making significant economic progress. As a result some other colonists, particularly members of the families of those already under excommunication from the Altkolonier church, have also been prompted to break with tradition. At the same time, there has been a serious decline in community solidarity. Many colony functions, such as the maintenance of roads and drains, depend on communal effort. However, since the conservative faction invokes ostracism against the excommunicants,

18. An occasional farmer saves rice chaff and broken rice to feed to horses during the periods of heaviest work, but, since little rice is grown, very small amounts become available to augment animal rations.

no negotiations for a detente have been possible. Many conservatives have, in fact, withdrawn from the issue by taking themselves off and relocating on Shipyard. In consequence, Blue Creek's population fell from 822 at the end of 1965 to 744 a year later. Partly for this reason, but also because other colonists—newcomers who held with the traditional view and were aware of the emerging conflict at Blue Creek—chose not to locate there, Shipyard is already experiencing serious crowding. Indeed, Shipyard colonists who own land at Blue Creek but will not live there, together with the remaining conservative group at Blue Creek, are now agitating for a transfer of property. They hope that their acreage at Blue Creek (some 9,000 acres), together with a substantial amount of land at Blue Creek owned by Altkolonier now resident in Mexico, can be traded to the Belize Estates Company for an equivalent amount of the company's lands adjacent to Shipyard. The company has, indeed, agreed to this proposal. All action is, however, stalemated because the named warders of the deeds to the Blue Creek property have both been excommunicated. They, together with the rest of the banned group, insist that the excommunicants have a right to be consulted on the proposed trade. Since they are under ostracism by the others, though, no negotiation is possible. The overall visible effects of the differences in ideological position have been the creation of an acrimonious atmosphere and the wasting of much material substance and physical and emotional energy.

Whatever the combination of reasons in each individual case, the trend among the conservative Altkolonier has consistently been one of gradual but pervasive economic attrition, and there are as yet few promising signs of a reversal of this process. Many of them brought very substantial amounts of capital—$10,000, $15,000, $20,000 (U.S.), and more—with them from Mexico and, their hopes of early success buoyed by the sight of the lush verdure clothing their new lands, built large and handsome farmsteads. But the soil has failed to justify their estimates of its fertility, and their struggle with the forest, the elements, insect and animal pests, and the ever-thriving weeds and fungi has been a largely unequal one.

As a result, then, consumption has consistently exceeded the rate of creation of new wealth, their capital has gradually been eaten away, and even the once well-to-do are now generally much reduced in circumstances. Among the few who appear to have considerably improved their situation are those who, by investing in heavy land-clearing machinery and then hiring out their services, have attracted a portion of the capital brought from Mexico. This, however, represents merely the distribution of existing wealth, not the creation of new. Others, former Anwohner, with little or no capital and no experience in running farms of their own, from the very beginning had little chance of succeeding and are now economically prostrate. Such persons are, by their own admission, worse off than they ever were in Mexico, where, however poor, they were by custom entitled to a small yard and grazing right in the communal pasture, at least occasionally found employment among the farmers of their village, and, if worst came to worst, could rely on the charity of relatives, neighbors, and the church.

Some Emerging Trends and Techniques

And yet, most colonists face facts realistically; lacking capital, they know they cannot return to Mexico, however much they might like to. There is little evidence of despair, and much of tenacious resolve that all will yet be well. There are those who would have the excommunicants responsible for all ills, for having, as they see it, invited divine retribution. Others, more realistically, are turning increasingly to livestock, particularly poultry, and are making limited use of fertilizers, with encouraging results. Market opportunities are broadening. Besides an improvement in the markets of Corozal, Orange Walk, and Belize City, Mexican traders from Chetumal, Quintana Roo, have taken to touring the colonies, buying cattle and hogs at good prices.[19] In 1966 the average gross cash income per family was on the order of $500–$600 B.H. ($350–$420 U.S.) at Shipyard and $700 ($490 U.S.) at Blue

19. Prices paid by traders from Chetumal in July 1967 were on the order of $.17 (B.H.) per pound for cattle and $.30 for hogs, on a live-weight basis.

Creek; these incomes contrast sharply with an approximate *net* cash income of $1,000 ($700 U.S.) per family at Spanish Lookout.[20] Yet, there are many aspects which may be regarded as hopeful in terms of the ultimate survival of the Altkolonier colonies. Common retail, service, and manufacturing functions are, if possible, performed on the colonies by members of their own group. Although these activities are themselves generally on a precarious economic footing, they nevertheless increase the impact of any wealth entering the colonies from outside. In sum, in this writer's opinion, the Altkolonier in British Honduras *will* survive. In spite of all the weaknesses inherent in their social system they still, in the main, individually and collectively possess the dogged determination and frugal habits by which they and their forebears have surmounted grim adversity before. Poverty may, however, already be making inroads with long-range implications. No obvious consequences of dietary deficiency, such as the presence of the protein-deficiency disease kwashiorkor, were noted. Yet, although there is some general availability of legumes—beans and peanuts—the diet among the poorer Mennonite colonists is particularly low in protein. Also, since milk is seldom available to them, there appears to be a prevailing calcium and vitamin deficiency which manifests itself in inhibited growth and lack of stamina among youngsters.

The greater economic success of the Kleine Gemeinde at Spanish Lookout, vis-à-vis the Altkolonier, reflects their greater flexibility in the adoption and adaptation of new techniques. Interestingly, however, despite their concerted drive to achieve a viable man-land relationship, and despite copious evidence of former Maya occupation of the region, the Kleine Gemeinde have not sought to understand the factors by which the Maya *milpero* determines and regulates his clearing, burning, and planting. Yet, compared to the Altkolonier, they have developed or borrowed many useful techniques. An early minor breakthrough was the ridging of fields to overcome the problem, in peanuts and beans particularly, of diseases and pests which were promoted by excessively wet

20. Family sizes on the three colonies are very nearly alike, being approximately 5.5 members per average family unit at Spanish Lookout, 5.6 at Blue Creek, and 5.7 at Shipyard. Income figures were supplied by the Vorsteher of each colony.

soils. It appears that the idea was first tested at the suggestion of one of the Central Farm technicians at Baking Pot. It was, however, subjected to ad hoc modification by the addition to the ridges of sawdust to improve soil texture, and chicken droppings or chemical fertilizers to increase yields. Ridging has also made it possible to propagate the potato, staple of the Mennonite kitchen, as a winter crop. The seed cuttings are set out on the ridge and are then covered with a heavy mulch of corn cobs, whereupon the tubers develop on the soil surface at the base of the mulch. At harvest the precariously anchored crop is simply lifted by hand.

Another promising technique relating to drainage was adapted from a very different source. A colonist who had continued to subscribe to the *Family Herald and Weekly Star*, a Canadian farm newspaper, read there how, on heavy clays in southern Ontario, subsurface drainage was being experimentally effected by running a tractor-mounted cable-layer (such as those used for laying plastic pipe or telephone lines at shallow depth) through the ground. The tool, which is similar to a well-driving point, is mounted on a heavy-beamed frame much like that of a pan-breaker, which is attached to the tractor's three-point hydraulically controlled drawbar. It is drawn along horizontally, below tillage depth, in the direction of slope. The soil around the point is compacted by its passage, leaving a "tube" which functions in the same way as weeping (subsurface drainage) tile and may last for a couple of years. Considerable optimism surrounds this development.

The techniques of wresting new land from the forest have also occupied considerable thought. Unlike the Altkolonier, who still strive for "clean" clearing prior to cultivation, canny colonists at Spanish Lookout have developed procedures—independently, it seems—which indeed bear some resemblance to those employed by the Maya. Initial felling, with machete and ax, may be done from November to February,[21] at a cost of between $10 and $15 per acre (B.H.) if the job is hired out. The burning takes place in April

21. This period is longer than the season for felling apparently used by the Maya *milpero*, who delays felling until February and March, then burns at a carefully selected "propitious" time in April. For a detailed account of Maya methods, see Ruben E. Reina, "Milpas and Milperos: Implications for Prehistoric Times," *American Anthropologist*, LXIX:1 (February 1967), 1–20.

or May, prior to the onset of the rainy season. Corn is then planted with the dibble or digging stick—a technique learned from the Central Farm. This costs $5 to $6 per acre, including $.50 to $1 for seed. By mid- or late June the corn may be two feet high. At that time *jaragua* (*Hyparrhenia rufa*) is seeded broadcast at the rate of five to ten pounds per acre, mixed with molasses grass (*Melinis minutiflora*) at one to two pounds per acre. The molasses grass, which is a vigorous grower, chokes out weeds. In September the corn is snapped by hand and normally yields from one-half to three-quarters of a ton (fifteen to twenty-five bushels) per acre. The field is then left fallow for a year or two, so that the grasses may re-seed and establish a thick stand. Near the end of the second year after felling—in January or February—cattle may be let into the field to graze it down. This is optional. Then, in April, before the onset of the rains, the field is fired, killing the molasses grass but leaving the hardy, deeper-rooted *jaragua,* and also consuming most of the deadwood left on the ground after the original firing. Corn is again dibble-planted. After this crop is taken off, the field may be used for permanent pasture or, if desired, residual stumps can be bulldozed and cleared for $10 to $20 per acre.

Another method of permanent clearing is to fell, burn, and plant a first crop of corn as described above. After the crop is taken, the bush is allowed to grow back in for a year or two and is then cut again. This second cut yields much light wood which burns well, so that most of the remaining old heavy deadwood is consumed with it. The total cost of felling by this method runs somewhat higher, being on the order of $20 to $25 per acre. On balance, then, the corn-grass-fire technique appears now to enjoy the most favor. As cultivated pasture, however, pangola (*Digitaria decumbens*), which was recommended by the Central Farm at Baking Pot, is winning considerable favor. It is both more nourishing and more palatable to cattle than either *jaragua* or molasses grass.

The original emphasis on poultry in the livestock sector has been maintained at Spanish Lookout. At the end of 1966, flocks totaled some 28,000 birds, of which approximately 20,000 were layers or pullets, and 8,000 were broilers. There has been a sustained effort, however, to broaden the livestock base, particularly through the keeping of cattle. Attempts to establish European breeds have met with very limited success. Both Holstein and Brown Swiss stock, although imported from Florida and supposedly conditioned to a climate not too different from that of British Honduras, have suffered from heat and insects—ticks and tick-borne diseases particularly—with resultant high rates of mortality. It is hoped now, with some apparent justification, that crosses of these milking breeds with tropic-conditioned Santa Gertrudis cattle will make it possible to establish a small dairy industry. This could prove a valuable adjunct to the colony's economy. Most milk is imported, almost all of it in tins. Fresh milk flown in from Guatemala costs $.60 (B.H.) or more per quart in Belize City. If production can be increased sufficiently to warrant it, the colonists hope to buy up the Butland cannery facilities, establish a pasteurizing plant, and sell fresh milk in Belize.[22] At present, though, there is a heavier concentration on beef production. In addition to beef raised for colony needs, some $1,000 (B.H.) worth of beef is marketed through the Mennonite center in Belize each week. Total cattle population at the end of 1966 was over 1,800. Hogs, of which there were some 320, are of little commercial importance, being kept mainly for the family table. Pork and ham are strongly enshrined in the Mennonite kitchen. Occasionally, however, a Mexican buyer may bring up a truckload of corn and take back hogs.

The emphasis on animal husbandry at Spanish Lookout is reflected in the cropping pattern, which is heavily biased towards corn in the summer or rainy-season phase. All of the approximately 750 tons produced each year is consumed on the colony, with most of it being fed to poultry. Additional purchases include such small surpluses as may from time to time be available at Blue Creek (Shipyard has yet to meet its own needs) and the occasional truckload from Mexico. Two privately operated feed mills import some seventy-five tons of concentrates and twenty-five tons of ready-mixed rations each month from New Orleans. Grain is expensive.

22. In the late summer of 1968 the Spanish Lookout colony began selling pasteurized milk in Belize City at $1.15 (B.H.) per gallon. They had converted the Butland cannery and its steam-generating facilities to this function.

The government marketing board's resale price for corn is around
$6.25 (B.H.) per hundredweight. However, the free market price
may fall as low as $3.00 per hundredweight just after the native
harvest, then rise to between $4.50 and $6.00 as this is absorbed and
reserves diminish. Imported feeds are even more costly: $9.85 per
hundredweight for concentrates and $8.95 for ready-mixed com-
plete rations.

Garden and orchard produce furnishes some small income, but
the other primary sources of revenue are lumbering and the winter
crop of beans. Lumbering is now approximately paced to the rate
of clearing—some 375,000 board feet per year. With the expansion
of the agricultural sector, it has had to become more of an in-
cidental activity. Beans are sown in December and harvested in
February and March. Often they are planted on corn land, which,
because it has been intertilled, is relatively free of weeds. Double-
cropping increases utilization of the still scarce arable land, and
winter-cropping avoids many of the problems with root disease and
fungus infestations which tend to severely affect beans in the wet
season. Success with both corn and beans is heavily predicated on
substantial applications—100 pounds or more per acre—of phos-
phate fertilizers, 12-24-12 or 10-40-10. They, too, are expensive:
the 12-24-12 analysis costs $10.25 (B.H.) per hundredweight laid
down in Belize, and the 10-40-10 costs somewhat more.

Expanding Production and the Search for Markets

It had been established by 1962 that without adequate
applications of chemical fertilizers there would be little success
with beans. Since then there has been a rapid rise in production,
from 30 tons in 1963 to 80 in 1964, 200 in 1965, and 500 tons in
1966. Although Spanish Lookout is the only surplus producer of
beans [23] in the country, the 1966 crop flooded the market, which

23. Most of the beans grown by the Mennonites in British Honduras are comparable to those they grew in highland Mexico. Market preference appears to favor
a brown bean very much like the common kidney bean.

could only absorb some 300 tons. The remainder was threatened with spoilage during the ensuing wet season. The government thereupon addressed itself to the problem and managed to find a market in Jamaica for the surplus 200 tons, at $.11 (B.H.) per pound. This was not really a very rewarding price compared to the $.12 to $.17 per pound normally obtainable on the local market. To the colonists this experience has once more driven home the point that they lack competitive capability, saddled as they are with high input costs and a local market characterized by low flexibility, at least in the range of prices that will cover production costs. Nevertheless, it is planned to increase production, since beans are one of the few crops suited to the winter season, and the land is therefore available. For its part, the government has given assurances of its concern and guaranteed its good offices in further exploring the export market. Indeed, Spanish Lookout has come to be regarded as something of a revolutionary phenomenon in productivity, and it is the expressed wish of the premier that the rest of his countrymen emulate it. That the colonists themselves have confidence in the future of Spanish Lookout is perhaps best expressed by their own willingness, of recent, to pay $100 (B.H.) and more per acre for improved land.

Incomes and Capital Expansion

Based on the yield in 1966 of the colony's internal general revenue levy of 2 percent on sales of agricultural and forest products, which was $8,838, it is possible to estimate that Spanish Lookout in that year created new wealth on the order of $441,900 (B.H.) This amounts to a gross productivity, per family unit, of approximately $3,700; in addition, each family derives certain subsistence benefits from its land, and these make up a large part of the day-to-day household economy. A 0.5 percent levy on wholesale purchases by businesses yielded $1,000, which is indicative of $200,000 worth of orders, almost all of which was absorbed at retail on the colony. Agriculture is almost entirely mechanized, with much modern equipment, including eighty-one wheel tractors and seven crawlers. According to one equipment dealer, Mennonites from Spanish Lookout in 1966 bought 60 percent of the new Massey-Ferguson tractors sold through Belize. The colony owns its own heavy equipment for the construction of roads and drains. A centrally located cooperative store handles most of the retail trade, except for that in fuel. A rural telephone system went into operation in July 1967. The sawmill is common property, but each man snakes in his own logs. Then, on an agreed day, once a week or as needed, all interested parties pool their labor to get the work done. In most of the economic sphere, private interest predominates. Produce may be sold on the farm to one or another of several private dealers who supply the retail trade in Belize City. However, much is consigned directly to the Mennonite center, for which Spanish Lookout acts as supplier for 80 percent of its turnover, or for roughly $280,000 (B.H.) in goods per year. Several heavy trucks offer freight service to and from Belize and Chetumal, at rates of $.45 and $.90 (B.H.) per hundredweight, respectively, one way. This service is also occasionally used by the Altkolonier at Shipyard and Blue Creek. Wages for day labor, between colonists, are set by general agreement at $5 per day, about twice the going rate elsewhere, for, it is held, it is better that the less well-to-do should be able to support themselves by their labor than be periodically forced to fall back on charity, and the cost to the community is no greater.

The Kleine Gemeinde community has been spared the ideological dissentions that have afflicted the Altkolonier from the beginning of the British Honduras venture. Only recently, however, some seven ultra-conservative families, who find the increasing secular involvement of the colony not in keeping with the tenets of the Mennonite faith as they interpret them, have withdrawn from the church, have renounced modern technology, and have formulated plans to set up a community of their own elsewhere, at a place not yet decided upon in 1967. The degree of consternation which has attended this development may be gauged from the avid way in which the other colonists have bought up their equipment—particularly tractors—at auctions.

The Amish and Old Order Mennonites

The one other Mennonite settlement in British Honduras, which has so far been mentioned only in passing, is a mixed group of Amish and Old Order Mennonites at Santa Elena, near El Cayo. They comprise some ten families from a variety of backgrounds, having come from Pennsylvania, Ohio, Arkansas, and Ontario. In each case they have emigrated because of irreconcilable differences with the established religious organizations of their home communities on matters of doctrine and the permissible degree of ongoing adjustment to the world at large. They have come to British Honduras, singly and in small groups, since 1965 as ordinary immigrants without inclusion in the Privilegium which covers the other Mennonite groups. In 1966 they arranged a joint purchase of a tract of some 4,000 acres near Santa Elena, where they hope to farm in the traditional and unobtrusive way. By the late summer of 1967, they had some 300 acres in various stages of cultivation. This is also the approximate extent of reasonably level land in the valley on which they have formed a rather disjointed linear settlement.

The survival of the Amish-Old Order group as an ethnic and religious entity would appear, at present, as a matter of conjecture. They have some contact with Spanish Lookout, but, according to their Elder, cultural and doctrinal differences are too great for any close connection to develop. Young people from Spanish Lookout, however, do occasionally make the twelve-mile trip to Santa Elena to visit their counterparts there. There was some thought given to the possibility of absorbing the ultra-conservative group which has recently emerged at Spanish Lookout, but language peculiarities and differences of doctrine proved to be such that, after a few exploratory contacts, it was deemed best to abandon the idea.

In the matter of achieving economic viability, the Santa Elena group is—except for language, since all speak English—in much the same position as the Altkolonier, for they are possessed of a certain cultural inflexibility which will be difficult to reconcile with material progress.

As has been shown, there are significant basic attitudinal differences between the several Mennonite denominations residing in British Honduras regarding the degree to which material involvement with the world at large may be reconciled with traditional religious doctrine. In the final analysis, though, past experience indicates that, in the matter of survival, tradition and reaction ultimately make some concession to economic viability and material progress. On this basis it appears justifiable to express cautious optimism that the Altkolonier will yet reverse the economic attrition of the first decade of colonization and that a very gradual economic recovery will ensue. It may be too early to hazard the same prediction with respect to the Amish-Old Order group. They are few in number. A comparable venture by people of their persuasion in the Mexican state of San Luís Potosí in the late 1940's ended in abandonment of the project and a general return to the United States. As for the Kleine Gemeinde, their colony is, in relative terms, already a very substantial success.

Relations with the Native Population

The fact that from the first there were few native people, either Maya or Negro, living among or even very near the Mennonites has left the initiative with respect to contact almost entirely with the Mennonites. True, the Altkolonier experienced considerable exposure to the people of Maskall and Orange Walk during the first months of settlement, when shelter and other facilities on colony lands could not yet accommodate them, but the language barrier kept interaction even then at a minimum. The Kleine Gemeinde at Spanish Lookout are effectively separated from nearby settlements by the Belize River. There has in any event been little attempt at contact beyond the requirements of official and business relationships. In part, the reason for this is one of attitude. The Mennonite groups in British Honduras have always maintained a considerable aloofness from people not of their own persuasion—other Mennonites included—a circumstance reinforced in the present situation by the pronounced ethnic difference.

The Mennonites do not sympathize with what they regard as the improvident and lackadaisical approach to life of many of the natives and do not, in general, approve of their apparent moral code. Attempts to engage them in regular employment in lumbering, land-clearing, or other labor have met with general dissatisfaction, mainly because of such employees' frequent absence from work from the moment any wages are paid them. Otherwise, though, relations are relatively harmonious within the narrow realm of mutual contact. Certainly there has been little of the harassment and banditry that characterized the early years in Mexico.[24] Of late, however, as Mennonite products increasingly infiltrate the national market, there have been mutterings from business interests and workers alike concerning the unfair advantage that comes of the Mennonites' toilsome habits. The government, however, in the words of the premier, hopes that the people may learn to follow the Mennonites' example with respect to thrift and toil.

Education

It is evident that differences in attitude and experience, as reflected in resiliency and flexibility in meeting the contingencies inherent in the adjustment to a new physical, cultural, and economic Umwelt, determine the degree to which successful accommodation to the conditions prevailing in British Honduras has been accomplished. It is curious, therefore, that even the most successful colony among them, Spanish Lookout, is adamantly reactionary in at least one crucial area—the teaching of English. It is freely and universally admitted by those of the Kleine Gemeinde who obtained their education in Canada that their written and spoken knowledge of English was immeasurably useful in bringing their colony to its present state of relative well-being. And yet, no English is taught in their schools. The failure to do so rests partly

24. There have been few robberies to date. In the course of one attempt, however, a Kleine Gemeinde colonist was killed. Although it is claimed that the assailant's identity was known, he disappeared into the bush and the constabulary failed to apprehend him.

upon the fact that German is the language of the church, and it is regarded as a matter of primary and overriding importance to perpetuate it. The root cause, as also with the Altkolonier, lies deeper though and is tantamount to a mental block with respect to the English language, for *it* was the vehicle of instruction whereby the Mennonites in western Canada were, in the early 1920's, forcibly inducted into secular education through compulsory attendance in the public schools. After protracted and bitter resistance, culminating in a futile appeal to the Privy Council in London, there followed the Altkolonier exodus to Mexico. The Kleine Gemeinde, for their part, at that time made an uneasy truce with the secular educational system, and those who departed Canada after the Second World War struck English from the curriculum of their schools. As a result, then, most of the younger people, who grew up in Mexico and British Honduras, have little or no command of the national language. Since this controls the kind and quality of contacts outside the colony, it inhibits acculturation to the Umwelt, a factor regarded by their elders as "good" in a measure which outweighs other considerations. True, those few of the rising generation who become actively involved in business do eventually obtain a speaking knowledge of the national patois, "Creole," but this still leaves them without that capacity to read and write English which has served the founders of the colony so well.

The Altkolonier, whose experiences during the course of the imposition of the public schools in Manitoba and Saskatchewan a half-century ago were on the order of the traumatic, have lapsed from a reasonable level of preoccupation with education to a denigration of learning which has progressed to the point where today, in Mexico as in British Honduras, few of the rising generation attain a state of functional literacy even in their mother tongue.

Conclusion

It is beyond argument that the state of the Mennonites' educational system limits the role that, because of their other qualities—particularly their frugality and toilsomeness—they might otherwise be expected to play in the national development of British Honduras. By the same token, however, because the positive qualities of the Mennonites are substantially at variance with the social nature of most of the country's population, it would appear unrealistic to anticipate the translation of Mennonite successes, particularly at Spanish Lookout (with which the government is especially impressed), into a general model for the rural population of the country. Moreover, the Mennonites, as *die Stillen im Lande*—"the unobtrusive ones"—are as reluctant to proselytize any part of their culture as they are loath to acculturate.

Bibliography

BENNETT, JOHN W. *Hutterian Brethren*. Stanford: Stanford University Press, 1967.

Boletín Meteorológico, No. 6, Estado de Chihuahua (August 1963).

BRAND, DONALD D. "Northwestern Chihuahua." Ph.D. dissertation, University of California, Berkeley, 1933.

BURKHART, CHARLES. "Music of the Old Colony Mennonites," *Mennonite Life*, VII:1 (January 1952), 20–21.

BURROWS, R. H. "The Geology of Northern Mexico," *Boletín de la Sociedad Geológica Mexicana*, VII (1910), 85–103.

CORRELL, ERNST. "Mennonite Immigration into Manitoba," *Mennonite Quarterly Review*, XI:3 (1937), 196–227.

————. "Sources on the Mennonite Immigration from Russia in the 1870's," *Mennonite Quarterly Review*, XXIV:4 (1950), 329–352.

DYCK, ARNOLD. *Verloren in der Steppe*. Steinbach, Manitoba: Selbstverlag, 1944.

Familienregister der Nachkommen von Klaas und Helena Reimer. Winnipeg: Regehr Printing, 1958.

FOSTER, GEORGE M. *Traditional Cultures*. New York: Harper and Brothers, 1962.

FRANCIS, E. K. *In Search of Utopia*. Altona, Manitoba: D. W. Friesen and Sons, 1955.

————. "The Manitoba School Problem," *Mennonite Quarterly Review*, XXVII:3 (1953), 204–237.

FRIESEN, I. I. "The Mennonites of Western Canada, with Special Reference to Education." M.A. thesis, University of Saskatchewan, 1934.

FRIESEN, P. M. *Alt-Evangelische Mennonitische Brüderschaft in Russland (1789–1910)*. 2 vols. Halbstadt, Taurien: Verlagsgesellschaft "Raduga," 1911.

Great Britain. *Report of the Tripartite Economic Survey of the British Honduras*. May 1966.

Great Britain, Colonial Office. *Land in British Honduras*. London, 1959.

HARDER, DAVID. "Chronik." A hand-written account of Altkolonier history in Canada and Mexico, 1920–1965.

HARTSHORNE, RICHARD. *The Nature of Geography*. Lancaster, Pennsylvania: American Association of Geographers, 1939.

HARTSHORNE, RICHARD. *Perspective on the Nature of Geography*. Chicago: Rand McNally, 1960.

HILDEBRAND, J. J. *Hildebrand's Zeittafel*. North Kildonan, Manitoba: J. Regehr, 1945.

INFIELD, HENRIK F. *Cooperative Communities at Work*. New York: The Dryden Press, 1945.

JAMES, PRESTON E., AND CLARENCE F. JAMES. *American Geography: Inventory and Prospect*. Syracuse: Syracuse University Press, 1954.

KEEN, BENJAMIN, ed. *Readings in Latin American Civilization*. Boston: Houghton-Mifflin, 1955.

LEIBBRANDT, GEORG. "The Emigration of the German Mennonites from Russia to the United States and Canada, 1873–1880." *Mennonite Quarterly Review*, VII:1 (1933), 5–41.

MACARTNEY, C. A. *National States and National Minorities*. Oxford: The University Press, 1934.

The Mennonite Encyclopedia. 4 vols. Scottdale, Pennsylvania: Mennonite Publishing House, 1955.

MILFORD, R. "The Nutritive Value of Pasture Plants," in *Some Concepts and Methods in Sub-Tropical Pasture Research*. Oxford: The Alden Press, 1964.

MORTON, W. L. *Manitoba—A History*. Toronto: University of Toronto Press, 1957.

NAVARRO, MOISÉS GONZÁLES. *La Colonización en México*. Mexico City: Talleres de Impresión de Estampillas y Valores, 1960.

PENNER, HORST. "The Anabaptists and Mennonites of East Prussia," *Mennonite Quarterly Review*, XXII (1948), 212–225.

PETERS, KLAAS. *Die Bergthaler Mennoniten und deren Auswanderung aus Ruszland und Einwanderung in Manitoba*. Hillsboro, Kansas: Mennonite Brethren Publishing House, n.d.

PETERS, VICTOR. *All Things Common*. Oxford: The University Press, 1967.

REDEKOP, CALVIN W. *The Old Colony Mennonites*. Baltimore: Johns Hopkins University Press, 1969.

REINA, RUBEN E. "Milpas and Milperos: Implications for Prehistoric Times," *American Anthropologist*, LXIX:1 (February 1967), 1–20.

REMPEL, DAVID. "Personal Diary." An Account of land-seeking missions sent by the Altkolonier to South America and Mexico, 1919–1921.

ROSS, DENMAN W. *The Early History of Landholding among the Germans*. Boston: Soule and Bugbee, 1883.

ROSS, HUGH R. *Thirty-Five Years in the Limelight: Sir Rodmond P. Roblin and His Times*. Winnipeg: Farmer's Advocate of Winnipeg, 1936.

SCHMIEDEHAUS, WALTER. *Ein Feste Burg ist Unser Gott.* Cd. Cuauhté-moc, Chihuahua, Mexico: G. J. Rempel, 1948.

Silvestre Terrazas Collection, Bancroft Library, University of California, Berkeley.

SIMPSON, GEORGE EATON, AND J. MILTON YINGER. *Racial and Cultural Minorities.* New York: Harper and Brothers, 1958.

SISSONS, C. B. *Bi-Lingual Schools in Canada.* Toronto: J. M. Dent and Sons, 1917.

SMITH, C. HENRY. *The Story of the Mennonites.* Newton, Kansas: Mennonite Publication Office, 1957.

SUDERMANN, LEONHARD. *Eine Deputationsreise von Russland nach Amerika.* Elkhart, Indiana: Mennonitische Verlagshandlung, 1897.

THIESSEN, JOHN. *Studien zum Wortschatz der Kanadischen Menno-niten.* Marburg: N. G. Elwert Verlag, 1963.

TREMEEAR, W. J., ed. *Canadian Criminal Cases.* Vol. XXXI. Toronto: Canada Law Book Company, 1920.

WARKENTIN, JOHN H. "The Mennonite Settlements of Southern Manitoba." Ph.D. dissertation, University of Toronto, 1960.

WILLOWS, A. "A History of the Mennonites." M.A. thesis, University of Manitoba, 1924.

Index

Index